Cultivating Music

Cultivating Music

The Aspirations, Interests, and Limits
of German Musical Culture, 1770–1848

DAVID GRAMIT

University of California Press

BERKELEY   LOS ANGELES   LONDON

University of California Press
Berkeley and Los Angeles, California

University of California Press, Ltd.
London, England

© 2002 by
The Regents of the University of California

Library of Congress Cataloging-in-Publication Data

Gramit, David.
    Cultivating music : the aspirations, interests, and limits of German musical
culture, 1770–1848 / David Gramit.
        p.   cm.
    Includes bibliographical references (p.   ) and index.
    ISBN 0-520-22970-3 (alk. paper)
    1. Music—Germany—18th century—History and criticism.   2. Music—
Germany—19th century—History and criticism.   3. Music—Social
aspects—Germany.   I. Title.

ML275.G66   2002
780'.943'09033—dc21   2001004562

Manufactured in the United States of America

10   09   08   07   06   05   04   03   02

10   9   8   7   6   5   4   3   2   1

The paper used in this publication is both acid-free and totally chlorine-free (TCF). It meets
the minimum requirements of ANSI/NISO Z39.48-1992 (R 1997) (*Permanence of Paper*). ♾

for Stephen Kelly

Contents

Preface   *ix*

1. INTRODUCTION: CULTIVATING MUSIC   1

2. SCHOLARSHIP AND THE DEFINITION OF MUSICAL CULTURES   27

3. THE DILEMMA OF THE POPULAR: THE *VOLK*, THE COMPOSER,
    AND THE CULTURE OF ART MUSIC   63

4. EDUCATION AND THE SOCIAL ROLES OF MUSIC   93

5. PERFORMING MUSICAL CULTURE: THE CONCERT   125

    Afterword   161

    Notes   167

    Bibliography   241

    Index   263

Preface

Musicology has only recently begun to view the culture of serious music not simply as the transparent medium in which both it and the objects of its study exist but rather as a complex of institutions and ideologies that have shaped in fundamental ways our conceptions of the nature of music and of music's role in society. With this book I seek to contribute to that re-examination by considering the values and motivations of one of the principal discourses that shaped that culture. In order to do so, I have drawn on the resources of social history, sociology, and ethnomusicology as well as historical musicology; if the result may equally dissatisfy practitioners of each of those disciplines, I hope it may also provide a perspective unattainable from a less eclectic approach.

If every book can be read as a compilation of the words and ideas that have preceded it, this is, in at least one way, more obviously true of the present one than of many others. Not only does it depend on the work of others in the usual sense, it is in many respects a selective compilation of writings that have defined the culture of "classical" music since its inception. It frequently proceeds by juxtaposing the diverse voices of advocates of German musical culture against one another in order to highlight not only the considerable common ground that they share despite various controversies but also the socially based insecurities that played as great a role in shaping that culture as did loftier and more familiar aspirations. Indeed, one of my principal claims is that those aspirations and insecurities are intimately linked. To demonstrate this, I have found it necessary to quote extensively from the sources rather than simply to summarize their arguments. In the admittedly sometimes tortuous but often surprisingly engaging prose of the period, the recurrent issues of establishing a musical culture come across with a vitality that no summary could reproduce. More important, though, the language of the sources is as critical as their summarizable arguments; images and turns of phrase recur with surprising regularity in discussions of ostensibly unrelated topics, and the common basis of the project of defining a culture of serious music is revealed as much in its rhetoric as in its intellectual premises.

Examining these documents has made me keenly aware not only of their formative influence on the field of musicology but also of the extent to which the project they delineate has shaped my own understandings of music. I must also acknowledge, however, the significance of another project, one that does not appear so obviously in these pages: the pioneering challenges to traditional musicology posed by scholars including Susan McClary, Richard Leppert, Lawrence Kramer, and others, especially since the 1980s. Although I have suggested both here and elsewhere that the continuing emphasis of much "new musicology" on the analysis of individual musical works is a heritage that a critical social history of music must look beyond, I also acknowledge with genuine gratitude the liberating and leavening impact of that work—I have no doubt that without it I could not have conceived the present volume.

I also owe a great debt to a number of individuals who have consistently supported my work. Stephen Kelly first introduced me to a critical approach to the history of music and has remained a dear friend and colleague; the book is dedicated to him. Tilman Seebass provided invaluable mentoring and a superb model of committed and humane scholarship, and Richard Leppert encouraged and supported my exploration of links between music and social forms at a critical point in my career. Students and colleagues at the University of Alberta have provided a uniquely vital environment in which the study of music as a social practice flourishes, and the university itself has consistently supported my research, most notably through a McCalla Research Professorship in 1997–98, during which I undertook the early work on this study, and through a sabbatical leave in 1999–2000, during which I completed it.

A grant from the Social Sciences and Humanities Research Council of Canada allowed both travel and support for research assistants. The librarians of the institutions at which I worked—including the Berlin Staatsbibliothek, the Bibliothek für bildungsgeschichtliche Forschung of the Deutsches Institut für internationale pädagogische Forschung in Berlin, the Library of Congress, the Boston and New York Public Libraries, and most especially the University of Alberta—all provided invaluable assistance. In particular, James Whittle of the University of Alberta's Music Library provided unfailing support in tracking down innumerable obscure requests, as did the university's interlibrary loan department. My research assistants, in particular Della Dennis and Joel Kroeker, helped compile and index sources in a way that has greatly facilitated my work.

I am also indebted to those who read portions of this work at various stages, including James Parsons, Tia DeNora, Regula Burckhardt Qureshi, and an anonymous reader at the University of California Press. William Weber not only read two chapters in draft form and provided thorough and stimulating responses but also provided valuable suggestions for the entire manuscript, as did Celia Applegate. Susan McClary's suggestions enabled me to develop what I hope is a considerably more effective introductory chapter. The comments of all these readers have contributed substantially to whatever virtues this book may have. The assistance of Lynne Withey and Mary Francis during the writing and reviewing of the book, and of Suzanne Knott and Bonita Hurd during its production, has made working with the University of California Press a pleasure, as well as resulting in a far more readable book. Finally, to my wife, Frieda Woodruff Gramit, and my son, Jacob Gramit, I give my thanks for the support and patience without which I could never have completed this project.

1   Introduction
Cultivating Music

One of the most suggestive of the many descriptions of musical activity in the autobiography of the Austrian poet Franz Grillparzer dates from his youth in the first decade of the nineteenth century, during the terminal illness of his father:

> In my melancholy mood at that time I truly felt the need for an external diversion. Poetry was then rather distant from me, and with its precisely expressed thoughts it would have been a less suitable expression for my uncertain feelings, reaching into the future. I hit upon music. The piano was opened, but I had forgotten everything; even notation had become foreign to me. Then it proved useful that Gallus, my first piano teacher, while he had me play figured bass in half-childish dallying, had imparted a knowledge of foundational harmony. I took delight in the harmony of the tones; the chords dissolved into motions and these formed themselves into simple melodies. I said farewell to notation and played from my head. Gradually I acquired enough skill that I could improvise *[phantasiren]* for hours.[1]

Grillparzer's account of his emotionally charged return to the piano draws upon a familiar understanding of music: more indefinite than literature, its value lies in its ability to express "uncertain feelings." Indeed, so conventional has this version of music's power become that it is easy to overlook its import as a claim for both the significance of the inner experience of the individual and the privileged role of music in voicing that experience. But not long before Grillparzer, such a claim would scarcely have been conceivable. Mary Sue Morrow has shown how Fontenelle's notorious query, "*Sonate, que me veux-tu?*" (Sonata, what do you want of me?) haunted German music criticism in the late eighteenth century.[2] That rhetorical question— implying that because it was nonrepresentational, untexted music could not convey a specific meaning—serves as a succinct reminder that music has not always been available for meaning of the sort ascribed to it by Grillparzer and many others during the last two centuries; the existence of a public culture of serious music in that sense—one that asserts the role of music in the construction of individual subjectivity and its place in intellectual discourse—is a relatively recent phenomenon. As William Weber has suggested, music's functions before the nineteenth century simply did not include those that we now easily associate with the classical music tradition. Music could celebrate occasions, display learning, or entertain, but to claim for it a serious role in human development seemed at best eccentric, at worst misguided.[3] It is, of course, unlikely that Grillparzer would have viewed this brief passage as making such a claim, but his account nonetheless rests on the assumption that music can bear that kind of significance. It both depends on and contributes to the existence of a discourse legitimating music as a suitable object in which to locate meaning—and arguably the most influential such discourse originated precisely in the period of Grillparzer's life, among the advocates of serious musical culture in German-speaking Europe in the late eighteenth and early nineteenth centuries.

But it would be a mistake to read Grillparzer's anecdote purely in relation to aesthetics, for it succinctly reveals that the availability of music as a meaningful object also depends on the social practice of music: without Grillparzer's piano teacher and the socially recognized harmonic conventions that he inculcated, Grillparzer would have had no music to act as an expressive medium. If we imagine the perspective of the teacher, Gallus, and his professional colleagues, however, yet another link between aesthetics and practice appears: without the ideology of music's significance, there would in all likelihood have been far fewer opportunities to teach. This last link is far from incidental, and it relates not only to music instruction but also to the entire institutional existence of music in a society in which aristocratic patronage no longer seemed to guarantee music a secure place. As I argue below, the claim that music—or, more accurately, a particular and limited form of music—was worthy of consideration as an essential part of human cultivation arose from a social situation in which that claim served to secure the existence of music as a legitimate activity and to maintain the livelihood of its practitioners. Both the aspirations of German musical culture and the defining boundaries that its advocates set for it were inseparably intertwined with the interests of music as a field of social practice, and the entire project hinged on the acceptance of music as essential to the cultivation of fully human individuals, the *Bildungsideal* so central to the self-identity of the German bourgeoisie.[4]

My goal in what follows is to explore this eccentric but ultimately pragmatic project, the eccentricity and the pragmatism of which have largely disappeared from view due to its longevity and influence. So definitively have both the repertoire and the discourse of German-speaking Europe in the late eighteenth and early nineteenth centuries shaped our own sense of what a culture of art music is, that perhaps only recently, as other forms of musical expression have begun to undergo long-overdue study, have we been able to recognize the impact of this culture and study it rather than frame our studies under its influence. In order to do so, I have found it necessary to practice throughout the shifting focus I have illustrated briefly in considering Grillparzer's report, reading the aesthetic in relation to the particular social relations of music making. Only by so juxtaposing these realms have I been able to address the questions that have most interested me: how and to what ends did participants in that culture define it for themselves, and how have those definitions continued to both shape our conception of that music-historical period and serve the ends of those who interpret the culture and its music?

THE SOCIAL CATEGORIES OF MUSICAL DISCOURSE

To approach these questions, I have worked from a deceptively simple premise: talk about music invokes and constructs social categories. It also, of course, accomplishes other, more conventionally musical ends, but if we take seriously the observation that music is inevitably a social practice, then musical statements are also social statements, whether or not the figure of the music teacher hovers as explicitly as it did in Grillparzer's memoir. The two realms of meaning need not, indeed cannot, exist apart from one another, even if individual interpretations of a given statement may direct our attention to one realm or the other. Consider, for example, the following well-known statement from E. T. A. Hoffmann's review of Beethoven's Fifth Symphony: "Music is the most romantic of all the arts; one might even say that it alone is purely romantic. The lyre of Orpheus opened the gates of Orcus. Music unlocks for man an unfamiliar world having nothing in common with the [world of the senses] which surrounds him." [5] As one of the most succinct summaries of the romantic understanding of music, Hoffmann's review (and this passage in particular) is familiar from a host of histories and text anthologies, and its evocation of a transcendent realm accessible through music seems resolutely asocial, just as the review from which it is drawn is focused not on social questions but on aesthetics and analysis of music. And in this way the review has contributed to the established and by no means inaccurate account of German romanticism in music. But even here, the social aspect figures, albeit negatively: the new world that music "unlocks for man" (and *music* here implies works identified with individual composers, just as *man* evokes the attentive listener who hears as the reviewer does) is valuable precisely in that it obscures the implicit but distracting relations that make the experience itself possible. Hoffmann's understanding of this transcendent power was not universally held, as Sanna Pederson's exploration of competing currents in German music criticism makes clear.[6] But even here, where the social seems most remote, the implicit categories of the composer and the reflective listener, mediated by the insightful critic, serve to make the discourse comprehensible by linking it to familiar roles.

Grillparzer's piano teacher, of course, embodies one such role, and still more are revealed in another statement claiming music's transcendent power, a lengthier and less familiar one written in 1782 by Hoffmann's older contemporary, Johann Friedrich Reichardt:

> No art has so great a need of support from rulers as music. The painter can bring forth the greatest work of art in his lonely chamber, and then needs only to exhibit it in order to delight the whole world. The same goes for the sculptor: he himself and his block of marble suffice for his most splendid creations. The architect finds his field of activity in a hundred ordinary requirements and occasions. If the musical artist, however, would bring about more joy than pleasant tickling, if he would work on entire peoples with the full, almighty power of his art, which enraptures the entirety of sensible nature with irresistible power and raises it heavenward, then the ruler must first grant him the great occasions and all the tools he needs: appropriate buildings, genuine singers, players with both knowledge and love of art for all the participating musical instruments, and the instruments themselves.[7]

Here, the unstated background to Hoffmann's evocation emerges as the focal point. As part of a direct plea—Reichardt titled it "To Generous Rulers"—this statement is calculated to elicit the support necessary to maintain and develop a musical culture that "would work on entire peoples with the full, almighty power" of music. As he makes clear, that is an elaborate and costly ambition for which someone must foot the bill—a mundane concern that Hoffmann had no need to raise. From the more familiar perspective of Hoffmann's review and the music criticism that has followed its example in the ensuing centuries, there is perhaps something unsettling, even vulgar about Reichardt's straightforward list of concrete requirements, and there can be little doubt that Reichardt himself would have preferred not to have to make such an appeal. In making it, however, he laid out a valuable map of his own conception of the social relations that could bring about the untroubled impact of music that his statement seeks and Hoffmann's assumes. That he felt compelled to do so indicates an insecurity about music's place that we will encounter repeatedly in this volume, and his ultimate appeal to ruling princes is an attempt to call on the traditional patrons of sophisticated music to fulfill their accustomed roles in changing circumstances. As we will see, however, that strategy was by no means the only one, nor even the most likely to succeed, for the musical world in which Reichardt had been raised was undergoing thorough transformation.[8] Reichardt's statement itself suggests something of that change, for the goal he sees for a well-supported musical life is not to provide entertainment for the court or to demonstrate the ruler's magnanimity and wealth but rather to "work on entire peoples" not with pleasing, superficial music but with serious, powerful art. Just how to accomplish that work was far from obvious, but Reichardt's concern for it constructs yet another social relation one I consider at some length below: that relation between the creative artist and the people as a whole, who encounter and benefit from the composer's art—in short, a musical public.

Conceptualizing an appropriately powerful music, defining a public, and establishing the musician's relationship to it were not simple matters, but the viability of music as a profession depended on their accomplishment. To explore these issues and the circumstances that gave rise to them, I have focused on a portion of the musical discourse of the period that has received relatively little attention. Although there has been an encouraging increase in attention to music criticism, a substantial body of musical writing has most often fallen outside the scope of such studies: writing that is concerned not directly with "the music itself" but rather, like Reichardt's plea, with the conditions necessary for its existence and propagation.[9] Those documents are numerous and scattered throughout the musical literature of the period, and selection from such a wealth of sources has inevitably depended on my own critical perspective and the boundaries that I myself have set. Since those boundaries bear so heavily on what follows, it is worth clarifying them here. This is not a study of German musical life (although it aims to contribute to that larger topic) but rather of aspirations for that life and the limits—some self-imposed, some unavoidable—of those aspirations among advocates of a culture of serious music in German-speaking Europe, a group that William Weber has called "musical idealists." I do not adopt Weber's term here, since Mark Evan Bonds has recently argued persuasively for a more limited and precise use of "idealism" in this period.

But Weber's depiction of a relatively small group of advocates acutely aware of the developing prominence and autonomy of instrumental music, suspicious of fashion and empty virtuosity and convinced of the moral superiority of serious music, remains a valuable orientation to one of the most enduring musical developments of the period.[10] Given that goal, then, I have focused largely on discourse by and for those interested in establishing that culture—writing that I have frequently termed "musical discourse" as a convenient form of reference. The bulk of my examples are drawn from the periodicals that sought to advance the cause, for those periodicals were crucial to the establishment (and later to the fragmentation) of a shared conception of a musical culture. Most prominent among them is the *Allgemeine musikalische Zeitung*, the long-lived model for serious music periodicals in the nineteenth century, but its eighteenth-century predecessors and contemporary competitors provided important material as well. A number of other publications, from textbooks to pamphlets and prefaces, also proved significant; I have largely omitted—except occasionally for the sake of comparison—writings directed to a general reading public, whether by musicians or others, and the more popular, entertainment-oriented music literature that began to appear near the end of the period under consideration. As I suggest several times below, the concerns of musical discourse often differ in surprisingly consistent ways from those expressed even in apparently related fields by authors with a serious concern for other forms of art. So, for instance, while Reichardt is clearly a central figure in that discourse, Grillparzer, as an amateur musician whose primary commitment was to literature, stands nearer its margins; with professional standing in both music and literature, Hoffmann straddles the distinction and serves as a useful reminder of its provisional nature.

MUSIC, THE PUBLIC SPHERE, AND ENLIGHTENMENT IDEOLOGY

The existence of such a discourse is, of course, predicated on a larger social development, the establishment by the later eighteenth century of a public sphere of discourse, of which music formed only a small part. Small, but not insignificant: as Weber has noted, the emergence of a public discourse on musical taste in England and France was closely bound up with, and often served as a barometer of, social and political developments in those kingdoms in the eighteenth century.[11] The far more diffuse political situation of central Europe meant that the development of musical discourse inevitably manifested itself differently there. As Pederson has noted, however, it was also crucially and inseparably enmeshed in the contradictions inherent in the concept of the public sphere, in which reason was held to be universal but was nonetheless effectively limited to adult male property owners, and in which the public was alternately idealized and held to lack the most basic civilized cultivation.[12]

The relationship of musical discourse to the public sphere is a particularly crucial issue, since music's role in that sphere was by no means assured, at least to the satisfaction of its advocates. The result was a pragmatic but inconsistent appeal to public taste on some occasions and royal or aristocratic authority on others. Although the development of a public sphere made musical discourse of this type possible in the first place, its uncertain associations meant that advocates of music long remained ambivalent about it. Validation by a literate public could verify a claim to universal value, but if, as often occurred, that public was represented instead as the common crowd (and the *Pöbel*, or rabble, is a label we encounter repeatedly), the same validation could undermine music's status.

In the end, however, there could be no evading the claims of the public sphere, because, as Pederson also notes, it was inseparably bound up with the cause of enlightenment, and without Enlightenment ideology, claims for the value of music would have been insupportable.[13] Enlightenment ideology and rhetoric pervade musical discourse of the period to an extent that has rarely been sufficiently recognized; even the romantic criticism that explicitly opposed many tenets of the Enlightenment project still depended on arguments for the institutionalization of public musical life that were solidly based on that project. Since those institutionalizing aspects of musical discourse are my primary interest, the significance of Enlightenment ideals beyond the ideology of the public sphere—and particularly those that took root in German-speaking territories—merits consideration here.[14] Most obviously, the frequently expressed view that highly developed, harmonically sophisticated music represented a progressive development over earlier and more primitive musics draws heavily on the Enlightenment's valorization of reason. In the words of an anonymous writer whose views I consider at greater length below, Oriental peoples "are still distant from genuine enlightenment," but "we Germans . . . must justifiably be proud of the accomplishment of having elevated music to a higher level."[15] This faith in the rational as the guarantor of music's value may seem at odds with the romantic idealization of the natural and of the medieval past, but those views found little sympathy among the advocates of musical culture. As I suggest below in considering the *Volkston*, only once music could confidently claim a place within educated culture could such ideas safely be considered. When they surfaced earlier, they were more frequently associated with writers who approached musical culture from positions (often aristocratic or literary) outside it.

Other aspects of Enlightenment ideology, however, are fully as significant as this dependence on rationalist arguments. The claim to universal validity that I have already noted, for instance, is a gesture characteristic of the Enlightenment and one closely bound up with the movement's social place. Its close association with the administrative and professional bourgeoisie, especially in Germany, has long been noted, and that link meant that the claims of rational thought and natural behavior that Enlightenment writers advanced were not only Eurocentric, as the above example suggests, but also shaped in the image of a particular segment of German society—that of the writers themselves. In one guise, this universalization of bourgeois values could be directed against the aristocracy, both as a moral critique of what was often represented as frivolity and depravity and as a claim that nonaristocratic culture was of equal or superior value (at least intellectually and morally).[16] The musical implications of this claim are familiar in the established narrative that sees middle-class concert life replace aristocratic patronage as the focus of musical culture, and as far as it goes, this perspective does indeed represent important developments. We will see, for instance, advocacy of institutions such as the concert and the choral society couched in terms that make clear the unsavory associations of aristocratic musical life and its institutions, especially opera. But the universalization of bourgeois values had broader implications: it shaped evaluations both of other cultures, which could easily be found wanting in the degree to which they had cultivated within themselves rational conduct and art, and especially of the lower orders of society, whose backwardness and lack of cultivation could explain their unsuitability for a role in the theoretically open public sphere. Understanding the implications of this last evaluation is complicated by another factor. The literate representatives of bourgeois culture have, of course, left behind a disproportionate share of the written record, and so, as social historians have had to note, the idea that their norms represent the actual activities of people, questionable even when dealing with the literate middle class itself, is dubious in the extreme when considering the lower classes.[17] This observation proves crucial because musical discourse of the period was by no means only concerned with marking itself off from the old ruling order but was also intent on distinguishing itself from, and considering its relationship to, the lower classes of society—a process that has attracted considerably less scholarly attention than the rise to prominence of the musical culture with which musi-cology itself has closely identified.

The all-too-obvious gap between claims to universal validity and the ev-ident backwardness of much of the populace gave rise, especially in Prot-estant territories, to another enlightened cause, one to which musical dis-course was heavily indebted: strong advocacy of pedagogy as the practical social consequence of enlightened thought.[18] Not only were many of the leading figures of the German Enlightenment closely associated with uni-versities (Kant is perhaps the most obvious example), but educational re-formers and model schools remained highly active and visible proponents of enlightened thought well into the nineteenth century. Although I deal at some length with only one such reformer—the influential Swiss peda-gogue Johann Heinrich Pestalozzi, whose approach attracted the attention of numerous music educators, including Hans Georg Nägeli—it is worth remembering that the program of cultivation that I discuss in relation to music was only part of a far more widespread movement to cultivate the population.[19]

But the cultivation most frequently envisioned was a very specific, lim-ited one, for the social situation of enlightened thought also conditioned the educational reformers. Anthony J. La Vopa's summary of the ways in which the hierarchical nature of growing bureaucratic states shaped the so-cial settings of the literate public provides a valuable reminder of the insep-arability of intellectuals from the state:

> The bureaucratic apparatus of the new state developed in partial fusion with the elites at the summit of the corporate hierarchy. Absolutist authority and power flowed downward through the court and its net-works of aristocratic families; through a corps of bourgeois adminis-trative and judicial officials . . . ; through the universities that trained them; through the established church and its clerical hierarchy; through local office holders. It was precisely this multi-tiered service elite, more or less directly implicated in the workings of "absolutism," that formed the center of gravity for the Enlightenment's new sociability. By and large the new social spaces . . . were occupied by the groups who consti-tuted the state. If they were private retreats from absolutism, they were also its informal extension.[20]

In such a context, it is not surprising that the result was not direct political activity but rather what Joachim Whaley terms "primarily a utilitarian re-form movement deeply committed to the traditional social order."[21] Both the external limits of state authority and the internal ones determined by the self-interest of a class dependent on the existing order dictated that *Volksaufklärung* (popular enlightenment, whether through self-help literature or the expansion and reform of schooling) equip the populace to fulfill more adequately its established role in the social and economic order rather than challenge that order. This tendency was clear from the start among German writers, but after the French Revolution seemed vividly to demonstrate the disastrous consequences of more radical enlightenment, it became a very nearly unquestionable starting point for German thought in general and education reform in particular.[22]

Even so brief an overview of the ideals and limitations of the Enlightenment reveals their role in defining the social and intellectual space in which musicians sought to establish a place for themselves; matters of immediate practical concern to musicians are close at hand in all of the areas discussed. The relevance of a concern for general education, for instance, is clear— or would be, if music were accepted as an essential element in that education and if the necessity of employing musicians to provide the necessary instruction were recognized. Chapter 4 explores this issue with respect to popular education, but for the present it suffices to note that the latter concern—that musicians themselves find employment through teaching— surfaces not only in the discourse on school music education and the training of teachers but also in that concerned with private music instruction, where one might expect that the need for a teacher would be self-evident. That expectation, however, like many of our inherited concepts concerning "classical" music, was a part of the cause of musical culture, as an 1807 review of teaching methods makes clear. To be sure, personal instruction had always been the standard medium through which one learned musical performance, but the development of print culture, on which both the public sphere as a whole and musical discourse itself depended, had, according to the reviewer, introduced an alternative: "We can say that good musical method-books are among the advantages of our time. Even a half century ago, these methods were as rare as they were incomplete."[23] This change had undoubtedly contributed to the quality of music teaching, but it had also made possible the dangerous opinion that methods could eliminate the need for personal instruction. In response, the author argues that as important as a rational, progressive pedagogy is, printed methods are inherently limited: they cannot replace the crucial element of the teacher's example. As a result, even the best method is of little use to the child attempting to learn music, and "without the help of a teacher, of none at all."[24] The argument is made in purely musical terms, but it is also true that the example of the master requires the master's remunerated presence, and so this musical argument is simultaneously an argument for the continuance of a traditional means of supporting musicians despite a significant new development in the production of instruction. If the need for one-on-one instruction has remained self-evident, it is precisely because of this intertwined complex of stylistic concerns—for the reproduction of such qualities as "good tone" and "musicality"—and professional self-advocacy.

The pragmatic orientation of musical discourse in relation to the social and intellectual setting of the Enlightenment is revealed as well in aspects no longer so familiar. As Reichardt's argument for the necessity of rulers' support for music makes clear, musicians were every bit as dependent on the hereditary rulers of the state as were its administrators, and the development of a public sphere by no means eliminated the important role of courts in providing positions for musicians. Although forms of patronage and the social standing of the musician were clearly undergoing change, securing the support of those patrons long remained crucial.[25] And this was no secret to musicians, as these "remarks from the diary of a practical musician" reveal: "Under current conditions, no artist is more often required to live among and with people of all kinds from the distinguished and rich classes than the musician—especially the practical musician, the virtuoso; but none, as a rule, fits less well among them than he does. Very rarely does he enjoy an upbringing for the finer world in his early years, and what is not at least sketched out and prepared to this end in early years can scarcely be made up for later."[26]

With its frank acknowledgment of the gap between musicians' and patrons' upbringings, this passage suggests in part a very traditional order of patronage in which the (presumably male) musician served his social better; but it also reveals a discomfort and uncertainty that the precisely defined social order of the traditional household would have prevented.[27] The current, more uncertain situation demanded the sort of counsel to the uninitiated that the article goes on to provide. As it does so, it effectively evokes the tension between independent thought and artistic activity, on the one hand, and social dependency, on the other. Although outwardly respectful, the musician as free subject evaluates his patrons: "Among fifty of the prominent and the rich who may gladly hear the artist occasionally and have him around them, and indeed also reward him, I have scarcely found five who *loved* art from their hearts, but scarcely one who really *respected it deeply*—however much many were able to fashion lovely words about it."[28] Under these circumstances, the musician must learn to give the patron what he desires (as, the author claims, Mozart had) but to reserve the finest products of his art for the few who will appreciate it and, beyond that, to conduct himself with full awareness of his own essential dignity:

> To each the respect, courtesy, and favor that he deserves, simply according to his relations and civil situation! But if he is so weak as to separate *himself* from those relations, to boast about them, to want to see you humble yourself before them, do *not* do it—or you will lose everything, even in his eyes. Rather, respond to arrogance with a manly but modest avowal of your freedom from artificial necessities! Believe me, those who continuously complain and are in need amid abundance and surplus nevertheless privately have respect [for such a response], and if you hit upon the *manner* in which to express such a thing, you will indeed be able to *accomplish* with him what another could not dare to *begin.* But this correct manner is *manly:* definite, without haughtiness, modest, without submission![29]

The claim that art is worthy of the highest respect in and of itself is here linked to a similar claim for the artist, but it is one couched not in terms of the special privilege of genius but rather of universal human dignity, independent of station—if not of gender, as the exhortation to manliness reveals. But again, this is a tactic for coping within the existing order, not a strategy for controlling or changing it; to critique morally depraved patrons for failing to meet a universalized standard of conduct was not to urge an end to the relationship of patronage, a step the dependent musician quite literally could not afford.[30]

THE STATUS OF MUSIC AND
THE INTERESTS OF MUSICAL CULTIVATION

Uncertainty and insecurity have already appeared repeatedly in my account and will continue to do so; it is reasonable, though, to wonder about the basis of those anxieties. On the largest scale, it is easy enough to answer that the transition from the essentially feudal relations of noble and church or civic patronage were giving way to a market-based culture of music, and this transition was indeed under way in music just as in society as a whole.[31] But when considered more closely, this response proves far less satisfactory: not only were the traditional relations of musical production by no means so comfortable that the prospect of their demise should automatically have been met with fear but also, as I have already suggested, noble patronage remained a significant source of support for musicians well into the nineteenth century.[32] Were the sources I have cited, then, simply, in the words of G. W. Fink (describing Johann Nicolaus Forkel's pessimistic evaluation of music in the 1770s), the views of "the many, who have been present in all ages, who, due to the constitution of music in their time, fear its complete ruin"?[33] In the absence of more extensive studies of the support of musicians than are currently available, the economic basis of these fears is difficult to evaluate, but in another respect their reality is difficult to deny—or at least, the situation in which musicians found themselves gave rise to such fears with remarkable frequency and consistency. Simply put, even if patronage continued, it did not guarantee musicians respect in society, and if patronage did in fact become less reliable, then that respect would be crucial to avoiding a fatal decline in music's standing.

Although the perception that music's standing was in jeopardy is often only implicit, occasionally it comes to the surface, as in this passage from Johann Samuel Petri's *Anleitung zur praktischen Musik* of 1782: "Moreover, deeper and more thorough learning of music is spoiled for many young people, and they are dissuaded from it. They are told that a person can only achieve a certain distinction in one area, and so anything else is all distraction, if one practices it too seriously—and the essential concerns for young people are certainly studies other than music; just look how few choral scholars have learned much thoroughly.—But tell me, were they really geniuses who without music would have become great learned men? Indeed, most of them don't accomplish very much in music, either."[34] Petri's characterization of his opponents' position reveals their suspicion that music is a distraction from more essential things. But note that the implication is not (as was sometimes the case in England at the time) that music diverts time and attention from more practical pursuits, but rather that it prevents devotion to learning;[35] the issue is the proper constitution of cultivation rather than industry against inefficiency. Petri's response, however, is unlikely to have offered much reassurance: by casting aspersions on the intellectual abilities of choral scholars (whose scholarships meant that they were among the few students from families with limited means who could attend schools otherwise serving a more prosperous and literate population), he would only strengthen suspicions that such choirs were outdated and musicians properly limited to a lower social order.[36]

The implication of social unacceptability is apparent in the title of an unusually forthright questioning of musical training: J. C. F. GutsMuths's "Wollen alle Deutsche Musikanten werden?" (Should All Germans Become Musicians?) of 1804.[37] It is difficult to believe that GutsMuths, a well-known pedagogical reformer who advocated gymnastic exercises as an integral part of education, was unaware that his use of the term *Musikanten* (musicians, but by the eighteenth century a term with strong implications of inferior class and dubious integrity) would be seen as a provocation. His article goes on to argue against what he sees as a dangerous fashion: "It is a completely unique phenomenon, not found in a single foreign nation that I am aware of, a genuine, constantly spreading fashion craze, that all children and young people, not only among the more cultivated classes of people but also even those of the burghers in the cities, ought to learn music."[38] Although he claims that he would be happy if children of all classes learned music if they had inclination and talent for it, he insists that most did not and that, for them, time and money spent on music instruction were simply wasted. Why, then, did parents continue this practice? GutsMuths offers five answers, each of which he proceeds to undercut. Although music might indeed make one more socially acceptable, so would a host of other activities and knowledge. The response that otherwise talent might go undeveloped could apply only to a very few who possessed that talent. Music could develop aesthetic sense—but attending concerts could do this more effectively and economically than could violin lessons, at which "the cats detect their equal."[39] Music could also be a pleasant pastime—but "I believe that German pedagogy has come far enough that it no longer needs to speak of [mere] pastimes."[40] And in any case, many forced to endure music lessons found it anything but a pleasant pastime. Finally, some instruction in music could in fact benefit public (i.e., church) singing—but nothing like extensive music instruction is required to meet this goal.

The social implications of GutsMuths's article were not lost on Christian Friedrich Michaelis, a prolific contributor to the music periodicals of the period who responded to it within two months of its appearance.[41] Indeed, social issues were the primary basis of Michaelis's reply; he agreed with a number of GutsMuths's other points, particularly those that stressed the illusory nature of claims for music's value based on sociability and recreation. Like those who had defended J. S. Bach against the criticisms of Johann Adolf Scheibe more than half a century earlier, Michaelis devoted a substantial portion of his reply to distinguishing between *Musikant* and *Musikus*, ostensibly to justify providing a negative answer to GutsMuths's title question but nonetheless upholding the dignity of music as a valuable art. Michaelis's distinction merits citing at some length, for it gives a sense of the precarious balance between claiming distinction for music as an art and advocating its broad dissemination:

> For in current usage one distinguishes between *Musikus* and *Musikant* approximately as one does between "actor" and "comedian." The former practices music as a noble, free art that is its own reward, or at least may not go begging for bread, is not degraded into art for hire,

even if it does not disdain rewarding encouragement for the artist, because and insofar as he, like everyone else, has basic needs and must sacrifice many a luxury for his art. The *Musikant,* by contrast, treats art simply as a source of livelihood and therefore accommodates himself completely to the arbitrary demands of his often very tasteless public of the moment, and is also content with the smallest gratuity. The *Musikus,* on the other hand, is either decently paid or trusts to the noble generosity of friends of art encouragingly to make known to him their respect for his art through their rewards; he often lives independently as a self-supported artist. Far from adapting his art to the whims of his listeners or using it to indulge the passions and needs even of the rabble, he will much rather always cultivate the taste of the public for his art, elevating it to that art's heights. He strives for the applause of the knowledgeable, and is proud of it; he would rather select a small number of genuine admirers than pursue the ovations of the great, common crowd. The *Musikant,* however, is basically simply a handworker, who works to order and is also free enough from artistic moods that he can play for money to suit every taste. Nonetheless, the *Musikant,* if he possesses true artistry and a rich musical memory, and knows how to play even the people's favorites with some taste, but especially if he knows how to circulate better pieces and songs with sense and selectivity, has real value. The despised and unknown *Musikant* can often approach the virtuoso in talent, and far surpass him in modesty and kindness. The lower classes of the people also want to be cheered, and sometimes need cheering more than the higher orders.[42]

Perhaps the most immediately striking feature of this discussion is that it construes the contrast between the two categories—and thus the concept of a "noble, free art"—in largely economic terms. Musicians who are genuine artists must have means of support—but must practice their art without regard for that need, depending on the discrimination and generosity of knowledgeable and well-off listeners. The circumlocutions Michaelis employs to avoid mention of actual payment in his initial contrast are remarkable. *Musikanten* represent the negation of this entire system of value, a system whose orientation toward the cultivated classes is revealed by Michaelis's dismissal of the values of the handworker. Ironically, this negation is also characterized by a willingness to accept even the smallest payment, while the disinterested *Musikus* is "decently paid." The *Musikant,* however, turns out to be necessary to provide music for the people, who are thus closed out of the opposition between cultivated and tasteless audiences—they turn out not to constitute a part of the audience of the *Musikus* at all. In this view, music is preserved as worthy of cultivated interest, but broad distribution is sacrificed, except in the most limited of forms.

There was, however, an alternative response, one that had the potential to maintain music's standing while insisting on the necessity of encouraging its practice at all levels of society, and another reply to GutsMuths's article noted that Michaelis had overlooked it: "Overall, that which seemed most important to me as an educator was not touched on at all in any of these articles, or only fleetingly. Namely, I am convinced that music is not to be recommended to youth simply as a means to develop taste, as a noble form of entertainment, etc.; it is infinitely more important (especially song) as the most excellent means of education, in order to develop a pure and noble spirit, to weave love of the good and beautiful in general, and of virtue and religion, deeply and intimately into our being, so that they remain forever inseparable."[43]

Here, firmly rooted in enlightened ideals of cultivation within the established order, was an enormously promising argument for the necessity of serious music. The development of discriminating taste and a capacity for pleasing entertainment perhaps smacked all too clearly of the self-indulgent habits of an internationalized and frivolous aristocracy, and the humble services provided to the lower classes by the worthy but unsophisticated *Musikant* perhaps did little to enhance the respectability of musical practice—in fact, they might simply reinforce the very associations that advocates of musical culture sought to defeat. But if so, insistence upon the serious value of music as a means of popular cultivation could offer a solution with potential not only to enhance music's prestige but also to provide a substantial and respectable place for musicians as those uniquely qualified to provide that cultivation. And as this excerpt suggests, music could claim to provide more than just one among many largely interchangeable means of cultivation. Its long-established associations with expressive and nonconceptual significance could support the claim that music could enhance spiritual and moral cultivation as a vital supplement to intellectual development. And as another article illustrates, such claims could easily mesh with faith in music's recent progress: "Recent music is far richer in melodies, our instruments are greatly improved and more capable of good performance and expression, [and] harmony, a substantial area of music, has been added to it; should we not therefore indeed be able to maintain about our music precisely what the ancients claimed about theirs with just as much propriety and even more: namely, that it has a cultivating influence on human character?"[44]

The utopian qualities of this aspiration will become apparent in the following chapters, for the hope that the entire population might be cultivated *through* music as a means of enhancing character and sociability inevitably conflicted with the desire to cultivate them to practice music as an end in itself, which was equally necessary to justify a culture of concert music. The latter cause would require a degree of cultivation that far surpassed the much more limited aims of state-supported education, to say nothing of the financial means that were often inadequate even to those limited aims; but substantiating music's claim to serious artistic and moral value required the prominence of just such a concert culture. Out of this tension arose a confusing variety of arguments and counterarguments, but the concern that music be recognized as an essential aspect of human cultivation—and, crucially, be supported by the state as a result—runs through the entire period I have considered. And for music's advocates, who were as inclined as we are to read their own concerns into their reflections on others, this particular concern ran through the entire history of music. Thus, A. B. Marx was eager to note that Chinese music (although it otherwise left much to be desired) "has been the object of state support for more than 4000 years," and the author of an overview of ancient Roman music attributed its overall insignificance in part to the fact that it "never became part of a general cultivation of the people." [45]

It may by this point seem as though I am attempting to paint the advocates of serious music as cynical opportunists dedicated to attaining material security through whatever means proved necessary, and that the necessary means involved denying those very material motivations. I am, in fact, arguing both that material interests are inevitably bound up in the development of high musical culture and that advocates of that culture sought to shape it in ways that seemed to have potential to attract support. To equate this pursuit of interests with either cynicism or insincerity, however, would be a serious misunderstanding of not only the sources themselves, which show remarkably little evidence of those qualities, but also, more fundamentally, the social processes I am claiming to be operative here. With respect to the former, there is simply nothing to suggest that the figures whose work I discuss doubted the inherent value of the cultivated musical tradition they tirelessly and prolifically sought to advance. Indeed, their utter lack of ironic distance, occasional self-doubt, or even awareness of the possible validity of other viewpoints is a fascinating if sometimes tiresome mark of the gap between their culture and ours.

The theoretical point, however, is more significant than my evaluation of the character of various writers or musicians. Simply put, to claim that participation in fine art is socially or economically interested is, contrary to

the familiar claim that disinterestedness is a prerequisite to genuine aesthetic experience, to say nothing at all about the sincerity of an individual's
or group's commitment to that art. The five true lovers of art whom the
"practicing musician" cited above claimed to have encountered derived the
same social benefit from it as the forty-five who simply followed fashion,
but this by no means implies that their interest in music was not genuine.
Even more, as Pierre Bourdieu's studies of the relations between social
classes and taste reveal, genuine commitment to the aesthetic marks high
social standing far more effectively than does fashionable imitation. It signals what he terms "investment," a deeply rooted commitment to the values of the "games" associated with the social field for their own sake; and
the investment of those born to the game (as opposed to those who "em-
bark on the game by a conscious act") "is made more total and uncondi-
tional by the fact that it is unaware of what it is." [46] To the extent that serious music had indeed become an integral part of the life of the cultivated
classes, then, the five music lovers more effectively signaled their membership in it than did the remainder—as the dismissal of the latter implicit
in the article suggests. But "to the extent" must be taken quite seriously
here: if musicians succeeded in placing their practice (and thus themselves)
within the realm of socially necessary cultivation, then such an evaluation
was socially meaningful; if not, it was largely irrelevant, except to the minority of musicians who clung to that view. Thus, as the sources themselves have already suggested by their nervous insistence, the social status
of music held the key to the ascent or descent of its practitioners within society, and the cause of serious music was for those practitioners a serious
business.

　　Understanding the mechanics of prestige within society becomes, therefore, an essential part of my project, and for that reason I have drawn on
Bourdieu, who provides the most nuanced account of the interactions
of status and social class. For although it may be true in the overall work-
ings of the global economy that, as Immanuel Wallerstein claims, "status
is nothing more than the fossilization of the rewards of past achievement,"
for a social group whose way of life as a status marker for the church and
aristocracy appeared threatened, the establishment of a new form of status
was of paramount importance. [47] This situation shows clear parallels to the
development of both aesthetic thought in general and the category of vernacular literature, in that, as a variety of recent studies have shown, these
emergent fields are also integrally related to the interests of the bourgeoisie
and to the interests of authors who wished to confirm their identification

with that class.[48] The differences in the case of music, however, are also important to recognize. Thus, for example, John Guillory's argument that literature constituted a reification of the cultural capital of the bourgeoisie reveals significant parallels to the developments that concern me here. But the link between literature and literacy, the latter essential to the working of bourgeois society, meant that literary production had a visibly central role in the constitution of that society that music did not.[49] As a result, the marginalization that seemed to threaten music was all the more frightening; although relations among literary authors, publishers, and the public were by no means secure, the field of written literature was established to a degree that separated it from that of serious music in an essential way. For example, in the 1770s, when a character in Friedrich Nicolai's *Das Leben und die Meinungen des Herrn Magister Sebaldus Nothanker* sought to correct the title character's high opinion of literary culture, he employed an analogy with art and music:

> Your imagination, my dearest friend, still flies a bit too high. Let yourself down and come closer to earth! The greatest mass of professional writers practice a trade just as do wallpaper painters or pipers *[Kunst-pfeifer]* and consider the few truly learned writers almost exactly as those craftsmen would a [Anton Raphael] Mengs or a Bach—as intrusive bunglers who aren't a part of the guild. Out of this trade and not out of a desire to illumine the human race has arisen the unspeakable multitude of books at which you so wondered; for, for more than a hundred years, Leipzig has clearly been the market city for the goods that these learned craftsmen *[Handwerker]* prepare for every trade fair.[50]

Nicolai allows music its genuine artists in the figure of (presumably C. P. E.) Bach, but the purpose of the analogy is to link the literary production the character seeks to denigrate to more familiar examples of non-artistic production, among them music. Even more than that, though, Nicolai ranks the status of literary hacks slightly higher than that of the wallpaper painter and the piper, noting that their views are *almost* identical but, presumably, not quite so degraded. Finally, note that the *Kunst-pfeifer* (and the term *Kunst* here is used in analogy with such terms as *Kunstreiter*, a trick circus rider) is distinct from the respected composer-performer in a way that the hack writer is not distinguished from his or her serious counterpart: the piper is simply not a part of the literary world at all, while the published and respected composer is. For musicians, the specter of descent not merely to a less respectable realm of literate culture but entirely below it, to the world of tavern fiddlers and wandering gypsies, loomed with an immediacy that had no direct literary counterpart. That prospect, however unlikely its actual realization may have been, conditions a significant amount of the writing I cite.

To summarize, then, my principal claims are these:

- The ideal of a high musical culture as it developed through the late eighteenth and early nineteenth centuries in German-speaking Europe must be understood in the context of the historically specific material and social concerns of musicians and those dependent on musical activity. Neither the gross developmental schema of a transition from feudal to capitalist relations of production, on the one hand, nor the privileging of a history of ideas and aesthetic developments, on the other, adequately characterizes this development, unless one also takes account of the local and practical concerns of those who constituted the social field of music, a field that came to be demarcated with increasing clarity during the early decades of the nineteenth century.

- Those concerns dictated that the status of music as a serious activity worthy of the attention and support of cultivated society was of paramount importance. Accordingly, reading the musical discourse of the period in light of the potential for ascent or descent of music and its practitioners offers insight into the cause of serious music and its advocates.

- The claim for music's status as a practice essential to literate and cultivated society was closely associated with both a hierarchical understanding of the development of musical cultures and a project of popular cultivation in music. Music's claim to deserve public support depended on this assertion of universal public utility.

- The project of musical cultivation that resulted from this claim can be understood both as a part of the larger Enlightenment goal of popular pedagogy within the established social order and, from a still broader perspective, as an element in the development of a populace disciplined (in Foucault's sense) and therefore better suited to participation in a society increasingly characterized by the rationalized and regulated forms of interaction associated with capitalist relations of production. These systemic perspectives, however, must ultimately be connected back to the specific relations and concerns of the musical field and the motivations and actions of those who constituted it.

- Both the concert of serious music and the musicological project of reflection on works of art music and their creation were also defined in essential ways by the situation of music and its practitioners during this time, and they continue to show the influence of that context—often redefined and in support of different ends—to a degree often overlooked.

- Ultimately, the status of German musical culture rested on a precariously double-edged claim: serious (and most often German) music was held to be universally valid, even though, at the same time, maintaining its prestige demanded limiting access to it along the lines of existing social divisions, prominent among them class, gender, education, and nationality. To ignore the significance of the claim to universality would not only obscure the ways in which the equally significant exclusions operated, but it would also distort the motivations of the advocates of serious music. To overlook those exclusions, however, as musicology all too frequently has, is to mistake the ideals of a culture for its admittedly less flattering but considerably more complex social dynamics.

Once again, it is worth emphasizing the fact that to support these claims I have focused on musical discourse. As invaluable as a thorough exploration of the practices that constituted those relations would be, my goal has been more modest but, I hope, more attainable: to explore the writing of advocates of serious music in order to contextualize both ideals and boundaries that have too often been given little consideration even as they have lived on to shape more recent attitudes and practices. I have thus sought to contribute, albeit in a preliminary way, to a larger project that Jörg Fischer, in an insightful critique of the original German edition of Carl Dahlhaus's *Nineteenth-Century Music*, describes as "a critical social history of music, in which the 'high music' of the nineteenth century would not so much have to fall under ideological suspicion as it would have the conditions of its existence, its place, and its social dependency more strongly accentuated."[51]

Because I have focused on the ideology of serious music rather than specific locations or events, my account has a generalizing quality. That is to say, it is not an examination of local particulars but rather of shared goals. This is by no means to claim that the situation in Vienna was interchangeable with that in Berlin, or that the geographical, political, and religious differences between Saxony, Switzerland, and Bohemia were either insignificant or unrecognized at the time, but simply to note that the advocates of a culture of serious music consciously sought to transcend those differences. Indeed, one of the persistent characteristics of the musical discourse I consider here is its insistence on the desirability of cultivating music for the good of both musicians and humanity as a whole. Neither have I provided a monographic study of a single period or individual. The period I have included intentionally embraces both the classical and the romantic periods of the standard music-historical narrative and takes into account the work of authors whose views on a variety of topics are sometimes in sharp opposition to one another. But as Lydia Goehr has noted of the only slightly later controversy between Wagner and Eduard Hanslick, even the most inveterate opponents within musical discourse shared a crucial premise: music's "proper purpose of human cultivation." [52] In order to suggest the social context and the implications of this shared premise, a general perspective proved essential, one that easily could have produced a relatively static representation of high musical culture as an entity—after the model, perhaps, of Friedrich Kittler's characterization of the discourse network he identifies with the arbitrary date of 1800. [53] But even though the aspirations of a Forkel in the 1780s and a Fink or even a Brendel in the 1840s were similar in a number of important ways, the drastically different social and musical circumstancs of the two ends of my period meant that I inevitably needed to come to terms with historical change as well.

For instance, by the 1840s no one writing about music would have conceived of the musical world as Johann Adam Hiller did in the introductory issue of his *Wöchentliche Nachrichten und Anmerkungen die Musik betreffend* (1766): "By announcing serious pieces of music at courts or in churches we will also seek to accomplish nothing but to commend the diligence of skillful masters in this area of musical composition as well, and to save them from a kind of obscurity, or even contempt, to which they appear to be condemned through no fault of their own, since the often far more trivial work for the operatic stage everywhere contests its superiority. The musical societies in cities certainly also deserve to be mentioned in their form and arrangement, since they are generally the nurseries of music, or ought to be." [54] To be sure, fears about the preponderance of opera remained, but by the end of our period, civic—that is, public—music making had definitively replaced the court and the church as the presumed location of the serious; the musical societies that Hiller mentions almost as an afterthought had come to dominate musical life, at least in the thinking of its advocates. To that extent, advocacy of serious music itself had served as an agent of change. If the concerts of the 1830s and 1840s were still far from being either as pure or as prominent as many writers would have liked, they were nonetheless considerably nearer the ideal than concerts had been only a generation earlier.

My focus on public, official musical life as imagined and represented by its advocates has another important consequence: it underrepresents both

domestic music-making and—partially (but only partially) as a result—
the role of women in musical life. Domestic music-making did indeed receive a share of attention; in 1842, for instance, August Kahlert noted that
it had provided a foundation for current concert life.[55] But Kahlert's reference is both retrospective and hierarchical. Although, as he was certainly
aware, domestic musical activity continued to play an important role—indeed, through the sale of music it effectively underwrote the existence of
musical culture as a whole—in his account it appears as both associated
with the past rather than the present and of less significance than the public, professionalized musical culture that is his primary concern. The presumption that men were the actors in this public musical world is pervasive, and thus the small place accorded to women in these sources is not
only a result of the exclusion of the domestic sphere in which they played
a dominant role. For although work such as that of Freia Hoffmann has
begun to make clear that women did indeed play a role in professional musical life in defiance (or perhaps more accurately, circumvention) of hege-
monic constructions of gender, the discourse I discuss here is precisely that
which helped establish and reinforce those normative conventions, both
overtly (as discussed in chapter 4) and, more often, implicitly (as I note
occasionally elsewhere).[56] Accordingly, my choice of masculine pronouns
in paraphrases and discussions of these texts is a conscious decision to go
against current conventions in the hope that the exclusion those pronouns
signal will more effectively convey the text's often unspoken implications.
The project of inserting music into the public sphere was in the end also a
project of masculinizing it.

The remainder of the book takes the form of a series of case studies focused on a selection of social relations, moving from the perceived outer
limits of music to the very center of musical culture. Chapter 2 explores
the relation of scholars of music—or better, given the multiple roles often
played by participants in musical culture during this period, of the scholarly *stance* toward music—to musical cultures as wholes in what might
appear to be the most disinterested and distant of cases: the representation
of the musical cultures of the world. But concerns for the status of German
music are rarely distant from such accounts and sometimes provide the
central focus of pieces ostensibly devoted to far more exotic topics—and
nowhere do attempts to conceptualize musical culture as a whole occur
with the frequency that they do in discussions of national musics. A variety of scattered individual accounts provides a sense of the developmental
hierarchy of musical cultures, but the most comprehensive view of the period is found in Gustav Schilling's quirky (and immodestly titled) *Ency-*

clopädie der gesammten musikalischen Wissenschaften, oder Universal-Lexikon der Tonkunst (Encyclopedia of the Complete Musical Sciences, or Universal Lexicon of Musical Art), a six-volume work of the late 1830s. The *Encyclopädie*'s articles on national musical cultures, many written by some of the most prominent musical authorities of the period, show this developmental hierarchy in conjunction with a concept of national cultural identity that betrays a clear debt to Herder. Despite the work's evident assertion of the musical superiority of Germany, though, most of its articles continue to premise their evaluations on an assertion of current sophistication that is more concerned with the cause of music than that of the state; to assert the Germanness of complex music was less a patriotic claim than a promotional one. Even in the area that appears most distant from the immediate oncerns of musical practice, then, the setting of boundaries served to enhance the position of domestic musical culture. This equation of sophisticated autonomous music with Germany was indeed, as Pederson puts it, an "exclusionary ideology," but one not so much "directed at other nations" as intended to secure recognition of the cultural significance of German music on the basis of its unique quality.[57]

Composers in relation to "the people" are the focus of chapter 3, whose subject is the ambivalent issue of popularity, especially as manifested in the concept of a musical *Volkston*. J. A. P. Schulz's characterizations of the qualities required for songs that would be acceptable to and meet the needs of a broad populace provide clear examples of the application of Enlightenment rhetoric of education dispensed by a knowledgeable elite to a needy populace. But as the writings of his contemporary Johann Friedrich Reichardt reveal, that position was an uncertain one, given the current position of musicians. An alternative view of the popular—the suggestion that the musician might learn from the music of the people rather than provide for them—was also risky: it threatened the distinction of the musician as a member of the cultivating elite by implying that value derived from qualities inherent in the people rather than from the authority of the trained musician. The greater prominence of this view toward the end of the period under consideration is a sign of the developing security of musical culture. The discourse surrounding the *Volkston* took place at a comfortable distance from what has become the canonic repertoire of the period, but its relevance is suggested by consideration of issues concerning the popular in the music of Haydn, Schubert, and Schumann. Finally, the rhetoric of more recent musicology shows that the issues of popularity and the relation of serious music to "the people" continue to shape critical understanding of "serious" music.

Chapter 4 continues to deal with popular cultivation, but from the perspective of the music teacher in relation to children—or of that relationship as imagined by the pedagogues most closely associated with the cause of serious music. This latter qualification proves crucial, for nowhere is the contrast between the utopian ideals of cultivation in music and the limitations—established both by the political and economic situation of general education and by the disciplinary process of cultivation itself—more evident than it is here. Hans Georg Nägeli's influential elementary singing method is the principal focus for this chapter, which proceeds from the details of systematic, "natural" pedagogy to consider that pedagogy's significance in a variety of contexts. Not only are Nägeli's links to enlightened ideals of cultivation clear, but his method also provides nearly a textbook example of a disciplinary practice in Foucault's sense. To suggest the larger set of relations in which such pedagogy was imbedded, I consider as well a variety of other writings on education, writings that, in conjunction with Nägeli's, reveal the ways in which the discourse on pedagogy addressed family and gender ideals, social boundaries, and economic concerns. Finally, a more general consideration of these issues in relation to the developing professional concerns of musicians suggests the interests shared even by those who appear to have had the most diverse goals for musical cultivation.

The final chapter returns to a topic more familiar to musicology, one at the heart of the period's musical discourse: the development of the concert. Familiar though the rise of the concert is as a distinct music-historical topic, the issues of cultivation and the setting of boundaries link it to the topics of the previous chapters. The perspective developed in those chapters helps to clarify the place of this institution within the larger concept of musical culture. Its central role made the concert a topic that was treated extensively throughout the period. I have, therefore, chosen not to focus on a single topic or author but rather to survey a broader variety of materials in order to suggest the ways in which the ideal of the serious concert served to objectify the relationships that constituted a well-ordered musical culture. The interaction of performer and audience is the most obvious such relationship, but a variety of others demand attention as well. Since the advocates of serious music saw the concert above all as a forum for the most advantageous possible presentation of the finest musical works, the system of generic values that determined which works were appropriate to that forum constructed a far broader network of social relations, one that built on the hierarchies on which the project of cultivation was based. Because those judgments took the form of musical evaluation rather than personal or explicitly social ones, however, the concert could appear as the showcase of absolute aesthetic value, free of outside interests and influences.

The ideology of the concert's autonomy had a variety of implications. It both demanded and reinforced the development of an institution that was formally independent of the social hierarchy rather than an overt reflection of it. It also helps account for musical discourse's increasingly negative view of virtuoso performers, whose personal charisma and reliance on their own compositions threatened the disinterested authority of the concert and musical discourse itself as the certifiers of the canonically valid. Moreover, it defined an event in which the musical public could be set apart with increasing clarity from the professionalizing performer. The cultivated and socially respectable standing of that public served to confirm the status of music as a contributor to general cultivation, while the distinction between the public and the professional performer (whose technical accomplishments were increasingly necessary) helped secure the economic basis of the field by reducing the status (and hence the prevalence) of concerts of dilettantes. Finally, the composer, whose genius confirmed the authority of the critics and demanded both the cultivation of the audience and the professional skills of the performer, emerged as the central figure around whom all the relationships of the ideal concert revolved.

All of this goes far beyond Franz Grillparzer's modest anecdote of private amateur improvisation. But it is ultimately an indication of the success of the project of institutionalizing a high musical culture of professional musicians that the image of an melancholy teenager improvising for hours seems so quaintly remote from the world of serious music. The tensions within and around the developing musical culture that Grillparzer's teacher represented meant that creative activity within that culture would finally become the prerogative of only a relatively few even within the class of professional musicians. If we still recognize the melancholy teenager absorbed in music as a cultural stereotype, the music in which he or she is apt to be absorbed is rooted in a very different culture. In that respect, at least, the success of the project of serious music in institutionalizing a place for musicians, critics, and scholars may be inseparable from its failure to become the universal expression that it claimed to be.

2   Scholarship and the Definition of Musical Cultures

A discussion of attempts to define the musical cultures of the world may seem an oddly remote place to begin a consideration of the strategies through which the status of serious music was established in one particular region of Europe. But although it is true that representing the music of the rest of the world was a relatively peripheral concern for most participants in German musical discourse, the role that those representations played was more significant than their quantity might suggest: they allowed a conceptualization of musical cultures as a whole, providing a space in which to imagine what was—or might become—unique about German music in particular. As Veit Erlmann argues in another context, because Europeans and non-Europeans have "represented each other for centuries, if not millennia, through a variety of media and objects, imagining common spaces and narratives, it follows that no 'local' identity can ever be constructed from grounds circumscribed by a bounded, defined place."[1] In their determination to develop such a local identity, the advocates of serious German music engaged with and reshaped a newly available body of knowledge about the world's musics, and in the course of that engagement their sense of their own place emerges with unusual clarity. Although images of other musics had played a role in the imagination of European music for centuries, sustained consideration of non-European music in German music literature developed precisely when the identity and security of that culture seemed most threatened; the scholarly enterprise of delineating it was inseparable from the development of an historical and developmental hierarchy that allowed a claim for its privileged status.

To see this, it will be necessary to move beyond the issues of disciplinary and intellectual history that have been the central focus of discussions of early ethnomusicology and to consider German discourse on other musics as a social practice through which a variety of interests were engaged.[2] As Philip Bohlman has noted, "Ethnomusicological thought in the nineteenth century was inseparable from the work of that century's foremost musical scholars," and since, at least in the early part of the century, those scholars were also among the foremost advocates of German art music, their perspective on musical cultures provides a valuable orientation to their cause.[3] Indeed, as Erlmann further suggests, without the confrontation with those cultures that Europe's colonial expansion provided, the reflexive understanding of that cause that constitutes musicology would be quite literally unthinkable: "Musicology, as a mode of knowledge about an object called European music, in fact could only have emerged in relation to colonial encounters."[4]

CONCERNING INDIAN — AND GERMAN — MUSIC

On 19 January 1803, the *Allgemeine musikalische Zeitung*, unquestionably German-speaking Europe's leading music journal at the time, featured a lead article that departed considerably from what had become the norm in the first five years of its existence. Instead of the usual article on aesthetics or musical life, or a review of a musical work or treatise on theory, history, or pedagogy, it ran a lengthy review (serialized over two issues) of *Ueber die Musik der Indier,* a translation of Sir William Jones's writings on Indian music annotated and supplemented by Friedrich Hugo von Dalberg.[5] Although, as we will see, discussions of the music of other cultures were occasional features of German music journals throughout the late eighteenth and early nineteenth centuries, such lavish and prominent treatment of a topic so apparently remote from the central concerns of the *Allgemeine musikalische Zeitung* was unprecedented: no such review had ever appeared in the journal. Nor did this article's appearance change the journal's focus significantly.[6] The book, though, had clearly touched a nerve, and the review's extraordinary defensiveness proves a useful introduction to a consideration of German scholarship's construction of the musical world and its own place in it.

The review begins by acknowledging the value of the book's effort to illuminate a previously obscure topic and goes on to provide an historically grounded justification for an interest in Indian music: since it is well-known that the people of the Orient had been the originators of culture, which Occidentals had received from them, their musical culture is of particular interest; we could only profit from "getting to know the situation of musical art among those nations from which the first culture originated and which were also prevented in various ways from participating in the later progress of the art."[7] The implicit assumption that other cultures preserved an earlier state of musical development was nearly universal among Germans who wrote about those cultures, and the assumption was often, as here, united with a faith in linear musical progress that formed one of the bases of evaluation of any musical achievement. Precisely with respect to this latter belief, the book's two authors—a British official who had taken an avid interest in Indian music and an accomplished German musical dilettante, a member of a distinguished family of long noble standing[8]—had, according to the review's author, made their crucial mistake.

Jones's work had dealt principally with Indian scales (his death had prevented him from completing a projected larger historical work), which he claimed showed similarities to the Western church modes; according to the review, this claim was part of a strategy to confirm the value of Indian music. But, the reviewer insisted, the character of Indian culture makes such a claim to value dubious:

> For the culture of the Hindus had more to do with the expansion of fantasy than with clarification of the intellect. Moreover, they remained fixed in that state, and from thence arises their marked tendency to make sensual, to symbolize, and to personify everything intellectual. Indeed, they have this in common with all Orientals, as with all peoples who no longer live in the primitive state but who are still distant from genuine enlightenment; but the Hindus seem to carry this further than other Asians. For they . . . are among the most harmless, peace-loving nations (one could also say the most passive and indolent or feminine). No wonder they have a delicate feeling for music! But also no wonder that, prevented by climate, religious and political circumstances, etc., from further development, they so drenched even the first elements of music with fantasy that they had their hands full with them and could not disentangle themselves from the magic circle they had drawn themselves, even if they had wanted to; rather, they became ever more absorbed in it.[9]

The volume's editor shows this himself through numerous examples of Hindu musical myths. But by failing to recognize the undeveloped state of Indian music, "the author and editor allowed themselves to be misled by (an excusable) partiality for their subject, to confuse poverty with simplicity and clumsiness with originality and sensible daring, in support of the value of Indian music."[10]

Given the familiarity of Orientalism as a critical category, such dismissals of non-European cultures are perhaps not surprising, nor is the way in which the review links the non-European with the unenlightened, the irrational, and the feminine. In a music journal, however, it may come as a surprise to find those latter qualities so bluntly associated with heightened musical sensibility. Enlightened rationality remains wary of the suspicious deviancy of musicality, and the review testifies to the aptness of Philip Brett's identification of "teutonic abstraction" as a "means of self-policing" through which musical education guards against this threat: by ascribing music's dangerous qualities to a foreign culture, the reviewer casts himself in the role of the guardian of the rational and abstract in music.[11] Since the reviewer makes no claim to have encountered any Indian music himself, the security of this evaluation is remarkable, and it would be easy to dismiss it as a close-minded reaction against a pioneering work that more recent ethnomusicologists have recognized as an important early work in their field.[12] But although that close-mindedness is undeniable, its origins merit closer examination: the disagreement between Jones (especially as Dalberg presents him) and the reviewer exemplifies a tension that not only pervades German accounts of the music of other cultures but also bears on the social and ideological concerns of the advocates of German high musical culture.

Indeed, the cause of serious music pervades the review, which turns out to devote considerably more attention to the status of European, and especially recent German, music than to its ostensible subject, and it is precisely Jones's and Dalberg's overenthusiasm for that subject that the reviewer takes as his principal target: "Whether thereby [through the material he presents] the *special worth* of Indian music is established, upon which the author insists so powerfully that he seeks to overshadow even our own progress in music by contrast, and in which the editor [Dalberg] supports him as strongly as possible—that is another question, which this reviewer has no hesitation at all in *denying*." According to Jones and Dalberg, Indian music is inseparably tied to words, "but," as the reviewer puts it, "an art deserves that name only if it is *independent*"; and since Indian music had no independent harmonic system and depended utterly on the text for its rhythm, it could make no such claim, however complex its scales might be.[13] Such a mistake can only be the result of a one-sided view of music, one that failed to recognize, for instance, that composition is not simply the translation of words into music but rather the expression in ordered tones of aesthetic ideas, "some of which are pleasing in and of themselves (for example, in quartets) and signify no feelings that can be specified through *concepts [Begriffe]*, and some of which, *bound* to concepts (words), express *more defined* feelings."[14] If this is denied, a whole realm of music is eliminated: "And this vast area of music . . .—ought we diligently to restrict it, if it were possible, in order to gain a supposedly greater energy in music, which surely could not be won with a small supply of artistic means, but rather only through a larger one, appropriate to *our* culture? Ought we— as would necessarily follow—. . . to declare the best compositions of a C. P. E. Bach, of a Joseph Haydn, among others, to be affectations, and satisfy ourselves with musical forage—or sweet pablum? No, Germany's genius will prevent that, even if it were not so obviously to be forbidden." [15]

Orientals, the ancient Greeks, and even the contemporary French might be indifferent to instrumental music, the review continues, but Germans are bound to disagree with Dalberg, who even went so far as to cite Fontenelle's famous question, "*Sonate, que me veux-tu?*"(Sonata, what do you want of me?) as a critique of empty "passagework and difficulties" in current music.[16] Granted, the reviewer counters, much instrumental music is shallow, "but is this evidence that we should give up our hard-earned and varied artistic means and lead our music voluntarily back into the dependence from which it has freed itself, especially in Germany?"[17] The answer, expounded at considerable length, is clearly no, and although the review goes on to note and correct a number of smaller points (and speculates on the dim prospects that British colonization will cultivate the Hindus to "greater humanity"), its focus is unquestionably on the defense of autonomous—and largely German—instrumental music against what it perceives as the challenge Jones and Dalberg offer to its validity. All of this, the reviewer declares, makes clear the need for a theory that would account for the value of this music.[18] It should by now be clear that more is at stake in this review than the nuances of Indian music—indeed, there is little evidence that its author is concerned about them at all. An alternative would be to read it instead as a straightforward argument for the superiority of German music, and certainly, passages like this one appear to support such a reading: "The same voice [like Kant questioning the validity of music as a fine art] sounds from England, Italy, and France, where, with few exceptions, there is little sense and talent for independent, aesthetically pure music. And we Germans, who must justifiably be proud of the accomplishment of having elevated music to a higher level, should we let others argue or belittle us out of it?"[19]

On this reading, both Kant and Dalberg come off essentially as traitors to the nation—a particularly damning judgment in the Napoleonic era in which the review appeared. But as Celia Applegate has argued, invocation of a German nation in the early nineteenth century most often has little to do with the state-oriented conception implied by the notion of treason, and even the anti-French stance of the review is less straightforward than the passages I have cited might suggest: as contemptuous as the author is of French taste in music, he writes with apparent approbation of Napoleon's invasion of Egypt as a contribution to that country's aesthetic and intellectual cultivation.[20]

A closer consideration of the review's context and rhetoric suggest an alternative that is less straightforward but ultimately, I believe, more plausible. The *Allgemeine musikalische Zeitung*, it is crucial to recall, was a "general" publication but one directed to a specific fraction of an already small audience: that portion of the literate German population with a serious amateur or professional interest in music. As such, it represented the dominant voice concerned with music within the German public sphere and would continue to do so until a variety of seriously competing journals began to appear in the 1820s and 1830s.[21] Given this context and the pervasive concerns for the status of music discussed in the introduction, the review's emphasis on German music as a touchstone of value takes on a different resonance; it is less a straightforward appeal to patriotism than an attempt to align a cause that centrally concerned only a relatively small group—the cause of serious, autonomous music—with a more general population, the German literary public, for whom a national cultural identity had, since Herder, become a familiar and powerful ideology. In effect, *wir Deutsche* (we Germans) is a wishfully invoked metaphor for *wir Musiker* (we musicians), a claim that the prestige associated with the former category applies to the latter as well.

On this reading, Dalberg escapes suspicion as a traitor, but the contrast between his perspective and that of the reviewer still demands consideration. There is no denying that Dalberg too had a serious interest in the cause of German musical culture: he was an accomplished pianist, a composer, the author of a number of theoretical works, and a patron and supporter of music, and he had dedicated *Ueber die Musik der Indier* to none other than Joseph Haydn. Why, then, should his perspective have differed so drastically from the review's? Once again, the position from which Dalberg wrote proves critical. A descendent of a prominent noble family, Dalberg had been given the most extensive education that his privileged position could afford him. His extensive travels included accompanying Herder to Italy in 1775.[22] All of this suggests that Dalberg was invested in music in a very different way than were those who depended on it for their livelihood. It seems highly unlikely that he would in any case have endorsed the extreme viewpoints the reviewer reads into his words, but his privileged standing nonetheless allowed him a detachment that made possible the disinterested—or, according to the review, insufficiently interested—consideration of so remote a topic, even at the risk of appearing to slight the activities of the musicians of his own culture.[23] The review's tendentious response makes clear the gap that set Dalberg's position apart from the perspective of those more directly bound up in German musical life, whose attention focused on the music of other cultures only when they could see an immediate connection to their own musical and social concerns. This clash between a privileged perspective, which often had literary associations and, frequently, aristocratic origins, and that of musicians or authors dependent on serious music for a livelihood is one we will encounter again; it serves as a warning against the too-easy equation of serious musical culture with German literate culture, an equation that would confound the aspirations of music's advocates with the reality they faced.

We are now in a position to understand the review's desire for a *"solid aesthetic theory of music,"* especially in contrast to what was currently available: "for up to now we have only those that deal with its *mechanical* parts, among them not only piano methods and the like but also texts on pure composition, fugue, and other things."[24] A genuinely philosophical theory of music would provide the justification to the literate world that music needed to establish its legitimacy; by equating even the ostensibly more prestigious literature on composition with conventionally devalued instruction manuals and labeling both "mechanical," the contrast between writing within a trade and literature about an art is drawn sharply and unmistakably. Whatever the utility of the former, it will not establish the legitimacy of music's claim to be a part of general literate culture without the latter, and unless that legitimacy is established, music (and, equally important, its practitioners) will remain vulnerable to the attacks that the reviewer so energetically parries.

MUSIC AND HUMAN CULTIVATION

Similar issues are evident in most German discussions of other cultures and their music, even brief, apparently incidental ones. In 1810, for instance, an article advocating broader training for composers introduced its subject with an object lesson drawn from world history: "Aesthetic culture, uniting the sensual with the intellectual, leads to humanity. Poetry cultivates most powerfully. For that reason art miscarried among the unpoetic [ancient] Egyptians and does so today among the unpoetic Chinese. Music does not possess this power, because it lacks objectivity and therefore easily produces one-sidedness."[25] In imagining a more cultivated future for composers, this essay too seeks to link music to a broader, literary culture, albeit at the cost of implying a parallel between current, uncultivated musicians and the unpoetic Egyptians and Chinese. Such parallels suggest that the link between conventional stereotypes of crude musicians and equally stereotyped representations of the music of crude peoples is more than one of common vocabulary: the concept of human cultivation provided a universally applicable standard by which music would be judged.[26]

Unless, of course, music itself could provide the standard of judgment. And that is precisely the approach taken by a number of publications that set the tone for German responses to other musics. Johann Nicolaus Forkel, for instance, published several articles describing the music of a variety of cultures during the 1770s and 1780s, including both the ancient Egyptians and the Chinese.[27] The brief account of ancient Egyptian music does little more than describe a number of Egyptian instruments, but its introductory summary, ostensibly defending ancient Egyptian culture against the assertion that it had no music whatsoever, provides a double comparison that places Egyptian music on the same plane as much contemporary non-European music while making clear that the writer judges from a position that allows dismissal of all those musics: "After such clear explanations, one would almost think that the Egyptians had had no music at all; but they did indeed, albeit very bad, and just as repulsive as music still is today among all peoples in Africa and southern Asia."[28]

Forkel's view of China is more subtle but equally revealing. Here, in an unusually lengthy article, he summarizes the writings of Joseph-Marie Amiot, a French Catholic missionary to China who had enthusiastically reported the complexities of Chinese music theory in a 1779 publication.[29] According to Amiot's report, the Chinese had discovered the division of the octave into twelve tones as early as 2637 B.C., long before the development of Greek and Egyptian music theory; since that system was the first to exist, Amiot concluded that those nations must have learned their system from the Chinese, perhaps as a result of a trip to China by Pythagoras.[30] Amiot's account of current Chinese music was far less favorable, however, and Forkel devotes considerable attention to the unsuccessful attempt of the emperor Kung-hi to introduce Western music, as well as to the strong Chinese resistance to that music; the emperor's attempt failed because "the imagined [i.e., Chinese music with its connections to the Confucian belief system] maintained its advantage over the true, and prejudices hindered persuasion."[31] After presenting a lengthy response by an imagined Chinese speaker to the purported advantages of European music, Forkel concludes, "So say the contemporary Chinese, clearly wrongly, but nonetheless with so much conviction that it is impossible to make them comprehend their error. They are the victims of the prejudices of an upbringing that teaches them that everything that is really good is found among them, and that the music developed by their ancestors is the most perfect in the world. Further, they recognize only their coarse and insensitive organs as judges of their feelings and will invariably laugh at us when we want to convince them that in order to be good, their music must be disposed according to the rules that we observe in Europe." [32]

Aside from expressing mild skepticism for some of Amiot's claims about the absolute priority of Chinese theory, Forkel presents his account relatively straightforwardly. Unlike the review with which I began, this article does not criticize the work on which it draws. The passage just cited, however, makes clear the absence of what Bohlman has termed "the unrestrained awe with which Amiot sometimes portrays Chinese intellectual and musical achievements." [33] Rather, Forkel's introduction frames the article in a way that makes it an object lesson in the cause of cultural and musical development:

> It is certainly worth consideration, when a people promises the most excellent prospects in the first bursting forth of the arts and, despite all those splendid prospects, remains fixed at one point. The Chinese, about whom Europeans are still uncertain whether they really ought to be considered clever or stupid, are a case in point. The music of their land is still today as it was many centuries ago; still just as stiff, unmelodic, unharmonic, and peculiar as one could possibly imagine, and as ever it could have been in its earliest childhood. Nonetheless it is capable of most powerfully moving the hearts of the natives.
>
> Now, with Chinese practical music in such a state, one could scarcely expect that the Chinese could have any particularly correct concepts about this art at all. Nonetheless, one finds a kind of theory concerning this art among them, a theory that contains such correct concepts that one can scarcely marvel at them enough. And still more, one finds that these correct concepts in their music theory stem from the very oldest ages of the nation. Now, how can it happen that this people, with such early good prospects, have until now still come no further in perfecting this art? [34]

That question, Forkel continues, can be answered only after closer consideration of Chinese music—hence his consideration of Amiot's work. Although he never returns explicitly to his opening question, his reflections on the Chinese as "victims" of their tradition-bound upbringing and unrefined reliance on their senses are clearly directed toward answering it—but also toward reinforcing the proper attitude about art and its development for all. The article, after all, had begun with a generalizing statement and had introduced the Chinese only as an example, and although it is tempting to dismiss this as a conventional opening gesture, it provided a crucial link between this article and a volume otherwise devoted (with the exception of a few historical accounts of European composers) to identifying and chronicling the activities and publications of current composers, performers, and writers on music. The link between a vital musical present and a rationalized cultivation in music that would break through traditional judgment, bound by the limits of unrefined sensation, justifies the article's presence.

I will continue to explore the issue of cultivation in relation to the place of musical cultures shortly, but Forkel's reinterpretation of Amiot bears further consideration before I do so. Amiot's enthusiastic account, as Bohlman notes, had "rephrased many of the basic arguments in the 18th-century aesthetic battle of the Ancients and the Moderns . . . , emphatically arguing that, if one is to engage in this line of reasoning, the only possible conclusion is that Chinese and other Asian musics are far superior to the music of either Ancients or Moderns in European history." [35] Although Bohlman sees this as a "new practice of cultural critique," it is also true that Amiot's learned speculations on connections between Chinese, Egyptian, and Greek music in antiquity place him in the position of learned authority that Edward Said famously characterized as essential to the constitution of Orientalist discourse, that academic beneficiary of, counterpart to, and justification for imperialist expansion. [36] Such discourse is inseparable from the increasing Western domination that produced it, as the review with which I began makes clear with its blithe references to British and French colonial exploits; still, that review, Forkel's account of Chinese music, and the vast majority of German treatments of the music of non-Europeans differ significantly from accounts like Amiot's or Jones's in that they are not firsthand accounts but rather redactions and translations of the accounts of others. [37] They adapted those accounts for a German readership whose interest lay less in the specific details of the music of "their" territories, for they had none to speak of, than in confirming the universal validity of their own music—a project ultimately no less Eurocentric than those of the French, English, and other authors on whom they drew, but one more directly grounded in the concerns of the musical field than in the overtly political. [38] And from that perspective, to champion Chinese over European music was as unthinkable for Forkel as the idea of the superiority of Indian music was for Jones and Dalberg's reviewer.

Cultivation, then, and specifically cultivation in a system perceptibly related to harmonically dominated European music, proved a useful standard for defining a musical world in which serious music—the music whose existence increasingly centered on the institution of the concert—occupied the highest level of a hierarchy. And the gatekeepers of that hierarchy were none other than those most interested and involved in that music. So blunt a formulation must inevitably render the work of these men (and men they were, to an overwhelming degree—another boundary whose ramifications I consider below) as more self-serving than may seem appropriate. After all, Forkel was sincerely convinced of the self-evident superiority of Western music, and his efforts on behalf of that music were tireless and, retrospectively, enormously influential—and the same is true of many of the authors whose works I consider below. But as I stressed in the introduction, to recognize that an aesthetic judgment is not disinterested is by no means to question its sincerity, nor even to suggest that those who make the judgment are aware of the interests it serves. As Bourdieu puts it, "Each taste feels itself to be natural—and so it almost is, being a habitus. . . . The most intolerable thing for those who regard themselves as the possessors of legitimate culture is the sacrilegious reuniting of tastes which taste dictates shall be separated."[39] Precisely the habitus—the internalized system of values and proclivities that inform a subject's actions—makes such judgment seem as natural as the upbringing that Forkel so regretted in the Chinese. But the closer judgments come to locally contested matters, the more apparent their interests become, as we have seen in the case of *Ueber die Musik der Indier*. One of the few references to non-European music in Heinrich Christoph Koch's *Musikalisches Lexikon* of 1802, the entry for *Janitscharenmusik* (Janissary music), illustrates this point in a way that makes clear the potential of the concept of cultivation and its resulting hierarchy to affirm critical authority. After a brief description of the style, then still widely imitated by European composers, Koch concludes, "Janissary music betrays the principal marks of the music of a still primitive people, namely its tumultuousness and the extremely perceptible representation of the rhythm by monotonous percussion instruments; and the enthusiasm for this music, which has spread for some time, seems to make no great compliment to good taste."[40] Once again, discussion of a foreign topic serves a double purpose: the larger hierarchy that places European music and judgment above the exotic is affirmed while, at the same time, the critic's own judgment on trends within his own musical world (involving the "reuniting of tastes which taste dictates shall be separated") is reinforced by the unflattering association of common taste for the novelty of imitation Turkish music with the crudity of its model.

The larger social and historical construct that consistently informs such references is succinctly summarized by C. F. Michaelis in an article of 1814 dedicated to assembling a variety of accounts of "the music of some wild and half-cultivated peoples." The diversity of the sources Michaelis assembles—including reports of music in Madagascar, the Palau Islands of the South Pacific, Turkey, and several other parts of Africa and Asia (including China, Java, and Kamchatka)—suggests that he too is less interested in the particulars of any one culture's music, or even in assembling an overview of a particular part of the world, than in gathering a collection of curious anecdotes that will affirm the thesis he lays out in his introduction:

> How deeply in human nature the ability and inclination toward entertainment with song, dance, and music lies is revealed not only by ancient history but also by the reports that travelers have given us concerning wild and half-crude peoples. For just as the oldest documents of the human race and the history books of the Greeks and Romans already mention the crude beginning, the increasing progress, and the growing prestige of the musical arts, so those who describe travels in our day also rarely forget portrayals of musical entertainments that they have encountered among wild and half-barbaric peoples. We usually find the feeling for harmony and melody developed among these people in proportion to their greater or lesser general development, and their music more or less simple, crude, and wild. Many give us an image of the poor and miserable state that the practice of this art may have had in the first times after its invention.[41]

The shifting balance between history and travel as sources of information is particularly revealing in this passage. In the first sentence, these sources develop in parallel—history demonstrates the pervasiveness of music, and so do travel reports. Already in the second, however, the balance shifts toward history, despite the parallelism implied by the sentence's construction, for history reveals the entire development of music, while travel reporters merely portray "musical entertainments." And by the end of the passage, travel reports have been reduced to a supplement, a representation of what might have been in the past. This imbalance, however, is consistent with the developmental premise of cultivation: if the European present represents the current high point of human cultivation, history can show the entire process that led to that state, while knowledge of peoples who have not yet reached that level can contribute only specific details about the more primitive conditions that, for Europeans, lie in the distant past. Between that primitive beginning and the present, though, lies considerable uncertainty, a situation suggested not only by the article's rather motley assemblage of topics but also by its terminology: its title refers to *halb cultivirte*

Völker (half-cultivated peoples), and within the first paragraph the same groups are also labeled *halb roh*—literally, "half raw," a term that also implies a need for completion of a process of development—and *halb barbarisch*, or "half barbaric," with considerably more negative associations. In-between status is clear, but this terminological muddle suggests considerable confusion about the direction of whatever development is occurring. History, however, presents no such puzzles, leading only to greater prestige for the art.

Another long-standing view of both the past and "primitive" peoples, however, had the potential to threaten that prestige: accounts of the overwhelming impact of music on the ancients and on current peoples easily led those who encountered them to wonder why our music had no such power. Friedrich Rochlitz anticipated that challenge to music in an essay he considered significant enough to revise and expand more than twenty years after its first publication.[42] Although the original version of the essay had treated the question of "the difference between the effect of music on primitive or cultivated people" in the abstract, the later version is altered in a way that taps into German expectations about discussions of other cultures: it is framed as a lengthy excerpt from a letter to a friend who had proposed a German edition of an unnamed foreign book. The book's author had annoyed Rochlitz in an introductory chapter that expressed astonishment at the overwhelming impact of the simplest forms of music among primitive peoples and regretted that our music had no such effect on us. Rochlitz proposes to deal with the issue not by directly answering the question of music's differing impact but by examining the assumptions that underlay it.

To do so, he begins with a question that precedes that of music's impact: "Is it really music, then, that has such an effect on the uncultivated? And if it is, does it make its effect *as music?*"[43] The question, he insists, can be decided on the basis of shared assumptions about the nature of the arts (here, the epistolary conventions of the article allow Rochlitz to postulate common ground with the reader): the arts build on elements inherent in human nature, but "as they are found in reality among more or less cultivated peoples, who have a history," the arts are built of "certain proto-arts *[gewisse Urkünste]*."[44] In the case of music, these include the art of rhythm *(Rhythmik)* and tonal art *(Tonkunst)*, which includes both melody and harmony. With this basis established, the problem is solved:

> Now, primitive peoples, as well as completely ineducable ones (if they exist) and completely uncultivated people among us, have absolutely no real tonal art nor any feeling for it, but rather only rhythm, and feeling only for that. What intones *[tönt]* to their ears does not really in*tone*,

but only sounds and resounds *[hallt und schallt]*; it is only there for them as the condition of noticing the rhythmic. The corollary questions, such as why our music has almost no effect on them and theirs is repulsive to us, are thus no longer questions. They have no *music*, and also no feeling for it. What affects them is something completely different . . . , even if it is one of the components of music.[45]

Rochlitz's emphasis on what seems a purely semantic distinction is significant to the remainder of his argument, but two further aspects of this passage merit comment before we trace that argument. First, although he acknowledges the possibility of ineducable peoples, he appears skeptical about their existence—enlightened faith in the viability of universal cultivation informs the essay. Second, that faith encompasses as well the uncultivated within Rochlitz's own society; as the rest of the essay will demonstrate (and as I will consider in more detail in subsequent chapters), the category of cultivation is not, finally, a geographical one.

Having dispensed with the issue of music among primitives, Rochlitz proceeds to consider the source of rhythm's powerful impact. Although he concludes that it is basic to all humans, indeed to nature itself, that fact argues against its power, which must then reside in the associations those rhythms have for the hearers. Among the North American Indians, the drum and pipe recall the agitation and pride of battle; among the Scottish Highlanders (a recurrent favorite example of primitive European music), strong rhythms are associated with national pride and the heroic deeds of ancestors, while gentler ones call forth memories of love and domestic happiness; even within Germany, in relatively uncultivated provinces like Swabia, the Tyrol, and Styria, the effect of local dances and *"completely common* marches" is similar.[46]

Even granting this, however, the impact of this rhythm on the uncultivated seems far greater than that of much more sophisticated music on the cultivated. To answer this objection, Rochlitz once again considers the nature of art, and questions whether such overwhelming impact is, in fact, its goal: "Is not much rather the purpose, the reward, of art to moderate everything violent in and of humans, to tame the passionate, to do away with the primitive?"[47] The more moderate impact of our music, then, which appeals to heart and mind as well as to the senses, is a virtue, in accord with the nature of human culture:

Otherwise, what is the purpose of all cultivation? Indeed, it is not only concerned with social relations and customs, and not only with knowledge and opinions. What is it, and of what value is it, if it does not also reach decisively into our willpower and morality, and thereby even into our internal and external creative work and activity? We all know and acknowledge "moderation in everything" to be, like a first fruit, the first sign of true cultivation. Moderation is impossible when only sensuality is excited—but it is not only possible, but also easiest, when and where all parts of our being are taken equally into consideration, equally excited and occupied.[48]

Rochlitz proceeds to the somewhat inconsistent conclusion that our music too is capable of great effect, citing well-known examples of acknowledged leaders (among them Frederick the Great, and George I and George III of England) who showed themselves greatly moved by musical performances, but his claim for the influence of musical cultivation remains the heart of his response. By 1824, when the expanded version of his essay was published, many might have disputed his claim for moderation as the goal of art. Among those who sought to establish a place for art music in German culture, however, his larger points—that music contributed crucially and uniquely to the cultivation that was essential to the development of humanity, and that the music that could do so was the sophisticated, harmonically based art with which they were familiar—remained largely beyond dispute.

NATIONAL CHARACTER AND THE DEVELOPMENT OF MUSIC: HERDER AND SCHILLING'S *ENCYCLOPÄDIE*

I have so far paid little attention to another crucial aspect of German conceptions of other cultures, one closely associated with the work of Johann Gottfried Herder: the concept of the unique character of a people or nation. Indeed, with the exception of our first review's insistence on the qualities of German music, little in these sources suggests that Herder's ideas played a significant role in consideration of the music of other cultures. As I suggest below, this is not true of a variety of later sources, for Herder's ideas became too well-known—and too clearly relevant to the issue of the music of other cultures—to ignore; so, although a full consideration of Herder's views is far beyond the scope of the present chapter, a brief consideration is necessary.[49]

Herder is best known in music studies for his advocacy of the volkslied, a topic that will more directly concern us in the following chapter, but underlying that advocacy was a concept of cultural identity that had significant ramifications for the issues I have so far considered. In its most radical formulation, the position Herder advanced totally undercut the developmental faith we have seen in virtually all our examples. In a well-known statement, he declared, "In a certain sense, every human perfection is na-tional, secular, and most closely considered, individual"[50]—that is to say, there is no absolute standard of conduct (or art) by which human activity can be evaluated. Instead, differing historical, geographical, and individual circumstances mean that both persons and societies will inevitably differ essentially from one another, and judging them by a single standard is fun-damentally misguided. Particularly in the realm of cultures, this led Her-der to insist that each nation or culture (not, it is important to note, each state) had a distinct character or spirit that could not be considered or eval-uated in the terms developed within another; and in his own words, "least of all can our *European culture* be the measure of general human goodness or value; it is no standard, or a false one."[51] That this apparently relativis-tic perspective was voiced in a work that included as well a withering cri-tique of European colonial practices would seem to align Herder far more closely with recent anthropology and ethnomusicology than with sources like those I have been citing, and indeed Herder is considered a significant figure in the history of both disciplines.[52] But note too that the immedi-ate occasion for Herder's essay was a debate concerning historiography—as we have seen, issues of history blend easily into those of cross-cultural comparison.

The degree to which Herder maintained this relativism is a matter of ongoing discussion among scholars, but it is clear that another aspect of his thought is in considerable tension with it, for Herder, like the enlightened authors with whom he often otherwise disagreed, also believed in the value and necessity of human development. This applied not only to individ-ual humans (and motivated Herder as an educational administrator and re-former) and individual cultures—which had their own youth, adulthood, and decline—but also to human culture, which had grown in stages from its infancy among the ancient Hebrews to its childhood in Egypt, and so on. Although it was, in fact, improper to criticize an apparently primitive cul-ture from the perspective of European development, the fault was compa-rable to criticizing a child for failing to exhibit adult behavior. The consis-tency of this position has been questioned, and with some justification, for it undermines considerably the claim for autonomous and unique value for every culture by reintroducing both a developmental hierarchy and an ex-ternal perspective for absolute evaluation of position within that hierar-chy.[53] However, it also allowed Herder to draw lessons from other cultures to apply to his own, particularly concerning the issues of education and cul-tivation that most concerned him—and at such times, as here, when he expounds on the beauties of ancient Greek art, his distance from Rochlitz, for example, is considerably less than one might expect: "And how did the Greeks attain all this? Only through *one* means: through *human feeling*, through simplicity of thought, and through a lively study of the truest, most complete pleasures, in short, through a *culture of humanity*. In this we must all become Greeks, or we remain barbarians."[54]

Given the tensions inherent in Herder's own writings, it should come as no surprise that discussions of music show no unified response to his ideas. The concept of a specifically German character evident in music, for instance, clearly had potential utility, as I have suggested above, and the German character of serious music unquestionably became a familiar topic during the first decades of the nineteenth century.[55] But if German music had a character valid on its own terms, so too did the music of other cultures and, if one took Herder's position to its fullest extent, so did the music of individuals or groups within one's own society who practiced other forms of music—such as the Swabian and Austrian folk musicians that Rochlitz insisted had no real music at all. Although such music did indeed begin to receive attention during the course of the nineteenth century (a process I consider in the following chapters), before the 1830s discussion of it in the major music journals is quite exceptional. And the tone of many of the relatively infrequent discussions of other musics that continued to appear differs little from the tone of those I have already considered.[56] However, the notion that development occurred on a universal scale, and that primitive peoples represented the childhood of humanity, was far more congenial, as was the need for intellectual and aesthetic cultivation that such a progressive view implied; here, Herder's ideas represented no real departure from views already well established in musical discourse.[57]

The articles I have so far cited provide a sense of the role of other cultures and their music in defining the limits and values of German musical culture, but their infrequency and marginal quality, while revealing the peripheral nature of German concern with other music, also make it difficult to develop an overview of how the musical world in its entirety might have been conceptualized. Histories of music by such authors as Forkel and Raphael Georg Kiesewetter provide overviews of a sort, of course, but another is provided by one of the most ambitious music encyclopedias of the period, Gustav Schilling's *Encyclopädie der gesammten musikalischen Wissenschaften, oder Universal-Lexikon der Tonkunst,* published in six volumes between 1835 and 1838, with a supplementary volume in 1842.[58] The encyclopedia's collaborative nature makes its perspective less unified than works by a single author, but the comprehensive ambitions signaled by its title make it particularly useful as a means of exploring the geography of the world's musical cultures as imagined by a number of Germany's leading scholars.

Schilling's project itself has a far from enviable reputation. Early reviews were mixed, and reports of inaccuracies and plagiarisms soon began to appear.[59] A by-now-venerable tradition of contempt for the work reaches into recent reference works, which dismiss the encyclopedia as useful largely for obscure biographical information, and Schilling's own reputation as a plagiarist whose claim to have earned a doctorate was dubious and who fled Europe to North America in 1857 to escape creditors has done little to enhance the work's credibility.[60] But criticism of the work at the time focused primarily on biographical inaccuracies and on Schilling's habit of omitting mention that long passages were drawn verbatim from previously published works. The topical and historical articles were considerably more favorably received, and their authors included leading figures such as A. B. Marx, G. W. Fink, and Ludwig Rellstab. In particular, Carl Ferdinand Becker, himself the compiler of an important bibliography of musical works, noted in a review of the encyclopedia for the *Neue Zeitschrift für Musik* that "the most excellent articles in the encyclopedia are almost all those that concern the history of the music of individual peoples."[61]

Those articles are the primary means through which the music of other cultures was discussed in the *Encyclopädie*. Relative to the size of the entire work, they, too, occupy relatively little space—just over two hundred pages in a work of over four thousand; the claim to universality by no means meant that European music, its history, and its practitioners were not to receive primary attention, or that the non-European world would be treated with anything approaching a proportionate degree of detail. But this imbalance is itself revealing, of course: what these articles, along with the numerous shorter articles on individual related terms and instruments, do provide is a sense of what constituted a complete view of the musical world from the perspective of Germany in the 1830s.[62] Although Schilling's article on Herder (3:558–59) makes no mention of his concept of national character, the article "Styl" (6:531–33, ascribed to "N.," most likely Gustav Nauenburg) makes clear that that conception is nonetheless fundamental to the encyclopedia's approach. The subjective meaning of style (as opposed to the objective, concerned with compositional technique) distinguishes first between the ancient and modern periods. The next category, though, receives considerably more elaboration:

Then one further distinguishes style in its subjective sense according to the nation to which the artist belongs, for almost every one of the various nations also possesses its unique qualities, not only in the style of representation of its art but also in the art itself and its various means. *Turkish music,* for example, is completely different from *German,* and *French* music again different from *Greek,* etc. Certain instruments belong uniquely to one people and one land, others to another, and the one has more ability in and inclination to the cultivation of vocal music, the other to that of instrumental music. As is well-known, in this book a separate account is dedicated to the music of each people and each land of the old and new [i.e., ancient and modern] world.[63]

Those articles are summarized in Table 1. As Nauenburg's description suggests, ancient and modern cultures each receive consideration (with the articles on current European nations generally beginning with their Christianization and referring back to relevant historical articles for earlier periods), and I have further separated European and non-European modern cultures, for, not surprisingly, the latter receive considerably different treatment than the former. In what follows, I will consider each category separately.

Antiquity and Pre-Christian Europe

Although (with the conspicuous exception of those on ancient Greece) these articles comprise a relatively small group, their role in establishing the encyclopedia's overall perspective on musical cultures is considerable. As we have seen, the ideology of progressive development meant that the past could be treated as a counterpart to contemporary primitive cultures, and the *Encyclopädie's* articles on ancient cultures do so consistently. The reputedly most ancient culture of all, that of the Hebrews, was claimed as a specialty by Schilling himself, although it is a specialty for which his article shows little enthusiasm: "If we speak of Hebrew music of the time of Moses, we must by no means imagine so completely rhythmically ordered an art as we are now accustomed to consider music to be. It was probably only a crude, *recitative-like* natural song, which was accompanied by imperfect instruments, and especially *percussion* instruments (along with which *string* and *wind* instruments also already existed), however it pleased the singers."[64]

This image of a primitive state, of course, accords with the place of the Hebrews at the very beginning of human development. But in order to confirm this assessment of their music against those who have claimed far

Table 1. National Articles in Schilling's *Encyclopädie*

Article	Location	Author
I. Antiquity and Pre-Christian Europe		
Aegyptische Musik[1]	1:69–71	
Briten—Britische Musik	2:23–24	G. W. Fink
Germanen	3:202–[7]	L. M. F. [Friedrich Baron de la Motte Fouqué]
Griechen:		
Griechische Musik (im Allgemeinen)	3:310–18	ABM. (A. B. Marx)
Griechische Harmonie	3:318–23	ABM.
Griechische Instrumente (ὄργανα)	3:323–27	ABM.
Griechische Kanonik	3:327–32	ABM.
Griechische Notirung	3:332–36	ABM.
Griechischer Rhythmus	3:336–40	ABM.
Griechische Tonarten	3:340–46	ABM.
Griechische Tongeschlechte	3:346–50	ABM.
Griechisches Tonsystem	3:350–57	ABM.
Hebräer—hebräische Musik	3:529–39	Dr. Sch. [Gustav Schilling]
Kelten—keltische Musik	4:71–76	G. W. Fink
Römer (Musik der) oder Römische Musik[2]	6:43–50	
II. European Nations		
Böhmen—Böhmische Musik	1:699–707	†b.
England—englische Musik	2:592–601	G. W. Fink
Frankreich—französische Musik	3:36–44	G. W. Fink
Irland—irländische (irische) Musik	3:747–48	

NOTE: The inconsistent capitalization of article titles as shown in the original has been retained. Bracketed page numbers indicate corrections of erroneous pagination in the original. I have not included articles that consist only of cross-references to other national articles.

[1] Although primarily devoted to ancient Egyptian music, this article also briefly considers contemporary practices.

[2] In addition to discussing Roman antiquity, this article examines the "Roman school" of composition in the time of Palestrina and his successors and concludes with a consideration of contemporary Roman musical life.

Table 1 *(continued)*

Article	Location	Author
Italien—italienische Musik	4:7–20	G. W. Fink
Niederlande—Niederländische Musik	5:161–74	G. W. Fink
Polen—Polnische Musik[3]	Supp. 339–41	
Portugal—Portugiesische Musik	5:517–21	Dr. Sch.
Rußland—Russische Musik	6:96–102	
Schottland—schottische Musik	6:253–58	
Schweiz—schweizerische Musik	6:300–304	Dr. Sch.
Skandinavien—skandinavische Musik[4]	6:393–402	F. und S. G.
Spanien—spanische Musik	6:433–37	Dr. Sch.
Teutschland—teutsche Musik	6:615–27	G. W. Fink
Ungarn—ungarische Musik	6:726–30	K.[5]

III. Non-European Cultures

Article	Location	Author
China — Chinesische Musik	2:204–10	ABM.
Eskimo	2:625–27	
Indien—Indische Musik	3:693–99	
Mauren (Musik der) oder Maurische Musik	4:607–9	K.
Neugriechen	5:147–48	M.
Orientalische Musik	5:296–305	T. u. M.
Türkei—türkische Musik[6]	6:708–12	

[3] A note explains the delay and brevity of the article as the result of a contributor who failed to provide a more substantial one as promised.

[4] This article includes sections devoted to Danish and Swedish music and a brief one on Norwegian and Icelandic music.

[5] Most likely, this was written by J. Krüchten, author of "Über das Musikwesen in Ungarn," *Cäcilia* 5, no. 20 (1826): 299–304, from which the encyclopedia article draws extensively (without acknowledgment).

[6] This article includes Persian music.

too much for Hebrew music on the basis of Biblical accounts, and who "seem to forget the obligation also to take into account the true nature of the thing, the character of the people and other relevant circumstances," Schilling notes that even today the peoples of the Orient do not possess the developed instruments that such music would have required. Moreover, "if we consider still further that the state of musical instruments is a standard whereby a people's degree of musical culture may be measured rather securely, from there emerges directly the most certain judgment of the low level of Hebrew music in comparison to our own."[65] Note that not only Hebrew music is evaluated by this means; the neighboring "Oriental" cultures with which Schilling makes his point—Arabs, Persians, Egyptians, and Greeks—are implicitly ranked as well. The childhood of human music lives on.

Egyptian music fares no better, in keeping with the view of it we have already seen in Forkel's *Bibliothek*. Here, however, its uncertain but likely deplorable state is ascribed to the character of the people: precisely what Egyptian music was like is forever lost, but "in any event, given the national character of the Egyptians, who, opposed to every innovation, would not depart even a hair from the customs of their ancestors, it can only have been such a music as lay in the utmost childhood."[66] When the article goes on to discuss current Egyptian music as characterized by Guillaume Villoteau, who had reported on it as one of the scholars who accompanied Napoleon's Egyptian campaign, the expectation that German music will without question be elevated above all others is undercut. Villoteau had compared Egyptian secular song to the screams of a man being beaten, but, the article's author adds, "Tacitus says little better of the songs of the [Germanic] bards, which, according to him are supposed to have been similar to the clatter of the wheels on a freight wagon braking as it travels down a steep mountain."[67] Although this reference does little to flatter the ancestors of today's Germans, it nonetheless reaffirms a more complex hierarchy with Europe at its apex: European culture, as represented by Villoteau (and thus the militarily supported expansion of European hegemony), stands in relation to that of modern Egyptians as Tacitus and Roman civilization had to the primitive Germanic past. Europe, in short, has inherited the place of leadership once occupied by Rome.[68]

As Table 1 makes clear, however, Greek music claims a massively disproportionate share of the attention devoted to ancient topics, indeed to national articles overall (except, of course, for the fact that the entire remainder of the *Encyclopädie* is devoted to the music of the nations of Europe). A. B. Marx, the work's principal contributor on theoretical topics, provided what is, in effect, a small monograph on ancient Greek music in the form of nine primarily theoretically oriented articles. In his introductory article Marx himself seems to raise the question of whether this relative wealth of attention is due to the absolute quality of Greek music; he begins by noting both the extensive attention Greek music has received throughout history and the hope that, given both literary and mythological accounts of the powerful effects of Greek music and the unquestioned sophistication of

Greek art and literature, Greek music would prove to be equally exemplary. That the answer will turn out to be negative is already suggested when Marx sounds a note of caution:

> The possession of one art does not follow from the possession of the other (or else Raphael would have been a great musician and Mozart a great painter), but rather much more likely the opposite. The Greeks are overall the people living *outwardly*, artistically active in *visual perception;* for that reason their sculpture reached perfection and all their poetry was oriented toward the visual; to them, thought and feeling are immediately concept, image; even their language bears the mark of this fundamental orientation. But precisely from this it may already be concluded that the other side, the preeminently *inward art* of tones, could *not* have come to the same degree of perfection among them.[69]

Although Marx immediately goes on to note that such a generalization cannot lead to reliable conclusions, his overall evaluation of Greek music fully confirms it.

Marx's article on Greek harmony provides a characteristic example of his approach. He begins by noting that if one defines harmony as every simultaneous sounding of pitches, or even every orderly (*regelmäßig;* 3:318) one, the Greeks undeniably possessed harmony. The matter, however, is not so simple, he continues:

> In a *deeper sense* that grasps the *essence* of the matter, we must understand by harmony the placing together of those *tones united by nature* through their origin and content, [and] the progression (leading apart and reuniting) of these tones according to natural law and artistic reason. When, for instance, our current harmonic system is able to derive its first chord from some original tone, C for example, to continue naturally from this chord to another, to lead back again to the origin according to definite natural laws [here Marx inserts a musical example of the pitch C followed by a simple I–V⁷–I progression, followed by a second C], and from this beginning (the correctness of which is not further discussed here) to unfold the entire system of harmony, polyphony, and modulation, then we possess harmony in that deeper sense, which, however, is then not a collection of coincidentally happened-upon simultaneities, but rather the rational and naturally necessary unfolding of the entire essence of pitch, insofar as it goes beyond barren monophony. The question of whether an individual or a people has a greater or lesser number of such simultaneities is of little significance; the question of whether it has harmony in this higher sense is equivalent to whether it has lifted itself out of the unconscious childhood of artistic life to independence and mastery in the art. For whoever does not have in hand—in the deep concept of harmony—the bridle of all

tonal motion must every moment fall victim to the conflict between his intention and the natural inclination of the tones.[70]

Here, enlightenment rhetoric of independence, rationality, and natural law sets up a condition that Greek harmony must inevitably fail to fulfill, for the only such natural system is of course contemporary Western harmony. In rhythm and notation, too, the Greek system proves wanting, and sophisticated work on musical proportions only confirms the childhood of Greek musical thought, since more sophisticated musical development leads to other musical topics (3:327–28).

Such extraordinarily detailed attention to Greek music (and many other brief articles deal with Greek musical figures and terms as well), despite Marx's low opinion of its achievement, points once again to the tensions in which advocates of musical culture were enmeshed. On the one hand, knowledge of ancient Greek culture was an essential prerequisite for participation in the discourse of learned society, and recognition as a part of that society was essential if serious music was to be a respected and supported activity. On the other hand, acknowledging the music of the ancient Greeks as exemplary—when all evidence suggested it depended heavily on text and placed great value on simplicity—would undermine the superiority of contemporary music, whose claim for a new, higher status rested in large part on what its advocates saw as a new autonomy and sophistication. To negotiate this dilemma, Marx seeks to provide—here in brief, but extensively in his theoretical output—precisely the justifying theory that the reviewer of *Ueber die Musik der Indier* had called for more than thirty years earlier. The devaluation of Greek music is a part of a larger justification for the musical present.

The pre-Christian music of Europe is treated considerably less extensively than that of classical antiquity, but the encyclopedia's two principal articles devoted to it—on Germanic and Celtic music—illustrate the unresolved tension between two different approaches to establishing the significance of German music: the progressive scheme apparent in views like Marx's and the approach of those who sought to idealize the past as evidence of inherent German character and achievement. The latter is distinctly a minority viewpoint, not only in the *Encyclopädie* but in German musical discourse as a whole, but it appears clearly in Baron Friedrich de la Motte Fouqué's essay on the *Germanen*—that is, the ancient Germanic peoples (and also in his article on the related topic of bards [1:435–38]). Once again, the author's position is distinct from that of the leading participants in musical discourse: a member of a Prussian military family and himself a Prussian officer, Fouqué was also a poet and novelist and a friend of the romantic author August Wilhelm von Schlegel. Like Dalberg's, then, his musical activities were those of a cultivated dilettante—and to an even greater extent than Dalberg's, they were subordinate to his literary work, for although his current reputation is relatively minor, at the time he was considered a significant romantic author. Given this background, it is not surprising that Fouqué stresses the virtues of the Germanic tribes, all of which had shared the same essential values: "faithfulness to one's word, honor to women, heroic defiance of enemies, humility before the gods." According to Fouqué, "These they celebrated in richly mythical form, but in significant reflection of the one authentic eternal light, so that perhaps no other mythology can compete with the Germanic in this. As among all brave peoples who delight in arms, poetry and her inseparable sister, music, lived and moved in happy honor among the Germans too."[71]

In the remainder of the article, the reader learns very little more about the music of the Germanic tribes, but the German-Christian culture foreshadowed by this remarkable claim about the religious truth of German mythology receives extensive attention. There is "so powerful a continuity in the flow of Germanic history and cultivation" that the great events of later German (i.e., *deutsche*) history, even the Lutheran reformation, can be understood as deriving from "the natural, healthy sense" of the Germanic people.[72] More than that, however, the dispersal of Germanic tribes through much of Europe meant that this healthy influence has had even broader ongoing impact, especially in music:

> Thus, while the name *Germanen* gradually disappeared as the name of a people and tribe in the progress of world history, Germanic cultivation maintained itself, even spread itself to an elevated life in the most varied ways in all European lands, indeed to a large extent still further afield than that. We have already indicated the fundamentals of this cultivation and need only point it out in order to permit recognition of the salutary qualities of its diffusion. Music, in particular, gained harmonic richness through the continuing progress and transformation of life that gradually followed. . . . Even if we do not in any way wish to restrict ancient music to melody alone, as has been attempted from many sides, granting it at most accompaniment at the octave, we must nonetheless recognize how the rich element of harmony lay only very undeveloped still, in bud. It has developed to its current flowering only through the success of Germanic cultivation, which indeed is often also called *romantic*.[73]

Here, a conclusion in some respects similar to Marx's—that ancient music was far less developed than its current counterpart—takes on a very different coloring. Rather than depending on rational development on the basis of natural laws, the progress of music derives from the Germanic spirit, concentrated in Germany but nonetheless also responsible for whatever development occurs outside it.

In sharp contrast, a representative of the established mainstream of musical discourse, Gottfried Wilhelm Fink (at the time editor of the *Allgemeine musikalische Zeitung* and contributor of the bulk of the encyclopedia's articles on European nations), presented a considerably bleaker—and more musically oriented—picture of ancient German musical accomplishment in his article on German music. Although he acknowledged that no genuine melodies from the pre-Christian period survive, this did not stop him from developing a rather elaborate characterization of early German musical achievement:

> Only through inference do we arrive at the highly probable view that the old German melodies may well have matched the generally disseminated norm of the Celtic (see *keltische Musik*). Just as the oldest art of music distinguished itself among all peoples more through power of rhythm than through beauty of tone, which first developed later, so we find it also among the old Germans. Indeed, they may have paid even less attention to pitch than, for example, the old Scots. The most varied descriptions of the song of the Germans that ancient authors have left us demonstrate this. It must have been more noise and screaming than real song, made effective by rhythm, a power that even now enjoys more general urgency and must be reckoned among the first powers of music.[74]

I will discuss Fink's views on contemporary European musical cultures shortly, but for the present it is important to note that he did not hesitate to give priority to the model that supposes progress from primitive origins even in the case of Germany, and at the cost of presenting a highly unflattering view of the ancestors of his own nation. As we have seen with the example of Friedrich Rochlitz, the cause of musical sophistication outweighed claims of loyalty to an imagined cultural nation; on it depended the claim for music's place in general culture, a matter of far more pressing urgency to Rochlitz and Fink than to Dalberg or Fouqué.

Fink's references to Celtic music provide a final, curious piece to complete the encyclopedia's picture of the European past and connect it to the rest of the ancient world. As we saw already in the review of *Ueber die Musik der Indier*, the origin of culture in Asia had achieved the status of an article of faith by the early nineteenth century; as Fink put it, "Out of Asia, from east to west, moved everything unsettled, searching, wandering, all power and everything troubled, as well as all culture, art, and religion."[75] Fink argued—as he had at length in his book *Die erste Wanderung der äl-testen Tonkunst*—that the Celts were the key to understanding how that art of music had reached Europe. Spreading out over the continent after 600 B.C.E., the Celts had brought with them the music they had encountered among the conquered Medes, which they in turn had learned from the Hindus. Aside from the Greeks, no one they encountered in their migration—including the Germanic peoples—possessed cultivation equal to that which they had encountered in Asia, so they spread their art wherever they went. The evidence for this development was still to be found in Europe: "In fact, wherever even a trace of ancient incipient art of European peoples still remains, it bears clearly the essential signs of Asiatic origin. . . . All remnants of peoples who, due to isolation or neglect, have still remained close to their earliest circumstances offer irrefutable evidence that the earliest art of music can have been nothing other than that which emigrated from China and Hindustan."[76]

Those isolated peoples inhabit remote areas of Switzerland, the Basque regions of Spain, Wales, and especially the Hebrides and the Scottish Highlands—and even folk melodies of remote parts of Prussia show similar traits. This is not to claim that the Celts had adopted the entire Asian theoretical system; rather, they borrowed what struck their ears: "Everything that had to do with speculation about it [the tonal system] lay too distant from their extremely active life."[77] Fink's primary evidence is the pentatonic scale common to the Chinese, Hindus, and other Oriental peoples, but the text-bound, nonmetrical rhythm still found in bards' songs in the Hebrides provides further support for his argument. Hindu music had gone on to further developments, but the Celts retained their simple music, as befit their level of development as a people. Despite the questionable merits of Fink's argument as historical ethnomusicology, it established an origin for European music that fit more comfortably into the prevailing paradigm than did Fouqué's Germanic heroes; it took account of available knowledge of Asian music, explained the origin of a musical art beyond "noise and screaming" in Europe, and perhaps most important, assured its readers that that art had existed in only a primitive state before the historical cultivation of European music had begun to develop toward the music of the present. It remains only for us to consider the various nations' roles in that development and the accounts of non-European musics that provided a frame for it.

European Nations

As I noted above, the article "Styl" laid out the basic concept of national character in music; it also established a distinct ranking within "*modern music . . .* by which indeed one understands the music of the Occidental or European peoples."[78] The three that have achieved "a certain supremacy, a preeminence" [*ein gewisser Oberherrschaft, einen Vorrang*] are, not surprisingly, German, French, and Italian. The characterization that follows (6:532) is equally predictable: German music is powerful, serious, and inwardly directed; French music is imposing and polished, but it never achieves more than elegance. Italy's music, finally, is lively and passionate—excepting the characterless music that has predominated since the appearance of Rossini. Although the national articles do not undermine these familiar stereotypes, they do offer considerably more than reiteration of them. The details of compositional history for each nation need not concern us here, but the common issues that these articles consider merit examination as a development of the ideas we have already seen in the articles on earlier nations.

I have already noted, for instance, that Fink's article on Germany takes a distinctly reserved view of the musical achievements of the early Germans. The article leaves no doubt, however, where Fink's loyalties lie, concluding that "still, among all peoples, Germany maintains the first rank in music, as it long has, a position that is also no longer disputed even by insightful foreigners. What there is to improve, and it is to be improved, will originate with Germany."[79] In contrast to Fouqué, however, Fink bases the development of that leadership on the supposed superiority of Germans in specific musical areas. Although Germans proved resistant to church-imposed plainchant, for instance, they were already recognized as skilled instrumentalists in the Middle Ages and had begun to perfect instrumental music by the fifteenth century (6:616, 619). Thus, the specific musical traits of the Germans account for their leadership in the developing field of autonomous instrumental music, and this occurs despite, rather than because of, the influence of the church.[80]

That anti-ecclesiastical tone carries consistently through Fink's national contributions. The most dramatic case in point is England, where the strictness with which the music of the Catholic Church was imposed helps account for the country's relative musical insignificance: "This consistently carried-out strictness in the equality and legal uniformity of church music has never yet been a blessing for art, neither among the Egyptians nor in Greece, and also not in England; *it brings unfreedom in art*, which, like lack of restraint, brings ruin."[81] Only the strength of English folk music kept the situation from becoming still worse. A similar imposition in France had less disastrous consequences for French national music only because of the stubbornness of the French (3:37). Italy, too, managed to maintain its musical identity—but again, despite rather than through the agency of the church (4:8-9).[82] In such passages, Herder's concept of specific culture is particularly clear: not only does national character receive a favorable portrayal against an international homogenizing force, but the greatest potential clearly lies in secular development. This is not to suggest simple parroting of Herder, however; by the 1830s these ideas were far from novel, and Fink's secularist rhetoric could equally be ascribed to his desire to write a history whose subject was the emerging culture of concert music as an autonomous entity free of externally imposed control.

The significance of that subject is borne out by further consideration of the place of folk music relative to cultivated forms. Here, Bohemia offers a particularly clear example. The nation's character, the article's author maintains, shows a mix of German and Slavic elements, respectively considered equivalent to progressive and conservative; but more significantly, a commitment to broadly based cultivation in music, combined with a natural inclination toward music, made Bohemia a leading musical culture by the eighteenth century. By the early nineteenth, however, the situation had declined—due in part to the dissolution of religious schools where music instruction had been important—and Bohemian musical life was considerably poorer. The author's closing assessment reveals the relative significance of folk and cultivated music in determining a nation's musical standing: "To be sure, the people still love music as always, and seldom does a commemorative or celebratory day pass without the sound of trumpet and drums, even in the country; the military music of the Bohemian regiments still belongs among the very best, like the Austrian; as before, the miners still love their triangle, various mountain regions their dulcimers, and the Eger region especially the bagpipe, and they all handle these favorite instruments outstandingly. But it will take more if the land is again to rejoice with justification in its old glory. Accordingly, with the exception of Prague, it is still the land of the mistuned harps."[83] A characteristic inclination toward music, and even vital folk and functional music, will not suffice to establish or maintain a nation as musically significant. Indeed, in the central nations, the topic of a separate contemporary folk music does not even arise. In contemporary Europe, cultivated music is the measure of a people's musical standing.

The tension between national characteristics and cultivation becomes more pronounced in the encyclopedia's treatment of peripheral European cultures. With remarkable consistency, the authors of articles on Hungary, Russia, Poland, Ireland, Scotland, Sweden, and Spain all deny the presence of any significant national quality in the cultivated music of the nation but point out that it survives in *Volks-* or *Nationalmusik* (the two terms are used almost interchangeably). The discussion of Sweden, more developed in its analysis than most, provides an otherwise typical example (note that division along class lines is presumed as the starting point):

> As in Denmark, and almost to an even lesser degree, music in Sweden has never reached significant heights. . . . The few leisure hours of the lower classes are partially filled with pleasures too loud and boisterous for the quiet Muse to dare show herself among them. She is more often to be found among the middle class; but the moments in which she appeared to individual, meditative souls were always fleeting, and the rare appearance could not build any lasting, living circle for itself, since everyone was too full of his daily goings-on to turn toward this lovely creature with undivided love. Musical cultivation is indeed supported by the upper classes in Sweden as in other lands; often it must even appear there completely unwillingly, but only in fashionable dress, by the constraints of which her life and activity are restricted and which does not allow the discovery of a single trace of *national* character. . . . Only if we follow Swedish music to the point where it appears in a more intimate fusion with the whole national character, to the *folksong*, do we arrive . . . at more satisfying results.[84]

Through passages like this, cultivated music itself becomes a sort of national characteristic, reserved to the central musical cultures, and especially to Germany.

Despite its rather harsh evaluation of lower-class musical life in the above passage, the article on Scandinavian music is also exceptional in that it is a rare case in which this limitation of the characteristically national to folk music does not appear in conjunction with a consistently higher valorization of the cultivated. The author notes that, in both Denmark and Sweden, recent decades have seen the publication of important collections of folksongs. In the case of Sweden, only the "more faithful memories of the lower classes" are credited with preserving what the "superficial, fashionable songs of the day" have driven from the awareness of the rest of society, and the editors of the Danish collection are criticized for attempting to "improve" their melodies.[85] Such views of the significance of the lower class as a storehouse of musical and literary memory not to be tampered with accord at best uncomfortably with the image of the same class's raucous, unmusical behavior; and the ideologies underlying these incommensurable views of the lower classes will concern us more in succeeding chapters. For the present, however, it is worth noting that this hasty revaluation of lower-class music is closely associated with a project whose orientation is first and foremost literary–folk song collection. Again, the tension between the values of literary and musical culture is palpable.

The Edges of Europe and Beyond

In discussing the peripheral cultures I have just mentioned, the *Encyclopädie* approached the boundaries of Europe, and at those boundaries, cultures began to depart in a variety of ways from the cultivated European model. As I have already suggested, Scotland provided a model of the primitive; enterprising Scottish character and a carefully developed educational system might seem to promise great things, but "nonetheless, if we strip away the value of nationality from the music that belongs uniquely to the Scots, it is as good as none at all, or exists in the condition of a most destitute childhood."[86] Fink's theory of Celtic music receives no mention here, but the link this most primitive of European musics provides to other parts of the world is not neglected: the author notes both that some Highlands melodies sound Chinese and that other writers have observed that Moorish songs in Morocco sound Scottish (6:255). Portuguese culture blends with the non-European world in a different, more literal manner. According to Schilling, the Portuguese people, like the Spanish, are "nothing but a mix of Celts (the original inhabitants), Carthaginians, Romans, Germans, Arabs, Jews"; their music has maintained no national character whatsoever, having been given over entirely to Italian influence.[87] Furthermore, the Portuguese have no educational institutions through which they might train native musicians and achieve independence from Italian influence. In this, they are outdone by their own colony, Brazil, where musical training schools founded by the Jesuits have produced a large number of successful black musicians (5:519–20). The most extreme example of the loss of European civilization, however, is its very cradle, Greece; a separate article on current Greek music *(Neugriechen)* treats the nation's modern inhabitants not as descendants of the ancient Greeks but as an example of primitive Oriental cultur. Their music is "coarse and repulsive," and even that of educated Greeks is "unbearable for cultivated ears."[88] Their musical activity is a model of irrational and uncontrolled physicality: "A Greek can rarely sing without dancing at the same time, and the other listeners can never resist the temptation to join in, as though driven by a natural impulse; and then, when they all sing together, this makes a truly horrible noise."[89] Although one might think that the church might have improved Greek music, it has not done so; and finally, conquest by the Ottoman Empire has meant that, for the last four hundred years, the Greeks "could take no part in European cultural development."[90] The implication is clear: to be cut off from Europe is to be eliminated from participation in the civilized musical world.

As even a cursory examination of Table 1 reveals, Schilling's claim to provide universal coverage proves far from accurate with respect to non-European music. Even allowing for considerable gaps in European awareness, the encyclopedia proves remarkably spotty; with the single exception of the Eskimos, the peoples of both the Americas and sub-Saharan Africa are written out entirely, and even areas that Michaelis, Rochlitz, and others had discussed more than twenty years earlier go unmentioned. Again excepting the case of the Eskimos, coverage of non-European cultures is limited to what could broadly be included under contemporary use of the term *Oriental.* Given Schilling's less than exemplary accomplishments as a scholar and editor, it is difficult to credit this pattern of coverage to a coherent plan, but it is nonetheless consistent with the understanding of the limits of "music" within musical discourse that we have seen throughout this chapter. Music worthy of that name is cultivated, at least partly rationalized. To the extent that such music is found anywhere outside Europe, it is found in those countries from which culture arrived in Europe—that is, the Orient. As the single exception to this principle, the Eskimos provide a foil against which the significance of true music is all the clearer.

In a number of respects, the view of music in these articles is already familiar. That the theorist A. B. Marx wrote the article on China, for instance, might appear surprising until one realizes that, despite a long introduction defending Chinese music against the European presumption that it is laughable and insignificant, his interest in and understanding of the importance of that music is precisely the same as Forkel's half a century earlier: the sophisticated ancient theory of the Chinese reveals the beginnings of musical cultivation—as does the existence of state support for music, a topic of considerable interest in musical discourse—but for the last four thousand years they have remained suspended without further development. The unsigned article on India also covers familiar ground. Drawing almost exclusively on the work of Jones and Dalberg, it reiterates the criticisms of that work with which I began; however, after noting the near absence of genuinely Indian musical practice in present-day India, it goes on to add a further argument against the claim that Indian music has "a perfection equal to ours": "If it had ever been so perfect, it would certainly have been preserved and adopted by the immigrating peoples, instead of being supplanted by them. In the English possessions the music is now almost completely European."[91] Although it is perhaps unsettling to encounter so utterly transparent a justification for the imposition of colonial culture, it is in many ways a straightforward corollary of the ideology of development and cultivation that was deeply anchored in the very concept of a universal culture of serious music. To that extent, the *Encyclopädie* does indeed present an undistorted overview of the *gesammten musikalischen Wissenschaften*, the "complete musical sciences" of its title.

Perhaps the most immediately striking characteristic about the remaining articles on Oriental musics is their apparent lack of discrimination in differentiating cultures. The ease with which Fink could write of the Celts as heirs of a musical system from both India and China is in fact typical; both Marx's article on China and Schilling's on the ancient Hebrews relate their respective topics to Oriental music in general, and the encyclopedia's article on Turkey also proves to include a discussion of music among the ancient Medes and the Persians. The most diffuse article of all, however, is that on Oriental music itself. Although primarily devoted to Arab music, it also evaluates the state of music among the Burmese, Siamese, and Singhalese. In all these cases, the idea is never absent that the standard against which this music must be measured is its acceptability to the European ear; nor is a negative evaluation of that acceptability ever missing. The instrumental music of Burma, for instance, can be pleasant enough when heard over the water at a distance, although it is largely unappealing at closer range (5:302). The constant quarter-tone motion of Arab melodies is "unbearable" (*unerträglich;* 5:298), but beyond that, Arab music is given a surprisingly nonjudgmental treatment, perhaps reflecting the influence of the French sources the author cites, as well as increasing interest in the historic sources on Arab music.[92] Of all the Oriental peoples, the Siamese are depicted most favorably: "The Siamese appear to have made more progress in music than all other Asian nations. Their melodies are usually lively and not without charm, even for a cultivated European ear."[93] The limit to this approval, however, is set through a by-now-familiar comparison; this most sophisticated of Asian musics reaches only the level of the most primitive of Europeans: "J. Crawford affirms that most of their melodies are comparable to Scottish and Irish ones."[94]

Insignificant though this achievement turns out to be, it suffices to distinguish the Siamese from such peoples as the Arabs, Indians, or Chinese, whose music has either remained static or declined. The cultural stagnation of the Orient, with its always inherent and always flattering contrast to European progress, not only justifies the primarily historical focus of the consideration of the latter three nations but also accounts for the otherwise puzzling mixture of past and present in this discussion of music among the Medes and Persians:

> For the rest, the music of the Medes remained mostly in the hands of women. They had female singers and cithara players who belonged to the entourage of the king and in his harem, a custom that is still found today in Persia. The best (or, so to speak, only) Persian musical artists are always in the service of the prince. In addition, the effeminate and seductive plays of the Medes had such a corrupting influence on the morals of the Persians that nothing more could be done to demean music. In Persia the female dancers and actresses, as well as most of the musicians who are not expressly reserved to the prince, form wandering bands that display their arts in private houses. Such a band consists of a prima donna and her entourage, who appear only occasionally to break up the main dialogue with choruses, dances, and songs.[95]

From this point, the article returns immediately to antiquity, observing that the introduction of Greek theory through Alexander's conquest of the Medes had no real impact on their musical practice. This passage is one of the few in the encyclopedia to touch on both the seductive potential of music and its link to the feminine—dangers safely contained not only by their location in the Orient and the ancient past but also by the immediate turn to the topic of abstract theory. But more than that, the almost dizzying alternation of past and present—from ancient Medes to Persian courts, back to Medean theater, and then, without transition, to Persian dramatic troupes and finally to ancient theory—vividly writes the Oriental past as interchangeable with its present.

Only if those stagnant cultures were to follow the European example could this be expected to change, as the same article noted in the case of Turkey: "Music is also an essential part of good upbringing among them, and we may expect much from the extraordinary striving for civilization of the current sultan with respect to the improvement of musical culture as well. Already he has assembled a significant number of the most outstanding musicians at his court in Constantinople, even if their art is still used more for pleasant dalliance, on the one hand, and military ends, on the other."[96] The final sentence's clear implication—that although progress has been substantial, the sultan has not yet really grasped the higher purpose of European music—reveals the limits of the otherwise laudable importation of civilized culture even as it praises the development. At the same time, as occurred in earlier examples we have seen, it also demonstrates and reinforces the writer's authority to make such an evaluation: it can originate only from the perspective of already achieved cultivation.

At the other extreme of non-European music lay that of the Eskimos; the brief article devoted to them is based on a single account from an English naval captain. If the brevity of this treatment and the apparent randomness of the choice of this particular culture would seem to argue for its insignificance, the article itself claims otherwise: "The music of the Eskimos, this wildest of all wild peoples . . . is admittedly as limited and impoverished as are the spirit, customs, form, etc., through which they are distinguished from all other nations; nevertheless it is music, and it also provides the most convincing proof that no people, even the most primitive, is devoid of all music, and of how this beautifying language was, so to speak, bestowed upon or given as an inoculation by Mother Nature at creation to every rational, feeling being as a most precious blessing—at least a capacity for it." [97] Although the account that follows emphasizes the poverty of Eskimo music far more than the universal musicality for which it provides evidence, it is the latter point that is emphasized elsewhere in the *Encyclopädie*. Both the general article on *Musik* and the article on the lied refer readers to the article on Eskimo music precisely in support of this point (5:61 and 4:387). The conclusion of Gustav Nauenburg and Georg Christoph Grosheim's article on the lied does so in a way that succinctly reviews the essential categories of the recognized musical world: "The Orient knows this expression of lively feeling [the secular song] as much as the Occident, and even the wildest of wild peoples does not do without its song, which cheers it and in whose tones it pours out its entire primitive heart. Simply compare the article *Eskimo*." [98]

Jonathan Stock has recently noted the continued resistance of musicology to the methods and interests of ethnomusicology, ascribing that resistance in part to musicology's role as representing cultural expertise within Western art music, in contrast to ethnomusicology's dependence on informants and knowledge gathered from outside a culture. [99] As we have seen, however, the claim of earlier music scholarship was considerably grander: to represent knowledge of cultivated European music was to represent the entire claim of music as an art. As untenable as this claim now appears, it is important to recognize that those who sought to establish serious music within German society accepted it very nearly without question; the extent to which the culture of serious music and the practices, if no longer the rhetoric, of historical musicology still bear the remnants of that attitude merits serious consideration, especially since, as I argue in the following chapter, important aspects of our understanding of that tradition have been shaped to a largely unrecognized degree by the views of its early advocates.

From the accustomed perspective of musicology, however, the musical world constructed by the sources I have been examining may seem remote from the concerns of the composers with whom that discipline has traditionally concerned itself. This is not to suggest that composers were unaware of the general outlines of this conception. While considering a possible opera on the subject of Bacchus in 1815, for instance, Beethoven made this note in a sketchbook: "Dissonances perhaps not resolved in the entire opera, or resolved completely differently, since our refined music is not to be thought of in these times."[100] But the real significance of the efforts of participants in musical discourse to define both the universality of music and the limits of its true, cultivated form lies elsewhere—as I have suggested, they helped legitimate a claim that music belonged among the fully developed products of European culture. And here, the intellectual interests of music scholarship overlapped a vital concern of practicing musicians, for as an unusually blunt evaluation of the situation in 1842 noted, only such an evaluation of music could justify its support:

> Are artists less deserving than officials, statesmen, and university teachers, that their external life should be made easier, so that they can direct all energy to the inner life, undisturbed and undistracted by base cares? Whoever is to give full effort to intellectual work must first have a full stomach. For that reason the Mongolians and Kamchatkans can have no artists and no scholars, for they must struggle constantly for their daily bread and have no surplus with which to feed useless thinkers and dreamers. By contrast, the lovely abundance that appears of its own in the civilized life of great cultivated peoples must be used for the benefit of the so-called *Zehrstand* [a class drawing its sustenance from the rest of society], among whom we have no hesitation in numbering ourselves [as artists], since we also contribute our portion to the general labor.[101]

Only if musical labor were recognized as a legitimate intellectual undertaking could it make such a claim, and only if a cultivated audience could appreciate the sophisticated music upon which that claim could be based would musicians be supported. For practicing musicians and others whose livelihood depended on a viable culture of cultivated music, then, the topic of the place of music within society had immediate ramifications; the following chapters explore a variety of efforts to establish such a secure place for music.

3 The Dilemma of the Popular

The Volk, *the Composer, and the Culture of Art Music*

The hierarchies and claims for value constructed by the scholars discussed in the previous chapter have a rather distant and abstract character, remote from the concrete concerns of everyday musical activity. The practical tenor of those concerns emerges vividly from this exchange within the Mozart family, dating from the period of Wolfgang's composition of *Idomeneo* in 1780. Leopold Mozart wrote to his son, "I recommend that in your work you think not only of the musical, but also of the *unmusical public*—you know there are *100 ignorant ones* for every *10 truly knowledgeable,* so don't forget the so-called *popular,* which also tickles *long ears.*" Wolfgang's reply to this paternal advice expressed (qualified) agreement: "Don't worry about the so-called popular, for there is music for people of all kinds in my opera—except not for the long ears."[1] If, as I claimed in the introduction, musical discourse inevitably evokes social categories, this brief exchange is no exception, but its categories are considerably more immediate than the entire nations that populate narratives of the world's musical development: here, attention focuses pragmatically on the distinction between the ignorant and the true *Kenner* (the technically knowledgeable), with the *lange Ohren* as a still more aurally challenged subset of the former. But it is important to recognize as well an implicit fourth category created by the existence of the exchange itself: the two Mozarts are set apart as the creators who are perceptive and skilled enough to know and cater to (or spurn) the tastes of those other groups. Clearly, neither Mozart was setting out to make a grand social statement; on the contrary, recognizing and working with such distinctions was part of the practical business of composing, a necessary skill in a trade dependent on the goodwill of patrons and audiences. But a closer consideration reveals the presence of categories that operate much like those we encountered in the previous chapter, for what separates the knowledgeable from the ignorant is nothing other than thorough cultivation in music. And it is finally only their still more thorough cultivation in music that authorizes the privileged perspective of the Mozarts themselves, just as positioning themselves among the most cultivated of peoples authorized the critical authority of the scholars who evaluated more primitive musics. Moreover, the ubiquity of a concept of a cultural hierarchy based on degrees of cultivation meant that the "popular" was itself a category fraught with social significance. In a society in which social distinctions were an integral part of life, such sociomusical categories could scarcely avoid coming to interact with, represent, and reinforce larger class distinctions, and those class boundaries are thus inevitably at issue in definitions of musical culture.

In the Mozart letters the "so-called popular" is still a rather nebulous category; it clearly has stylistic associations, but it can by no means be taken to suggest appeal to the general populace, who would hardly come into consideration as a potential audience for opera, particularly *opera seria*.[2] In this case, popularity must rather be understood with reference to a far more limited and privileged group. But beyond the operatic world, the issue of popularity in relation to the cultivation of musical taste was played out with considerably broader social referents, although, as we will see, it was no less bound up with the material concerns of practicing composers. The extent of the discussion surrounding popularity, particularly in the context of the lied, has been thoroughly documented by Heinrich W. Schwab, to whose work any consideration of this topic is heavily indebted.[3] Schwab, however, considers popularity primarily as an aesthetic influence on the development of a genre; in the present context, it is of interest rather as a concept in which musical discourse explicitly overlaps social categories. Discussion of the popular, especially as it crystallized around the issues of the *Volkston* and the volkslied, illustrates the degree to which such categories resonated with social meaning, serving to define the lower boundaries of high musical culture and the place of the musician and, especially, the composer within a larger society.

These topics, however, have had little visibility within musicology. The folksong has been relegated to disciplines distinct from it (ethnomusicology and folklore), while the *Volkston* proper has been at best a subsidiary topic removed in several ways from the focus of disciplinary interest. Its principal theoretical and compositional advocates, Johann Abraham Peter Schulz and Johann Friedrich Reichardt, are marginal to even the most charitably broad canon of late-eighteenth-century music, and the North German locus of *Volkston* theorizing is geographically far removed from the

Viennese repertoire that dominates both the canon of performance and the attention of scholarship. Neither *Die Musik in Geschichte und Gegenwart* nor *The New Grove Dictionary of Music* accords the *Volkston* an article, and Schwab himself finally subordinates his discussion of popularity to the development of art song and Schubert's transformation of the genre.[4]

This lack of familiarity means that a preliminary consideration of terms is in order. *Volkston* and volkslied were both used with considerable inconsistency during the period I will discuss, and precisely those inconsistencies indicate the tensions that issues of popularity invoked. A *Lied im Volkston*, literally, a song in the tone of the people, might be understood to be an imitation of the singing of the people, but more often, as we will see, it implied a song written by a cultivated poet or musician in a style thought to be simple enough for the people. The social hierarchy of cultivation thus comes into play in the concept itself. Furthermore, the identity of the *Volk* was by no means self-evident—did it refer to all the people of a nation, or to the common, unspoiled people, or to the ignorant in need of the cultivation that volkslieder or *Lieder im Volkston* might provide? Each of these possible identities had drastically different implications for the nature of the song in question and for its creator's relation to a public. The *Volkston*, then, is not a concept that can be defined in purely stylistic or aesthetic terms; although the simplicity that had become a standard rallying cry of eighteenth-century aesthetics was rarely absent from discussions of the *Volkston*, the concept implies considerably more than just a simple tone, for notions of the popular are inevitably bound up with social distinctions.[5]

Precisely because it was so charged with social implications, the concept of popularity implicit in the *Volkston* proved difficult to contain in the context of the developing culture of serious music. Although it held obvious appeal for composers seeking to reach larger audiences and claim the universal validity of their art, it held dangers as well: an accessible art with truly universal popularity would leave no basis for claiming distinction based on appeal to an elite, whether defined socially or artistically. This dilemma has resulted in an ambivalence toward the popular that not only informed discussions of the *Volkston* and the volkslied from the 1780s until well into the nineteenth century but also continues to shape the study of that period's music.

THE POSITION OF THE COMPOSER: THE *VOLKSTON* AND POPULAR CULTIVATION

The most extensive recent discussion of the *Volkston*, by Margaret Mahony Stoljar, sets sharp bounds to its final significance: "The *Volkston*, however optimistic the vision that gave it birth, remained a short-lived moment in musical history that ended with the still persisting division of musical experience into separate categories of high and low art."[6] Stoljar's analysis is oriented toward the social to an unusual degree, but this statement reveals some of the limitations of her perspective. The discursive act of positing a *Volkston,* far from providing opposition to a division between high and low, itself presupposes and reinforces it by imagining a *Volk* from whom the speaker is separated by both the ability to abstract such a class and the desire either to address or to emulate it. And as I suggest below, the persistence of the topic at the margins of the issues of concern to musicology suggests that that act of distinction, of separating a class of musically significant, active, and individualized subjects from an undifferentiated *Volk,* is a moment in musical history that has proven far from short-lived. Rather, it was instrumental in the constitution of a distinct high-art culture of music, and it has remained essential to the continued process of citation through which that culture has maintained its identity and authority.[7] It provides a necessary lower term against which a literate, knowledgeable musical culture can be defined while, at the same time, because of the ambiguity of the concept *Volk* itself, it allows a claim for universal validity for an art nonetheless in some way rooted in that *Volk.*

Although she rejects attempts to understand Schulz's songs as popularizations of the style of "the traditional folksong," Stoljar interprets his efforts at accessibility in highly charged political terms: "The popular tone as conceived by Schulz and Reichardt was the precipitation in art-song of the democratic ideas that permeated later eighteenth-century thought and which sought to bring the experience of art within the grasp of all the people"; and more generally, the entire movement was "a product of the socially progressive thought of the late-eighteenth century." The *Volkston* thus comes to play a role in a familiar narrative—the ultimately successful struggle of the (good) bourgeoisie against the (oppressive) ancien régime—as an expression of the "belief that the life-blood of the age belonged to the people as a whole."[8] Because the *Volkston* is directed at the people and their needs, it is aligned with anti-aristocratic values.

Schulz's own publications on the *Volkston* and music among the people, however, make his democratic loyalties considerably less clear. The defining locus classicus of the *Volkston,* Schulz's preface to the second edition of his *Lieder im Volkston* (1785), for instance, is at first glance strikingly devoid of overtly social rhetoric:

> In all these songs it is and remains my goal to sing more in the manner of the folk than in the manner of art, namely, so that even unprac-

ticed lovers of song (as long as they don't completely lack a voice) can easily sing along and keep them in their memory. To this end, I have selected only those texts from our best lied poets that seem to me made for this folk singing *[Volksgesang]*, and sought in the melodies themselves for the greatest simplicity and comprehensibility, indeed sought in every way to attain the *appearance of the familiar [Schein des Bekannten]*, because I know from experience how helpful, even necessary, this appearance is to the quick reception of the volkslied. In this appearance of the familiar lies the entire secret of the *Volkston;* but one must not confuse it with the familiar itself; the latter awakens boredom in all artists. The former, by contrast, has its place in the theory of the volkslied as a means of making it alive and quickly comprehensible to the ear, and is sought by the composer, often diligently and often in vain.

For only through a striking similarity of the musical and poetic tone of the lied; through a melody whose progression never exceeds the pace of the text, nor sinks below it, that molds itself to the declamation and meter of the words like clothing to the body, that flows on in very singable intervals in a range suited to all voices and with the simplest modulation; and finally through the greatest perfection of the relationships of all its parts, which gives the melody that rounding that is so crucial to every artwork in the realm of the small—does the lied obtain the appearance under discussion here, the appearance of the unforced, the artless, the familiar, in a word, the *Volkston*, whereby it impresses itself on the ear so quickly, returning unceasingly.[9]

Here, Schulz indeed expresses a desire to reach a broad audience: the "appearance of the familiar" is required to reach "even unpracticed lovers of song." Note, however, that this statement is not directed *to* that segment of Schulz's imagined audience. On the contrary, the opposition of folk and art is established in the first sentence, and the remainder of the passage continues in the tone of an composer-initiate instructing other connoisseurs of what he has discovered; this is less an invitation than an explication. Because of that tone, what might otherwise seem an abrupt shift can be seen as a fitting continuation: the second paragraph not only dispenses with reference to the *Volk* until its final phrase but also first adopts a far more technical vocabulary (pace, declamation, meter, intervals, etc.) and then has recourse to the language of aesthetics (perfection of relationships, rounding, the artwork) in the context of a weighty periodic sentence that seeks to impress upon its readers the supreme artistry and aesthetic consequence of the apparently artless. Such passages serve as reminders that Schulz was not only a guiding figure of the *Volkston* but also a pupil of the theorist Johann Philipp Kirnberger and a contributor to Johann Georg Sulzer's codification of Enlightenment aesthetic theory. And this connection is of more than biographical relevance, for in this text, enlightenment descends from above as the knowledgeable composer dispenses the fruits of his learning to a broader (if still socially undefined) public. Only the extent to which we have naturalized the expectation that music is defined by a composer providing works to a public allows a set of relations that closely mirror those of enlightened monarchy to be read as democratic.[10]

The enlightened and authoritative rhetoric of the preface suggests very different associations for the collection than those drawn by one early reviewer, Carl Friedrich Cramer, whose discussion appeared in the first volume of his *Magazin der Musik* in 1783. Indeed, the preface may have been intended to clarify Schulz's own perspective and the context in which he intended his work to be heard, for Cramer suggests two very different ones for it, neither of which aligns directly with Schulz's own explanation, although the second does share some common elements. The first, however, derives from a literary milieu of which Schulz would give no hint in his later preface:

> It has now been about a decade since Herder—who strolled about all sorts of regions of literature in his foraging—following the scent of the *Reliques of Ancient Poetry*, came across the fallow field of *Volkspoesie*, which previously no one at all had tread on. He immediately made his adventure known in the *Fliegende Blätter über deutsche Art und Kunst*. Bürger, who at just that time was occupied with the same reading, did something even more important than the theorist; although independently and without needing that impetus, he realized these ideas in his splendid *Lenore* and various other ballads. Immediately in his footsteps came Hölty and Stolberg with some equally very beautiful pieces. And then, finally, Bürger, in his essay "Daniel Wunderlich" in the *[Deutsches] Museum* put forward his misconceived theorem *of the unique grandeur of Volkspoesie:* and behold! every swamp at the foot of Parnassus awakened, and their tiny little inhabitants croaked out on all sides so much *Volksgesang* that finally even Bürger's ears rang with it, and he found it necessary . . . to demand silence of the mob of frogs. . . . The epidemic also spread to musicians; they copied down street songs, and wrote them themselves—and even lauded it as the non plus ultra of musical art, and as the first *Consolations des Miseres de la vie humaine.* Now that, in a nutshell, is the literary history of the mania of the *Volksgesang*, which raged for some time, and—thank God—is mostly past; and in a few years its former existence will only be remembered through perhaps a few good deposits that the passing fermentation left behind.[11]

In this contextualization of the musical *Volkston*, the original impetus is the well-known revival of the volkslied, here presented as a project initially theoretical and poetic; the role of musicians comes under consideration only after Cramer has moved from the revival's respectable origins to its far less successful popularization. Cramer (like Schulz) shows no interest in the idea of direct imitation of popular song that the literary example suggested to the unnamed musicians he introduces. Indeed, it turns out that Schulz's songs are quite unrelated to this phenomenon, and that their virtues are, in Cramer's view, rather to be ascribed to qualities specific to all good examples of the genre; these specifically musical qualities constitute the second contextualization, which employs some of the same vocabulary as Schulz. According to Cramer though, Schulz's label is simply an affectation dictated by the market for lieder:

> The content of this introduction, one would think, would also concern Herr Schulz, who here publishes *Lieder im Volkston*—but by no means! The addendum *"im Volkston"* is not much more for him than a vehicle with which he has sought to prepare the way for easier access for his extremely praiseworthy, genuine, well-thought-out, and deeply felt songs to the ears of good listeners who are nearly frightened away by the host of song-compositions that is appearing. True, one notices in all of them the not unsuccessful striving for true comprehensibility, popularity, and ease that he has sometimes sought to achieve even through the adoption of the familiar progressions and turns of phrase of the simple manner of good folk melodies—but these are all also qualities of the good lied in general, which can have a great many nuances of affect; accordingly, we will consider them as lieder in general.[12]

If Cramer's evaluation served to rescue the reputation of the *Lieder im Volkston* from the danger of association with what was, for Cramer, a largely discredited literary movement, Schulz's preface suggests that Cramer had gone too far in dissociating Schulz from the literary world and placing him in the musical. The familiar tone Cramer adopts is a far cry from Schulz's more elevated style, and Schulz has recourse not to the qualities of a good lied but rather to the essential characteristics of a work of *art*. The tension between musical and literary culture that we have seen elsewhere, then, appears here in yet another guise: Cramer seems to have sought to enhance Schulz's reputation by stressing that he was not simply following a fashion handed down to musicians by poets and theorists. Schulz, however, seeks to stress the claims of music—even apparently simple music—as art that is complex and demanding, and its creators (who might in Cramer's version still have been liable to dismissal as "mere" musicians) as knowledgeable participants in an aesthetic discourse capable of defining the needs of the populace.

If my reading of the preface to the *Lieder im Volkston* still seems to burden with overly ponderous significance what is, after all, a single relatively brief passage, consider it in light of another, less widely read text by Schulz. In his *Gedanken über den Einfluß der Musik auf die Bildung eines Volks* (1790), written to encourage the introduction of instruction in music in the Danish school system, Schulz deals more explicitly with the theme of cultivating the common people. The introductory passage, in which Schulz seeks to establish the value of musical cultivation, also proceeds through sharp juxtapositions:

> That music, when it is appropriately practiced and employed, could soften manners, ennoble feelings, spread joy and sociability among the people, and in general have a great influence on the cultivation of the moral character, can only be doubted by those who have never had occasion to reflect on the essence and effects of this art, or by those who have still not discerned that the culture of a nation promotes its happiness.
>
> Music affects the most excitable part of the human being, the sensual faculties [*Sinnlichkeit*], the direction of which is one of the first goals of a medium for the cultivation of a people. Enlightenment of the intellect alone has its effect on this often only slowly, often only weakly, often not at all; music, by contrast, does so at all times, and often so powerfully that it can inspire to unimaginable deeds. Just one example: the soldier instructed about the glory of dying for the Fatherland may perhaps on that account go into battle no less disheartened; to the sound of powerful battle music, by contrast, even without such instruction, he will go courageously into the face of death. The witness of a young but experienced army commander, whose name it would be boastful to mention here, gives the above complete support: encouragement to sing is the most effective means of allowing soldiers not to feel the difficulty of a forced march. One can easily think how much more effective still song would be for an army if for every such occasion, and others as well, appropriate war and soldier's songs were sung.
>
> In the provinces of Denmark, and particularly among the country people, little or nothing is known of music. Even general chorale singing in the churches is still a crude clamor without pure intonation and unity. When a people are so indifferent to the pleasures of the most noble human sense, hearing, that screaming and singing, false and pure, are one and the same to them—but that is impossible among Europeans; rather, when a people knows music in name only, or knows at most only the lowest level of its magical power, and has no further experience of the impression it would make on its feelings than that which its crude screams or falsely played instruments bring forth, then one can conclude that moral cultivation has made no significant progress in

this people; at the least, many of the most pleasant feelings that elevate the enjoyment of life are still unknown to it, and it is therefore lacking a great portion of its happiness. If, however, one makes known to it gradually the higher powers of music—to be sure, only those that remain suitable to its comprehension and its feelings, and that principally have as their focus the advancement of its moral pleasure—if one provides it [the people] with the frequent enjoyment of the same in so many situations of its life, it is not to be doubted that, precisely to the degree that a people's hearing is cultivated and made receptive to the higher powers of this salutary art, feelings for beauty will also be awakened in it, feelings whose influence on the morals, on all domestic and social pleasures, on its spirit and on its way of thinking, on the sweetening of labor and the easing of every burden and sorrow, on the enjoyment and happiness of its life, is undeniable.

   But how can music become commonly known among a people? Through the schools. Music instruction must be linked to school instruction.[13]

The theme at which Schulz arrives by the end of this passage—education—is one to which I return in the following chapter, but I have cited his approach to that topic at length here because it provides a more explicit social and intellectual grounding for the relations touched upon only briefly in the preface to the *Lieder im Volkston*. Its first paragraph not only extols the virtues of music but also (once again) makes clear that he is not writing for the unreflective or the uninformed ("those who have never had occasion . . ."). Instead, it establishes as its concern the welfare of an entire people, thereby implying an address to the authorities on whose decisions that welfare rests. Recognizing this implicit address clarifies the import of the following paragraph, which begins by taking as self-evident the value and propriety of controlling the sensual faculties of the people and asserts that (conventional) intellectual enlightenment is a relatively ineffective means to that end. This perspective also helps explain the text's seemingly bizarre juxtapositions, through which softened manners, ennobled feelings, joy, and sociability lead quickly to mindless but ferocious soldiers and forced marches. From the ruler's perspective, a softened and ennobled populace is a docile and obedient one.

   Any temptation to equate the *Volkston* with the music of the people is effectively quashed by the remainder of the passage. Schulz's description of rural musical practice makes his distaste abundantly clear,[14] and his appeal to the people's European identity as a guarantor of their ultimate educability still further emphasizes that it is the cultivation provided by Western civilization rather than any natural qualities of the people that must be developed if music is to render palatable their necessary labor. These values link Schulz's views to the prominent strand of German Enlightenment discourse that viewed cultivation of the people as a means to promote not equality but contentment with appointed social roles.[15] When, at the end of his pamphlet, Schulz calls for introduction—in the schools that he envisions for training teachers—of "song compositions . . . and other pieces on appropriate sacred and secular texts, such as farmer's songs, citizen's songs, soldier's songs, family songs, rounds on all the subjects that interest a people,"[16] his benevolence is of the sort that Gotthold Ephraim Lessing had earlier praised in the *Volkslieder* of the poet Johann Wilhelm Ludwig Gleim:

> Only you have really understood the people, and kept in view those among it who are more active with their bodies, who are not so much lacking in understanding as in the occasion to show it. You have mingled with these people, not to lead them away from their work through profitless contemplation but rather to encourage them in their work and to make their work the source of ideas appropriate to them and also the source of their enjoyment. In particular, in consideration of the latter, most of these your lieder breathe that which was so desirable and honorable a thing to the wise ancients, and which daily seems to be disappearing from the world—I mean that happy poverty, *laeta paupertas*, which so pleased Epicurus and Seneca, and in which it matters little whether it is forced or voluntary, if only it is happy.[17]

The link between Schulz's position and Lessing's is difficult to deny, and yet this corrective against the absorption of Schulz and the *Volkston* into the narrative of social progress could easily drift to the opposite extreme of portraying Schulz as an apologist for absolutist power or, at best, its unwitting tool. However, both the biography of Schulz written by his friend Reichardt and Schulz's own correspondence, especially with the poet Johann Heinrich Voß, reveal him to have been anything but a pliant servant of royal courts: his impatience with courtly affectations, his petty bourgeois background, and what Stoljar aptly characterizes as his "generous temperament" would appear to lend credence to her populist interpretation.[18] At issue, however, is not Schulz's character but the forces at play in the system of social relations in and through which he acted and to which the ideology of the *Volkston* contributed. Reichardt's account makes clear that to be taken seriously as a musician (rather than as the common tavern fiddler his father feared he would become) required that Schulz obtain a credible music education[19]—and through that education he learned not only the practical skills of the trade but also an appropriate understanding of the relationship of the music to power. Ideologically, these two categories are not as exclusive as they might appear: the goal of musical practice was to master the musical skills that would allow the musician to appear (as Schulz did in the preface to the *Lieder im Volkston*) as an authority who dispensed the products of his learning to a less cultivated public; with respect to power, the musician served those who stood in relation to the people as a whole as the composer stood to the musical amateur. Both personal success and broader influence depended on success in both categories. Schulz, in short, chooses a discursive stance that assumes the same authority for musical knowledge that, as Rudolf Vierhaus recognized, marked more firmly established discourses of knowledge and power: "Common to both sides, the ruling as well as the writing, was the inclination to understand the 'Volk' as the object of rational examination and [beneficently provided] happiness, and to believe that they understood its true interests better than it did itself."[20] If Schulz's notions of musical cultivation through the *Volkston* proceed downward from beneficent authority, they reveal his internalization—or at least prudent reflection—of the relations of both musical practice and the larger society in which music played a role.[21]

THE *VOLK*, THE ARTIST, AND
THE THREAT OF SOCIAL DECLINE

The explicitly conservative role of many such pedagogically oriented collections of folksongs and lieder in the *Volkston* led Ernst Klusen to dismiss them harshly: "They bracket out everything problematic, everything critical, present a positive side to every circumstance of life, and contribute to popular education in that they train obedient subjects."[22] But Klusen also recognizes that the concept of the folksong has served a variety of functions; in particular, he interprets its role in art music far more favorably: "The artist seeks new means and forms of expression with the goal of personal development; the composer is led, like a sailor by the North Star, to new shores. This is an individual, subjective creative problem of the autonomous artist, which can lead to very complicated creations."[23] This assertion returns the issue to territory more comfortable to musicology— the composition of unique works by autonomous creators. The simplicity of Klusen's binary, however—in which the pedagogical uses of the *Volkston* are manipulative and oppressive, while its employment by autonomous artists is liberatory—once again overlooks the system of social relations in which musical composition takes place.

To disregard those relations was a luxury that composers in the late eighteenth century could ill afford; the voluminous writings of Schulz's friend and colleague Johann Friedrich Reichardt make that point emphatically. In particular, Reichardt's understanding of the folksong, although it advocates the sort of creative use by genuine artists that Klusen upholds as exemplary—and in this departs significantly from Schulz's position—also reveals the extent to which that position itself arose from a specific and problematic social situation.

At first sight, Reichardt's view shares a great deal with Schulz's. In 1782, the year of the first edition of Schulz's *Lieder im Volkston* (and thus before the publication of Schulz's preface), Reichardt published "An junge Künstler" as the first article in his *Musikalisches Kunstmagazin*. In the course of outlining the requirements of a developing musician-composer, Reichardt turns to the need to follow nature, which in turn leads to an extensive digression on the necessity of a widely available body of volkslieder for both a healthy society and genuine art. He identifies his own *Frohe Lieder für deutsche Männer* as contributions to the cause and wishes that Schulz would publish more of his "genuine folksongs *[wahre Volksgesänge]*." Further, both his requirements for these songs and the position he adopts in enumerating them—the educated professional prescribing for the less informed public—suggest an alignment with Schulz's project:

> Song melodies with which everyone who has no more than ears and a throat will be able to join in must so exactly strike the tone *[Weise]* of the [poetic] lied—as *Herder* more aptly terms what one otherwise just calls its melody—in the simplest progression of tones, in the most certain motion, in the most precise agreement of divisions and sections, that once one knows the melody, one will no longer be able to think of it without the words, nor the words without the melody; that the melody will be everything for the words and nothing for itself.
>
> Such a melody—to say it to the artist in a single word—will always have the character of unison, and thus require no accompanying harmony or else allow it only as a concession.
>
> This is the way all lieder were created in the times when our German *Volk* was still rich in song.[24]

And yet this passage introduces a new complication. Reichardt's turn to the volkslied in the context of following nature suggests that the direction of learning found both here and in Schulz's writings—from the educated musician to an educable public—is supplemented by another, in which the musician learns from nature and "natural" song: that is, what was created in the unspecified past of the excerpt's final sentence. That final sentence (and, of course, the mention of Herder that precedes it) links Reichardt's cause to Herder's advocacy of the literary volkslied, which urged that the spirit of a people found purer, more spontaneous expression in those texts, whether printed, orally transmitted, or newly written.[25] Herder himself declared this position enthusiastically in the essay to which Cramer had referred in discussing Schulz: "Know, then, that the wilder, that is, the more lively and freely acting, a people is (for this word means nothing more than this!), the wilder, that is, the more lively, freer, more sensual, more lyrically conceived, its songs must be, if it has songs!"[26] The aesthetics of the Sturm und Drang that such statements evoke, however, did not coexist comfortably with the practical concerns of musical culture; to argue simultaneously that the composer ought to provide worthy songs for an uncultivated public and that that composer ought to look to the *Volk* for models of genuine creativity produced a tension that Reichardt's transference of the source of that inspiration to the past (again following Herder's model) only masks. This ambivalent attempt to identify with the *Volk* while also claiming professional competence as a form of distinction from the general public makes Reichardt's rhetorical task considerably more challenging than Schulz's, as well as more relevant to the problem of defining the bounds of musical culture as it developed in the nineteenth century. It is an ambivalence with which Herder himself was familiar, as he revealed in the historical overview that introduced the second volume of his own collection of volkslieder: "It is not necessary that the folksinger come from the rabble *[Pöbel]* or sing to it, any more than it insults the most noble poetry to sound from the mouth of the people *[des Volks]*. 'People' does not mean the rabble on the streets, who never sing and create, but rather scream and mutilate."[27]

Reichardt never gives voice to such overtly contemptuous evaluations, but his discomfort with the state of popular musical culture becomes clear as his essay continues, as does his understanding of the social situation that gave rise to it. An idealized view of the *Volk*, a despairing evaluation of popular musical taste, an ideal of high art, and an acute awareness of socioeconomic demands on the composer all find expression in a single remarkable passage:

> But why does even the most attentive observer find among the European peoples no new genuine volkslieder? Clearly, the constitution of the state has much to do with it—but this oppressed in the past as well. I think the most important thing is that that beautiful natural necessity [i.e., the creation of volkslieder] has become an art, and art nothing more than a trade *[Handwerk]*. From the prince's *Oberkapellmeister* down to the beer fiddler who brings operetta into the farmer's tavern,

virtually everyone is now an imitative manual laborer [*Handarbeiter*] for the going market rate. Most unfortunately, there are so many of them that there can never be competition among the buyers, but always among the sellers. Therefore, then, even the highest goal of today's so-called artist is this: to satisfy the greatest quantity of his payer's follies at once. And this has so generally fatal an influence on the entire people that when anyone—whether ruler or tenant—once lets a happy human feeling well up, he no longer has enough direct, untroubled sense to express it from himself and according to his own nature; the ever-ready wandering musician [*Spielmann*] sings forth from him instead—instead of old hunting songs expressing completely the character of the nocturnal stalkers and trappers, instead of the cozy life on the water breathing from fishermen's songs, calm cheerfulness from shepherd's songs, and from all sounding the living expression of true joy and true pain.[28]

Perhaps the most striking feature of this paragraph is the opposition it establishes between the past as a powerful but vague ideal and a troubled present dominated and contaminated by economic necessity. In that (again, unspecified) past, even art was not yet necessary; the common people, from whom the creative artist is clearly separated, naturally expressed themselves in the form of folksongs appropriate to their station. Art, then, comes into existence only when this properly stratified social order breaks down and spontaneous expression is no longer possible (a parallel to Schiller's opposition of the naive and the sentimental). But even this situation offers no real solution, for art, too, degenerates as soon as it is introduced in Reichardt's extraordinarily compressed sketch. Reduced to mere *Handwerk*, it falls victim to the free market. Music, in short, has become a commodity and, still worse, one whose supply far exceeds demand, to the extent that the musician (no longer artist but rather common *Spielmann*) is reduced to displacing the genuine music of the people with popular tunes simply to procure an existence. It would be difficult to imagine a more graphic characterization of the alienation of the worker in the realm of music.

At issue here is not the historical accuracy of Reichardt's scenario: even if Reichardt himself believed that such an ideally free and satisfied world had ever existed, few would seriously argue that the ancien régime had provided either such ideal creative freedom or such cozy and cheerful conditions for its peasantry.[29] Reichardt's urgency stems rather from the precarious insecurity of the present and its consequences: the very freedom that Reichardt sought in creativity emerges as a threat in the social sphere. His solution—the cultivated artists' creating and returning genuine volkslieder to the people, thereby cultivating them to appreciate the high art that the same musicians created, having learned to be natural from genuine folk music—imagines a reuniting of the creative and the social that would overcome the specter of downward mobility that hovers over the passage.

These concerns link the issue of the *Volkston* and the place of a high-art culture of music to concerns well outside the strictly aesthetic; as Julia Moore has observed, the socioeconomic circumstances of the late-eighteenth-century musician were in fact those of the petty bourgeoisie,[30] and this position made a life devoted purely to autonomous art unthinkable. Thus Reichardt wrote that Schulz's father, a baker, beat his son in an effort to dissuade him from a musical career that he could only imagine would create a *Bierfiedler;* Schulz's reply was disarmingly straightforward: "Father, in the future it will be a trifle for me to earn a thousand *Thäler* a year with music."[31] The darker side of this situation is suggested by Schubert's expression of relief, several decades later, at having found even a temporary musical position: "Otherwise I would yet have become a ruined *Musikant.*"[32] Schubert's fears were likely realized more frequently than Schulz's hopes; as Tia DeNora has pointed out, in the transformation of musical arrangements among the Viennese aristocracy at the end of the eighteenth century, the number of musicians who emerged to success under a system dominated by prominent stars rather than stable and ongoing domestic musical establishments (*Hauskapellen*) was small indeed.[33]

But Reichardt's references to *Handwerk* and the *Handarbeiter*—examples of what became a conventional contrast between devalued *Handwerk* and genuine *Kunst*—do not fit comfortably with this assessment of the musician's place. Rather, they reveal a view of work far removed from the pride in productive labor of the traditional craftsmen, whose guilds had secured the place of the petty bourgeoisie.[34] But precisely the same economic forces that Reichardt saw as threatening the security and freedom of the musician were those that had long threatened to undercut the traditional privileges of the guilds—and as Sabine Schutte has noted, it was among the petty bourgeoisie threatened with assimilation to a developing class of common workers that the most vocal rejection of the volkslied as the crude song of the common people would develop.[35]

The freedom of the true artist and his relation to the volkslied, then, are socially loaded topics. Reichardt had chosen as the first keyword for the developing artist a term fraught with significance for any contemporary reader of the German press: *Freyheit.* As Jürgen Schlumbohm has documented, that term became a keyword summarizing rising bourgeois aspirations across all fields of public life—embracing social mobility; free enterprise and free, commodified labor; free trade; and the free dissemination of ideas—all in contrast to the dependence and obligations of the old social order. If, as Schlumbohm notes, the German bourgeoisie pursued these goals both out of immediate self-interest and a desire to establish "the legal foundations of a full and unimpeded establishment of capitalist relations of production," for Reichardt, given the uncertain social status of musicians, the idea that changing relations of production could be equated with self-interest was less clear.[36] To claim freedom as the necessary prerogative of musician-artists (not musician-craftsmen) was to use the language of universality to claim for musicians membership in the cultivated, professional bourgeoisie in whose image that universality was shaped.[37] Such a hope for upward mobility required precisely the sort of contrast, a gesture of setting boundaries, that the *Volkston* could provide: in it, the composer appears not as a worker but a free intellectual securing his identity against the common people both by providing for their cultural well-being and by drawing on an idealized *Volk* past to guide his creation of works of art whose appeal will be as universal as is adequate cultivation.

The relevance of Reichardt's social origins (as the son of a court musician) and concerns about the future of his trade-cum-art become clearer through comparison with the perspective provided by Ludwig Achim von Arnim, who addressed the afterword of *Des Knaben Wunderhorn*, "Von Volksliedern," to Reichardt. Although the two shared a common interest in the topic, Arnim's place as a man of letters and member of a noble family gave him a perspective significantly different from that of even a literarily active professional musician like Reichardt. Arnim's opening praise of Reichardt itself establishes a social distance to be traversed: Reichardt, who has "done more for old German folksong than any other living musician," has "communicated it, in accord with its value, to the literate classes."[38] And Arnim's own perspective as a representative of those classes is one in which the experience of folksong confirms a privileged upbringing. His first memory of encountering folksong (in the form of its religious counterpart, *Kirchenlieder*) was "from my nurse, as she cleaned the room" (*von meiner Wärterin beim Ausfegen der Zimmer*). He goes on to note that he later encountered Schulz's songs "in sociable circles" (*in geselligen Kreisen*), and that his tutor praised them as second only to the poems of the highly respected Enlightenment poet Christian Fürchtegott Gellert. His first experience of the full power of folksong occurred in the country, as he listened to court servants and village people through his window on a summer night singing before joining their regiments and marching off to war. For Arnim, then, folksongs are situated as the music of people who serve, overheard and remembered in the context of a stable social order in the tradition of Schulz and Lessing.[39] Arnim's response to what he too recognizes as the undermining of that stability is thus markedly different from Reichardt's:

> In this whirlwind of the new, in this supposedly instant birth of paradise on earth, in France too (even before the Revolution, which was perhaps first made possible thereby) almost all folksongs were obliterated; they are still impoverished in that regard—what will bind them to that which is permanent to them as a people? In England as well, folksongs are more seldom sung; Italy too sinks in its national song—opera— through idle people's thirst for novelty; even in Spain many songs are said to be lost and nothing significant circulates. Oh, my God, where are the ancient trees under which we still rested yesterday, the ancient signs of stable borders—what happened to them, what *is* happening? They are almost forgotten among the people, and, sadly, we strike at their roots. If only once the mountain peaks are stripped of timber, the rain drives away the soil and no wood will grow there again; let it be our endeavor that Germany not be so fully mismanaged [*verwirtschaftet*].[40]

The remarkable claim that the French Revolution could have been made possible by the decline of French folksong only underscores the link between happily singing people and stability. The perspective of the leading voice of the romantic folksong revival is thus closer to that of the leaders Schulz sought to address than to Reichardt's threatened would-be professionals: although the final sentence still adopts economic terms, its patrician "our" acknowledges a leader's established responsibility rather than making new claims for the status of a profession.

THE *VOLKSTON* AND MEANING IN THE CLASSICAL CANON

The ease with which such authors as Schulz, Reichardt, and Arnim shifted from artistic to social and economic concerns blurs Klusen's distinction between pedagogical (mis-)uses of the *Volkston* and its authentic appearance in autonomous, self-expressive art. However, both the geographical removal of *Volkston* discourse from the still-canonic repertoire of the late eighteenth and early nineteenth centuries and the relative obscurity of the music of its leading advocates have ensured that little musicological attention has been directed to any relation between that discourse and the Viennese classical canon. Direct links between these worlds do exist—Schulz's visit to Haydn, Baron Gottfried van Swieten's familiarity with the North German lied, Mozart's direct experience of the socioeconomic insecurity of the independent, "free" musician[41]—but the musicological insulation of the canonic repertoire and its history from the larger musical culture of the period requires a more direct demonstration of the relevance of the concerns I have traced above, even at the risk of yet again reinforcing that insulation by appealing to the canonic repertoire to validate the significance of the issue.

One obvious starting point is Haydn's *Die Jahreszeiten*, in which the *Volkston* figures perhaps more extensively than in any other work in the classical canon. That work's opening tableau, the chorus of country folk welcoming spring ("Komm, holder Lenz") followed by the aria "Schon weilet froh der Ackermann"—a transparently clear example of the *Lied im Volkston*—establishes immediately the existence of a contented peasantry going cheerfully about its proper work; a review of the first performance notes that the aria "breathes the most unaffected cheerfulness." [42] The familiar themes of the literary *Volkston* run throughout the oratorio, reaching an apotheosis of sorts in the trio with chorus, "So lohnet die Natur dem Fleiß (no. 20—"thus nature rewards diligence"); its near ecstatic tone, with concertante winds that were more often associated with far loftier subjects, is an indication of the central importance of that virtue in the ideological world of the *Volkston*—at least, that is from the perspective of Gottfried van Swieten, the noble patron and educational reformer who prepared the text. Haydn himself was reportedly less enthusiastic, famously complaining that "it had never occurred to him to set 'industry' ('Fleiß') to music." [43] This response, however, is less the sign of van Swieten's poetic incompetence that it is often taken to be than it is further evidence of the contrasting social positions of the musician, most of whose long career had been spent as the servant of a noble family, and the cultivated patron from whose perspective the diligence of the peasantry was evidence of the proper ordering of society.

The oratorio's close lays out the place of the *Volk* and their music within society even more explicitly: the daughters' spinning song (no. 38) is introduced as a work song to facilitate labor ("and cheered is their task by plain and artless, jolly song" *[und ihren Fleiß belebt ein ungekünstelt frohes Lied]*)—here presented as integral to traditional peasant life but in fact more closely associated with the textile cottage industry that was crucial to the preindustrial development of central Europe.[44] The final folksong, a product of the peasants' evening recreation, tells the comic story of a lecherous nobleman's foiled scheme to corrupt the honor of an "honest country girl." These tableaus of productivity and virtue set the stage for the work's concluding meditation on the transience of life and the endurance of virtue (Simon's final aria, no. 42), but they also effectively mark the end of the work's representation of peasant life. The closing double chorus transcends the *Volkston* in its Handelian splendor, just as its exhortation to seek the reward of eternal life confirms the limited place of the peasants' world in the larger divine order; the virtues it enumerates (helping the poor and oppressed and protecting the innocent) are those of the benevolent ruler, not the ruled.[45] Similarly, Haydn's music confirms the familiar musical hierarchy, a point that the reviewer of *Ueber die Musik der Indier* recognized as well: "And [as Haydn's folksong settings unite primitive melodies with our harmony] so too the *beauty* that results from the choice of a genuine folk song . . . or a folklike, simple theme in the works of Händel, Haydn or others, results not because these men, perhaps for lack of anything better, had to take their refuge here, but rather because in the course of their composition they show how much can be made out of a simple or simple-seeming phase through their *own* wealth of ideas and according to the nature of *our* music."[46]

The idyllic image of a contented and diligent lower class is familiar from Schulz and the popular pedagogy of the German Enlightenment—and hardly surprising in Haydn, whose connection to important figures in the Austrian Enlightenment (van Swieten prominent among them) David Schroeder has made clear.[47] But it would be a mistake to view this work, premiered, after all, not in a public concert but before an elite noble audience in Vienna's Schwarzenberg Palace, as a purely personal statement by Haydn. The report of the premiere cited above makes no such assumption; it closes with praise not for Haydn but for the informal society of noble patrons of art (led by van Swieten) who had made the work possible: "In this circle Haydn's genius found love of art, a cultivated and receptive public, and encouragement such as is unusual in Germany. May the taste of this school live long, be spread far and wide, and bring forth such fruits everywhere!"[48] This audience (like Haydn's patrons, the Esterházys, who had long appreciated the widely recognized rustic elements in Haydn's symphonic minuets and rondos) was plainly positioned to appreciate so accomplished a representation of happily productive subjects; but to be recognized at the same time as perceptive patrons of the most sophisticated high art added further distinction: the popular had social meaning both in its representation and in its transcendence, particularly in the case of a work through which "from beginning to end the spirit is involuntarily swept away from the most moving to the most fearful, from the most naive to the most full of artifice, from the most beautiful to the most sublime."[49]

Works like *Die Jahreszeiten*, however, were clearly exceptional and were recognized as such: by its 1801 premiere, Haydn was a revered master, and his new work in the prestigious genre of the oratorio was eagerly awaited. More typical of the place of the *Volkston,* and less obviously linked to maintaining the social status quo, are a series of songs by Schubert; largely written between 1815 and 1817, they set to music eighteenth-century texts by poets including Matthias Claudius and the poets of the *Göttinger Hainbund,* among them Ludwig Hölty, Friedrich von Stolberg, and Johann von Salis-Seewis. Their topics include idealized presentations of the activities of peasant farming (*Pflügerlied,* D. 392; *Erntelied,* D. 434), fishing (*Fischerlied,* D. 351, D. 364, and D. 562), and traditional craft work (*Tischlerlied,* D. 274), as well as contentment, diligence, and the pleasures of life among the characters who practiced those activities (*Morgenlied,* D. 266; *Abendlied,* D. 276; *Lied,* D. 362 and D. 501; *Herbstlied,* D. 502; *Das Lied vom Reifen,* D. 532; *Täglich zu singen,* D. 533). Written well before Schubert could have had any hope of reaching patrons at the social level of Haydn's, these songs have no obvious biographical motivation, nor does any discussion of them among Schubert or his friends survive. In the absence of such explanations, they might easily be dismissed as evidence of Schubert's indiscriminate choice of texts or as an effort to assimilate an established stylistic convention. Both of these possibilities are solidly rooted in the conventions of musicology, but the larger context I have sketched above suggests that even if undisciplined reading (itself a familiar assessment of attempts by those outside the educated classes to achieve intellectual validation) and stylistic exploration are not to be dismissed, these songs would not have been experienced as neutrally as such explanations would imply.

The songs themselves present by-now-familiar values. The *Pflügerlied,* for example, replicates in the space of eight strophes the progression of *Die Jahreszeiten* as a whole, from the concrete activity of plowing (undertaken, of course, "diligently and bravely"—*arbeitsam und wacker*) to the ultimate reward of eternal life, and gives no more hint of the far less idyllic reality of preindustrial agricultural labor than does Haydn's text.[50] What sets them apart is the context in which they arose: what could explain an interest in such songs among Schubert and a small circle of largely young, educated middle-class auditors, urban dwellers connected neither to the landed aristocracy nor to agricultural laborers? As I have elsewhere suggested, the ideals of productive activity and virtue that these texts present link them to values of self-cultivation that a number of Schubert's friends pursued, but the possibility that the songs had a more purely recreational function should also not be overlooked.[51] In either case, the process through which meanings could be derived from them deserves closer consideration.

If these works are taken as simple entertainment, their significance is relatively straightforward. If the songs were considered to be examples of role-playing or even mockery of the simple characters they represent, the texts and stylistic gestures of the *Volkston* create a distance from the familiar, unmarked texts and gestures (unmarked, that is, with respect to this particular field of meaning) with which composer, performers, and auditors would more regularly identify. Performance of such a song would create a temporary, socially distinct alternative self whose effectiveness depends on its clear distance from the "real" self, the security of which is reinforced by contrast with the briefly imagined one of the song: however uncertain Schubert's existence as a young, unrecognized composer (still threatened by descent to the status of a "ruined *Musikant*"), or that of his friends as aspiring artists and unestablished members of the Austrian administrative bourgeoisie, such play could reassure them of what they were *not*.

Alternatively, if these songs were meant and experienced in earnest, the situation is more complex but still bound up with social identity. While the comic interpretation depends on a literal understanding—the auditor imagines a "real" farmer or fisherman—a moral application (which many of these texts explicitly invite) demands abstraction: Schubert and his friends clearly would not have understood these texts as exhortations to diligently plow or fish. Instead, of course, the texts would be applied metaphorically to advocate diligence and contentedness in the activities in which they did in fact engage. Goethe's brief poem "Hoffnung" (set by Schubert as D. 295) provides a model of this level of abstraction, leaving only the unspecified "daily work of my hands" to recall the metaphor of physical labor:

> Schaff', das Tagwerk meiner Hände,
> Hohes Glück, daß ich's vollende!
> Laß, o laß mich nicht ermatten!
> Nein, es sind nicht leere Träume:
> Jetzt nur Stangen, diese Bäume
> Geben einst noch Frucht und Schatten.

> Grant, daily work of my hands,
> the great joy—that I complete it!
> Oh, let me not grow weary!
> No, these are not empty dreams:
> now only sticks, these trees
> will one day yet give fruit and shade.

Conventional and familiar though this process of abstraction is, I have sketched it explicitly here because the process itself effects the same confirmation of self-identity that a comic understanding manifests more overtly; that is, both effectively establish a distance between the performers and audiences and the laboring classes that are the songs' subjects. In this case, a metaphorical interpretation of labor serves as a reminder that the work one is engaged in is *not* simple *Handwerk,* for otherwise no such abstraction would be required. Even more, however, the very act of abstracting to a universal value instantiates the qualities required of a member of the cultivated administrative class, particularly in the wake of the educational and bureaucratic reforms advocated by Herder and Humboldt.[52] In abstracting a universal human value, the interpreter effectively marks himself off from the imagined laboring class from whose actions the value was abstracted. As Schiller recognized, to partake of the universal—which Schiller required of the artist as much as the reformers did of the administrator—*demands* such abstraction, which must leave open the possibility of exclusion: "But in order [for the poet] to be assured that he really does address himself to the pure [human] type in individuals, he must previously have extinguished the individual in himself and elevated himself to the type. Only then, when he feels not as this or that particular person (in whom the concept of the type would always be limited) . . . but as a *human being in general,* is he certain that the entire type will feel as he does—or at least he can insist on this effect with the same right as he can demand humanity of every human individual." [53] The final sentence's implicit recognition that not all humans are, after all, fully human generalizes the means through which the *Volkston* could retain its relevance in a context removed from the conservative Enlightenment's popular pedagogy. In the case of these songs by Schubert, as with Reichardt, that relevance is intimately related to the social identity it could help secure.

VOLK AS PRIMITIVE OTHER

The *Volkston* was far from a new style when Schubert wrote these songs, but its survival (at least in name) until near midcentury is revealed by its occasional appearance in the works of Robert Schumann.[54] The most extensive examples are the *Fünf Stücke im Volkston,* Op. 102, for cello and piano, but the term also appears to characterize the "Nordisches Lied" (*Album für die Jugend,* Op. 68, no. 41), and several other pieces in that collection—including no. 9 ("Volksliedchen"), no. 10 ("Fröhlicher Landmann von der Arbeit zurückkehrend"), no. 18 ("Schnitterliedchen"), no. 20 ("Ländliches Lied"), and no. 24 ("Erndteliedchen") [55]—are clear descendants of the idealized folksong. But Schumann's usage also indicates something we have not yet encountered. In the *Fünf Stücke im Volkston,* the term marks these pieces as exceptional; the *Volkston* is a kind of stylistic exoticism, here divorced from explicit association with a class of people. In the *Album für die Jugend*, the "Nordiscnes Lied" offers a similar case: its *Volkston* evokes a foreign style just as its opening melody (G-A-D-E) names its dedicatee, the Danish composer Niels Gade. The remaining examples, however, perform a more straightforwardly pedagogical function, introducing the young pianist to characteristic styles as much as to pianistic challenges. Schumann's purpose is suggested by an aphorism from his "Musikalische Haus- und Lebensregeln" of 1848: "Listen diligently to all folksongs; they are a rich source of the most beautiful melodies and will open your eyes to the character of the various nations."[56]

Schumann's perspective on the *Volkston* is rooted in concerns that differ substantially from those expressed by Reichardt more than half a century earlier. Whereas Reichardt had written as a member of a threatened class of professional musicians seeking to secure a future amid changing relations of musical production, by the 1840s the reordering of the musical world was a fait accompli; the bourgeois musical public could support (if still often precariously) a musical career in a variety of forms.[57] Schumann's campaign against musical philistines did not aim to secure a place in the bourgeoisie for musicians but rather to maintain a privileged place within a larger bourgeois musical culture for devotees of high art. The utility of the *Volk* in this campaign is suggested by an essay by Carl Alexander, "Ueber das Volkslied, insonders das Italiänische," which appeared in the first volume of Schumann's *Neue Zeitschrift für Musik*. Before turning to his ultimate purpose of characterizing Italian folksong, Alexander orients his reader to the broader issue in terms that may initially call Reichardt to mind, in that they set up the past as the locus of true folk music. But Alexander's past is by no means purely ideal, as his comments on primitive language make clear; his views instead recall the views of the primitive discussed in the previous chapter: "Language is the affect of the soul, attested to by particular sounds. The first signs of this may well have differed little from the sounds of animals and have signified little more than pain and joy. Hence we still hear the languages of peoples who are young or who have sunken back into deep childhood in the hot regions of Africa and America, similar to an elongated howl consisting of [vowels], extended according to the power of their passion to unpleasant monotony, while those of the northern peoples, given the reserve and brevity of their nature, are much more like a [consonant]-heaped hissing, rattling, or rumbling."[58] The reason for this evocation of the crude and primitive becomes clear when Alexander turns to music. Folksongs, we discover, may be valuable as a source, but art is a matter of much greater sophistication:

> Just as language, with respect not only to euphony, but also to characterization, richness, and capability of inflection, directly represents the cultivation [*Bildung*] of nations, so the lied is the most faithful mirror of its soul, its character, and its ability to feel; it is as well the most important source for all poetic and musical, indeed, more broadly, of all historical and philosophical investigations, and the folksong must be for all musical artists an honorable monument of a classical youth, an example of simple, natural feeling—without requiring that we believe that something other than lack of experience, of flexibility of spirit, enforced the boundaries of noble simplicity. What the gifted, simple spirit finds instinctively, the highest cultivation finally returns to, through error and hesitation, but also with certainty and conviction.[59]

Here, the distancing evident in Reichardt's evocation of an unspoiled past of healthy folksong is both elaborated and inverted: the past rather than the present becomes the location of tension, now between crudity and the beautiful, if naive, art that primitives unreflectively produce. For the *cultivated* musician, folksong is less an ideal than an object of study, a pedagogical tool that the artist will transcend. This perspective is consistent with both Schumann's compositional uses of the *Volkston* and his own hortatory aphorism: folk music could provide a bulwark against the merely fashionable, and thus a form of distinction through which the truly dedicated and cultivated could be recognized—but only if it could be understood to reinforce rather than challenge the hierarchy of value that culminated in high art.[60] Revaluing the folk as primitive and exotic and the *Volkston* as a raw material and a teaching tool accomplished just that. Like Klusen's two categories of the *Volkston*, this gesture reinforces a distinction between two cultures of music, only one of which achieves the category of art, understood as free individual expression.

THE MUSICOLOGICAL HERITAGE OF THE *VOLKSTON*

German Scholarship

The similarity between Klusen's conclusions and these from the mid–nineteenth century will be less surprising if we consider the degree to which Schumann's understanding of a canonic high musical culture has held sway since that time and has exercised a powerful influence on the received understanding of music history. The existence of a distinct culture of high art music—for Schumann the motivation for extensive journalistic and critical efforts—has long been taken as a given and is presumed in the once dominant (and still frequently encountered) belief that the stylistic history of that music is as autonomous as the music itself is often heard to be. In this, the music-historical enterprise reveals its debt to the largely North German critical, theoretical, and aesthetic discourse on music in which the *Volkston* too was rooted.[61] The persistence of that discourse has meant that the *Volkston* and the issues surrounding it have exercised an influence on the construction of music history that has continued far longer than has musical interest in the repertoire about which the discourse originated.

Once again, Haydn provides a useful starting point. In his *Historisch-Biographisches Lexikon der Tonkünstler* (1790–92), Ernst Ludwig Gerber wrote of Haydn in terms that are strongly reminiscent of Schulz's: "He possesses the great artistry to often appear familiar in his compositions. Thereby, despite all the contrapuntal artistry found in them, they are popular and pleasant to every amateur [*Liebhaber*]." [62] Not surprisingly, then, in his article on Schulz, Gerber noted that "among the living masters of the first rank, my idols are *Schulz* and *Haydn*. Every young composer of talent should seek to hold up these two as examples. Both are just as classically correct as they are not to be equaled in their beauty." [63] Although Gerber's equal valuation of the two composers contradicts current opinion, Haydn's familiarity and accessibility have remained central to our image of the composer. For instance, they color E. T. A. Hoffmann's characterization of Haydn as the first great romantic composer: "His symphonies lead us into a boundless, green glade amid a lively, jovial throng of happy people. Young men and women swing past in round dances, and laughing children, eavesdropping behind trees and rose bushes, throw flowers teasingly at one another." [64] By the time of Adolph Bernhard Marx's biography of Haydn for Schilling's *Encyclopädie* (1836), the composer had assumed a character transparently indebted to the ideology of the *Volk;* indeed, he *becomes* the simple, loyal subject-peasant: "He was *completely* the expression of his people, fully and purely. Simply honorable and upright, in natural contentedness, which beautiful Austria pours into every breast, in the innocent cheerfulness of heart of an enjoyment of life untroubled and undisturbed from without or within, free of distant longings and ideas to carry him away, loving and pious as a child, gladly open to the most inward feelings of nature and to cheerful, *comic* moods: thus are the people [*Völkchen*] in the closest circles about the fatherly ruling throne of Austria, and so was their most characteristic singer." [65] This nature governed Haydn's work, as well: "The realm of thought gave him only as much insight as was compatible with the undisturbed activity of his temperament, his folklike thought, feeling, and faith; it let him remain an unabashed child of his land and lifted him above the surface of unconscious instinct without alienating him from his secure, natural ground." [66] The ambivalence of this elevation of the innocent and the folklike is confirmed, however, when Beethoven appears to set the limit of Haydn's accomplishment just as art transcends the volkslied: "Due to the power of his deeper idea, Beethoven—and first he—was led to newer, higher revelations. But in that which Haydn did give, he stands alone and indispensable."[67]

Such discussion of the role and limits of the simple in relation to artistic accomplishment has remained central to definitions of what we now call the Viennese classical style. James Webster has drawn attention to the crucial role it has played in constructing that style as a perfect synthesis "of harmony and counterpoint, traditional and galant, strict and free, *Kenner* and *Liebhaber.*"[68] And according to Guido Adler, one of the pioneering figures of the academic discipline of musicology, the simplicity essential to that synthesis had one essential source: "Their art rests on the ground of folk music."[69] Adler's student and colleague Wilhelm Fischer had sought to confirm this viewpoint in an extensive study that established the familiar distinction between what he termed the *Fortspinnungstypus*—the characteristic melodic style of the high baroque (that is, almost exclusively J. S. Bach)—and the *Liedtypus* of the Viennese classical style. The term Fischer chose for periodic phrase structure carries with it implications of simplicity, and the source of that simplicity is by now predictable: "The '*Liedtypus*' derives from the dance- and song-melodies of the people."[70] Webster notes the conservative musical values that such constructions of the classical style served in the early twentieth century,[71] but Fischer was careful to set bounds to the role of the popular and folk-derived in his ideally synthetic repertoire. He preserves the transcendence of the style and distinguishes it from the genuinely popular without compromising the purely stylistic orientation of his study by contrasting forms unquestionably associated with high art with those of the dance: "The role of dance pieces in the formation of sonata form is thus twofold: the modulatory framework and the construction of the principal melodies are dancelike. All the other formal elements owe their origin to forms that stand distant from dance music. Thus, with complete justification Guido Adler refers to the great importance of the influence that descendants of the polyphonic vocal forms had on the development of sonata form."[72]

Although it is tempting to dismiss such statements—written while a virulent form of populism dominated Viennese politics and while popularization of the classical canon was a controversial issue in Viennese musical life[73]—as testimony to issues long since laid to rest, the example of Walter Wiora's 1957 study, *Europäische Volksmusik und abendländisches Tonkunst,* reveals the continued presence of those issues in post–World War II

German scholarship. Within a larger study investigating the interaction of the distinct layers *(Schichten)* of European musical culture since antiquity, Wiora devotes a chapter to establishing the validity of Adler's and Fischer's view of the significance of folk music for the Viennese classical style, largely through melodic comparisons. When, in his introduction, Wiora touches on what made the Viennese style exemplary, he reveals a nervous awareness of the social dangers of drawing on the *Volk* to bolster the prestige of high art in terms strikingly reminiscent of authors from nearly two centuries before, now bearing the mark as well of postwar, divided Germany: "The degree to which a composer manages to realize the ideal of genuine, substantial *Volkstümlichkeit* does not depend only on his goodwill and on the political principles that he follows. He must, like an orator, have an instinct for what 'gets across'; he must have gotten used to a listening audience and be able to distinguish '*Volk*' from 'mass' and 'rabble.' Alongside numerous failed forms, such as vacuously simple, populist, and primitivist pieces of music, there are noteworthy types of genuinely *volkstümlich* art. In this way the Viennese classical masters united the things of the spirit with the claims of their contemporaries."[74] Heinrich Schwab's study elaborates on this position, explicitly linking the Viennese style to the concept of the *Volkston,* and, in a final reversal of terms, applies labor, the necessity of the common people from which so many commentators had sought to separate music as an art, as a metaphor not for the common term of the synthesis but rather for the artistic: "Through such procedures, the masters understood how to include a broad spectrum of contemporaries. Along with the comprehensible *Volkston,* the 'appearance of the familiar,' difficult labor on the musical material itself stands as the goal of intensive organization of the work. Thus their works fulfill both components of the 'classical' style-concept: the social and the qualitative."[75] Classical *quality,* then, is attained despite, not through, popularity.

Veiled Persistence: North America

The *Volkston* and the German volkslied tradition have held a far less prominent place in English-language musicology. Nevertheless, both because of their (largely unrecognized) role in defining the classical style and because of their usefulness in defining an elite—whether social, intellectual, or artistic—they remain visible on its margins. Stoljar's effort to enlist the *Volkston* for the cause of bourgeois democratic values is an unusually direct and socially oriented confrontation of the subject; more in line with the music-critical orientation of much North American musicology are a variety of briefer discussions of the popular or folk styles within studies of the canonic repertoire.[76] Walter Frisch, for example, in an article that is unusual for explicitly evoking the *Volkston*, does so primarily as a foil to reveal Schubert's greater creativity: "In a work like *Heidenröslein* (D. 257) formal design and melodic content seem perfectly coordinated. The song manages to attain sophistication without ever overstepping the aesthetic bounds of its folklike idiom. . . . But *Nähe des Geliebten* (D. 162), a strophic Goethe setting composed on 27 February 1815, manifests a compelling dialectic between form and content. The harmonic and melodic aspects of the song utterly transcend the folk style associated with a strophic framework."[77] Not surprisingly, despite this moderate praise for the successfully folklike, the study so introduced goes on to investigate the means through which the *Volkston* was transcended so convincingly.

Joseph Kerman's study of Beethoven's *An die ferne Geliebte* deals at greater length with the issue of a great composer's interaction with the ideal of the volkslied.[78] In it, Kerman interprets the cycle from the perspective that "Beethoven seems to have been caught between an innate allegiance to *Kunstgepränge* [artistic ostentation—a term drawn from the cycle's text] on the one hand and a growing sensitivity to the attractions of *Volksweise* [folk-style melody] and strophic setting on the other" (133). Once again the gesture is familiar: the attraction of the folkish and simple is acknowledged, but real mastery lies in successfully integrating it with the artistic and complex. Kerman thus recapitulates the conventional account of the genesis of the classical style in the course of demonstrating how this song cycle marks Beethoven's departure from that style, for the synthesis of the simple and the complex proves essential to Kerman's characterization of Beethoven's idiosyncratic late style. The cycle itself shows "that Beethoven could not accept the *Volksweise* ideal in its pure form" (154), as does the Ninth Symphony's complex treatment of the simple *Ode to Joy* theme, and the essay's conclusion suggests that Kerman has the same sympathies: his final discussion of *An die ferne Geliebte* is bracketed first by a reference to the surprising simplicity of a variety of unnamed late "sonata and quartet movements" (154) and afterward by a discussion of the elaborate cyclical structure of the Quartet in C-sharp Minor, Op. 131, interpreted as a descendant of the extended continuous form of the song cycle (156–57). Simplicity's role is again fulfilled in its transcendence.

Perhaps the most striking difference between this account and the others I have cited is its complete avoidance of social referents—the *Volksweise* concept appears as a purely stylistic convention in the context of an individual's creative efforts. Even Kerman's introduction of the lied ideal avoids the social relations central to that concept, largely by focusing on a single great figure, Goethe, despite the absence of any direct link between Goethe and the work in question. Personalizing the issue of the *Volksweise* thus clears the way for a purely stylistic consideration of the song cycle's significance.

Focusing exclusively on three individuals—Haydn, Mozart, and Beethoven—Charles Rosen provides a similarly style-dominated account in his influential 1972 study, *The Classical Style*.[79] As Webster has noted, Rosen's account is heavily (although inexplicitly and perhaps unknowingly) indebted to the German musicological tradition's construct of the classical style as an ideal synthesis.[80] In dealing with the popular style (329–50, in the course of a section dedicated to Haydn), Rosen also follows the plot established by that tradition: popular elements increase accessibility while providing a foil for the artistic complexity and subtlety that give the music its overriding interest. The result is a series of evaluative statements opposing the two elements:

> In short, the "popular" tune is used for its squareness and symmetry as a substitute for the banal cadence formulas, for the "filling" that would otherwise have been needed in its place. . . .
>
> The folk style has significance in Haydn's music mainly as an element of popular style in general, and this, as it appears in Haydn's music, is used largely for its stabilizing effect. . . .
>
> The popular material retains its character exactly because Haydn's technique isolates what it intends to develop. . . . This enabled Haydn to exploit the most characteristically popular side of his material while using it as the basis for the most sophisticated structures, provided only that the material had a strong tonal orientation. (Yodelling is so obsessively triadic that it might easily have been invented by the classical style if it had not already existed, and it is difficult to take seriously the formative stylistic influence of something structurally so inevitable and so logical.)[81]

The parenthetical conclusion of the last statement reveals unambiguously where Rosen's interests and loyalties lie by granting creative agency to a stylistic abstraction rather than allowing a challenge to the thesis that forces internal to the music are ultimately generative. Indeed, the conclusion of the chapter (344–50) abandons the consideration of popular materials and treats instead the issue of compositional subtlety in introductions.

Unlike Kerman, however, Rosen acknowledges the social, in a manner that anticipates Stoljar. Thus, "melodies of marked popular character" (for instance, those in Haydn's minuets and trios) are interpreted as "moments that the traditionally aristocratic form is made democratic—or at least available to the new audience" (340). Such elements, however, are ultimately subordinated to a higher artistic goal: "No doubt the ostentatious presence of the rhythms and turns of phrase of the popular dance forms are heard as a frank extra-musical reference—the irruption of the ideals of the non-aristocratic classes into the world of high art; but the style that Haydn had elaborated was, by 1790, one of such power that it could accommodate these ideals without loss of its own integrity" (341).

The autonomous integrity of that style and its products is the result of the propitious coincidence of a broad public audience and a stylistic language that enabled "the creation of a popular style which abandons none of the pretensions of high art." In short, this phenomenon, "perhaps unique in Western music" (332), is the product of a past golden age in which, as in Reichardt's, happy social circumstances made possible uniquely powerful music; only the historical setting and the structuralist interpretation of that music's power are new. The linking of folk elements primarily with a broad popular audience, however, obscures the possibility that popular elements could equally serve both aristocratic ideologies and those of musicians themselves, just as the use of terms such as *popular* and *democratic* downplays the elite status of such music both at the time of its origin and in the present.

This is not to suggest that these authors are using the *Volkston* and the concept of the popular to advance antidemocratic ideologies or even consciously to advance any political stance at all. On the contrary, their stance is quite determinedly apolitical. The boundary-defining concept of the *Volk*, however, still serves to define a social relation, placing the informed critic, sensitive to the nuances of stylistic coherence and artistic complexity, in close relation to the individualized composer-genius, whose work the critic explicates for the less knowledgeable reader. This placement of the critic within the small creative group—which, in the exchange between the Mozarts that opens this chapter included only composers—sets the critic too against the people and their simple music, now a raw material for both the compositional and the interpretive process. And so the critical evocation of the past asserts its authority not only through citation of the authoritative works of the past but also by adapting for itself the claims of distinction that musicians developed along with those works.

4 Education and the
Social Roles of Music

The continuing influence on musicology of concepts developed in the discourse around the *Volkston* has been possible in large part because that discourse centers on the relationships with which musicology has dealt most comfortably and extensively: those between the composer, musical works, and imagined ideal audiences. The concept of a populace cultivated to comprehend and participate in music, however, embraced relationships well beyond that familiar core. Even in the context of a discussion of a centrally important work by an exemplary composer, for instance, A. B. Marx touched on a number of those other relationships; consider his introduction to one of the most famous moments in all of Western art music, the entry of the chorus into a previously purely instrumental genre in the finale of Beethoven's Ninth Symphony:

> As in his outer life he longed fruitlessly for the sweetly satisfying
> bonds of the family and deluded his heart with paternal concern for
> ill-disposed relatives and again and again returned gladly to delusion,
> so in his art he turned with longing, remembrance, and wishes of love
> toward humanity, so grew his desire for human music, for song, and led
> him to the pinnacle of his creation. The Ninth Symphony, with chorus,
> was written. . . . With gigantic force he conjured up the gigantic powers
> of the fullest, most powerfully moving orchestra. . . . All that can no
> longer suffice. It shatters—and the instruments themselves take hold
> (in recitative form) of the tune *[Weise]* of human song. Yet again all
> those float past, dreamlike, human voices grasp the recitative, and they
> lead to Schiller's song of joy, to him a song of union for all people.
> Nothing can be more moving, nothing lets us gaze so deeply into his
> breast, than the way first the basses, then [all] the singers begin to sing
> "Freude schöner Götterfunken" so simply, so folklike, so given up to
> gentle longing and love, which seeks only humankind—humankind!—

needs only community with humankind, and no longer knows or seeks anything higher.[1]

It is precisely Marx's extravagant evocation of relations beyond the composer-music-audience triad that sets this passage emphatically apart from what has since become the musicological norm: Marx's vision embraces not only the personal and familial bonds of the composer but also a patently utopian "union of all people" and a desire for "community with humankind." Furthermore, those two extremes—the cozily domestic and the universal—appear to be causally linked: Beethoven's personal relational failures account for the intensity of his utopian longing, and the medium of expression for that longing is the universally accessible *Volkston* of *An die Freude.* Marx's resort to the biographical may seem reminiscent of Victorian sentimentality of the sort that colors George Grove's interpretations of the symphonies, but I would argue that, in conjunction with the all-embracing vision of unity to which it leads, the appearance of the domestic is here rather an indication of the almost unbounded aspirations of Marx's ideal for musical culture. And as Marx himself recognized, any hope of realizing those aspirations, even in the most approximate form, required cultural activity well beyond that of the composer.

One of the most crucial of those activities—the systematic cultivation in music that alone could ensure the reproduction and dissemination of a culture of music—provides the subject of this chapter. Of the many forms of music education that merit more careful study in the context of the social history of music, I have chosen beginning instruction in singing for school children as a focus. Like most forms of music education, singing instruction provides an opportunity to examine in some detail the disciplinary processes through which music educators sought to shape individuals who would both carry on the practice of music and embody the claims of music's advocates that that practice contributed to a more highly cultivated society. As we will see, discipline and embodiment are precisely the methods of that pedagogy, which provides a remarkably consistent example of a disciplinary practice in Foucault's sense; the ideal singing community that Marx (and many others) imagined could be realized only through systematic training that would reshape its pupils in the image of that ideal. More than that, however, the discourse on school singing instruction represents the broadest ambitions of music pedagogy, and as such it does indeed embrace the extremes of social relations. Although it inevitably centered on the teacher and his students in the classroom, this discourse touches as well on the roles of family life through which the student could be prepared for education and on the public social roles for which children were to be trained. Elementary music education thus occupied a crucial role in a vision of music as part of a larger project of cultivation.

Despite this significance, to raise the topic of elementary school music instruction in relation to Beethoven's final symphony is, from the perspective of musicology, to juxtapose the sublime and the invisible. With a single notable exception focused on issues of baroque performance practice, German music education in the eighteenth and nineteenth centuries has had virtually no presence at all in recent English-language scholarship, and although a long tradition of German scholarship (without which the present chapter could not have been written) treats the history of music education, links between those specialized studies and considerations of the larger musical culture are exceedingly rare.[2] When the pedagogy and pedagogical music of this period do find discussion, they most often figure negatively. So, for instance, John Butt concludes his study of German Lutheran music education with a chapter devoted to "the decline of the Lutheran cantorates during the eighteenth century," and Charles Rosen contrasts the pedagogical masterworks of Bach with a far bleaker view of later efforts: "The more private educational works of the Romantic composer produced little of any considerable musical interest, even for those of us with a nostalgic feeling for the days when we played 'The Happy Farmer' and other pieces from Schumann's *Album for the Young*. By the late eighteenth century, there is a sad and permanent decline in the quality of music written for young performers or beginners: one has only to compare Bach's *Album for Anna Magdalena Bach* with anything that came later."[3] From perspectives such as these—and both are informed and convincing in their own terms—studying the pedagogy of the period would appear to offer little to the discipline.

Even a cursory examination of discourse on music from this period, however, suggests an alternative perspective. Reichardt and Schulz, discussed in the previous chapter, were by no means unique in their concern for educational institutions and methods: the subject occupied a prominent place in the same periodicals that reviewed recent music and chronicled the concert and operatic life of the cities. To be sure, the topos of decline was already familiar, but most frequently as a conventionalized introduction to proposals to remedy a situation depicted as deplorable. Although discussion of education became less prominent in general music publications by the 1830s, it nonetheless occupied virtually every significant writer on music, including Marx himself, who not only wrote on it in his *Berliner Allgemeine musikalische Zeitung* (1824–30) but also published several books on various aspects of education—and as I discuss below, the social upheavals of 1848 made the topic current once again among the reform minded.[4] The topics of interest ranged widely, from the need for new institutions to train professional musicians to ways to develop musical taste among amateurs, and from the role of mechanical devices to guide keyboard hand position, which was debated intensely, to the level of education suitable for women.[5]

The topic of elementary school instruction in singing in particular occupies a prominent place within discussions of education, and although it has a long history that both predates and continues beyond the period under discussion, it was treated with particular intensity in the first two decades of the nineteenth century. Unlike most other discussions of music education, which presumed students (or at least parents) with an established interest in music and a background that motivated their study, the problem of the role and method of music instruction within general education brought its theorists and practitioners face-to-face with the challenge of constructing a general populace with a taste for and ability in music. In other words, to return to Marx's vocabulary, it demanded that whatever the bonds of the family that had produced a student, that student should emerge from study trained to join together in the united human music, in song.

This aspect of music education bears with particular relevance on the joining of voices and instruments that Marx—and many other nineteenth-century commentators—found so overwhelming in the Ninth Symphony.[6] From the perspective of musical activities and their associations, more was at stake in this joining than the blurring of generic compositional conventions. In a culture that increasingly linked instrumental music with virtuosity and complexity, vocal music itself developed strong associations with popularity; as Hans Georg Nägeli, whose educational work provides a focus for much of this chapter, wrote in 1812, advocating the establishment of distinct vocal and instrumental concerts, "The more instrumental music tends toward the sublime, the further it is removed from popularity; vocal music, on the contrary, approaches it [popularity] the more completely it appears."[7] And the particular style of song Beethoven chose allowed no mistaking the mixture of popular and complex: as Marx noted, the vocal tune is self-evidently folklike *[volksgemäß]*. Note, however, that Marx further qualified his description: the entrance occurs *"so simply, so folklike, so given up to gentle longing and love."* This is a far cry from J. A. P. Schulz's description of singing among the common people as "a crude clamor without pure intonation and unity," and numerous later writers provided evaluations of popular singing similar to Schulz's.[8] The gap between these two representations of a singing *Volk*—one an imagined ideal reflected in high art, the other a conventional response to actual song as heard through the standards of that art—constituted the challenge set for popular instruction in singing: how to transform a crudely singing rabble into a genuine representation of a *Volk* worthy of art.

The means by which to achieve such a transformation are suggested in the following account of another foundational act—this one, however, unlike Beethoven's definitively singular and individual creative one, is presented as a prescriptive fiction rather than a concrete musical event and is designed to be infinitely repeatable:

1. The teacher, standing at the blackboard opposite the children, speaks: "Children! You are to learn to sing! Assume the correct position for that, as I prescribe it: Stand upright! Chest out, head not thrown back."
2. "Stand still! Feet not too close to each other!" Because they need to change the position of the body slightly from time to time, he has them place now the right foot, now the left, a bit forward, in alternation.
3. "You should never stand at an angle. Those on either side must turn only the eyes, and if necessary the head, a little toward me."
4. "To sing, you use the same organs (parts of the body) as in speaking. I am now raising my hand; as I bring it down, pronounce the vowel 'a' [i.e., 'ah']"—[they speak:] "a." (The raising of the hand to signal the beginning of an exercise must occur somewhat slowly, in contrast to the rhythmic upbeat introduced later. The hand must always stand still for a little while, so the children have time to think, but always be brought down quickly, as if with a start.)
5. "I am raising my hand again; as I bring it down, say 'a' twice"—"a.a."
6. "Once more! As I bring it down, say 'a' several times—five or six"— "a.a.a.a.a.a."
7. "And once again! Connect several such 'a's for me without a break; that way, avoid stuttering!" The children attempt it without success. Finally he says: "Pay attention! I will produce such a continuous 'a' for you." Now he sings at approximately the pitch at which the "a" had been pronounced by the group (the totality of voices)—actually a purely held tone. He speaks: "Imitate me," and sings the tone in the same way. The children sing "a."
8. "Now, children, you have brought forth a tone. When one continues a vowel for a certain while in this way, and without the slightest interruption, what results is what one calls a tone; and just so one begins to sing." [9]

With this classroom vignette, Nägeli and Michael Traugott Pfeiffer began their course of instruction in the *Gesangbildungslehre nach Pestalozzischen Grundsätze* (1810). As one of the most widely discussed and longest-lived elementary singing texts of the period—Gustav Nauenburg, the leading German authority on vocal pedagogy, still recommended its use in 1836[10]—the *Gesangbildungslehre* provides a starting point for an investigation of the ideologies and relationships that enmeshed school music instruction with both high musical culture and more general social concerns. To be sure, this was only one among many introductory methods, but many of the features that concern us were common to many authors' approaches.[11] And as an introduction to the *Gesangbildungslehre* itself, this scene touches on a variety of central themes, which I develop in what follows.

SYSTEMATIC AND PROGRESSIVE PEDAGOGY

Pfeiffer and Nägeli's text—and Nägeli's extensive writings as an advocate of music pedagogy—is bound up with the German educational reforms of the late eighteenth and early nineteenth centuries, which themselves developed not only from the Enlightenment project of cultivation but also from the civil reforms initiated in response to Napoleon's German campaigns.[12] Ideals of universal education and the development of individual potential motivated reformers from Berlin (including Wilhelm von Humboldt, and Carl Friedrich Zelter in music) to Vienna (where Gottfried van Swieten played a prominent part in establishing guidelines for mandatory universal education) and beyond. Among the leading reformers was Johann Heinrich Pestalozzi (1746–1827), the Swiss author and pedagogue whose vision of a society humanized through educational reform was extremely influential; Nägeli's methodology is explicitly based on Pestalozzian principles, and, as Eckhard Nolte has noted, although Nägeli's aesthetic positions found relatively few followers, his methodology was extremely influential.[13] In the words of Johann Gottfried Hientzsch, writing nearly two decades after the work's publication, "An extraordinary number of teachers gradually learned from this work what 'method' means in singing instruction, and hopefully many more will still do so. It is and remains a central work on singing instruction in schools of every type."[14]

The basis of Pestalozzi's approach—the "method" that Nägeli offered—was systematic development from the starting point of sense impressions *(Anschauungen)*, which Pestalozzi took to be universal. Strongly influenced by Rousseau's ideal of the natural development of children, he maintained that effective elementary education required leading children systematically from that which was already familiar in their own experience to ever more complex concepts:

> Learn therefore to classify observations and complete the simple before
> proceeding to the complex. Try to make in every art graduated steps of

knowledge, in which every new idea is only a small, almost impercep-
tible addition to that which has been known before, deeply impressed
and not to be forgotten.

. . . Again, bring all things essentially related to each other to that
connection in your mind which they have in Nature. Subordinate all
unessential things to the essential in your idea. Especially subordinate
the impression given by the Art to that given by Nature and reality;
and give to nothing a greater weight in your idea than it has in relation to your race in Nature.[15]

Pestalozzi's understanding of that nature further prescribed that all knowledge *(Erkenntnis)* derived from three fundamental human faculties: the
power to generate sound, which made speech possible; an ability to conceive in indeterminate, purely sensual images, which provided a basis for
the knowledge of form; and a determinate, "no longer purely sensual" con-
ceptual ability, on which quantitative knowledge was based.[16] To follow nature, then, required breaking down traditional subjects to their most basic
elements and slowly reassembling them for students, guided by the principle that number, form, and language provided the means through which
humans perceived reality.

In 1809, Nägeli provided an extensive theoretical justification for his
particular adaptation of these principles to singing instruction in an article
published simultaneously in the Pestalozzian *Wochenblatt für Menschenbildung* and the *Allgemeine musikalische Zeitung.* This double publication
signaled Nägeli's desire to convince pedagogical and philosophical readers
of the value of instruction in music for general human cultivation and to
convince musicians of the need to reform what he characterized as a traditional but pedagogically ineffective means of conceptualizing music. The
latter group, he anticipated, would prove more resistant to his approach:

We ask nothing less of the genuine musician than that he for once
attempt to forget his inherited tonal system as well as the art of composition he has learned, and especially that which the systematizers—
oddly enough—have tried to provide as grammar and rhetoric; that
with our use of technical terms he never think of that system, and in
general not think beyond the simple definition. Indeed, we cannot even
permit him his theoretical division of the realm of music into harmony
and melody. He must leave behind his old perspective utterly and completely for the sake of the present investigation, in order to gain entrance into the realm of art and its scholarship from a new perspective.
Let him trust us.[17]

This type of exhortation addressed to musicians—favoring greater intellectual subtlety over unreflective adherence to tradition—again reveals the

gap even advocates of music recognized between literary-philosophical and musical culture. The passage also provides a graphic demonstration of the distance between Nägeli's theoretical discourse and that which was to be imparted to children: as the scene given above reveals, they were to receive no such courteous introduction. Although the text's "General Rules for the Teacher" opens with the admonition that "the teacher himself should express joy in music at the beginning of the first period of instruction," instruction itself was to begin neither with aesthetic discourse nor with links to prior experience.[18] Indeed, the book's twenty-second rule for the teacher prescribes that "the teacher should avoid speaking to the children about expression of feeling, tasteful performance, or artistic beauty in a higher sense. . . . All indefinite musical-aesthetic ideas should remain completely foreign to the children in our music method."[19] Rather, the children were simply to experience singing as the production of sound in its most basic form. At the educational ground zero of the first "a," the method would begin its progressive course. To understand the implications of that course requires considering at least its outlines in more detail.

The first basic principle to be developed is number, in a lengthy section of "Elementary Instruction in Rhythm" (Elementarlehre der Rhythmik). Here, students learn first to end their sounds together, as they began them, then to pause as directed, and then to recognize three types of written notes —slow, medium, and fast (quarter, eighth, and sixteenth notes)—and their corresponding rests. After a transition to singing on "la" instead of "a," the method introduces a series of exercises to drill a variety of rhythmic patterns. The progression continues through half notes, dotted halves (and exercises in triple meter), dotted quarters (and duple compound meter), whole notes, double dotting, ties, triplets, thirty-seconds, sixty-fourths, and the entire range of meters, including the "very rare meters" of 6/2, 6/1, 12/4, 9/16, 12/16, and 24/16, which are introduced without the by-now-usual drills. The conclusion instructs the teacher that, since the later section on notation will reinforce this one and ensure that each individual has mastered rhythmic concepts, he can proceed "without hesitation" *(ohne Bedenken)* to the "Elementary Instruction in Melody" (Elementarlehre der Melodik) (40).

After a preliminary examination of each child's voice, classifying each according to range, strength or weakness, accuracy, and quality (41–47), the teacher proceeds to introduce—again through drills—height and depth in pitch and to build first a diatonic tetrachord and then two linked tetrachords to form an octave. At first, pitches are represented on a fragmentary, clefless staff of two, then three and four lines, and then through the numbers one through seven. With this system, students are to practice drills, including leaps up to a seventh; the teacher then introduces pitches beyond the range of the octave, letter names for pitches, and the standard, five-line staff with C clef. Sharps and flats are introduced first by beginning tetrachords on pitches that require alteration to produce the proper pattern of intervals, then through exercises of up to five consecutive halftones, both ascending and descending. Exercises in leaps involving chromatic alterations introduce "progressions of dissonant intervals," which are, "as is well known, by far the most important and difficult part of the art of intonation."[20] To conclude the section, the teacher has the children sing an ascending and descending chromatic scale through an entire octave. Before proceeding further, however, the teacher is again to examine each student individually, for the sake of "purification, correction, and amplification of his ability with pitch."[21]

The final basic element, dynamics, is introduced in a similarly systematic, albeit mercifully shorter, way (71–82), beginning with three levels—mezzo, forte, and piano—and progressing through exercises that introduce the full range of standard dynamic indications, including crescendi and diminuendi. Another individual examination for purification, correction, and amplification ends the section.

At last, having introduced rhythm, pitch, and dynamics separately, the three are combined in the fourth section of the *Gesangbildungslehre* (83–119). As usual, a simple beginning—in this case, application of dynamics to rhythmic patterns to produce metric pulses—leads through a series of exercises, and eventually the three elements are combined in dauntingly complex ways, including swelling, inflection of pitch in anticipation of succeeding pitches, and "the so-called *messa voce*" (das sogennante *messa voce*; 115).

Nägeli ascribed special significance to the following section, on the art of notation:

> The musical sense, first comprehensively aroused by the rhythmic, melodic, and dynamic courses, then expanded many times over by the combining of the musical elements, should now be raised and refined to genuine artistic sense; the ability *inwardly* to call to mind the art object (the actual succession of pitches or practice phrase) in the most precise way as a conceptualized and felt object *[Begriffs- und Gefühlssache]* should here—considered in this particular application—receive its completion. The succession of pitches that the child hears should hover before it so clearly that it still mentally hears the pitches in their relationship sounding in its ear a moment—even half a minute—later,

and sees the notes that correspond to them standing there before its eyes, just as if it saw them externally, written on the board. To a limited degree, everyone who is able to sing a musical phrase from memory possesses this ability, for in order to sing it from memory, one must call it to mind internally, *hear* it, and if one has learned it from notation, in fact *see* it as well. Indeed, everyone, as a human being, has this intellectual sense, a spiritual ear and a spiritual eye—in a word, the ability to *perceive* art. So here, the perception of art will be cultivated precisely through the art of notation.[22]

Once again, the procedure through which this final stage in the progression from the simplest experience of tone production to full-fledged, if admittedly limited, inner receptiveness to works of art is progressive and comprehensive. The book's remaining sections deal with combining music and poetic texts, first from the perspective of diction, then of the interaction of musical and textual accent, and finally taking account of poetic meter and overall structure.

I have summarized Nägeli's method at some length in order both to establish what such a systematic and progressive musical method entailed and to provide a concrete example of a "natural" method in Pestalozzian terms. The *Gesangbildungslehre* was neither unique nor unprecedented; its interest lies precisely in the unusually detailed expression it gives to practices and values that were increasingly widely accepted among "progressive" music educators. As John Butt notes, during the eighteenth century instruction books in singing show increasing attention to progressive pedagogy that sought to develop students' understanding; in particular, Johann Adam Hiller provided a carefully gradated series of lessons in his *Anweisung zum musikalisch-richtigen Gesange* of 1774 and in a simpler version for basic school instruction published in 1792.[23] And although the *Gesangbildungslehre* was by no means universally adopted or greeted with uniform enthusiasm, its critics rejected not the basic principle of experience-based, progressive instruction but rather particulars such as its often-ponderous prose style, its strict segregation of rhythmic and melodic elements, the style of its musical examples, and the like. The summary dismissal by the work's first review in the *Allgemeine musikalische Zeitung* encapsulates such criticism aptly: "In its form, the work is a deluxe edition, realized through expansion and verbosity, of the already-available and the better understood."[24]

Despite criticisms, the longevity of the *Gesangbildungslehre* suggests that it did indeed meet a widely perceived need, offering a systematic alternative to the traditional reliance on rote memorization that Butt supposes still to have been widespread in the mid–eighteenth century.[25] To judge by this report from 1822 by Bernhard C. L. Natorp, another reformer, the practice lived on far longer even than that: "In many schools, one has previously been satisfied to *drill* youths *mechanically* in singing some of the most familiar church melodies and some popular school songs, through repeatedly singing them and having them sung back. One intended only that the youths ought to grasp some songs simply by ear and impress them in their memories. No musical notation was employed, nor did practices follow any sequential order."[26]

The link this report makes between outdated pedagogy and the singing of chorales is revealing, for although reformed singing instruction was often linked to improving the state of music in churches, the new pedagogy had a fundamentally secular—and often statist—orientation. A rationally systematized "nature" effectively replaced the received chorale as the ground of musical knowledge, just as new methods of teaching reading replaced traditional dependence on the Bible or the catechism as the foundation of literacy.[27] Thus Nägeli's distinctly unenthusiastic acknowledgment of the chorale's significance after a far lengthier discussion of its inappropriateness for elementary instruction signals a fundamental change in the orientation of both the methods and the aspirations of singing instruction:

> We too honor the chorale as something that has lasted for centuries in the church. As a song of the people, it may not be taken from them until there is something better with which to replace it, until it becomes, in part, superfluous. It should never and will never pass away completely. Nor would we by any means wish to see it banned from higher art. It has its particular effect only when it is partially augmented with other artistic genres or musical movements (as in Graun's well-known passion oratorio), or is intermingled here and there as a cantus firmus (as, for example, in C. P. E. Bach's "Heilig"). In any case we must seek to ensure that it is henceforth no longer used pedagogically in such a detrimental way, nor elevated so exaggeratedly in the philosophy of art.[28]

A FOUNDATIONAL DISCIPLINE

To teach singing in this "natural" way, then, was to make a new beginning, to establish a pedagogy distinct from both the traditional training of musicians and the church school tradition. This observation allows a more precise identification of the novelty of approaches such as Nägeli's, for, in and of itself, singing instruction in the schools was not a novelty: it had long had a place in both Catholic and Protestant territories. The long and illustrious history of the Thomasschule in Leipzig was well-known, and in 1773 Charles Burney noted that Bohemia's musical culture owed a great deal to training provided in parish schools.[29] But the new music pedagogy had very different roots, located in the enthusiasm for popular pedagogy that became one of the central concerns of the German Enlightenment. Although laws requiring mandatory universal schooling had been established in parts of Germany as early as the seventeenth century, only in the latter part of the eighteenth did the cultivation of the whole population occupy the attention of a variety of German intellectuals. By the end of the eighteenth century, school was obligatory—and controlled, at least in principle, by the state—in virtually every German-speaking jurisdiction.[30] Only through such cultivation, according to the reformers, could the nation as a whole live up to its potential, as each individual became a full, literate participant in civil society. The essentially secular orientation of such efforts at popular cultivation meant that the place of music was by no means secure, for instruction in music was easily linked with the church's long-standing preference for inculcating belief by nonliterary means in order to avoid the dangers of free thought that literacy might encourage.[31] Thus, for example, in 1800, less than thirty years after Burney's trip, a report on the condition of music in Bohemia lamented the decline of choral singing, a decline it attributed to the end of monastic choral foundations and still more to the introduction of state-run normal schools that gave no thought to musical instruction.[32] The challenge for those concerned with music in the schools, then, was to reestablish the necessity of the arts in terms of the new orientation of education. Here, Nägeli's efforts had counterparts throughout German-speaking Europe. In Josef II's Austria, a court commission under the direction of Gottfried van Swieten, proposed in 1783 that future *Volkslehrer* (elementary instructors in the state's schools) would need to be trained in aesthetics not only so they could render attractive the truths of religion but also because "the cultivation of taste, which is precisely the concern of aesthetics, is a national opportunity, for taste perfects reason and morality, and spreads charm and sociability over all of life."[33] In Berlin, Karl Friedrich Zelter drafted numerous proposals urging the integration of music into the Prussian Academy of Arts and arguing that improved music instruction would have a beneficial effect on all levels of society.[34] And in 1812, Natorp, whose evaluation of the old style of singing instruction I have already cited, proposed while an official in the Brandenburg school administration a two- to three-year training program for elementary schoolteachers that included rigorous musical training along with a wide variety of other subjects.[35]

Nägeli himself provided one of the most enthusiastic evocations of the goal of this new beginning in music instruction, one unique in its elevation of choral singing and its overtly utopian aspirations but typical in its linking of improved music instruction with the common good. In what he characterizes as the forthcoming "age of music," the ideal society is realized in aesthetic form, far surpassing the admittedly impressive accomplishments of recent opera and sacred music, whose basis Nägeli describes as dramatic, conceived for viewing rather than active participation:

> In all of this [the heights of recent music] is only the beginning of joy.
> The age of music begins only where higher art is practiced not just by representatives—where higher art has become the common possession of the people, the nation, indeed the whole company of European people, where humanity itself is taken up in the element of music. That becomes possible only through the advancement of choral singing. . . .
> Take hosts of people; take them by the hundreds, the thousands; try to bring them into human interaction, and interaction in which every individual gives free and active expression to his personality through feelings as well as words, where he at the same time receives uniform impressions from all the others, where he becomes aware of his human independence and solidarity *[Mitständigkeit]* most intuitively and from so many sides, where he receives and circulates enlightenment, where he radiates and inhales love instantaneously, with every breath—do you have anything other than choral singing? Do you find a single thing among the thousand springs that the Giver of all good things opened up to you that could even be remotely similar?[36]

From the perspective of Nägeli's nearly ecstatic vision of universal human joy through singing, the evocation of universal brotherhood in the Ninth Symphony seems uniquely appropriate, and the sense in which the entrance of a chorus could be heard to herald a new beginning is expanded. But if we contrast the utopian language of the vision with the concrete instructions of the opening lesson, we are brought abruptly back to the process through which these singers were to be cultivated: if, as we have seen, the new pedagogy sought to establish new institutional foundations for music instruction, it was also to be foundational—a new beginning—for each individual student. Indeed, one of the remarkable features of Nägeli's opening scene is the complete absence of any acknowledgment that these schoolchildren may previously ever have sung anything at all. This is a singing distinct from all prior experience beyond the school, and Nägeli intended that it should remain so, according to his twenty-ninth rule for teachers:

> Insofar as his power or authority allows it, the teacher must see to it that the children do not damage their voices by singing outside the school before they are secure in pitch. Private practice in rhythm, of course, would be harmless. Premature singing of melodies (musical babbling of every kind), on the other hand, makes the child's voice unsteady and impure. For this reason, the teacher must certainly also prevent the children in the meanwhile—before they are sufficiently secure in pitch to sing correctly and without perceptible drop in pitch a song of several lines or strophes without an instrument—from showing by singing at home what they have learned in school.[37]

This extreme directive has been seen as evidence of the basic impracticality of Nägeli's method, and in fact, it is doubtful that such measures could have been enforced outside of exceptional situations, such as orphanages or boarding schools.[38] Nonetheless, the conception of a clean break with previous experience is fundamental to the progressive method. Thus, for example, Natorp, whose methodology was in many respects less rigid than Nägeli's, encouraged teachers to permit students to sing at an earlier age than that at which their formal instruction began, but he prescribed for the purpose not the immediate singing of familiar songs but rather yet another series of progressive preparatory exercises [*Vorübungen*] that would only gradually lead to carefully selected songs:

> [The *Vorübungen*] are limited simply to singing *only by ear*. Instruction consists of *singing to the students*, and practice in *singing back*. One should introduce to the students through singing for them first individual tones then shorter and longer sequences of tones, first only with all the short and long vowels, then with syllables and words to be sung back clearly, certainly, powerfully, and gently, in various degrees of stronger and weaker expression and in various degrees of slower and faster motion. Soon they can be taught to sing by ear such songs as are appropriate to their comprehension and their youthful spirit.[39]

Even in this less rigid system, then, song can begin only once properly regulated sound production has been established as a foundation, replacing uncontrolled habits developed prior to schooling. The goal is quite simply a reconstruction of the singing subject.

Stated in these terms, the reform of singing is revealed as a discipline in precisely the sense of the term used by Foucault. The *Gesangbildungslehre* departs from traditional pedagogy by prescribing in minute detail the manner in which students are to use their bodies to produce music and in insisting on the critical importance of the instructor's overseeing every step of the process with each individual. Foucault's own description of the novelty of such disciplinary practice and its larger ramifications effectively conveys the scope of the change:

> To begin with, there was the scale of the control: it was a question not of treating the body *en masse,* "wholesale," as if it were an indissociable unity, but of working it "retail," individually; of exercising upon it a subtle coercion, of obtaining holds upon it at the level of the mechanism itself—movements, gestures, attitudes, rapidity: an infinitesimal power over the active body. Then there was the object of the control: it was not or was no longer the signifying elements of behaviour or the language of the body, but the economy, the efficiency of movements, their internal organization; constraint bears upon the forces rather than upon the signs; the only truly important ceremony is that of exercise. Lastly, there is the modality: it implies an uninterrupted, constant coercion, supervising the process of the activity rather than its result and it is exercised according to a codification that partitions as closely as possible time, space, movement. . . . The historical moment of the disciplines was the moment when an art of the human body was born, which was directed not only at the growth of its skills, nor at the intensification of its subjection, but at the formation of a relation that in the mechanism itself makes it more obedient as it becomes more useful, and conversely. What was then being formed was a policy of coercion that acts upon the body, a calculated manipulation of its elements, its gestures, its behaviour. The human body was entering a machinery of power that explores it, breaks it down and rearranges it.[40]

To speak in terms of coercion, manipulation, and breaking down may seem extreme in this context, but that is precisely what many of Nägeli's instructions involve. The opening scene provides an example of the precision with which students were to position their bodies. Immediately thereafter, attention to the process (rather than the end) of singing becomes even more directly manipulative of the components of the body, as the children are instructed in the proper means of shaping the mouth to produce "a": after opening their mouths as if to produce the vowel, they are to regulate the opening, inserting their little finger and touching it gently with their teeth, then removing it. Repeated practice, the teacher is informed, will be necessary to ensure that everyone can satisfactorily accomplish this. In the case of thin-lipped children or those whose lips quiver when held open, the teacher will need to take special measures, in the latter case directing children to practice before a mirror until they can conform to the standard (10). Similar precision is required to produce the remaining sounds (161–83).

Time is likewise regulated and its most efficient use calculated. According to Nägeli's general rules, singing should never occur before 9:00 A.M. or after 7:00 P.M., and instruction ought to occur three times weekly. Each hour of singing should be divided by a break, during which the teacher demands complete silence; it should fall between the thirty-first and thirty-fifth minute of the hour.[41] In hours during which particularly difficult work is undertaken, the hour should be divided into three by two breaks of at least four minutes. Once a week for fifteen minutes, and once a month for an entire hour, the teacher should hold a review in order to determine the students' mastery of materials. Corrections are to be made as precisely and consistently as possible, according to a prescribed vocabulary; so, for example, *richtig* and *unrichtig* are reserved for the evaluation of rhythm, *rein* and *unrein* for that of melody, while *getroffen* and *gefehlt* refer to verbal answers to the teacher's questions (1–2). The examinations that conclude the course's major sections ensure that each student has made proper use of this regulated and systematized time and thereby successfully internalized the principles of singing. The goal of those examinations is "purification, correction, and amplification," precisely the bringing of disciplinary power to bear on the individual that Foucault noted as the essential role of the examination.[42]

Nägeli's constant use of brief, frequently repeated exercises rather than larger musical pieces and his desire to banish evaluative aesthetic language from preliminary instruction likewise attest to the disciplinary character of the *Gesangbildungslehre*. Once again, the temptation to dismiss the rigors it prescribes as aberrations should be tempered by the realization that what Nägeli spells out in excruciating detail typifies a far larger pedagogical trend, one whose legacy will be familiar to any pianist who recalls early encounters with Czerny. From this perspective, Rosen's observation of "a sad and permanent decline in the quality of music written for young performers or beginners" takes on a new significance: if "constraint bears upon the forces rather than the signs," it is no longer necessary or even desirable that students learn by means of whole (if simple) works of art. Rather, careful analysis of the necessary physical components of performance allows the whole to be built up more efficiently, even mechanically, "for there is a mechanism in every art, of which the spirit must have command, if it is to express itself easily and clearly."[43] Little wonder, then, that even educators outside of music recognized the utility of singing instruction; F. A. W. Diesterweg, a pioneer in the education of young children, put it bluntly: "*Singing is a most excellent means of discipline*. It forces crude and intractable children into quiet contemplation and self-examination."[44] It promised, in other words, the internalization of precisely the behaviors and attitudes that the surveillance of the teacher could impose only from the outside.

MUSIC EDUCATION IN SOCIETY

The docile Foucauldian body created through musical discipline is a powerful image, but an incomplete one; relying on it too heavily in this instance would risk overlooking significant distinctions that the new pedagogy enacted within the social hierarchy in which it arose. Foucault himself notes that through military training "one has 'got rid of the peasant' and given him 'the air of a soldier'" but beyond that has little to say about the interaction of discipline and social class.[45] Precisely that interaction, however, is crucial to understanding the relationship of music pedagogy to the developing culture of art music.

Nägeli's desire to prevent children from singing outside the school provides a convenient point of entry into this issue. Ostensibly, such singing was to be avoided because it "makes the child's voice unsteady and impure." Nägeli does not suggest that such unauthorized practice might bring about physical damage to the voice; this is not a question of guarding against overexertion by enthusiastic children. The more likely source of harm— one consistent with Nägeli's use of the term "purity"—was contamination by the unmentioned music that the course of instruction is designed to supersede: the vernacular practice that Nägeli's contemporaries so frequently denounced. Only the development of musically literate singers who could produce sounds in a reliable, uniform manner and hold a musical work of art precisely in their minds to the level of each securely defined pitch could hold the line between proper, cultivated singing and an orally transmitted music subject to vagaries of pitch, unregulated vocal production, and unauthorized ornamentation.[46] To allow students to sing outside the teacher's supervision before they had sufficiently internalized "correct" singing risked further habituation to the impurity of uncultivated practice.

The link between purity of expression and cultivated singing is reinforced by the link between singing instruction and proper pronunciation. On the importance of the latter Nägeli was unambiguous: "It is agreed that only through precise, razor-sharp, elementarily beautiful phonetic art does singing receive definition, contour, and form; and only when the singer overcomes the difficulties of the language and has learned to make use of its strengths, when he knows how to leap about with consonants—that is to say, with his sounding organs—as a pianist does on the keys, only then does the art of singing become alive in and through him."[47] Uncharacteristically, however, Nägeli has little to say about what this accomplishes in a larger context; for that, we can turn to texts written by his contemporaries. Zelter, for instance, came to the topic of pronunciation in the context of his prescription for remedying the declining quality of long-established school choirs:

> Regular singing classes must take place in the schools, as they previously did. Cantors . . . must instruct boys in singing from an early age; thereby every cantor will develop a small choir for his church; the cantors will compete with one another, and young people will already be able to sing something when they enter the higher schools.
>
> If this instruction occurs under a good general directive, German pronunciation (which is in general faulty) will thereby be improved; for those who have better pronunciation and articulation easily come to a better end and develop themselves more easily.
>
> In the higher schools, then, the matter could soon achieve still more: for variety, choruses in ancient languages, for example by Latin and Greek poets, could be sung instead of sacred songs.[48]

Zelter's reference to classical literature was no doubt influenced by his knowledge of the preferences of Wilhelm von Humboldt, who had recently been appointed a privy councillor to the king, but it also indicates the broader educational context of singing instruction, as does the linking of good pronunciation not to musical quality but rather to students' overall success. In an 1804 article on the need for early childhood training in music, C. F. Michaelis reveals a social grounding for that success; in an exhortation to a mother to develop her children's sense of hearing he urges that she have them identify sounds and imitate her own singing: "You will soon be rewarded for these cares by the dexterity and security of the child's voice, the euphony of its speaking, and its receptivity to singing. You will soon rejoice in its pure, melodic speech and will no longer wonder at the monotonous, coarse dialect [*Mundart*] of the savage or badly educated children of careless neighbors."[49] Music and speech are here closely linked to the child's escape from the savagery signified by unregulated, common dialect—Zelter's claim that diction leads to success is valid to the extent that standardized high German diction could serve as an audible marker of distinction from the uncultivated.

At issue was nothing less than the development of animals into humans, as a speech by Herder makes unmistakably clear:

> When we come into the world we are of course able to scream and cry, but not to talk or speak; we emit only animal sounds. These animal sounds remain with some people and races throughout their entire lives. . . . Youths who have acquired this unpleasant dialect of merely animal sounds should make every effort in school to acquire a human, natural speech possessed of character and soul and to rid themselves of their peasant or shrieking back-alley dialects. They should leave off the barking and yelping, the clucking and cawing, the swallowing and dragging together of words and syllables and speak human rather than animal language. Happy the child, the boy, who from his first years onward hears understandable, human, lovely sounds that unnoticeably mold his tongue and the sounds of his speech. Happy is the child whose caretaker, mother, older siblings, relatives, friends, and finally first teachers speak to him in their bearing and speech with reason, decorum, and grace.[50]

The same urge to differentiate human from animal sound through precision and definition appears in Nägeli's introduction to the teaching of pitch: "The song of humans differentiates itself from that of the nightingale through precise gradation. The latter is a simple flow, undulation, the former a transformation, an articulation. The nightingale, following its artistic instinct, lets its undulation run its course, once it has opened its throat, as long as its breath, one exhalation, lasts according to physical laws. . . . Humans, according to their artistic instinct, produce a scale, they direct their physical ability with tones, they break off the tone, elevate it, rise, fall—all in one breath."[51]

Purified singing, like Herder's purified speech, is thus "natural" to humans—and yet both are the products of cultivation through schooling: they can be produced only through rejecting the sounds that the child of an uncultivated family hears all around. And in both speech and music, only through literacy, through written and precisely reproduced sounds, can imprecise, animal-like noise be replaced by fully articulated, measured (and thus regulated) human vocalization. As a result, despite the undoubtedly sincere desire of the reformers for universal cultivation, for a fully humanized society, such education inevitably served a classifying, socially articulating function. As both Herder and Michaelis imply, those children who encountered cultivated language and song in the home, before entering school, were marked for success in advance, while those who first encountered the practice in school could rarely internalize it as fully or as comfortably. Thus the effort to make speech and song uniform through schooling could itself reinforce the distinction between those from cultivated families and those of common heritage.

This process might have been a temporary one if the aspirations of reformers like Michaelis, Nägeli, and Pestalozzi himself had been fully realized, if they had indeed, through an effective system of universal education, trained a generation that in turn cultivated its children to the point that they reached "fully human" status. But even Pestalozzi declared repeatedly that education must fit each person to that individual's ordained station, and that the manual labor central to the lives of the lower classes required less intellectual development than the roles of the higher.[52] And even limited aspirations like Pestalozzi's were far beyond those of many of the authorities who actually funded education and whose primary concern was to produce obedient subjects untroubled by an excess of useless and potentially dangerous ideas. This combination of limited aspirations, even more limited investment, and the avoidance of political confrontation by educational reformers bounded the spread of literacy well into the nineteenth century.[53] Nor were the presumed beneficiaries of popular education always eager to embrace schooling for their children. Families dependent on child labor for essential income or farm labor saw little benefit to formal education, especially when it was linked to mandatory school fees, and even among the lower bourgeoisie, apprenticeship long remained more significant than formal schooling.[54] This is not to suggest, however, that the efforts devoted to singing instruction in the first decades of the century were without effect. On the contrary, they are bound up with the development of what Carl Dahlhaus aptly characterizes as an "untold number of amateur choruses: the singing academies, *Liedertafeln*, and *Liederkränze* that formed an increasingly dense web of musical societies mingling companionship and music in equal measure."[55] G. W. Fink was able to point with some pride to school music education as a contributor to Germany's superiority to France in general musical accomplishment: "Music instruction, such as every village school in Germany has, is even now not to be thought of at all in France."[56]

Fink's boast, however, must be tempered by awareness that literary cultivation and, even more, musical literacy remained prerogatives of the still quite small educated classes, and that "proper" speech and music retained their potency as class markers. And beyond that, both Nägeli's two-tiered conception of musical performance—with complex instrumental music ranked above popular choral music—and the distinctly subsidiary place of reports on choral music and performance within general music periodicals of the 1830s and 1840s suggest that it provided the lower term of a status binary within the literate classes. An 1842 report on the condition of music in Swabia, for instance, begins by discussing the pervasiveness of choral societies *(Gesangvereine)* and noting that "it is certainly heartening when thus, not only the more educated, but also people from the lower classes expend time and effort on the development of their musical talent, when even the common people rises above its natural song and seeks to ennoble the same to a beautiful polyphonic song." It goes on, however, to observe that most such organizations never achieved anything significant in musical terms, and that the song festivals at which they performed were "not as much of general musical significance, but much rather simply musical folkfestivals." The next (and considerably longer) section of the article begins with a transition that makes the hierarchy explicit: "Let us go from the *Liederkränze* to the higher artistic institutions and associations of our land." [57]

The opposition of simple choral music and sophisticated instrumental music among the literate could also contribute to an increasingly complex stratification of musical styles within society as a whole. If literate musical practice could be understood to embrace its own opposition of high and low, then uncultivated music—*Volksmusik* understood as music *by* the people instead of *for* them—could be understood as something entirely outside the system, a resource for aspiring artists, just as Schumann envisioned it in the aphorism from the "Musikalische Haus- und Lebensregeln" I have already cited in discussing the *Volkston:* "Listen diligently to all folksongs; they are a rich source of the most beautiful melodies and will open your eyes to the character of the various nations." [58] Defining that which was not a part of literate culture as folk music made it exotic enough to recuperate for use by the culture that had defined it by exclusion.

MUSIC EDUCATION, THE FAMILY, AND THE NATURE OF WOMAN

Another practice of social classification is at work in singing instruction, less obviously although arguably more pervasively: the production and reproduction of the members of an idealized family. With this, we have finally arrived at A. B. Marx's point of departure for his discussion of the Ninth Symphony: "the sweetly satisfying bonds of the family." Nägeli himself provides little explicit discussion of this topic; its significance is revealed only by a few passing references. The *Gesangbildungslehre* itself consistently discusses *Kinder* (children) and envisions instruction to girls as well as boys. In one of the few passages that indicate the end to which those girls were being trained, Nägeli's assumption that early childhood education is the role of the mother suggests that the matter was so self-evident that it needed no special justification; Nägeli's tone is, in fact, considerably more matter-of-fact than Michaelis's plea to mothers:

> No more [than children are expected to be exposed to extraordinarily accomplished musical performances] do we demand that the mother who wishes to make her child receptive to musical cultivation from its early youth by letting it hear her singing voice be an artistic singer in the higher sense of the word. That the child hear pure voices, pure song, pure playing of purely tuned musical instruments—that is the main thing. Every mother who proposes to educate her child herself in this art must therefore above all ask a musician—and demand a conscientious answer—whether she sings what she has learned properly. . . . Only if the answer is satisfactory may she let her child hear her voice for the awakening of its musical sense; if not, she must avoid it, and must completely forego self-instruction of the child in singing.[59]

The ascription of the crucial role in preschool education to the mother is entirely consistent with Nägeli's Pestalozzian orientation, for the mother's early teaching in the home was, according to Pestalozzi, both the model for his "natural" method and the first crucial locus of cultivation for children. Nor was Pestalozzi unique in this; both historians and literary scholars have long recognized the enormous influence of the gender roles that prescribed this occupation for the mother, particularly in the later eighteenth century and after. The ideology of the family on which such models were predicated placed the mother at the center of the family's domestic life and redefined domestic labor, especially including child rearing: such labor was no longer simply the economically necessary work of the household that earlier models had described but became as well the natural fulfillment of the role to which women were destined.[60]

If mothers were to carry out this role effectively, they too would need to be educated—those responsible for the crucial early education of the next generation would themselves need to be able to speak properly and sing purely. Like other aspects of his system, Nägeli's audition of the mother before a competent musician who could certify her qualifications likely never occurred outside his imagination, but the subordination of the mother to authoritative evaluation that it enacts succinctly encapsulates a process that was widely advocated, if often less bluntly. Van Swieten, for instance, argued that mandatory education must include girls precisely because of their role in rearing children, not only for the sake of the development of their children's mental ability but also because mothers who had themselves been to school would be less apt to be hostile to their children's schooling. Numerous books on basic education, especially reading, were addressed to mothers in order to train them for this "natural" role.[61]

In musical discourse, that role was far more often assumed than debated. In 1798, for instance, Carl Gottlob Horstig, another frequent contributor to the *Allgemeine musikalische Zeitung*, argued for the inclusion of girls in singing instruction, asking, "Wouldn't the singing teacher deserve particular gratitude from his fellow citizens if he developed among their promising daughters a talent that will make their good fortune—some time in the future to be amiable wives and good mothers—infinitely sweeter?"[62] The same assumptions also inform two articles by Friedrich Guthmann from the following decade, articles that outline the bounds of appropriate music education for women mindful of not overstepping their "limited but lovely femininity." For women lacking the leisure to cultivate music throughout life, any training beyond the basis required to sing and play simple pieces independently was not only superfluous but most likely doomed: "I must still appeal to experience, which has all too often shown that in art, too, stepping beyond the limited feminine circle fails to a greater or lesser extent a hundred times for each success."[63]

Although Guthmann's articles thus justify the limits they set for appropriate education by appealing to the nature of women, they also exempt certain classes of women from those limits: first, those "who through outstanding talent or due to other circumstances make practical music their principal occupation"; with an unusual degree of explicitness, Guthmann specifies that he means rather to address the needs of "the good girls of the middle class."[64] In so acknowledging the varied circumstances under which women did in fact learn music, despite the norms that pressed for limitation, Guthmann provides an example of the complex tensions between ideology and practice that Freia Hoffmann identified in her exemplary study of women instrumentalists; her work suggests that the unidentified "other circumstances" that Guthmann offered as an extenuation for a few women's pursuit of virtuoso careers were most often the fact of having been born not to the administrative middle classes but rather to a musician, a socially less respectable but musically less restrictive position.[65] If Guthmann's exclusion of women seeking a professional career in music provides a lower limit to the status of those for whom he prescribes, his other qualification provides an upper one. Through the contrast between the "gute Mädchen der Mittelstände" and the "Damen, welche . . . lebenslang eine Kunst zu ihrem Vergnügen kultiviren" [ladies who all their lives cultivate an art for their enjoyment], an unmistakable boundary between the middle and the upper classes arises, not only through the explicit identification of the middle classes but also through the implied contrast of *gute Mädchen* (virtuous young girls) with more fortunate *Damen* (ladies). To describe the latter's practice, Guthmann chose not the inevitably positive (and indisputably German) *bilden,* but the French loanword *kultiviren,* with all its attendant associations of aristocratic idleness and otherness. Between these two limits lay the ideal, the model bourgeois woman who would "not shine, but indeed move and cheer." [66]

Like the desire to cultivate "natural" speech and song, then, the vision of the place of women within the ideal of music education reveals its orientation toward bourgeois society as the locus of the natural. As Karin Hausen notes, this consistent orientation meant that the ideal of *Geschlechtscharakter,* the distinct nature of the sexes, was by no means lived out consistently throughout society: only among the cultivated bourgeoisie, suspicious of aristocratic manners and not in possession of inherited estates but leisured enough to afford the relative luxury of a mother largely devoted to child rearing, was it even possible to approach that ideal.[67] But just how powerful an attraction that model exercised is suggested by Marx's evocation of Beethoven's longing for the "sweetly satisfying bonds of the family," bonds conspicuous by their absence from his earlier, matter-of-fact description of Beethoven's youth as the son of a court musician. Besides the element of pathos Marx's effusion on the Ninth introduces, then, it also characterizes Beethoven in terms most comprehensible from the perspective of the class-bound but universalized ideal of the nuclear family, figuring Beethoven's artistic struggle as a displaced striving toward that ideal from a social origin that Marx regarded as outmoded.[68] By way of contrast, J. F. Reichardt provides a full evocation of the ideal for which Marx's Beethoven longed in his "Advice to Young Artists" of 1782; the freedom and stability that the artist requires, Reichardt insisted, could exist only in conjunction with the domesticated love of the nuclear family:

> Let all-encompassing love fill your whole soul. In everything, wherever pure love leads you, you move surely toward the summit of your art, as of your happiness.
>
> Do not fear social ties, either, if pure love leads you into them. There is no true freedom where there is no rest for the spirit. And you will find this rest only in the solid, indissolubly woven bond with the wife that your soul loves. And a thousandfold new, never suspected feelings of love come to life in your soul and strengthen your being and your happiness, when you recognize yourself and your wife in beautiful dear

little ones. Oh, it is unspeakable bliss, unnameable peace for the soul, to have in [my] little house a better, a self-created better world, to be able simply to step over my hospitable threshold to see every discontent produced by worldly corruption vanish at once, to be able freely to apply every power for the perfection of my love, power that I often may not, cannot, apply in larger society!

Only in this way does love beget and preserve a noble drive to action.[69]

MUSIC, THE STATE, AND THE ECONOMY

As Reichardt's effusion suggests, by prescribing a bounded, domestic role for women, the ideology of the character of the sexes reserved for men the sphere of public activity. Nägeli affirmed this role when he addressed his appeal for the adoption of his method simply to "deutsche Männer."[70] As the natural actors in both the state and the economy, men were the agents who would achieve the goals of music education once the child grew beyond the initial nurture provided by the mother. Nägeli's image of choral singing as an ideally cooperative model of human interaction presents one aspect of this goal—the symbolic expression of a universal brotherhood—but the boundaries of that universality, as we have seen, link it inextricably to the experience and interests of the cultivated bourgeoisie. Remembering this affiliation will be crucial to an understanding of other goals of singing instruction, goals that seem far removed from an ideal of aesthetic interaction.

The strict obedience Nägeli required of students and the discipline of the singing class, for instance, are far removed from the cooperative utopia of the idealized choir—but in the context of school as a state-controlled institution with the goal of producing obedient, productive subjects among the lower classes and capable, broadly educated administrators among the cultivated middle classes, both the cooperative ideal and the strict discipline of institutional practice were necessary. Nägeli's vision, after all, was directed to well-educated readers, while his instruction was intended for students for whom obedience was an essential lesson, regardless of their eventual station, for it was a prerequisite to the internalized self control (*Selbstbeherrschung*—literally, command of the self) that he saw as an essential benefit of his method.[71] For once, other writers are even more explicit than Nägeli. An 1828 directive on singing in the elementary schools of Cologne, for instance, recognizes the power of singing instruction to cultivate the feelings and train and strengthen the will, and goes on to link it to obedience and proper social interaction quite directly. Singing instruction "is one of the most essential means of educational instruction, through the proper and uninterruptedly continued application of which even the crudest spirit can be made receptive to more gentle feelings, given over to their influence and accustomed to subordination to general laws through common activity with others."[72] The *Erziehungslehre* of Friedrich H. C. Schwarz states the matter even more bluntly: good hearing, which a progressive course of musical instruction develops, leads to receptivity to the spiritual but also to obedience, as the language itself demonstrates through the relationship of *hören* (to hear), *horchen* (to listen), and *gehorchen* (to obey).[73] More advanced humanistic education could develop the administrator, but the basic common ground of education, of which singing could be a vital component, lay in this internalization of obedience.

The administrative state, however, was by no means to be the only beneficiary of the discipline inspired by music, which required, after all, far more than obedience for its mastery. Another requirement is suggested by a directive from another set of guidelines from 1828: "Singing instruction, however, must appear in a serious and worthy form, requiring effort and providing difficulties to overcome. For people must learn early that there is no pleasure without work, and that work itself must become pleasure for them."[74] Such diligence had a clear economic value, particularly in light of the dramatic expansion of manufacture (largely, until the mid–nineteenth century, domestically based) in German-speaking countries during the eighteenth century; in this context, music education meshed naturally with an economically oriented educational policy that sought to create a disciplined but docile labor pool.[75] J. A. P. Schulz's claim, cited earlier, that music could sweeten the labor of the people could easily be extended to this concern for productivity, as when, for instance, instruction in industrial work was made more palatable at the Brandeis Hauptschule in Bohemia through the singing of songs.[76] As an art that developed the "disposition for regularity, accuracy, order, and harmony" and provided a "bond of sociability," music could supply an ideal mode through which to socialize productive workers.[77]

But these same qualities could be used to argue for a very different role for music in relation to the working class. In a striking example of the survival and reapplication of these issues, Theodor Hagen argued in 1845 that music was an essential means to prepare workers oppressed by industrial civilization for the responsibilities that would await them in a justly reordered society. In their current state, no such change could succeed: "Everything within them is broken; struck by a poisoned arrow, they bear their fate on the one hand with bestial indifference, on the other with moving resignation. A great many of them are inwardly and outwardly so exhausted, so morally and physically benumbed, that a sudden material improvement of their situation, a sudden experience, would have an unhealthy effect on them.—Music purifies and strengthens the human, prepares him for the better; *it is music, too, that must prepare the reorganization of the factory system.*"

Hagen's solution is to extend the already healthy development of the *Volksliedertafel* (folksong society) both to agricultural workers and to all levels of urban workers; currently, he maintains, only the more highly placed workers participate (an observation consistent with the limitation of musical culture to the literate classes discussed above). He is careful to distance such music from the enervating (and foreign) practices that would hinder progress: "Clearly, a singing people is a very weak one, given up to sinking into stupidity, but only when, like the Italians, it gives itself up to romances and cantilenas, when it sings out its pain *in isolation* in the night. . . . But a people that after its completed day's work assembles in larger divisions and lets its strides sound happily and freely in the open, to the powerful, healthy melodies that sound from its mouth—such a people is strong; for it is united."[78]

It is only fitting, in this light, that the Prussian national assembly of 1848 met in the hall of the Berlin Singakademie and that the uprisings of 1848 brought about a renewal of interest in proposals for the reform of music education.[79] The impact those uprisings had on music education, however, was no more thoroughly revolutionary than their impact on society as a whole. The *Gesangvereine*, like many other bourgeois associations, were indeed a powerful social force, but singing instruction was no more able to produce successful revolutionaries than it did uniformly productive and obedient peasants and workers. In both cases, the pliability of the underclass proved less complete in the event than in the theoretical imagination.

MUSIC EDUCATION AND THE MUSICAL FIELD

The ease with which the same arguments for the utility of training in music could be used to argue for both conservative and revolutionary ends suggests that those political alignments were only secondary motivations for the advocates of education; the "social meaning" of this practice is no more directly explainable in terms of the social and political development of German society as a whole than is the social meaning of individual works of music. This is not, however, to claim independence or radical autonomy for either music or musical practice but simply to recognize that within the field of music, with all its undeniable links to other activities and its roles in constituting the society of which it was a part, there operated a hierarchy of values and distinctions—as well as very immediate material concerns—that served to define that field and the players within it, orienting them and assigning meaning to their activities. And within that musical field lie motivations that help explain the intensity of the advocacy for singing reform as well as its limitations.[80]

A primary concern of the members of any social field is that field's continuing existence—that is, the material existence of its players—and in this case, the insecurities attending the transformation of the relations of musical production are again widely in evidence. Zelter, whose critical role in establishing the institutions of serious musical life in Berlin has recently been emphasized by Celia Applegate, provides an example that displays the intertwining of personal material concerns and advocacy of musical training with unusual clarity. Trained by traditional apprenticeship as a mason, he pursued another, secret but otherwise equally traditional, musical apprenticeship to a local *Stadtpfeifer* against his father's wishes. But such a background was no longer sufficient for a prominent public career as a musician: only after Zelter had also studied with Johann Philipp Kirnberger, the recognized master of learned musical style, did he pursue such a career.[81] Successful enough in the artistic field to correspond with the likes of Schiller and especially Goethe, he nonetheless found that his musical work, including leading both the Berlin Liedertafel and the Singakademie, produced insufficient income to support himself and his family. His proposals for educational reform are thus directly linked to his efforts to secure himself a position in which he could adequately support himself through music. And Zelter's concerns were by no means unique. Discussions of music education routinely pointed out the need to support those who would provide it, or otherwise to secure the living of professional musicians. In this respect Hagen, whose proposal includes state support for both rural and urban music teachers, does not depart from a variety of earlier schemes: in 1782, for instance, Reichardt had called on rulers to support training schools; an 1805 proposal that the state use music to ennoble the rural population proposed that only certified *Stadtmusiker* (civic musicians) be allowed to perform at local festivities, in order to secure their income against the encroachment of disreputable wandering (folk) musicians; and in 1811 Amadeus Wendt advocated hiring teachers who could devote themselves entirely to teaching singing.[82] Political allegiances aside, support for school music instruction was inseparable from concerns about the recognition of the professional nature of music as an occupation and the provision of adequate positions for its practitioners.

Defining a musical field involved more than providing adequately for musicians, however, and the practice of music education was also concerned with the establishment of a hierarchy *within* that field. The implicit exclusion of nonliterate folk practices discussed above provides one example of this process, continuing a long tradition of efforts by educated musicians to dissociate themselves from popular musical practices—an expression in the realm of education parallel to the rejection of *Bierfiedler* and *Gassenhauer* in discussions of popular and folk music.[83] But if the existence of a hierarchy in the field was not a new development, several new factors contributed to the particular form it took in the later eighteenth and early nineteenth centuries. First, the Enlightenment concern with popular pedagogy provided a new, more varied social field in which issues of classification and hierarchy could be laid out, for, as we have seen, schooling acted unequally on subjects from differing social backgrounds, even when it was not explicitly designed to provide more limited educations to those of lower stations.[84] In addition, as musicians increasingly sought to confirm their membership in the cultivated middle class, they themselves participated in the discourse on popular pedagogy, prescribing their educational solutions from above: that is, from a position that enacted their claims to a higher status than those for whom they prescribed, a process as apparent in the cases of Nägeli and Hagen as it was in the case of J. A. P. Schulz discussed in the previous chapter.

Another new circumstance is more familiar within music history: the revaluation of instrumental music, which reversed the long-standing hierarchy that figured vocal music, both in sacred genres and in opera, as superior to instrumental. The orientation of musicology to aesthetics and intellectual history, and to composers and works, has directed explanations of this shift largely to either developments in philosophical aesthetics or qualitative developments in compositional style (most often through the agency of the Viennese classical composers). A consideration of popular education, however, reveals the limitations of such explanations. For Nägeli, for instance, the ordering of instrumental music above vocal was essentially social and required for its plausibility that the latter no longer be immediately associated by his readers with prestigious, aristocratically supported opera. Expanding singing instruction in the schools could contribute to this reversal to the extent that the popular accessibility of singing would come to replace the splendor and refinement of opera or the transcendent value of sacred music as the primary association for the concept of vocal music.[85] Carl Dahlhaus's claim that the position of the amateur choral movement (and the educational process that underpinned it) "in the evolution of music as art remained dubious" is thus misleading to the extent that it fails to acknowledge that the existence and vigor of that movement both helped redefine vocal music and provided a lower term within the field of literate music against which instrumental music (and only later opera) could be conceived as the locus of artistic autonomy.[86]

A final consideration deals with the social location of the discourse I have been examining and its links to the continuing enterprise of musicology. Despite the continuing significance of aristocratic involvement in musical life well into the nineteenth century, public discourse on music, and more specifically discussion within the field of music concerning music education, was dominated to a large extent by authors with a keen interest in solidifying the links between music and education—including both formal schooling and general cultivation. That is to say, this discussion was dominated by the German intelligentsia who, as Norbert Elias has observed, established their ideals of serious high culture in marked opposition to what they saw as frivolous and worldly aristocratic values.[87] So both Schulz and Zelter, for instance, stressed their links to the most learned of North German musicians, Kirnberger and Friedrich Wilhelm Marpurg. It is symptomatic as well that the two leading and longest lived music periodicals of the nineteenth century, the *Allgemeine musikalische Zeitung* and the *Neue Zeitschrift für Musik,* originated not in a capital or in the seat of a significant court but rather in Leipzig, the center of the German publishing trade and a prominent university town. The significance of that location was suggested in 1840 by Gustav Keferstein:

> What effect hasn't Leipzig, for instance, had on the furthering of musical cultivation and on the shaping of musical taste, not just in Saxony, but in all of Germany! But who would question that it owes at least the greater part of its musical significance, effective near and far, to its universities and other learned institutions? In this city, so exceptional with respect to music, thousands of youths and young men achieved, along with their scholastic education, a higher musical one as well, which they then later, as officials of the state or church, were able to spread farther in the circle of their influence—and a substantial number of more gifted musical talents here found the first powerful stimulus to the decision to dedicate themselves more earnestly to an art they would oth-

erwise have either neglected completely or have pursued only superfi-
cially as dilettantes.[88]

The musical world, as defined in this paragraph and implicitly addressed in
the period's musical discourse, is situated firmly among the men of the bu-
reaucracy, separated from the lower segments of society by education and
the necessary means to pursue it and from those above by the rejection of
superficial dilettantism—and from women, implicitly, by their natural exclusion from this active sphere.

Such education brought with it not only practical skills in music but also
the capacity to understand music on the aesthetic level. Nägeli's insistence
on the crucial importance of the literate conceptualization of musical art-
works links his pedagogy to this goal, which remained central throughout
the period. In 1841, for example, the *Allgemeine musikalische Zeitung*, by
then well-known for its conservative position, published an address by Keferstein on the relationship of music to pedagogy in which he established
four ascending steps in the process of teaching: the first is simple sensual pleasure; the second, (mechanical) understanding; the third, feeling;
and the fourth, ability to comprehend the succession of states of feeling
brought in relation to one another by the higher musical forms, especially
the sonata.[89] This scheme is more elaborate and ambitious than Nägeli's
(and arguably even less achievable on any broad scale), but it shares with
its predecessor the privileging of cultivated comprehension. On the other
side of the musical spectrum, Franz Brendel, journalistic leader of the self-
identified progressive musical forces of the 1840s, expressed the same concerns; a repeatedly expressed goal of his efforts to secure the requirements
of a musical culture through the organization of *Tonkünstlervereine* (musicians' societies) was to develop an audience with sufficiently broad cultivation to appreciate current music.[90]

Poles apart in musical taste and very likely as well in the means by
which their proponents sought to cultivate those tastes, these positions
merge on one point: the culture they envision is one of cultivation, from
which those who have not benefited from a period in Leipzig or another
musical-academic center would effectively (but silently) be excluded. This
exclusion not only defines a milieu for the culture of serious music but also
establishes music as a field of employment for cultivated men: as Keferstein
suggested, university towns had encouraged substantial numbers of young
men (likely from backgrounds other than traditional musical families) to
pursue musical careers. At a time when an excess of educated men was a se-

rious problem, such a redefinition of the qualities required of a musician helped assure that the field of music was open to such people, as opposed to the products of traditional musical apprenticeships—hence the protests of authors like A. B. Marx in favor of *Gewerbefreiheit* in music, the freedom to practice music as a profession without guild restrictions.[91] From the other side, the expectation of cultivation preserved the field against the literate, but not fully cultivated, products of even the generalized schooling in music envisioned by authors like Nägeli (not to mention those produced by the far more limited instruction that the overextended Volksschulen could actually provide). And the academic tradition from which musicology developed is, of course, rooted in precisely the same cultivated stratum; its long history of loyalty to the canon and ideologies of that fraction of society, then, is not surprising.

These considerations have moved us far from the evocation of universal humanity with which this chapter began, but we are now in a position to understand another aspect of the powerful appeal of the moment Marx evoked. Through his use of the folklike, singing voice, Beethoven could be heard to declare universal brotherhood by means of the very medium through which many sought to achieve that universality in music. And yet, to understand that moment fully required a cultivation that inevitably excluded by far the greater portion of the people; the terms of the sought-after transformation themselves render it impossible. And so the "community with humankind" that Marx heard in the finale of the Ninth Symphony achieved its impact by giving voice to a dream all the more poignant because it was unattainable.

5 Performing Musical Culture

The Concert

But given the undeniable decline of church and theater music, concerts are now the single remaining means whereby both taste can be propagated and in general the higher purpose of music still occasionally be achieved. They must therefore be all the more important to us, and all the more precisely must one determine what they really should be and what they have become through neglect of the true concept that one must have of them.

—Johann Nicolaus Forkel, 1783

Why pay so much attention to these miseries, one might ask. We answer: it is indeed miserable, what the rabble performs for the rabble . . . ; but sacred is the hall of art where the spirit speaks to the spirit, where the genuine, pious artist, full of love for humanity, full of care for the needy disciples of art, with inspiration creates, and recreates what immortal spirits have sung before. And for the sake of such more serious things one may well be angry when the impure defile them. Nothing but seriousness is conducive to the true propagation of art, nothing but frivolity pernicious to it; every piano teacher, even every dancing or reading instructor, can discover that for himself.

—Eduard Krüger, 1847

If the problematic notion of the popular and the project of popular music education defined the margins of a culture of art music, the concert played a different but nonetheless crucially related role. Widely recognized as that culture's essential event, at once the proof of its claims to transcendent value and the forum through which those values were reproduced, the concert constituted the center toward which musical education would lead those who received the benefits of proper cultivation. Within the musical sphere, it embodied the universal values attained by those who had successfully reached beyond both the limitations of their particular upbringings and the common understanding of music, tainted as it was by fixation on the merely sensual. Because of this central role and the pervasiveness of the dangers that threatened it, the concert became the object of a rich (if widely diffused) literature that sought to define it, establish its significance, and secure both its position in society and its purity. My goal in the present chapter is to examine that literature, not primarily to provide a history or theory of the institution's development—tasks well accomplished by existing literature—but rather to explore the processes through which the concert was secured as the ideological core of high musical culture and through which it served both to instantiate and to provide an ideal representation of the relations of music making within that culture.[1]

Twentieth-century scholars are by no means the first to have noted the significance and novelty of the concert in the eighteenth and nineteenth centuries; those who wrote during that period, from Forkel on, were well aware of it too. As Nägeli put it in 1812, "Concerts, as we have them now, as all of cultivated Europe has them, are a creation of the previous century, arisen partly from developments within art itself, and partly from the expansion of social life."[2] Like so many aspects of German high musical culture, this awareness has remained within the musicological tradition that developed from it, leading to a variety of historical studies of an institution whose place as the centerpiece of bourgeois musical culture is firmly established and whose association with the canonic repertoire (sometimes referred to simply as "concert music") is a given. But there is a danger to such familiarity, which can easily give rise to a view of the concert as the inevitable expression of bourgeois musical culture and of the musical experience it promotes as paradigmatic, a starting point for music history rather than its object. Whether or not one views the concert as developing inexorably within bourgeois society, there can be little doubt that its establishment seemed far less inevitable to its advocates, for whom it appeared rather as a fragile hope threatened both from within and without, as this chapter's epigraphs suggest.[3] Few doubted that there would be concerts, but whether those concerts would be worthy of the hope they represented, the ideal experience they promised, was anything but certain. The processes of defining boundaries and establishing hierarchies, of advocacy and exclusion, that we have seen in more peripheral areas of musical culture were equally active at its center.

Such a reexamination of an apparently familiar topic can take advantage of a recent surge of interest in the study of musical performance, a development that embraces a remarkably wide range of scholars, from traditional musicology, theory, and performance practice to feminism, cultural studies, and philosophy.[4] In a number of these studies, the activity and venue of performance is seen to be as meaningful as the work performed and essential to the ascription of meaning to that work. In the words of Christopher Small, who uses the term "musicking" to include all types of musical behavior,

> The act of musicking establishes in the place where it is happening a set of relationships, and it is in those relationships that the meaning of the act lies. They are to be found not only between those organized sounds which are conventionally thought of as being the stuff of musical meaning but also between the people who are taking part, in whatever capacity, in the performance; and they model, or stand as a metaphor for, ideal relationships as the participants in the performance imagine them to be: relationships between person and person, between individual and society, between humanity and the natural world and even perhaps the supernatural world.[5]

Small's succinct insistence on the relational nature of musical performance can orient our consideration of the concert, even if that institution figures largely as a negative example of the dehumanization of music in Small's own work.[6] For the formal concert too can be viewed as the locus of both overt and covert human relationships—overt ones between members of the audience, between the audience and performers, among performers, and even between people who participate in the concert and people who do not, and covert ones represented as relationships to works or among works themselves. And this, in turn, can help explain why the nature of the concert was so fervently discussed during our period, and why those discussions so frequently touch on or become discussions of social relations. For a different genre and period (*opera seria* in the earlier eighteenth century), Martha Feldman has provided an example of what such a relational study might entail, considering audiences as well as performers as part of a larger ritual of performance.[7] As Feldman points out, the sometimes riotously interactive relations that characterized *seria* performance were replaced in the later eighteenth century by the more subdued and respectful demeanor with which we are familiar. But as we will see, there is still much to be gained by considering the interaction of all participants in the concert event, even if those who sought to prescribe its nature insisted on a rather different focus.

The complexity and volume of the discourse on the concert dictate several features of what follows. First, my discussion can offer only a sampling of an enormous literature. The centrality of the concert meant that virtually everyone had a view of its nature, and those views found expression in discussions of all manner of musical topics, relatively few of which were framed as explicit discussions of the nature of the concert. Simply put, if the concert was conceived as the focus of musical life, then virtually any musical discussion could lead to reflections on aspects of it or the activities it encompassed. Among such a superabundance of sources, my own priorities will be even more than usually apparent in my choices of examples. The same is true of the relational categories through which the chapter is organized: they are by no means exhaustive and could easily be conceived in other ways. To suggest the concert's central position in the ideology of serious music, as well as to reveal the links between that central position and the boundaries I have examined in previous chapters, I begin with the social and hierarchical implications of relationships within music—generic and stylistic distinctions—before considering the explicitly social relationships of the concert event. The chapter concludes by examining the implicit role of the composer, the person whose dominance finally authorizes the substitution of the objective for the personal in the validation of the concert and whose achievement justifies setting apart the concert from lower musical practices.

THE PROPER MUSIC AND THE IDEAL OF THE CONCERT

For the advocates of serious musical culture, a concert's value was defined above all by the worthiness of the music performed there. Because, as we will see below, this was certainly not the universal view, another issue writers faced was how to educate audiences to desire what was in fact best for them. Some, like Nägeli, accepted the inevitability of higher and lower forms—in his case represented by instrumental and vocal music, respectively[8]—but one of the defining traits of advocates of high musical culture was their insistence on a hierarchical distinction between worthy music and that which should be excluded, at least from concerts with true claims to value. This is not to suggest that the hierarchy was uniform: despite general agreement on a core of the most prestigious genres, considerable variety remained in what was considered admissible—but the need for generic boundary-setting was rarely questioned.

A Space between the Frivolous and the Crude

I have already discussed one of the basic distinctions in the previous chapter: opera's place was at best ambivalent in the concert. Some, like Gottfried Weber, offered an aesthetic justification for limiting its presence: in the absence of dramatic representation, operatic excerpts lost their sense in a way that sacred music, which is not sung by a specific character, did not. But beneath this apparently evenhanded judgment and despite his example of an unquestionably valuable opera (he cites concert performances of the first act finale of *Don Giovanni*), Weber passes implicit judgment on operas and their audiences when he raises the question of why audiences resist sacred music in concerts: "The answer lies written in the heart of these gentlemen (but they simply prefer that it not be read): church music just bores us, not only in concerts, but also in church itself; and that because it is too deep, too serious, and too lofty, not luxurious or trifling, not superficial, or what we call amusing!"[9] Just which music is luxurious and trifling enough is left unstated, but given the article's earlier contrast of sacred music and opera, no such statement is needed. Similarly, A. B. Marx criticized the inclusion of operatic excerpts on the grounds that their impact could never match that of the work onstage, but went on to discuss "the genres of composition that occupy the highest rank in the concert, and whose performance is the only justification for calling a concert *great.* That is the *symphony* and the *cantata.*"[10] Without overtly dismissing opera, such evaluations clearly distanced it from the core of the serious concert.

At the basis of the rejection of opera most frequently lay associations with frivolity and lack of serious purpose. An 1813 review of a Viennese performance of Spohr's oratorio *Das jüngste Gericht,* for example, opened with a definition of the oratorio that makes clear that the genre represents precisely the opposite of the operatic: "*Oratorio,* sacred cantata, comprises the greatest sublimity and dignity, complete unity in the genre, with the greatest possible avoidance of heterogeneous parts; thus, manly, powerful, strict, dignified composition with well-considered use of the chamber style and complete avoidance of the true theater style." The review went on to criticize Spohr's work for failing to live up to this standard and including operatic passagework. Spohr replied by citing the example of Haydn's *Schöpfung* as a precedent, but the attitude was well enough established that such criticism could not so easily be defused.[11] In an 1829 article, choral societies too were exhorted to avoid the frivolity of opera in favor of masses and oratorios; the author's point was driven home by a revealing anecdote. An opera director hired to direct a choir had splendid success with operatic choruses, but too great a focus on solo singing in operatic excerpts soon shrank participation. Choral singing in the city, however, was not yet completely undone: "A year later the new organist of the principal church, who had earlier participated in the famous Singakademie in B[erlin], attempted to found an organization on the model of that noble example, and, not without great pains, accomplished it. But most of the members had belonged to the [earlier,] dissolved group, and, spoiled by easy-to-perform, agreeable, and flashy opera music, they could not reconcile themselves to the serious, strict tone of the director and his masses and oratorios: one after the other stayed away, and by the end of the year the *Singverein* had once again come to an end." [12] Although the author again makes a gesture at evenhandedness—in his introduction, he rejects the views of "some strict friends of art, all too averse to the operatic style" [13]—the language of the anecdote makes clear the potentially damaging effects of immersion in opera. Nor was this view confined to the conservatives whose opinions the *Allgemeine musikalische Zeitung* increasingly came to represent. In 1842, in the *Neue Zeitschrift für Musik*, August Kahlert implied many of the same views in a discussion of career options for professional singers. Those who want to dedicate their lives to singing often believe that "they can do nothing better than go into the theater." Once again, the contrast with a higher form is made clear when Kahlert goes on to note that, although few think of a concert singing career, "perhaps the greatest proportion of our most outstanding vocal works of German musical art nonetheless belong to the concert hall or the church." [14]

As we have seen in previous chapters, accusations of frivolity and lack of substance are frequently associated with attempts to distance the musical values of the middle classes from stereotypes of an effeminate, internationalized aristocracy and its pastimes. The distancing of the concert from opera offers another example. Once again, Nägeli abstracts a grand conclusion from this observation; the paean to the participatory ideal of the choir cited in chapter 4 is followed immediately by a stark contrast: "Previously, the theater was the focal point where human existence and activity appeared in its most powerfully concentrated form. Here, however, higher art is practiced only by representatives. . . . The artistic essence of drama in the broadest sense is aristocratic in nature." [15] A different form of the same association appeared as early as 1801 in an overview of German music of the eighteenth century, which likened the rising prominence of instrumental music (initially within opera itself but later also in independent forms) to class unrest: at first, "instrumental music showed itself only as [the voice's] companion, or, when it wanted to rule on its own, borrowed the charm and splendor of the voice. But gradually it too aspired to higher rank. It relied (like the people on its superior physical strength and on the cultural achievements of the formerly lower classes) likewise on the increase and development of its tools. So first did the ruled become rulers." [16] This account is still ambivalent—it still gives opera a central place and goes on to wonder whether the democratic "struggle of all against all" that has resulted from the rise of instrumental music "delights or deafens"—but as the discourse of high musical culture crystallized increasingly around the serious and the instrumental, opera was increasingly marginalized within it. As William Weber has pointed out, the project of Richard Wagner can effectivel be understood as an attempt to impose on the operatic world the newly developed values of the serious concert.[17]

If distance from opera bounded the concert in relation to older high culture, the new predominance of instrumental music brought with it threats of its own, in the form of the potentially damaging associations of instrumental music with popular dance. Like opera, dance was too firmly established as a part of the musical world to make its elimination a conceivable topic, and in any case, the concert and the dance were distinct enough as events to render dance a relatively mild threat. Nonetheless, the topic recurs with enough frequency and consistency to suggest lingering discomfort.

In 1804 and 1805, Friedrich Guthmann outlined the associations of dance in a pair of articles that, although their explicit goal is to defend the activity and its music, nonetheless reveal its tenuous position relative to high musical culture. Dances, he argues, deserve more careful attention than they usually receive; in fact, "whoever believes that they are unworthy of a great genius is very much in error." But the terms of that attention are quite specific. First, even within dance, social distinctions are essential: "In dance music one ought, indeed, to distinguish clearly between the folk dance and that of the more cultivated classes."[18] Beyond that, though, the class distinction here broached gave dance lower-class associations that made its distance from the concert essential for the prestige of the latter. Although Guthmann rejects the views of those who are interested only in "products from a higher sphere," his defense of the genre is not to claim that it in fact belongs to that sphere but rather to note that among the works of dance composers are found "right many pretty and pleasing things, which are just right for cheering the people, plagued with burdensome work and the cares of subsistence."[19] Not only do the terms "pretty and pleasing" *(hübsche und gefällige)* effectively distance such dances from works with more serious goals, but the by-now-familiar perspective of the learned author prescribing for the less fortunate *Volk* also places dance primarily within the sphere of the uncultivated.[20]

Guthmann's tolerance from above finds a later counterpart in an 1834 discussion of the phenomenal success of Johann Strauss. Again, the theme of appeal to broader-than-usual audiences appears, although the term the author chooses is "the masses" *(die Masse)* rather than "the people"—a reflection of a gradual shift in conceptions of society since the early part of the century. Strauss's success, however, had made an explicit boundary necessary; the article includes a report from Leipzig noting that "one found that Strauss's dances were well performed by the well-arranged orchestra, but one also discovered that such music does not belong in the concert hall. . . . The best dance, we say, appears boring after several repetitions, when it is not to be danced to, when hearers must listen to it in solemn passivity, like an artwork whose comprehension occupies the understanding." Luckily, though, the reporter concluded, Strauss knew his place: "Strauss is a brilliant waltz-composer and virtuoso whom we like all the more because he doesn't want to be anything else."[21]

The presumption this report reveals—that a music to which one ordinarily responded physically (and thus, like the uncultivated classes) could not occupy the mind like true art—surfaces as well in the context of music education, whose ultimate goal, after all, was elevating the student to comprehension of the highest forms of art. Thus the pedagogue Johann Gottfried Hientzsch, for example, concluded an exhortation to teachers to pursue higher goals by citing dance as part of an opposition that had by then become conventional: "So, gentleman music teachers in the larger and largest towns, what do you think? . . . Do you want forever to remain for the fingers what dance teachers are for the feet, or do you want to elevate yourselves and be elevated into a higher region, indeed maybe into one of the highest, where you contribute to the noble idea of the aesthetic-Christian education of mankind?"[22] When dance appeared to threaten the development of musicians, making them unable to appreciate higher art, hostility could be considerably more overt. Another essay on education criticized ignorant teachers who knew no better than to teach their pupils simple dances; the students' parents were equally culpable:

> What an injustice the parents too do, clearly for the sake of a low fee, allowing their children to be spoiled musically, surely requires no mention; likewise, how little it says here too to find that a little waltz has been drummed into the dear little ones, for precisely dances are the basis of all later errors. The youthful spirit yields all too easily to the simpler, especially when in some respects earlier approval can be earned with it; it loses the seriousness necessary to make its own the classical products of art, even with the goodwill and more genuine knowledge of the teacher, and thereby thwarts every well-meaning effort.[23]

Here, dance is no longer a harmless pastime but an active threat.

The economic concerns discussed in earlier chapters play into this metonymy of concert and dance as placeholders for high and low musics and classes. Given what could appear to be an overwhelming preponderance of common music, cultivated musicians could fear that their security required protection—and this fear too found expression in terms of concert repertoire in opposition to dance. In 1837, for instance, an anonymous correspondent to the *Allgemeine musikalische Zeitung* complained that in Prussia, "since the paid, public practice of music has been placed in the class of handiwork, and every fiddler who buys a license is permitted to earn money with any band he pleases in dance halls and the like, it has become impossible to assemble an orchestra that is at all worth listening to, even in provincial cities of 20,000 to 30,000 inhabitants." To solve this problem, he recommended not only that each city maintain a competent string quartet as a core for an orchestra of dilettantes but also that no musician be granted a license to perform publicly unless he demonstrated his ability to perform serious music adequately; a violinist, for instance, ought to be able to perform adequately the first violin part of a Haydn string quartet and the first violin part from a symphonic movement "of a more recent good master."[24] The concert could thus set the standard for entry into the profession.

This view of dance kept the instrumental music of the concert free of the taint of the merely physical, and it formed the backdrop for a text whose influence lasted well beyond the period in which it was conceived. First published in 1854, Eduard Hanslick's *Vom Musikalisch-Schönen* became one of the foundational statements of formalism in music. It has, of course, long been associated with an anti-Wagnerian campaign to elevate music's formal relations above its potential for emotional manipulation; in the present context, however, passages like the following reveal that one of Hanslick's strategies was to associate the emotional with the physical and its disreputable vehicle, dance. In its anxious concern to exclude the crudities of music (and people) too closely associated with the physical, Hanslick's project thus reveals its roots in the earlier process of defining the bounds of acceptable concert repertoire:

> The creditor who, when pressing for repayment, was so moved by the sound of his debtor's music that he forgave the whole debt is activated in no other way than the sluggard who is all of a sudden prompted by a waltz tune to dance. The former is moved more by the intellectual elements, harmony and melody; the latter, by the sensuous rhythm. Neither proceeds out of free self-determination, however; neither is yielding to the promptings of spirit or of love of beauty, but both are stirred as a result of neural stimulation. Music loosens the feet or the heart as wine the tongue. To undergo unmotivated, aimless, and casual emotional disturbances through a power that is not *en rapport* with our willing and thinking is unworthy of the human spirit. When people surrender themselves so completely to the elemental in an art that they are not in control of themselves, then it seems to us that this is not to the credit of that art and is still less to the credit of those people.[25]

A Hierarchy of Genres and the Cultivation of an Audience

If the concert's firmly established boundaries with opera, on the one hand, and dance, on the other, circumscribed its basic realm, a great deal remained to be determined within that realm. Here, specific discussions of genres and their relationships to one another are particularly informative; from them emerges a distinct sense of a hierarchy: music which was clearly detrimental to the concert and its audience, that which could lead its listeners to better things, and that which represented the pinnacle of worthy music. The extreme ends of this progression were widely agreed upon—the trivial and dancelike were to be shunned and the symphony and the oratorio represented the ultimate goal—but the intermediate steps were considerably less well-defined. If an unambiguous and widely accepted generic hierarchy never emerged, however, these stylistic and generic discussions are nonetheless revealing because the terms in which they were conducted —the concepts of triviality, seriousness, and degeneracy to which they gave expression—map unambiguously onto the character types that the advocates of the serious concert sought to promote or discourage. The generic hierarchy on which the concert was premised meshed closely with the larger educational program; in the view of a wide variety of advocates, the concert itself could be both the final instrument of musical cultivation and its ultimate reward.

Thus, just as educational reform was premised on the need to cultivate students to develop their human potential, the most appropriate concert music was that which engaged the highest human faculties. Precisely what music did this and how those faculties were defined could vary, however. In the 1780s, Forkel still saw serious vocal music as the most appropriate, since those exceptional instrumental works that offered more to the truly knowledgeable than mere pleasing sounds were beyond the ability of the amateur listener to grasp.[26] And Hanslick's criterion of "free self-determination" under control of the will, with its emphasis on self-control, is far removed from the earlier conception of Bernhard Natorp, who in 1805 advocated concerts that focused on the highest of his four categories of music: not music for the understanding, nor "for the fingers, the breath and the voice," nor even for the ear, but "music for the heart."[27] Nägeli's position, that the intellectual is crucial, places him closer to Hanslick: "Not only was Lessing correct in saying 'a thinking artist is worth twice as much to me;' one could go much further and maintain that a work of art that is not simply aesthetically grasped (with the senses), but rather contemplated intellectually, indeed genuinely thought through, is worth a thousand times more to the viewer of the latter kind [i.e., cultivated ones]."[28] The 1841 address of Gustav Keferstein cited in chapter 4 is effectively an attempt to synthesize the positions staked out by Nägeli (and later Hanslick) and Natorp. Keferstein's progression moves from simple sensual pleasure to understanding and emotion but culminates in comprehending the "artistic idea" *(künstlerische Idee)* of the work through "conscious integration of the received and perceived individual impressions, stimulations of the feelings, emotional impact and so on."[29]

Such aesthetic reflections were directly linked to conclusions about the concert and its music. Natorp went so far as to include an entire sample program to show how a fully unified and effective concert might be realized, and Nägeli moved directly from his consideration of the value of the best music to a discussion of concerts as the center of public musical life. For Keferstein, the hierarchy was tied instead to specific generic and stylistic issues —the highest level of meaning could be drawn from music "in its higher forms, and especially advantageously in the most complete and highly developed of all, namely, sonata form." And as the most exemplary works in that area, Keferstein offers what was by 1841 the thoroughly conventional, even obligatory reference to "Beethoven's immortal master-creations in the realm of sonata form, among which are of course also included the symphony, the overture, the trio, the quartet, etc."[30] As we will see below, reference to an authoritative composer is a crucial element of this passage, but equally important are the genres Keferstein elevates: the core genres of serious instrumental music, which together with the oratorio or cantata (the nobility of which we have already seen extolled in contrast to opera) occupied the summit of the concert repertoire in virtually all accounts.

The alternatives to these high genres are clear in an imaginary conversation between a music director and his antagonists, a virtuoso and a dilettante, published in 1842. The music director, who clearly gives voice to the approved position, summarizes his demands: "In a word, play sonatas, symphonies, quartets instead of your doodling harmonics, instead of your breakneck variations, instead of your stupendous arpeggio etudes, instead of your glittering runs in thirds and sixths, instead of your melting, groaning, dying-out, roaring-out expression, emphasis, and delivery."[31] Of particular significance is this brief passage's inconsistency. Sonatas, symphonies, and quartets are opposed not only to devalued genres like the variation and the etude but also to modes of performance. The insistent repetition of the possessive pronoun reveals the outburst's true target: genres are at fault only insofar as they act as vehicles for "your" personal display, and the approved genres remain pure, unattributed to a devaluing person.

Even those genres, however, could be threatened through inappropriate use, especially in the form of arrangements—through which, once again, the idiosyncratic and personal could contaminate the work of art. The arrangement proved a particularly difficult topic. First, it was associated above all with the piano, which, although it was valued as a crucial instrument, was also occasionally viewed with suspicion for discouraging the study of other instruments. That this criticism masked a more substantial fear that most often went unidentified is suggested by two widely separated articles, each of which preface their concerns about the piano by raising the specter of too-casual treatment of music. In 1800, a report on the state of music in Bohemia lamented the decline of instrumental music, noting that "thorough teachers are becoming rarer, and since learning music becomes simply a pastime, one pays it no heed and always sets oneself an easily attainable goal." Forty-five years later, the very same concerns about the piano replacing other instruments recur, this time prefaced by an even more pointed contrast of the trivial and the worthy: if the public really prefers "Lanner- and Strauss-fests and the like" to "Mozart's or Beethoven's tone-creations," then it is the duty of criticism to develop more discriminating taste.[32]

The problem with an overabundance of arrangements was precisely that it could blur these distinctions. Thus, although discussions and reviews of arrangements sometimes acknowledged that they could serve a serious public, particularly if made by musicians who were themselves accomplished, fear of devaluation also found frequent expression, as Thomas Christensen has noted in the case of four-hand piano transcriptions.[33] And it was precisely the piano's omnivorous habits that were worrisome: "The one true social tone-tool . . . is and remains the piano. A thing may be written for the stage or consecrated to the church; it may be created for half a hundred players of a Beethoven symphony or a band leading Strauss dances; nothing can prevent that its imminent appearance in a piano arrangement, its entire value pressed into that form of a bill of exchange, must be put up with."[34] The process of degeneration that this practice threatened is sketched even more graphically in a review of small ensemble arrangements (with piano) of Mozart and Beethoven. The mania of arranging, once again, could not be stopped: "Nothing is protected: the greatest symphonies and overtures, masses and church cantatas, oratorios and operas, etc. etc. etc. must bear the brunt of it, and are offered to us in the most varied forms and shapes: as piano arrangements with and without voice; arranged for military band; as quintet, and quartet, trios, duos, and solos for individual instruments, *scilicet:* violin, guitar, flute, czakan, etc. (*per parenthesin:* the mouth harp, vulgarly *Maultrommel*, offers a still

uncultivated field—take note, gentlemen!); finally, yet again, metamor-
phosed into waltzes, gallops, polonaises, and eccosaises."[35] Here, devaluation takes several forms simultaneously: arrangement itself removes works
from their elevated venues, reduces the church, stage, and concert hall to the
level of the dance floor, replaces serious with popular instruments, and, finally, degrades serious music into dance forms.

Such fears of degeneration, constant throughout the period that the concert was in fact establishing itself as centrally important, reveal yet again the
insecurity that haunted the advocates of high musical culture. And according to numerous reports (including this one from 1837), degeneration was
not just a fear but an observable reality: "For that very reason [overempha-
sis on empty virtuosity] the term concerto, a showpiece, is gradually disappearing from the concert poster, like the old and revered silver basins are
from the table, replaced by colorfully stamped fragrance jars *(pot-pourris)*,
amusements *(divertissements)*, alterations or decorative borders *(variations)* and trivial wares of that sort, which can properly be surrounded by
Auber's dance overtures or Strauss's waltzes."[36] The parallel between generic and material decline (from traditional luxury items to cheap, mass produced knickknacks) conveys both status concerns and nostalgia, a frequent
combination among the prophets of degeneration. But earlier accounts
rarely suggest that the past had been radically different: the decline of taste
and quality in concerts had been bewailed repeatedly in Vienna nearly
twenty years before this report, and long before that, a Viennese author held
forth in 1787 on "the imminent downfall of music."[37] As early as 1778,
Forkel had devoted the foreword to his *Musikalisch-kritische Bibliothek* to
a detailed consideration of music's decline, the reasons for it, and the means
by which to prevent it. For Forkel, the problem was essentially stylistic
(and heavily gendered), and it was not theoretical but practical: "Never has
more been declaimed than now about the great, the sublime, the beautiful,
the expression of a manly and strong feeling; and when have we indeed had
less expression of the great, the sublime, the truly beautiful, and of manly
strength of feeling?"[38] The public, it would seem, proved stubbornly and
enduringly resistant to the gravity and greatness that would improve it.

A stylistic solution, however, continued to have its advocates. In 1820,
for instance, Friedrich August Kanne concluded a lengthy consideration of
"what is to be feared from current taste in music" with a straightforward
answer: "But what is the greatest bulwark against the ruin of music? Counterpoint!"[39] And as late as 1842, A. B. Marx's treatise on composition was
advanced as a similar bulwark against a familiar array of adversaries: "In
part, one can consider Marx's teachings an attempt to explain genius. But

be that as it may, if the new method does no more than cultivate musically well-disposed dilettantes, it will have done enough; it will have accomplished the highest, most salutary service possible in the present, when dilettantism has become so important a force in the state of music. Theory would thus heal the wounds that the practice of a host of abominable composers have given musical taste. In fact, dance- and virtuosity-composers, French and Italian opera-writers and their German imitators work unceasingly toward its corruption." [40]

In the face of such threats, segregation or cultivation appeared to be the only viable alternatives—and even most who advocated or at least acknowledged the reality of different concerts for different tastes still hoped to lead the public toward the higher forms. [41] Although, as we have seen, critical discourse was one means to cultivate an audience, the concert itself was often viewed as the essential educational tool. And as in the case of the other educational projects I have discussed, the goal of the concert was nothing less than to cultivate the audience to the point of full humanity. Thus, A. B. Marx could summarize the flaws of current concert life (after a lengthy enumeration of those flaws) with a simple and loaded parallel: "But what a heap of music is all this taken together, imparting nothing to the listeners but admiration of a mechanical facility and that sensual pleasure that is as distant from the enjoyment of art as—the animal is from the human." [42]

The link Marx's parallel suggests between the larger project of human cultivation and the improvement of the concert is amply confirmed by the conclusion of Natorp's earlier proposal for concert reform. The passage is a relatively lengthy one, but I include it as an unusually forthright account of the trickle-down effect of the concert in its most optimistic form:

> One of the most important advantages of such an arrangement
> of concerts would undoubtedly be that thereby all inauthentic music
> would gradually be completely supplanted, and true music, the music
> of the heart, would gradually claim such value that one would have
> to ask oneself how it was possible to bear a musical—or much rather,
> antimusical—jumble for so long a time. . . . Without a doubt, the true
> musical spirit would then gradually spread itself more generally; music
> would again flow over into schools and churches, into the workshops
> of the laborers, into the cottages and fields of the farmer; and the lovely
> hopes with which C. R. Horstig concluded his article on the "Practice
> of Student Teachers," hopes with which all friends of the beautiful
> and the good heartily concur, would be fulfilled: "Would not nature
> be transformed into a temple, and many lands into an Arcadia, if the
> gentle flute greeted the morning with lovely songs and the tender horn
> sounded out to us from the woods' twilight? Wouldn't work be com-

pleted more happily and the hour of leisure used better, if the magic of music made humans more human and tore them from the animal condition of torpor, through which they lull their finer senses to sleep through enjoyment of the coarser entertainments? But who knows whether the new century will not in this too bring with it a new, significant step toward the ennoblement of humanity."[43]

If most discussions of the educational function of the concert were more restrained, they nonetheless expressed the same progressive hope. Justus Thibaut's influential *Ueber Reinheit der Tonkunst* (1825), for instance, hoped that concerts (especially of the vocal genres with which he was most concerned) could develop audiences through pragmatically small increments: "But it would certainly be very wholesome if it were made a duty to give some selected pieces in the serious style (clearly not in the pure church style) in every concert. People must come to know in an easy way that with which they will be brought into closer contact, and if they befriend themselves almost playfully with it, one can use their good disposition for the sake of further progress."[44] In Schilling's *Encyclopädie*, similar advice to programmers of instrumental concerts noted that "of instrumental music it is especially *symphonies* that profoundly support and elevate artistic sense and artistic taste." But again, audiences could reach this level only gradually, for currently, "the greater part of the so-called fashionable world rebels against [symphonies] as though they were the most boring musical genre." Even given careful and progressive training of the audience, however, the author had no illusions that anything close to goals as utopian as Natorp's might be achieved on a large scale, and "if worst comes to worst, however, it is not the larger public but rather the quite small public of the select few that has a voice in this."[45] A public that refused to be educated ought at least not to be catered to.

The Threat from Within: The Virtuoso

If the education of the public remained uncertain, there was little doubt about the most immediate threat to its cultivation: the virtuoso was so firmly established as a corrupting force that, by the 1840s, writers who were quite serious in their rejection of what virtuosos represented could nonetheless play with the topic with easy familiarity. In 1844, Heinrich Paris, for instance, wrote, "For my part, I too have come so far that I would gladly add to the litany that prays for the aversion of all calamities, after 'war and pestilence,' 'and from piano virtuosos protect us, Lord our God!'"[46] And in the conversation cited above between a music director, a weak-minded dilettante, and a virtuoso—a piece with an impeccably high-minded conclusion—the virtuoso could even mock the standard ambitions of the advocates of serious music: "Haven't I told you that professional jealousy shines through? That we hardened sinners, as he [the music director] often represents us privately and publicly, corrupt the mind of the public by luring them out from participation in sublime oratorios into the sinful world?" [47] Unlike opera or dance, the virtuoso's place was undeniably the concert itself, and the threat was therefore all the more intense.

Intense but not immediately obvious—a number of relatively early sources reveal the virtuoso as still residing within the imagined community of musicians whose concerns needed addressing. An essay on traveling virtuosos of 1802 credits them with genuine usefulness, both in smaller towns, where virtuosos developed the artistic sense of an otherwise deprived public, and in cities, where they could combat the tendency to narrowness of taste; further, they could provide examples of accomplishment to both dilettantes and professionals. These services, however, were not adequately rewarded, except in the largest cities—accordingly, an alternative means of support needed to be found. [48] Another brief discussion noted that, whereas musicians formerly could count on establishing themselves through their own efforts, an oversupply of virtuosos and would-be virtuosos had "spoiled the market." [49] Neither of these accounts overlooks the flaws of many individual virtuosos, but their contrast to the enormous and overwhelmingly negative literature of the following decades is striking. By 1811, Nägeli could still recognize that a few virtuosos served the cause of good music, but condemnation outweighed concern, and thereafter far more sources from within the literature of serious music viewed the virtuoso as an abjected other than as a member of the community of worthy colleagues. [50]

This is by no means to suggest that the virtuoso was unanimously dismissed from the musical world. On the contrary, virtuoso concerts continued to exert a fascination that finds its way even into generally serious periodicals, particularly in concert reports. Thus the *Wiener allgemeine musikalische Zeitung* could publish a review of an 1812 concert by the flutist Anton Bayer that focused exclusively on his technical and interpretive accomplishments, noting, "The purity and speed of his double-tonguing leaves nothing to wish for. In general, Herr B. possesses a rare ability in the performance of passagework, during which the physical construction of his breathing mechanism supports him most advantageously, since it enables him to perform the greatest part of a variation without a breath." [51] Here, admiration of technique leads to an unusual reference to the body of the performer—precisely the sort of misguided emphasis that the genre of the variation set could lead to, according to its critics. Such accounts, too, became rarer as the century progressed—or, more accurately, they became the stuff of journals like the revealingly titled *Zeitung für Theater und Musik zur Unterhaltung gebildeter, unbefangener Leser* (Journal of Theater and Music for the Entertainment of Cultivated, Unbiased Readers) or the long-lived *Wiener Zeitschrift für Kunst, Literatur, Theater und Mode* (Viennese Journal for Art, Literature, Theater, and Fashion), which were unambiguously directed to a less serious audience.[52]

For the advocates of serious music, the too-obvious physicality of virtuoso performance could only distract from the real significance of music and lead to the neglect of those genres that truly had such significance. And as we have seen in the case of dance, the physical threatened to associate musicians with classes of activity (and classes of people) from whom they were eager to distinguish themselves. The image of music as handiwork *(Handwerk)* rather than art—and thus the product of the working rather than the cultivated classes—appears once again, for instance in the 1818 account by a Viennese critic of what he called "current concert abuse," in which virtuosos (again, with a few unnamed exceptions) were heavily implicated. To remedy this situation, art "must once again begin to show itself not as a daily tightrope walker, but rather in its entire value and power."[53] The image of the tightrope walker—inherently embodied, reliant on physical skills in a precarious situation, and unmistakably associated with popular entertainment—proved irresistible to numerous critics of virtuosity, including Thibaut, who halfheartedly "excused" virtuosos for pandering to common taste: "If need be, one can pardon the fact that our touring virtuosos . . . almost inevitably reveal only their most superficial aspects and nothing more, because the public as a rule prefers when a tightrope walker stands on his head to when he seeks to illustrate in beautiful, easy motions the ideal of the most lovely forms."[54] The low status only implicit in this analogy is unmistakable in August Kahlert's later use of the same image: "Dexterity, bodily skill, singularity now entice and bring something salably unartistic into the sphere of art. The tightrope walker stands no lower at all than a virtuoso who has set only the so-called 'unbelievable' as his goal."[55]

Mere physicality, however, does not explain the vehemence and persistence of the antivirtuoso discourse; dance, after all, had similar associations in this regard and excited much less resistance. As a flurry of recent scholarship on virtuosity has revealed, however, more was at stake: the virtuoso raised issues of individual subjectivity that were closely related to those of the creative (compositional) genius. From the perspective of a developing culture of high musical art, however, the virtuoso represented precisely the wrong approach to subjectivity, one that threatened the order of the concert and the bourgeois society it stood for. As Susan Bernstein perceptively summarizes it, the virtuoso's "deviations are errors that refer only to the particular performer and do not lead to the idea of the work, just as the instrumental manipulation of journalism and public opinion circulate, by means of money and applause, back into the fame of a particular individual. The arabesque of the nongeneralizable *I* is a deviant from the idea of originality—the idea of origination in the idea. . . . In virtuosity, the idea digresses." [56] Bernstein draws this conclusion from an analysis of Heine's music journalism, but she sounds a theme that was thoroughly familiar to numerous writers. Nägeli too saw the origin of the virtuoso in precisely the miscarriage of individual creativity. Having asserted that the rise of the individual can account for the creative splendor of recent music, he proceeds to explore its negative consequences: "As great, as highly effective and edifying as is this gain for art won by individuals, however, just as great, as highly damaging is that which has also been accomplished by individuals in the world, indeed by a great number of individuals: I mean the *touring virtuosos*." [57] Such a threat to the fundamentally compositional basis of serious musical life helps account for the intensity ofthe rejection of virtuosos as usurpers of legitimate musical practice who arrogantly prostituted themselves for personal glory. [58]

Like discussions of degeneration, the virtuoso discourse often posited a past untroubled by current woes: "If before one wanted compositions by the masters elucidated and called into consciousness by the performance of a virtuoso, now the interest has reversed itself, and one would much rather admire the dexterity of the individual. From the earlier perspective it was the *object*, but it is now the *person* that is the main point." [59] If the cancerous individualism that Kahlert here outlines progressed through time, however, it could also potentially be remedied in time. Conservative authors hoped this might be accomplished by simply returning to earlier practices; in this spirit, Heinrich Paris upheld as a model the performances of an aristocratic dilettante, the Archduchess Stephanie von Baden, who exemplified the ideal "through her truly classical performance of classical music." [60] More progressively minded authors, however, sought to offer new challenges. A. B. Marx, for instance, after asserting that mere mechanical virtuosity could be attained by anyone willing to apply himself, suggested that real distinction lay rather in the service of revealing the legitimate individuality of the artwork: "The public will feel that it has a true artist before it as soon as a performer allows every tone of the work to come forward easily, freely, and truly, as it lived in the soul of the composer." [61] In 1847, a consideration of the demands of choral singing made explicit the redefinition Marx here implies, reappropriating the term *virtuoso* for high art after decades of efforts at exclusion: "The frequently heard exclamation, 'After all, I can sing along in the choir!'—lacking in many cases a real basis—rests on the admittedly very common misunderstanding of the idea of virtuosity. The choral singer too must be a virtuoso. But this kind of artistic ability I would like to call a more internal one." [62] If virtuosity could be redefined as inner understanding, the damage of the virtuoso could be undone—at least in the ideal world of the imagined concert.

THE RELATIONSHIPS OF THE CONCERT

The ideal of the concert focused all attention on the works presented in it—hence the disruptive power of the virtuoso, whose presence undermined the work's proper centrality. Achieving that centrality, however, required that the elements that constituted the event and those who participated in it be properly ordered. If that ordering is implicit in discussions of the concert repertoire, it is fundamental to considerations of the concert as an event. Small's concept of musical performance as a representation of idealized social relationships bears recalling here, albeit with a caveat: musical performance may represent idealized relationships, but it is composed of present, concrete, and often unsatisfactory ones. As a result, discourse on the concert as event can usefully be read as an attempt to rescue an ideal in the face of experience of a far more resistant network of relationships and interests. To see this, it is useful to work back toward the concert's ideal center from aspects apparently far removed from it. Accordingly, I will begin with a single concert report that is atypical in a number of respects: not only was the event it describes far grander than most concerts, but it also evokes the social space of the concert considerably more explicitly than do many such reports. Indeed, its focus on social hierarchy rather than music marks it as an event more representative of an older order of performance than of the new, work-centered concert culture. Precisely because of its explicitness and its departures from what would become the norm, however, it can highlight the relational issues the concert evoked:

> On November 29 of this year [1812], Vienna celebrated a great musical festival, unique of its kind. It was the performance of the cantata *Timotheus, oder die Gewalt der Musik*, composed by Handel and provided with the accompaniment of a variety of wind instruments by Mozart. The holding of this great concert, by 621 friends of art of all classes, occurred in the Imperial and Royal Riding School with the special high permission of His Majesty the Emperor. The principal vocal parts were taken by Frau *v. Geymüller*, Fräulein *Bahrensfeld* and *Riedl*,

Herr Hofrath *v. Kiesewetter,* the Imperial and Royal Councillor and Doctor of Law Herr *Sonnleithner,* the silk manufacturer Herr *Soini,* and Herr *Hoffmann.* Herr *Streicher,* well-known as a teacher of the pianoforte and as a maker of that instrument—who was tireless in carrying out all preparatory arrangements, especially in the formation of the choir, and who is to thank above all for this concert's coming to be—led from the keyboard the choir that he had trained. Herr Hof-concipist *Mosel* of the Imperial and Royal Household Office, most well-known for his theoretical and practical knowledge of music, led the whole most admirably. Herr *J. Tost,* the merchant, oversaw the direction of the violins. The other solo and principal instruments, which stood near the keyboard, were taken partly by dilettantes and partly by the very best artists [i.e., professional musicians]: the cello by Herr *Hauschka,* the contrabass by Herr *Langhamer,* the two violas by Herr *Tœuber* and Herr *Kratki;* Herr *Bogner* and Herr *Baron v. Knorr* played the flutes, Herr *Czerwenka* and Herr *Kiess* the oboes, Herr *Graf v. Troier* and Herr *Friedlovky* the clarinets, Herr *Romberg* and *Prince Corolat* the bassoons, an Herr *Radezky* and Herr *Gowerlovsky* the horns. In addition to these, His Highness the ruling *Prince Joseph v. Lobkowitz* appeared among the solo singers at the second performance; overall one noted in the vocal as well as the instrumental choir several dilettantes of high rank, which elevated the value of the whole still more. Concerning the perfection of the performance there was only one opinion among nearly five thousand hearers. The whole event provided a delightful sight and a powerful impression, which cannot be described but only felt. Invitations to the friends of art were issued by *Joseph Fürst v. Lobkowitz, Moritz Graf v. Fries, Maria Anna Gräfin v. Dietrichstein,* and *Fanny Freyin v. Arnstein.* By general desire the cantata was repeated on December 3; both times it pleased the entire high court to attend the performance, which took place at noon on each day. The income from both performances came to 30,000 florins (Viennese currency), the allocation and distribution of which was entrusted to the *Society of Noble Women for the Advancement of the Good and the Useful.*[63]

Supporting the Concert: Patronage and Money

Perhaps the most immediate impression left by this report is the degree to which the event it describes is bound up with the imperial court and the nobility: it occurs by special permission of the emperor, it is attended by the imperial court, its status is elevated by the participation of noble (and even royal) amateurs, and its proceeds are directed to charitable ends by a society of aristocratic women. As a representation of an idealized society overseen by a beneficent ruler whose subjects of all degrees cooperate for both aesthetic and social good at the invitation of the aristocracy, it reveals how effectively musical performances could support the ideology of monarchy, even without the direct patronage of the crown in the form of court ensembles.[64] And in a traditional view, the reverse was true as well: the value of secular authority could support the ideology of serious music, as Forkel asserted in 1783: the highest goal of art could "no more possibly be a private matter than it could be left to the caprice of every individual, but rather only be preserved by official [*obrigkeitlichen*] events." [65] Even in Vienna, however, a city notorious for its social conservatism and elaborate hierarchy, the relations of patronage upon which this mutual support depended had been uncertain for decades before this event. In 1787, Amand Wilhelm Schmith had predicted that, due to decreasing support from great courts, "one can hardly expect Handel, Gluck, Gasmann, Paisiello, Sarti, Naumann, Salieri, Haydn, Dittersdorff, Mozart, etc. in the future." [66] And in 1818, within a few years of our performance, similar concerns received an even more specific social grounding: "But when the first class of the state [i.e., the nobility], upon which the fine arts always formerly depended to support their progress for the sake of cultivation of the spirit and of taste, no longer knows how to appreciate their essential value, then the entire burden of supporting the disciples of the arts falls upon the middle class, and if in the end they prove too weak, then music, poetry, painting, and sculpture are degraded, and give way to the rustic." [67]

Such fears for the security of the material basis of the concert provide a context for the anxiety over stylistic decline discussed above: in a social context in which the significance of musical performance was no longer reliably established by aristocratic patronage, the inherent value of art could replace the patronage of the highest classes as a guarantor of value. The report just quoted, in fact, itself suggests that this process was already taking place, despite the author's protests; note that although the arts depended on the aristocracy, the author uses recognition of their "essential value" as a standard by which to evaluate the patrons, rather than the reverse. By mid-century, one writer urged that the continued existence of court musical establishments should be justified not by its association with the nobility but by its use to further the state's goal of cultivating the people by developing their musical taste in widely available performances.[68] The prestige of music itself, such sources suggest, had effectively replaced the prestige of the patrons it had once signaled.

But the same forces that enabled that substitution also threatened its effectiveness. Just as Reichardt's appropriation of the ideal of freedom for the working musician had occurred in the face of the economic insecurity that accompanied the weakening of the ties of patronage (see chapter 3), concerts independent of the overt support of the aristocracy both relied on and were threatened by the increasingly monetarized wealth of the middle and upper classes. The image of stylistic cheapening we have already seen—the replacement of ancestral silver by cheap manufactured goods as an image for the decline of concert repertoire—suggests the danger: a musical economy based on money, both in the circulation of printed music and in the increasingly public form of the concert, meant that the best or the most prestigious could be inundated by the merely popular. Reichardt had already complained in 1782 that "a single written page many a true artist gave me from his hidden store during my travels was often infinitely more valuable than twenty engraved and printed works of the same man, prepared for the constricted heart of his gracious buyer and the iron-mongering of his music printer."[69]

If the problem of these altered relations of musical production was widely recognized, however, its solution was far less clear. One possible response to these altered relations of production was to attempt to reestablish the prestige of music by appealing to the leaders of the new order. Nägeli employed this tactic with unusual directness in addresses that linked the development of industry and art and that flattered his audience by acknowledging their leading roles in both areas: "I *know* and *prize*, in the same persons who in our circle strive to lift art higher, those who in other circles, in general and specific, patriotic ones, have long and repeatedly proven their public utility in *pedagogical, economic*, and other forms—all of them credits to our fatherland."[70] If Nägeli's reference to pedagogy serves as a reminder of the progressive ambitions of those who attempted to universalize high culture, another response to the threat of uncultivated popular taste is more directly linked to conservative social stances. Thibaut's prognosis is typical of such views: "For where all the world has a seat and a voice, and where each must also have something refreshing for his money, the classical can never fully prosper."[71] And in an 1839 article remarkable for its thoroughgoing rejection of virtually every aspect of contemporary musical culture, Heinrich Paris identifies the underlying cause unambiguously: "Because we have destroyed the worship of all *ideas;* everywhere we have made only *material* interests the single mover [*Mobil*] of all social relationships; because in everything *money* has become our only god."[72]

Paris's complete rejection of change sets him apart from many who sought to establish the prestige of the concert independent of the social guarantee of aristocratic patronage, but his diagnosis of the problem—social fluidity resulting from an increasingly commodified economy—was a factor with which all advocates of the serious concert had to contend. The ideally ordered world of the Viennese concert report bore increasingly little relation to the world in which concerts were produced, and that change accounts for the intensity of defenders of the concert's prestige in the face of the threat of the popular. To maintain the claim for the universal validity of the culture represented by the concert in a setting in which social hierarchy was no longer explicit would demand a quality Theodor Adorno characterized as "tact": "For tact, we now know, has its precise historical hour. It was the hour when the bourgeois individual rid himself of absolutist compulsion. Free and solitary, he answers for himself, while the forms of hierarchical respect and consideration developed by absolutism, divested of their economic basis and their menacing power, are still just sufficiently present to make living together within privileged groups bearable. . . . The precondition of tact is convention no longer intact yet still present."[73] From this perspective, one might understand the central problem of the concert to be the preservation of the "hierarchical respect" suggested by the seriousness of the Vienna event in the absence of the structuring presence of the monarch. As we will see, solving that problem demanded a framework that allowed the reconception of virtually every aspect of the event, from its geographic situation to the roles of participants and their interaction.

The Site of the Concert

The emperor's presence gives the concert not only a social center but also a physical location: a royal hall in the imperial city. In this way, the traditional nature of this event is further revealed; Charles Burney had recognized this feature of German musical life long before:

> I was somewhat tired of going to imperial cities [i.e., free cities not under the rule of a local prince] after music; as I seldom found any thing [*sic*] but the organ and organist worth attending to, and not always them. . . . These cities are not rich, and therefore have not the folly to support their theatres at a great expence [*sic*]. The fine arts are children of affluence and luxury; in despotic governments they render power less insupportable, and diversion from thought is perhaps as necessary as from action. Whoever therefore seeks music in Germany, should do it at the several courts, not in the free imperial cities, which are generally inhabited by poor industrious people, whose genius is chilled and repressed by penury; who can bestow nothing on vain pomp or luxury; but think themselves happy, in the possession of necessaries. The residence of a sovereign prince, on the contrary, besides the musicians in ordinary of the court, church and stage, swarms with pensioners and expectants, who have however few opportunities of being heard.[74]

The role of court musical establishments remained significant, as the presence of reports summarizing their personnel and activities well into the nineteenth century makes clear, but later musical discourse makes equally clear that those establishments no longer retained their unquestioned centrality. In the face of declining courtly support for music, the absence of that support might be bemoaned or redefined as a virtue, but to a large extent Burney's opposition between court and free cities was supplanted by one between major cities (often but not always also the seat of courts) and small cities or villages.[75]

Many of the points made through this opposition are predictable: musical performances in small locations, for instance, are held to be more difficult to organize successfully than they might be in large cities. An 1826 report in the *Berliner allgemeine musikalische Zeitung*, to give one example, criticized a festival in remote Demmin in Hinterpommern for programming works (including Beethoven's Mass in C Major and part of Handel's *Messiah*) beyond the ability of the relatively uncultivated audience to grasp and too grand for the limited forces available.[76] A later report on Berlin's concert life, by contrast, held that "even when the concert is reminiscent of [an evening at] a bar and flows into the same, the performances are often still better than concerts of the first rank in many smaller cities," and larger cities figured as the preferred destinations of the better virtuosos, further limiting the quality of provincial musical life.[77] Near midcentury, reports also begin to characterize small towns as places where older musicians and practices remained relatively unchanged by the transformations of urbanization—genuine amateur performance, for instance, was reported in 1842 to survive only in small towns, an indication of growing awareness of the role of professionalism in urban musical life.[78]

Cities, however, were by no means presented as ideal locations for music. The opposition could equally be used to critique the superficiality of the major centers. A. B. Marx, for instance, could note that even in "significant locations, namely in Berlin too," insubstantial programming marred concerts.[79] Others went considerably further; in 1839, Eduard Krüger maintained that, if anything, the urban musical public was more problematic than the rural: "The public is the same everywhere, from the smallest little city to Vienna—except that in the big cities infection with the cancer of dilettantism tends to have spread further."[80] From this view it is only a small step to the idealization of small-town musical life that Nägeli offered in an 1820 address.[81]

Both the rewards and the seductions of urban life are indeed conventional figures of the imagination of modern society. But noting this should not blind us to the significance of the increasing tendency of musical discourse to oppose cities to towns: through such means, the geography of musical life was effectively reconceptualized, with urban centers replacing courts as focal points, and the tours of virtuosos of varying reputations replacing the hierarchy of courts in defining the periphery. Their very conventionality is evidence of the degree to which this re-visioning has remained a part of our awareness.

The Concert's Participants

Nowhere is the transitional nature of the concert in the early nineteenth century more obvious than in the variety and fluidity with which categories of its participants are discussed. Even apparently straightforward distinctions like that between audience and performer prove uncertain, and both audience and performer are the objects of conflicting claims and definitions. Once again, our Viennese concert provides a useful starting point. Just as it presents an untroubled social order on the largest scale, with the monarch overseeing his cooperating subjects, the ideal of cooperative interaction of all classes also informs the particular arrangements of the concert. Not only do merchants, officials, and members of the nobility receive prominent mention (for "all classes" is here understood to include only the cultivated classes—a fundamental boundary to which I will return), but "artists"—that is, professional musicians—are acknowledged as part of the whole, and it is a professional, the instrument maker and teacher Andreas Streicher, who is singled out as the one person most responsible for the concert's existence. If our report still preserves a distinction between dilettantes and professionals, however, another familiar distinction, that between performers and "public," has little applicability: "friends of art" are found both in the audience and among the performers, and the status of the event is enhanced equally by the high rank of its amateur performers and by the presence of the court in the audience. Little wonder, then, that the audience's approbation was represented as unanimous. The image of cooperative interaction is an image of the recreational activities of the higher classes, aided insofar as necessary by professional musicians of lower standing, who are the sole representatives of the otherwise excluded lower order of society.

As flattering as this ideal of performance was for its participants, it proved difficult to sustain. The public concert of dilettantes was essentially a re-creation of domestic upper-class music making on a larger scale, and that change in scale could easily expose inadequacies of performance that might be overlooked in a salon. Richard Leppert has documented the extent of complaints about gentleman amateur performers in England, and in Vienna the amateur performances of the Gesellschaft der Musikfreunde, the organization that grew from the 1812 Handel concert, came under severe criticism in the decades that followed.[82] If serious music was to validate itself independently of patronage, it would require performances that made that value clear; high art demanded more respectful treatment than was accorded to it when used as amateur recreation: "Art is too noble to be a handicraft of boredom."[83]

All of this amounted to a thorough redefinition of the concept of the dilettante, and one that was recognized at the time; by 1842, August Kahlert could note that concerts had grown out of the expansion of domestic amateur music-making: "These worthy gentlemen played far worse than our paid orchestras do today, but they took sincere pleasure in the matter. Something similar is now found at most in small cities, for the dilettante has moved from the circle of practitioners to that of the critics."[84] Indeed, already near the turn of the century, reports that played up the active role of cultivated dilettantes as the basis of musical life tended to originate in remote areas, and no less an authority than Friedrich Rochlitz, the founding editor of the *Allgemeine musikalische Zeitung,* had written discouragingly of the difficulty of becoming genuinely knowledgeable about music, something few but the true (professional) artist could attain.[85] Like any fashionable activity, music lost prestige according to the extent that it was widely imitated. In 1819 one author, voicing a by-then-common complaint about the superficiality of most dilettantes' knowledge, could scarcely contain his contempt: "Only the very fewest have even the slightest idea that true musical cultivation contributes essentially to the ennoblement of the inward being and is capable of drawing the spirit cleansingly out of everything common; most drag the queen, born to rule and govern on one of the most splendid thrones in the realm of the spiritual, down with their unconsecrated hands into the filth of their own sinful lives, and force her, stripped of her heavenly beauty and made up like a common strumpet, to dance around them and so draw the eyes of the curious rabble upon them."[86]

Even more moderate critics acknowledged that performance by dilettantes demanded "critics who do not judge too harshly," and by 1840 a report on concert life in Berlin could place concerts by a society of dilettantes unhesitatingly among "concerts of the second rank."[87] Despite occasional attempts to uphold the value and necessity of dilettantism, by the 1830s and 1840s the more dominant image combined features of the moralistic disapproval so evident above with narrowness and superficiality. One correspondent, for instance, blamed Stuttgart's "tiresome dilettantism," which had reached "dreadful heights," for audiences' lack of interest in and familiarity with even prominent artists. Eduard Krüger, whose diagnosis of the "cancer of dilettantes" is cited above, gave this warning to artists: "Let him never be a *servant* of the public, for that is vulgarly *[pöbelhaft]* dilettantish and devalues the majesty of the idea in order to serve the realm of flesh and of darkness."[88] That dilettantism could so blithely be associated with the rabble *(Pöbel)* and contrasted to the majesty of ideal art reveals the extent of the devaluation of the noble dilettantism of earlier decades.

Clearly, this process could work to the benefit of professional musicians. Few writers put the matter as baldly as the author of an 1824 report on musical life in Vienna, for whom the abundance of amateur performances had straightforward economic consequences: "One can now hear so much music—and in part very good music—for free in Vienna that few want to spend money for it."[89] If amateur performance were restricted largely to *Hausmusik,* however, professional musicians could be not only public presenters of high art but also teachers of amateur performers and aspiring professionals, a dual role still familiar to performing musicians. The redefinition of dilettantism thus occurred alongside a simultaneous redefinition of the performing musician; the latter is evident in Krüger's determination that the artist not be content to be a servant. No reader at the time would have been unaware of the tradition of musicians in the service of noble families, nor of the facilitating role they played in amateur performances like the Vienna Handel concert. To assert that such service *(Dienst)* was unworthy of the artist was to contribute to a new definition of the professional musician.

Characteristically, those accounts that drew on the old image of musicians as guild-bound, narrow, and uncultivated also upheld the ideal of dilettantism. G. W. Fink, for instance, derided critics of dilettantism as *Zunftgenossen* (guild members), and another author compared the skills of many *Zünftler* unfavorably to those of dilettantes.[90] Once again, the history of music as a craft is linked to low prestige for its practitioners: for musicians to be seen as worthy of an art of inner cultivation required breaking the association of the profession with craft work and other manual labor and forging new links to cultivated society. Reichardt expressed his desire for this reclassification clearly when he pleaded for the founding of "genuine art schools . . . where the young pupil would not only be instructed in his art theoretically and practically, with insight and feeling and taste, but where his heart too would be nobly and grandly developed through genuine religion, enjoyment of nature, history, and the example of noble teachers, his head enlightened through knowledge of nature, the ancients, and the world, and thus high, noble artistic sense would be produced in him—O that I might still see such art schools!"[91]

In a similar vein, a reporter praised the efforts of Wirtemberg's Duke Carl not only for founding a first-rate orchestra with *Landeskinder* (literally, "children of the land," i.e., locals) trained in the school he had established but also for providing those students with broad training and cultivation, with the result that "among them a certain tone of humanity, of moral decency, and a harmony among themselves still remain, so that one is as at ease and comfortable in their social circle as one is in their concert hall."[92] Kahlert acknowledged the significance of these and similar efforts in his later overview, placing it in the context of larger social upheaval: "The older musician, mindful of a certain guild mentality [*Zunftwesen*], out of which all art, especially in Germany, developed, kept more to his own work and efforts than does today's, who demands to have his right to so-called *general* cultivation. Just as all classes and all occupations mingle more and more, the musician too is far more of a man of the world than he was previously."[93] After the revolutions of 1848, August Müller summarized what he called the "emancipation of the reproducing musician" in even loftier terms, citing the ultimate musical authority as the origin of the change. The musician's servitude—at least in the imagined musical order—was unquestionably at an end: "Beethoven, namely, challenged the orchestral musician to be an artist in the true sense of the word, and grants to everyone capable of reproducing well the sublime ideas of this creative spirit a patent for this quality, a patent which, sealed by a divine hand, will be honored throughout the entire artistic world."[94] The substitution of Beethoven for the ennobling monarch is an unmistakable claim for the autonomy of a professional musical world, a claim that would have been unthinkable a half century ealier.

If professional performers gradually made a distinct place for themselves, that development created a corresponding category that existed neither in the world of court ensembles nor that of dilettantism: a musical public, an audience distinct from but vital to the performer. This is not to suggest that awareness of the characteristics of listeners was a new development; on the contrary, documents like a satirical letter in Forkel's *Musikalisch-kritische Bibliothek* of 1778 demonstrate acute sensitivity to the motivation and musicality (or lack of it) of concertgoers. But characteristically, Forkel's satire is directed against an individual, a musically incompetent, social-climbing lout, rather than against a musical public that can be considered collectively.[95] The changing nature of music's audience, however—what one chronicler of eighteenth-century music recognized as the result of increased middle-class access to music, which "would no longer be raised as a hothouse plant but rather set out and divided along with the other fruits for the enjoyment of life"—brought about a corresponding reconceptualization of that audience.[96] Nägeli, for example, still recognized a clear distinction between cultivated listeners and others, but instead of castigating the latter, he proposed providing the distinct concert series I have already mentioned: one of sophisticated (instrumental) music for cultivated listeners and one for popular audiences. Such a plan depended on a collective conception of an audience—what slightly later writers commonly called a public—rather than the collection of individuals of differing qualities that Forkel's satire implies.

Once such a collective entity is conceptualized, it can be ascribed qualities and influence. Often, from the perspective of serious music's advocates, those qualities were negative ones. One of the most common accusations was that audiences were frivolous: "At concerts, nothing more than a pastime and an entertainment is sought. People would call it cheating them out of their good money, and they would be completely against it if the orchestra wanted to go further than that." [97] The public, however, could also be used to pressure performers, as did a correspondent who in 1837 criticized a poor performance of Beethoven's Seventh Symphony by the Braunschweig court orchestra: "Truly, the public is justified in completely overlooking such impure performance; it demands more care for its judgment. Beyond that, it does not pay its money for rehearsals, but rather demands that these be taken care of beforehand." [98] Opposed though these two statements are in their evaluation of the public's judgment, both show an awareness of the basis of its power: money or its absence was the final evidence of public approval or rejection.[99]

Precisely that leveling economic power, however, could make the public a threat, especially to those committed to serious music that was widely recognized to have limited popular appeal. Few went as far as Heinrich Paris in their rejection of the broadening of the public, but his diatribe reveals the class-based anxiety that the transformation of musical life could arouse:

> For everything that is offered to the masses that leaves the *mind* and *spirit empty*, in that it arouses the *senses*, is, in my opinion, always a blow to public morality; and the more that today's leveling of the classes and the ever-growing taste for artificial and artistically performed music bring about the vanishing among the lower classes of the good old, sociable *folksong*, sung from their own throats, as well as of the happy, natural *dance* tunes accompanied by their own delight, but on the contrary increase their half-civilized thronging to the theater, concerts,

and noisy music festivals, all the more do I consider the tumultuous, dizzying, deafening tendency, shifting at every seam—in a word, the *materiality* of today's music—a sign of the time that I do not hesitate for a moment to consider nothing short of a calamity of the time with respect to cultivation of the people and of youth.[100]

Note that what Paris rejects is not popular resistance to concerts and other musical events but rather the *presence* of the lower orders, which signals the end of proper social hierarchy—of the world as envisioned in our Viennese concert report.

If Paris's intolerance is extreme, his connection of issues of the musical public to cultivation is entirely typical; more mainstream views of the artist in relation to the public differ not in seeing concert life as an issue of public cultivation but in their bourgeois optimism that that cultivating project might successfully universalize taste for high art and the values it represented. In this view, publicly supported subscription concerts could act as a kind of museum that would develop the public's taste.[101] And the artist, in the end, finds a more exalted role than ever—not just as a member of the cultivated classes but as its very soul, as Eduard Krüger concludes: "We recognize the people as the body, the unconscious and unknowing sensuality of art-loving humanity, as the innocent congregation in relation to the knowledgeable priest, who gives them a soul. . . . Laity and artists form the integrating moment of the entire life of art; one cannot exist without the other, and may not desire it: each should nourish, refresh, and mutually support the other. In this way, genuine artistic life is engendered and perfected."[102]

Although Krüger's imagery is religious, it also clearly depends on the ideology of cultivation: the priests of music are not holy but rather knowledgeable. If, as Dahlhaus notes, music became religion in the nineteenth century, it was crucial for musicians that that religion be predicated on the mediation of a professionalized priesthood.[103] Not only, then, was cultivation essential both to establishing the limits of high musical culture and to defining the proper content of the concert, but it also proved invaluable to reconceptualizing the relations of the concert as an event: as the privileged possessors of the knowledge necessary to realize that event, musicians could hope to escape the undignified role of popular entertainer to assume a privileged status at the center rather than the margins of cultivated society.

The Concert as Model Interaction

As the concert developed its identity (at least in the ideology of the advocates of serious musical culture) as a site of performance by musicians be-

fore a public from which they were clearly differentiated, the model of interaction of the concert's participants took on new significance as well. In a
broad survey, John Spitzer has drawn attention to the rich variety of metaphors used to describe orchestras from the seventeenth through the twentieth centuries.[104] Although Spitzer suggests an historical succession, with
the dominant metaphor changing from that of orchestra as civil polity or
army (favored in the eighteenth century) to that of orchestra as nature or
machine (both favored in the nineteenth), all of these metaphors—along
with frequent references to the orchestra or other ensemble as a household
or an integrated body—were used in the early nineteenth century for a variety of ends. Sampling some of those metaphors can reveal both their usefulness and their limitations to the advocates of serious music and can
highlight the new authority of the composer and his works as the center of
the center—the final justification and authority for the concert as the focal
point of musical culture.

Discussions of performance as social interaction range from the
straightforward to the extravagant. The author of a brief article from 1841
on the role of an orchestral cellist, for instance, leaves the political implications of symphonic performance largely implicit with this statement:
"Here, the whole works in union; there is only one goal for which all strive,
so that one can properly call the symphony a purely social conversation of
the various instruments among themselves."[105] Nägeli (despite his odd dis-
claimer) makes the political more explicit in a more general parallel of the
social with musical performance:

> In order to organize an art-state, we must, just as in a political one—
> but I am not speaking politically here—have a nobility and a people, a
> nobility as the flowering of the individual, a people as the basis of na-
> tional cultivation. The nobility must always lift itself higher, the people
> make its total power always more powerfully effective. On the other
> hand, a nobility without a people, like a people without nobility, would
> be an ignoble and ineffectual condition of public life.
>   The core of our people are our choristers and orchestral players, the
> representatives of our nobility our solo singers and players.[106]

Nägeli seems blissfully unaware of the tension implicit between a perpetu-
ally self-developing nobility and a people developing its own power, but
August Müller was considerably more careful by 1849: his political metaphor is that of a constitutional monarchy in which the piece is the constitution, musicians are officials, and the kapellmeister is the presiding min-
ister—both monarch and people are conveniently absent.[107] The polity
could thus provide a model for several kinds of regulated interaction for the

common good, a goal made explicit in one of the most extravagant of such metaphors, that by which G. W. Fink sought to explain the symphony: "If we consider then these completely necessary demands for such a work, it follows for tone poetry that every orchestral instrument must be grasped according to its unique type as a distinct individual, each must be allowed its own particular singing and sounding, as if the most perfect freedom of a republican state of high priests reigned, in which each shows himself gladly subject to the idea as to a divine one. In the end the ground of the highest sovereignty, the highest legality, lies in the closest possible union with individual freedom." [108] Fink's high priestly republic not only captures an interactive but freely obedient ideal, but it also sets the priestly elect off from the (unmentioned) commoners, thus effectively bounding the space of performance. This effect may well have been unintentional—Fink, after all, was one of the late defenders of dilettantes—but it reveals how pervasive ideas of the work as a set-apart realm and the concert as a sacred space had become.

Other metaphors highlighted different aspects of performance. Not surprisingly, discipline and order were the most frequent objects of comparison to the military, even if the discomfort with which authors made them is occasionally palpable. By the coming together of the various parts, wrote one, "the greatest, I might even say, military, precision must reign—as much as military arrangements otherwise go against the character of art." [109] The military metaphor could also demand physical control, precision, and dignity from the director, as when another author introduced a caricature of a ludicrously overactive orchestra leader along with the counterimage of a dignified director, who, "conscious of his own power and that of those under his command, stood there something like a field marshal must stand at the front of his army before a battle." [110] In contrast, metaphors of the ensemble as a household or body tended rather to emphasize hierarchy, with metaphors of the household satirically detailing identifications of the different sections with various domestic roles (to the reiteration of traditional domestic virtues and mockery of social blunders) and metaphors of the body noting the interaction of all parts but also the necessary leadership of the head—usually in the person of the director.[111]

Serviceable as all these metaphors could be in highlighting various aspects of orchestral performance, and as suggestive as they are to later readers rediscovering the significance of performance as a model of interaction, their generality limited their usefulness for advocates of the concert as the highest of forms. Most could apply to any competent musical ensemble—even, for instance, that of Johann Strauss: "His orchestra is superbly rehearsed, which is easier because of the narrow scope of their goal: its soul is Strauss, whose spirit rules the bodies of all the participants." As though to underscore the qualification already provided by the mention of the group's limited aspirations, this passage goes on to ensure that what might otherwise have been read as a favorable metaphor ends in low comedy: "That this influence announces itself rather physically may have to do with the physical genre of his people; if his strings were somewhat too weak, we explain this as the result of his having left some violinists at home as too-confirmed gluttons."[112] Cooperative interaction under the direction of a competent leader was not enough: the leader must himself be informed by the highest goals.

Those goals could be ensured only by adherence to the repertorial standards of the serious concert—the musical criteria with which I began. Given the transitional nature of the concert and the traditional linkage of music to power, however, writers also occasionally drew on external authorities, as when Friedrich Rochlitz used the prestige of no less a figure than Frederick the Great to bolster his argument for the necessity of silence unmarred by rehearsing and tuning immediately preceding the opening of a concert.[113] More typical, though, were straightforward appeals to the authority of the work to validate the practice of performers: "Who can deny that the high respect that members of the orchestra have for the scholarly knowledge of their director powerfully electrifies musical performances? Isn't it as if the spirit of the composition shined its rays from the podium over the orchestra?"[114] This more extended example, concerning the Müller quartet in Braunschweig, makes the work's final authority still more explicit: "These incomparable four have—as soon as it has to do with their quartet—only *one soul,* like conspirators. That such a harmony can be achieved more easily [by a quartet] than a similar one in symphonies, where, as it were, a whole people arises to realize a great idea (theme), does not demean the excellence of the Müller quartet; the reproducing artist has satisfied all conditions as soon as he has learned how to set himself in harmony [literally, unison—*Einklang*] with the artwork *lying before him.*"[115]

Ultimately, a personal authority lay behind the work as well, the ultimate replacement for the monarch of Rochlitz's anecdote or the emperor of the Viennese concert. That person is, of course, the composer, most often not physically present at the concert but its proper focus, nonetheless; as Suzanne Cusick has stated in a reflection on the classical performance in the present, through the performer one seeks to achieve "a vicarious intimacy with the dead [composer's] thoughts."[116] In our period, writers were less apt to assume that the authoritative composer need necessarily be dead (although in practice he often was, and the retrospective quality of the canon was increasingly established during this period), but they did not hesitate to use the figure of the recognized master composer to bound the limits of proper performance. Nägeli, for instance, in a passage replete with imagery of emasculation, characterizes impoverished virtuosity (the bad individualism that countered the good of individual compositional creativity) as neglecting the authoritative composers; typical virtuosos are

> sweet little things, who melt away even more than their tones; weak-lings, who can't even stand upright, and who have as little rhythm and poise in their bodies as in their playing. And what sort of music do they usually produce in the halls that otherwise resound with the master-works of *Haydn* and *Mozart?* Concertos, by themselves; variations, also by themselves; divertissements, entertaining, also by themselves; even concertante pieces, may Heaven have mercy, also by themselves: everything, naturally, with a claim for great applause, which does not elude them either, if they perform even so miserable a composition prettily or brilliantly. . . . Note well that precisely the better artists play their own work more rarely, and all the more often the works of great masters.[117]

More positively, the purpose of the body assembled from diverse parts, of the militarily precise ensemble, is often explicitly to serve the composer (a purpose that may seem self-evident to us but, like much in our concert culture, is so precisely because of the developments under discussion). The closing out of alternative functions for the performer is particularly evident in a discussion of choral performance from 1847, in which the absence of performance indications from earlier music is attributed not to the existence of a variety of options for realization, nor to conventions or collaboration, but to a still higher expectation on the part of the creative genius: "The composers said: 'Understand and feel my work and an attractive performance will come of its own accord.'"[118]

The preeminent model for such a compositional authority, both during and after his life, was of course Beethoven. Lydia Goehr's identification of the post-1800 concept of the composer as "the Beethoven paradigm" is particularly apt in this context—recall that, according to August Müller, Beethoven himself had issued the patent freeing the performer to be a genuine artist. But the privilege could prove an ambivalent one, as a summary of Viennese concert life in 1824 suggests. The otherwise thoroughly conventional report, which details the activities of the city's various performances and musical establishments with relatively evenhanded attention to performers and composers, concludes with a description that not only attests to the lionizing of Beethoven during his life but also reveals that the same power that could bestow artistry on performers could also thoroughly eclipse them, leading to what Cusick calls "a ritual of disappearing Selves":[119]

> The current musical winter season could not have been closed more worthily and brilliantly than by a great musical academy in which the greatest genius of our times demonstrated that the true artist knows no stagnation. Forward, upward, is his watchword, his cry of victory. *Beethoven* offered a grand overture, three hymns from his new mass, and his new symphony, whose last piece ends with a chorus on Schiller's lied, "An die Freude." One can say nothing more than what the connoisseurs recognized and unanimously declared: *Beethoven* has outdone everything we have previously had from him; *Beethoven* has advanced still further onward!!
>
> These new artworks appear as the colossal products of a son of the gods, who has just brought the holy, life-giving flame directly from heaven.[120]

And yet this disappearance could serve the interests of both the advocates of high culture, for whom the quasi-divine authority of the genius could provide the apex of a hierarchy that claimed universal validity and required thorough cultivation to ascend, and the professional musicians—and not just composers, for performances of less than professional quality would not be sufficiently transparent to allow the necessary focus on the work and the genius who created it.

As a final counterpart to the relationships evoked in our Viennese report, then, consider those in this equally idealized account from twenty-five years later, written as a standard against which to judge the (considerably less ideal) accomplishments of the Braunschweig orchestra:

> The first duty of an orchestra is clearly to consider itself as a strongly articulated, united whole. Here no member has significance for itself alone. It is the duty of every one to offer up his peculiarities insofar as they do not relate to the greater whole. This demands an agreement about the performance of significant instrumental works, be it through the dominating agency of an outstanding director or through a collective agreement of individuals. In any case, nothing purely technical may be left to chance. If this is properly attended to—moreover with great diligence—it is possible that the masses will appear enlivened by *one* spirit. Then occur such unbelievable successes as those that have recently been achieved in the performance of symphonies, and especially *Beethoven's*. So the cities of *Paris*, *Vienna*, *Berlin*, and *Leipzig* have distinguished themselves before others through good perfor-

mances of great instrumental pieces. The author had the occasion to experience that splendid success in one of these cities. What inspiring energy was in the orchestra, in the public! A mutual encounter on behalf of a powerful genius brought the most magnificent to light. As the stone sprays sparks when steel touches it, so the fire of inspiration sprang from these tightly packed, listening masses. Imagine a public that prepares itself as if for worship in order to grasp the gigantic structure of a Beethoven symphony. It was completely so during the performance. Here, a barely repressed cry of the highest wonderment and joy, or of terror, when Beethoven in his demonic way makes night of day or day of night in the quickest transitions. There experts, with score in hand, making a sign at this or that when it seizes them as with ghostly arms. And no disruption of any sort, everywhere like-minded ones, brothers in the best sense of the word. That was brought about by an orchestra attentive with its whole soul, from its oldest to its youngest member. The author saw—as in the fourth movement of Beethoven's C-Minor Symphony, when a violin passage traveled down from the highest to the lowest like a tear—the gentlemen of the *Capelle* enter into a community with the public, so that they exchanged glances, forgetting all customary form.[121]

Here, the setting is not a court but an urban center, the metaphor of organic performance is explicitly in service of a work of genius, and the boundary between professional orchestra and listening public is securely drawn.[122] Note, however, that after Beethoven himself becomes an acting subject, making night of day and day of night, a new union of audience and performers appears, a union that depends on the previous separation, which allows the professional dedication of the performers and the worshipful preparation of the public. The union of humanity that Marx heard in Beethoven's Ninth seems here to be realized—if one forgets, as the author's rhetoric urges the reader to do, that the public is, here, no more the whole of society than it had been for the Vienna Handel concert. The failure of the Braunschweig orchestra and public to achieve these standards attests to the gap between ideal and experience, but the ideal of the concert essentially as we have inherited it shows itself to be fully formed, the imagined pinnacle of a cultural hierarchy, offering a spirit in whose image its advocates sought to shape a worthy society. If we can read in such accounts their genuine enthusiasm and commitment while remaining aware of both the professional interests that they served and the exclusions on which the culture they advocated was predicated, then we may find ourselves better prepared to appreciate both the achievements and the limitations of that culture.

Afterword

Nearly a century after the end of the period I have discussed, Theodor Adorno wrote a blistering condemnation of one of his era's most prominent attempts to popularize classical music, the *NBC Music Appreciation Hour*. One of that essay's most revealing passages characterizes the experiences that, Adorno claimed, could genuinely lead one to appreciate music, something he insisted the radio program could never do: "A person who is in a real life relation with music does not like music because as a child he liked to see a flute, then later because music imitated a thunderstorm, and finally because he learned to listen to music as music, but . . . [rather] the deciding childhood experiences of music are much more like a shock. More prototypical as stimulus is the experience of a child who lies awake in his bed while a string quartet plays in an adjoining room, and who is suddenly so overwhelmed by the excitement of the music that he forgets to sleep and listens breathlessly."[1] It is difficult to read Adorno's prototypical stimulus as anything other than a perhaps idealized autobiographical account of his own awakening to the power of music, a power that became a central fascination of his career.

If an acquaintance with Adorno's published work already lends credence to this interpretation, it becomes nearly inescapable if one considers as well his posthumously edited notes on Beethoven, published in English translation as *Beethoven: The Philosophy of Music*.[2] To an even greater extent than Adorno's finished works, these sketches and aphorisms reveal a critic whose thought was fundamentally shaped by engagement with the culture of German art music, and they demonstrate that Adorno's grounding in that music was not only complete but also the product of immersion in it from birth. Several fragments (placed by their editor at the opening of the collection) reflect on his musical experiences in childhood, including his terse reminder to "reconstruct how I heard Beethoven as a child";[3] and both the familiarity with which Adorno traverses the German classical repertoire and the confident ease with which he presents his hearings of music as self-evidently valid can be ascribed in part to this early and continuing experience. In Bourdieu's terms, Adorno represents a clear example of a subject born to a culture, one whose knowledge is "produced by early, domestic, 'practical' acquaintance" that leads to a form of mastery that scholastic knowledge can supplement, but for which it cannot provide a substitute.[4] Despite the suspicion with which academic musicologists have long viewed Adorno—perhaps precisely because his pronouncements claimed an intangible social authority that academic pedigree could not equal—he embodies to an unusual degree what Jonathan Stock has recently and perceptively identified as the basis of traditional musicological authority: the "personal authority" of "a musical expert within the culture."[5] And the highest ambition of the fragments on Beethoven reveals Adorno's conviction that the pinnacle of his musical culture was effectively the summit of human achievement; he hoped to demonstrate that "Beethoven's music is Hegelian philosophy: but at the same time it is truer than that philosophy."[6]

There is of course another side to Adorno's immersion in German art music, one apparent in the elitist dismissal of anything that, like the *Music Appreciation Hour,* smacked of pandering to uncultivated taste. This side of Adorno is all too familiar to students of popular music, for whom his name is virtually synonymous with intolerance for jazz and popular song as well as for their audiences. He could see that unfamiliar musical culture only as a world of "standardized products, hopelessly like one another except for conspicuous bits such as hit lines," songs to which "concentrated listening" was impossible, and listeners who were in any event incapable of such an effort; they "surrender themselves resignedly to what befalls them, with which they can come to terms only if they do not listen to it too closely."[7] Such attacks were a central component of Adorno's critique of mass culture, and their extraordinary vehemence suggests that what lay outside his musical world not only appeared deficient by its standards but also seemed to threaten its very existence; only such a danger could provoke so sustained and visceral a response.[8] But yet, only by contrast with its negation in the realm of mass music could the world of authentic music and concentrated listening be defined.

The dialectic subtleties and pervasive despair of Adorno's writings are indeed remote from the style and tone of the German musical discourse that predates him by a century and more. But I hope that it is by now clear that the two sides of Adorno that I have just sketched reproduce a tension that also pervaded that discourse: between a conviction that music expresses—or should express—something of vital importance to everyone, and thus has genuinely universal significance, on the one hand, and, on the other, a form of advocacy of musical culture that limits that culture and makes clear that only a select few are capable of appreciating and benefiting from its significance. Adorno's insistence on the supreme and unique achievement of Beethoven, the paradigmatic great composer; his naturalized familiarity with the German canon and its interpretation; and even his conviction of the tainted inferiority of the music and the listening habits that lay outside that culture's most accomplished representatives mark him as a product of the cultivating project I have described.[9] In that respect, Adorno's lifework embodies the triumph of that project—the ultimate example of a reflective and cultivated life in which music was a vital element—while his anguished awareness that that music was also inevitably the cultural property of a limited and privileged group, and even his infamous intolerance itself, serve as reminders of the exclusions on which that culture is predicated.

But Adorno's relevance to this study lies not only in his relationship to the culture that has been its focus but also in what Rose Subotnick aptly termed his attempt "to remove music from its technical isolation and reintegrate it into a totality of human relationships."[10] This aspect of Adorno's work has brought him renewed attention as musicology in recent decades has examined the social aspects of music with unprecedented vigor. My own work and that of many others has benefited from the encounter with his. And yet Adorno's descent from the culture of serious music has not proven unproblematic in this respect, either. From the culture of the concert and the great composer, he inherited a pervasive habit of locating the significance of music first and foremost within individual works of music and through the focused experience of apprehending the musical whole; his work—like many recent rehearings of the canonic repertoire—is unthinkable without the implicit privileging of the perspective of the cultivated listener.[11]

In making this observation, I by no means want to suggest that a focus on the meaning of individual works is in some way invalid or replaceable, and even less that the project of interrogating the structure and affective impact of works of music in light of social relations and ideological systems is misguided; indeed, that project has accounted for some of the most intriguing and challenging music studies to appear from the time of Adorno to the present. I am convinced, however, that it also represents a continuing and often unrecognized inheritance of the very culture that produced many of those works, and that we ignore that heritage at our scholarly peril.

A single example of recent scholarship must suffice to support this point. Lydia Goehr's *Imaginary Museum of Musical Works* has drawn together an impressive body of materials to demonstrate that around 1800 a fundamental change in the focus of the aesthetics of music brought about just the single-minded focus I have been discussing: "All references to occasion, activity, function, or effect were subordinated to references to the product—the musical work itself." [12] I have discussed at some length some of the ideals and interests that motivated this change, and Goehr provides a thorough examination of its aesthetic implications. But even in Goehr's account, it proves surprisingly difficult to keep in view the human social relations that constituted those activities, functions, and effects. On the very page from which I have drawn her summary statement, she notes that one of the developments associated with the emergence of a concept of fine art is the distinction between art and craft: that is, works with aesthetic value and those with practical usefulness. These product-oriented definitions accurately portray the relevant development in aesthetics, but they omit to note an important relational element: as we have seen repeatedly, craft— *Handwerk*, literally handiwork, the product of *Handwerker*—is a socially loaded term, closely associated with the petit bourgeois craftsperson rather than the ascendant cultivated middle class to whom the more prestigious concept of "art" is linked.[13] In privileging—even momentarily—the aesthetic, the social distinctions on which it is built vanish all too easily.

This is not to criticize Goehr nor to denigrate her remarkable work, but simply to point out that the habit of overlooking the social relations of musical production is so naturalized that it pervades the field of music scholarship. Because the cultivated and reflective listener is firmly established as the focus of the scholarly tradition, the hierarchical social implications of even so heavily freighted an opposition as that between *Kunst* and *Handwerk* simply do not arise. The problem is not willful disregard but rather a failure to perceive that the social situation of scholarship has so nearly duplicated that of the culture of classical music that the very issue of social position has seemed uninteresting. The result has been yet another duplication: like the authors I have discussed, musicology has, in effect, assumed the universal validity of central practices of the musical culture in which it originated.

In examining the ideology of that culture, I have sought to contribute to a growing body of work that seeks alternatives to the conventional practices of musicology not by reading musical works in a social context but rather by broadening our consideration of musical practices. As long as the study of works remains synonymous with the study of music, the price we will pay is the obscuring of the myriad other relationships and activities that make possible the existence of a distinct musical culture in a complex, stratified, and internally conflicted society. If music is indeed the meaningful cultural practice that many of us claim it to be, that meaning is constituted not only by the encounter of the cultivated, critical listener with the work but also by the entire network of relations that bring the privileged moment of critical listening into existence and ensure its privileged status. Exploring those relations will not mean that the academic study of music is no longer an activity of the socially privileged, but it may strengthen our awareness of the tensions and interests inherent in that activity.

Notes

CHAPTER 1. INTRODUCTION

1. Franz Grillparzer, *Selbstbiographie*, edited by Arno Dusini (1853; reprint, Salzburg: Residenz Verlag, 1994), 49:

> In meiner damaligen trüben Stimmung fühlte ich wohl das Bedürfniß einer Ableitung nach Außen. Die Poesie lag mir zur Zeit ziemlich fern, wäre auch mit ihren scharf ausgeprägten Gedanken ein wenig geeigneter Ausdruck für meine in die Zukunft greifenden unbestimmten Empfindungen gewesen. Ich verfiel auf die Musik. Das Klavier ward geöffnet, aber ich hatte alles vergessen, selbst die Noten waren mir fremd geworden. Da kam mir nun zu statten, daß mein erster Klaviermeister Gallus, als er mich in halb kindischer Tändelei bezifferten Baß spielen ließ, mir eine Kenntniß der Grundakkorde beigebracht hatte. Ich ergötzte mich an dem Zusammenklang der Töne, die Akkorde lösten sich in Bewegungen auf und diese bildeten sich zu einfachen Melodien. Ich gab den Noten den Abschied und spielte aus dem Kopfe. Nach und nach erlangte ich darin eine solche Fertigkeit, daß ich Stundenlang phantasiren konnte.

Unless otherwise noted, all translations of German texts are my own.

2. See Mary Sue Morrow, *German Music Criticism in the Late Eighteenth Century: Aesthetic Issues in Instrumental Music* (Cambridge: Cambridge University Press, 1997), 4–13.

3. See William Weber, "The Contemporaneity of Eighteenth-Century Musical Taste," *Musical Quarterly* 68 (1984): 175–94.

4. For a succinct discussion of the ideal of *Bildung* in relation to bourgeois identity in Germany, see Wolfgang Kaschuba, "Deutsche Bürgerlichkeit nach 1800: Kultur als symbolische Praxis," in *Bürgertum im 19. Jahrhundert: Deutschland im europäischen Vergleich*, edited by Jürgen Kocka, with Ute Frevert (Munich: Deutscher Taschenbuch Verlag, 1988), 3:9–44, esp. 29–34. For

a more general study in English, see Walter Horace Bruford, *The German Tradition of Self-Cultivation: Bildung from Humboldt to Thomas Mann* (London: Cambridge University Press, 1975).

5. Ernst Theodor Amadeus Hoffmann, review of Symphony No. 5, by Ludwig van Beethoven, translated by F. John Adams Jr., in *Symphony No. 5 in C Minor*, by Ludwig van Beethoven, Norton Critical Scores, edited by Elliot Forbes (New York: Norton, 1971), 151. Hoffmann's review first appeared in the *Allgemeine musikalische Zeitung* 12 (1810): 630–42 and 652–59. I have substituted "world of the senses" for the translation's "external material world" in order to express more precisely the original "Sinnenwelt."

6. See Sanna Pederson, "Enlightened and Romantic German Music Criticism, 1800–1850" (Ph.D. dissertation, University of Pennsylvania, 1995).

7. Johann Friedrich Reichardt, "An großgute Regenten," *Musikalisches Kunstmagazin* 1 (1782): v:

> Es bedarf keine Kunst so sehr die Unterstützung der Regenten um großgutes zu wirken, als die Tonkunst. Der Mahler kann in seiner einsamen Kammer das höchste Werk der Kunst darstellen, und darfs denn nur aussetzen, um alle Welt zu entzücken; eben so der Bildhauer, er selbst und sein Marmorblock, sind ihm genug zu seinen herrlichsten Schöpfungen; der Baumeister findet in hundert bürgerlichen Bedürfnissen und Veranlassungen seinen Wirkungskreis. Der Tonkünstler aber, soll er mehr als Freude angenehmen Kitzel wirken, soll er mit der ganzen Allgewalt seiner Kunst, die die ganze fühlende Natur mit unwiderstehlicher Macht hinreißt, und zum Himmel erhebt, auf ganze Völker wirken, so muß der Regent ihm erst die großen Veranlassungen und all die Werkzeuge die er bedarf liefern, ihm zweckmäßige Gebäude, ächte Sänger und kunstsinnige und kunstliebende Spieler aller wirkenden musikalischen Instrumente, und die Instrumente selbst liefern.

8. For a succinct summary of this transformation, see Celia Applegate, "How German Is It? Nationalism and the Idea of Serious Music in the Early Nineteenth Century," *Nineteenth Century Music* 21 (1998): 274–96, esp. 281–87.

9. For studies of music criticism, see Robin Wallace, *Beethoven's Critics: Aesthetic Dilemmas and Resolutions during the Composer's Lifetime* (Cambridge: Cambridge University Press, 1986); Pederson, "Enlightened and Romantic German Music Criticism"; and Mary Sue Morrow, *German Music Criticism in the Late Eighteenth Century*. Pederson's study, however, takes a broader institutional perspective and, therefore, does consider a broader than usual variety of documents.

10. See William Weber, "Wagner, Wagnerism, and Musical Idealism," in *Wagnerism in European Culture and Politics*, edited by David C. Large and William Weber, in collaboration with Anne Dzamba Sessa (Ithaca: Cornell University Press, 1984), 28–71, esp. 28–40; and Mark Evan Bonds, "Idealism and Aesthetics of Instrumental Music at the Turn of the Nineteenth Century," *Journal of the American Musicological Society* 50 (1997): 387–420.

11. Weber, "L'Institution et son public: L'Opera à Paris et à Londres au XVIIIe siècle," *Annales: Économies, Sociétés, Civilisations* 48 (1993): 1519–39.

12. Pederson, "Enlightened and Romantic German Music Criticism," 62. For a more detailed consideration of the public sphere and its historiographic legacy, see Anthony J. La Vopa, "Conceiving a Public: Ideas and Society in Eighteenth-Century Europe," *Journal of Modern History* 64 (1992): 79–116.

13. Pederson, "Enlightened and Romantic German Music Criticism," 54.

14. On the character of the Enlightenment in German-speaking Europe, see Paul Raabe and Wilhelm Schmidt-Biggemann, eds., *Enlightenment in Germany* (Bonn: Hohwacht, 1979); and Samuel S. B. Taylor, "The Enlightenment in Switzerland," Joachim Whaley, "The Protestant Enlightenment in Germany," T. C. W. Blanning, "The Enlightenment in Catholic Germany," and Ernst Wangermann, "Reform Catholicism and Political Radicalism in the Austrian Enlightenment," all in *The Enlightenment in National Context*, edited by Róy Porter and Mikuláš Teich (Cambridge: Cambridge University Press, 1981), 72–89, 106–17, 118–26, and 127–40, respectively.

15. From a review of *Ueber die Musik der Indier: Eine Abhandlung*, by William Jones, translated and annotated by F. H. von Dalberg, *Allgemeine musikalische Zeitung* 5 (1803): 283: "von eigentlicher Aufklärung noch entfernt sind"; and 293: "wir Deutsche, die wir mit recht auf den Vorzug, die Musik zu einem höhern Range erhoben zu haben, stolz seyn müssen."

16. This argument is developed, for instance, in Gerhard Kaiser, "The Middle Class as the Agency of Culture," in *Enlightenment in Germany*, edited by Paul Raabe and Wilhelm Schmidt-Biggemann (Bonn: Hohwacht, 1979), 62–78.

17. See, for example, Karin Hausen, "Family and Role-Division: The Polarization of Sexual Stereotypes in the Nineteenth Century: An Aspect of the Dissociation of Work and Family Life," in *The German Family: Essays on the Social History of the Family in Nineteenth- and Twentieth-Century Germany*, edited by Richard J. Evans and W. R. Lee (London: Croom Helm, 1981), 51–83, esp. 57–58 and 68.

18. See Whaley, "The Protestant Enlightenment in Germany"; Rudolf Vierhaus, "The Historical Interpretation of the Enlightenment: Problems and Viewpoints," in *Enlightenment in Germany*, edited by Paul Raabe and Wilhelm Schmidt-Biggemann (Bonn: Hohwacht, 1979), 23–36, esp. 27–29; and, for individual case studies, Hanno Schmitt, "Philanthropismus und Volksaufklärung im Herzogtum Braunschweig-Wolfenbüttel in der zweiten Hälfte des 18. Jahrhunderts," in *Das Volk als Objekt obrigkeitlichen Handelns*, edited by Rudolf Vierhaus, Wolfenbütteler Studien zur Aufklärung 13: Kultur und Gesellschaft in Nordwestdeutschland zur Zeit der Aufklärung I (Tübingen: Max Niemeyer, 1992), 171–95; and Ernst Wangermann, *Aufklärung und staatsbürgerliche Erziehung: Gottfried van Swieten als Reformator des österreichischen Unterrichtswesens, 1781–1791* (Munich: Oldenbourg, 1978).

19. Just how widespread and long-lived is suggested in the comprehensive

bibliography by Holger Böning and Reinhart Siegert, *Volksaufklärung: Bibliographisches Handbuch zur Popularisierung aufklärerischer Denkens im deutschen Sprachraum von den Anfängen bis 1850,* volume 1 (Stuttgart: Holzboog, 1990).

20. La Vopa, "Conceiving a Public," 89.

21. Whaley, "The Protestant Enlightenment in Germany," 117.

22. On the limits of educational reform, especially in Germany, see ibid., 108–9; Gerhard Sauder, "'Verhältnismäßige Aufklärung': Zur bürgerlichen Ideologie am Ende des 18. Jahrhunderts," *Jahrbuch der Jean-Paul-Gesellschaft* 9 (1974): 102–26; and W. Daniel Wilson, "Enlightenment's Alliance with Power: The Dialectic of Collusion and Opposition in the Literary Elite," in *Impure Reason: Dialectic of Enlightenment in Germany,* edited by Wilson and Robert C. Holub (Detroit: Wayne State University Press, 1993), 364–84.

23. Petiscus, "Ueber musikalische Lehrbücher und die neuesten unter denselben," *Allgemeine musikalische Zeitung* 10 (1807): 163: "Wir können sagen, dass gute musikalische Lehrbücher zu den Vorzügen unserer Zeit gehören. Noch vor einem halben Jahrhundert waren diese Lehrbücher eben so selten, als unvollkommen."

24. Ibid., 165: "ohne Hülfe des Lehrers, gar nichts."

25. On courts as employers of musicians, see Richard Petzoldt, "The Economic Conditions of the 18th-Century Musician," and Christoph-Hellmut Mahling, "The Origin and Social Status of the Court Orchestral Musician in the 18th and Early 19th Century in Germany," both in *The Social Status of the Professional Musician from the Middle Ages to the 19th Century,* edited by Walter Salmen, annotated and translated by Herbert Kaufman and Barbara Reisner, Sociology of Music 1 (New York: Pendragon, 1983), 158–88 and 219–64; on the changing but still significant role of noble patronage, see Mary Sue Morrow, *Concert Life in Haydn's Vienna: Aspects of a Developing Musical and Social Institution* (New York: Pendragon, 1989); and Tia DeNora, *Beethoven and the Construction of Genius: Musical Politics in Vienna, 1792–1803* (Berkeley and Los Angeles: University of California Press, 1995), 37–59.

26. "Bemerkungen aus dem Tagebuche eines praktischen Tonkünstlers," *Allgemeine musikalische Zeitung* 8 (1806): 705: "Kein Künstler ist, nach den gegenwärtigen Verhältnissen, mehr genöthigt unter und mit Menschen aller Art aus den vornehmen und reichen Ständen zu leben, als der Musiker—vornämlich der praktische, der Virtuos; und keiner passt in der Regel weniger dahin, als er. Sehr selten geniesst er in frühen Jahren einer Erziehung für die feinere Welt: und was für diese nicht in frühen Jahren wenigstens angelegt und zugeschnitten worden, wird schwerlich in spätern zur Genüge nachgeholt."

27. On the precise ranking of musicians' precedence in court households, see Petzoldt, "Economic Conditions," 164–65.

28. "Bemerkungen aus dem Tagebuche," 721: "Unter fünfzig Vornehmen und Reichen, die den Künstler manchmal gern hören und um sich haben mögen, habe ich kaum fünf gefunden, die die Kunst von Herzen *liebten,* aber kaum

Einen, der sie wirklich *hochachtete*—so viel schöne Worte Manche auch darüber zu machen wussten."

29. Ibid., 724–25:

> Jedermann die Achtung, Höflichkeit und Gefälligkeit, die ihm, auch schon seiner blossen Verhältnisse und bürgerlichen Lage nach, gebührt! Ist er aber so schwach, *sich selbst* von diesen Verhältnissen zu trennen, auf sie zu pochen, gegen sie dich demüthig sehen zu wollen: so thue das *nicht*—du verlierst sonst allemal, selbst in seinen Augen; sondern setze der Arroganz ein männliches, aber bescheidenes Geständnis deiner Freyheit von künstlichen Bedürfnissen entgegen! Glaube mir: sie, die mitten in Fülle und Ueberfluss noch immerfort klagen und bedürfen, haben in geheim dagegen Respekt, und wenn du die *Art* triffst, wie so etwas zu äussern ist, so kannst du schon darum mit ihnen *ausführen,* was ein Anderer *anzufangen* nicht wagen dürfte. Diese rechte Art aber ist: *männlich*—bestimmt, ohne Hochmuth, bescheiden, ohne Unterwerfung!

30. On the distinction between the tactics of those in socially inferior positions and the strategies of those with institutionalized power, see Michel de Certeau, *The Practice of Everyday Life,* translated by Steven F. Randall (Berkeley and Los Angeles: University of California Press, 1984).

31. For studies that take essentially this view, see Eberhard Preußner, *Die bürgerliche Musikkultur: Ein Beitrag zur deutschen Musikgeschichte des 18. Jahrhunderts,* 2nd edition (Kassel: Bärenreiter, 1950); János Maróthy, *Music and the Bourgeois, Music and the Proletarian,* translated by Eva Róna (Budapest: Akadêmiai Kiadó, 1974); and Lutz Neitzert, *Die Geburt der Moderne, der Bürger und die Tonkunst: Zur Physiognomie der ver-öffentlichten Musik* (Stuttgart: Franz Steiner Verlag, 1990).

32. On the difficulties of patronage relations, see Petzoldt, "Economic Conditions," 166–75 and 178–83.

33. From Fink's article on Forkel in *Encyclopädie der gesammten musikalischen Wissenschaften, oder Universal-Lexicon der Tonkunst,* edited by Gustav Schilling (Stuttgart: Franz Heinrich Köhler, 1836), 3:9: "die Vielen, deren es zu allen Zeiten gab, welche von der Verfassung der Tonkunst ihrer Zeit einen gänzlichen Verfall besorgen." Forkel's article is discussed below, in chapter 5.

34. Johann Samuel Petri, *Anleitung zur praktischen Musik* (Leipzig: Johann Gottlob Immanuel Breitkopf, 1782), 196: "Vielen jungen Leuten wird ohnehin die tiefere und gründlichere Erlernung der Musik verleidet und widerrathen. Man sagt ihnen, der Mensch könne nur in einer Sache es zu einiger Höhe bringen, daher sey alles alle Zerstreuung, so bald man es zu sehr treibe, und die Hauptsache der jungen Leute seyen doch andre Studien, als die Musik. Man sehe ja, daß wenige *Chorales* was rechtschaffenes gelernt hätten.—Aber man sage mir doch, ob sie wirklich *Genies* waren, und ohne Musik zu lernen große Gelehrte geworden wären?—Die meisten bringen es ja auch selbst in der Musik nicht gar zu weit."

35. On English attitudes, see Richard Leppert, *Music and Image: Domesticity, Ideology, and Socio-Cultural Formation in Eighteenth-Century England* (Cambridge: Cambridge University Press, 1988); and David Gramit, "Constructing a Victorian Schubert: Music, Biography, and Cultural Values," *Nineteenth-Century Music* 17 (1993): 68.

36. The fate of school choirs long remained a contentious matter. See, for example, [Carl Gottlob] Horstig, "Vorschläge zu besserer Einrichtung der Singschulen in Deutschland," *Allgemeine musikalische Zeitung* 1 (1798): 166–74, 183–89, 197–201, and 214–20; Klein, "Vorschläge zur Verbesserung der gewöhnlichen Singschulen in Deutschland," *Allgemeine musikalische Zeitung* 1 (1798): 465–71; and K. W. Frantz, "Singechöre, eine nützliche Anstalt," *Allgemeine musikalische Zeitung* 4 (1802): 673–79. On the background to this controversy, see John Butt, *Music Education and the Art of Performance in the German Baroque* (Cambridge: Cambridge University Press, 1994), 166–92.

37. J. C. F. GutsMuths, "Wollen alle Deutschen Musikanten werden?" *Bibliothek der pädagogischen Literatur* (November 1804): 295–99.

38. Ibid., 295: "Eine ganz eigen, bey keiner einzigen ausländischen Nation, so viel mir bekannt ist, sich wiederfindende Erscheinung, eine wahre, immer mehr um sich greifende Modesucht ist es, daß alle Kinder und jungen Leute nicht bloß der gebildetern Volksklassen sondern selbst der Bürger in den Städten Musik lernen sollen."

39. Ibid., 297: "die Katzen ihres Gleichen wittern."

40. Ibid., 298: "Ich glaube, die deutsche Pädagogik sey so weit gekommen, daß sie von Zeitvertreiben nie mehr zu reden brauche."

41. Christian Friedrich Michaelis, "Ueber einen Aufsatz mit der Ueberschrift: Wollen alle Deutsche Musikanten werden? (in der Bibliothek der pädagog. Literatur, herausgegeben von Guthsmuths [*sic*], November 1804)," *Allgemeine musikalische Zeitung* 7 (1805): 229–37.

42. Ibid., 230–31:

> Denn man unterscheidet, nach gegenwärtigem Sprachgebrauch, den *Musikus* vom *Musikanten* ungefähr so, wie den Schauspieler vom Komödianten. Jener übt die Musik als edle freye Kunst, die sich selbst belohnt, wenigstens nicht nach Brot gehen mag, sich nicht zur Lohnkunst herabwürdiget, ob sie zwar für den Künstler, weil und sofern er, wie jeder Andre, Lebensbedürfnisse hat und seiner Kunst manchen Aufwand opfern muss, belohnende Aufmunterungen nicht verschmäht. Der Musikant hingegen behandelt die Kunst blos als Erwerbzweig, bequemt sich daher ganz nach den willkührlichen Forderungen seines jedesmaligen, oft sehr geschmacklosen Publikums, und nimmt auch mit den kleinsten Gaben fürlieb. Der Musikus hingegen wird entweder anständig besoldet, oder er überlässt es edler Freygebigkeit der Kunstfreunde, durch Belohnungen ihm die Achtung für seine Kunst aufmunternd zu erkennen zu geben; oft lebt er unabhängig als privatisirender Künstler. Entfernt, seine Kunst nach den Einfallen der Zuhörer zu bequemen, oder mit ihr

den Leidenschaften und Bedürfnissen selbst des Pöbels zu fröhnen, will er vielmehr den Geschmack des Publikums immer mehr für seine Kunst bilden, es zur Höhe derselben emporheben. Er strebt nach der Kenner Beyfall und ist stolz auf denselben; lieber wählt er sich eine kleine Zahl ächter Verehrer, anstatt nach dem Zuklatschen des gemeinen grossen Haufens zu jagen. Der Musikant aber ist im Grunde blosser Handwerksmann, der nach Bestellung arbeitet, und auch von Künstlerlaunen frey genug ist, um für Lohn nach jedes Belieben aufzuspielen. Indess hat der Musikant, wenn er wahre Kunstfertigkeit und ein reiches musikalisches Gedächtniss besitzt, und selbst die Lieblingsstücke des Volks mit einigem Geschmack zu behandeln, vorzüglich aber mit Sinn und Auswahl die bessern Stücke und Gesänge zu verbreiten weiss, seinen guten Werth. Der verachtete, unbekannte Musikant kann sich oft durch Talent dem Virtuosen nähern, und durch Anspruchslosigkeit und Gefälligkeit grosse Vorzüge vor ihm behaupten. Die niedern Klassen des Volks wollen auch erheitert seyn, und bedürfen der Erheiterung bisweilen noch mehr, als die höheren Stände.

43. Engelmann, "Musik als Erziehungsmittel," *Allgemeine musikalische Zeitung* 7 (1805): 635: "Ueberhaupt—was mir, als Erzieher, am wichtigsten schien, war in allen diesen Aufsätzen gar nicht, oder nur flüchtig berührt. Musik nämlich, ist, nach meiner Ueberzeugung, nicht bloss für die Jugend zu empfehlen als Mittel zur Geschmacksbildung, als edle Unterhaltung etc. unendlich wichtiger ist sie (ist vorzüglich der Gesang) als das trefflichste Erziehungsmittel, um das Gemüth rein und edel zu stimmen, um die Liebe zum Guten und Schönen überhaupt, zur Tugend und Religion, tief und innig mit unserm Wesen zu verflechten, so dass sie ewig unzertrennlich bleiben."

Engelmann refers to GutsMuths's article, Michaelis's reply, and Michaelis's "Einige Gedanken über die Vortheile der frühen musikalischen Bildung," discussed in chapter 4, below.

44. "In wie fern kann die Erlernung der Musik etwas zur sittlichen und gelehrten Erziehung beitragen?" *Wiener allgemeine musikalische Zeitung*, no. 1 (1813): 359: "Die neuere Musik ist weit reicher an Melodien, unsere Instrumente sind weit vollkommener und des guten Vortrags und Ausdrucks fähiger, die Harmonie, ein beträchtlicher Theil der Tonkunst ist noch dazu gekommen; sollten wir daher wohl nicht mit eben dem und mit mehrerem Rechte von der heutigen Musik eben das behaupten können, was die Alten von der ihrigen behaupteten: daß sie nämlich eine bildende Kraft für den Charakter der Menschen habe?"

45. A. B. Marx, "China—Chinesische Musik," in *Encyclopädie der gesammten musikalischen Wissenschaften, oder Universal-Lexicon der Tonkunst*, edited by Gustav Schilling (Stuttgart: Franz Heinrich Köhler, 1835), 2:204: "seit mehr als 4000 Jahren ist sie Gegenstand der Staatsfürsorge"; the quotation on Rome is from the same encyclopedia's anonymous article "Römer

(Musik der) oder Römische Musik" (6:45): "niemals Theil einer allgemeinen Volksbildung ward."

46. Pierre Bourdieu, *The Logic of Practice*, translated by Richard Nice (Stanford: Stanford University Press, 1990), 67.

47. Immanuel Wallerstein, "Class Conflict in the Capitalist World-Economy," in *Race, Nation, Class: Ambiguous Identities*, by Etienne Balibar and Wallerstein (London: Verso, 1991), 118.

48. See, for example, Terry Eagleton, *The Ideology of the Aesthetic* (Oxford: Basil Blackwell, 1990); John Guillory, *Cultural Capital: The Problem of Literary Canon Formation* (Chicago: University of Chicago Press, 1993); and Martha Woodmansee, *The Author, Art, and the Market: Rereading the History of Aesthetics*, Social Foundations of Aesthetic Forms (New York: Columbia University Press, 1994).

49. See Guillory, *Cultural Capital*, 85–133. On the role of vernacular literacy and print culture in the rise of bourgeois society, see Benedict Anderson, *Imagined Communities: Reflections on the Origin and Spread of Nationalism*, revised edition (London: Verso, 1991), 76–77.

50. Cited in Evi Rietzschel, ed., *Gelehrsamkeit ein Handwerk? Bücherschreiben ein Gewerbe? Dokumente zum Verhältnis von Schriftsteller und Verleger im 18. Jahrhundert in Deutschland* (Frankfurt am Main: Röderberg, 1983): 21: "Ihre Einbildungskraft, mein liebster Freund, fliegt noch ziemlich hoch. Lassen Sie sich herunter und kommen Sie der Erde näher. Der größeste Haufen der Schriftsteller von Profession treibt ein Gewerbe so gut als die Tapetenmaler oder die Kunstpfeifer und sieht die wenigen wahren Gelehrten fast ebenso für zudringliche, unzünftige Pfuscher an, als jene Handwerker einen Mengs oder Bach ansehen. Durch dies Gewerbe und nicht durch die Begierde, das menschliche Geschlecht zu erleuchten, entsteht die unsägliche Menge von Büchern, die Sie so bewundert haben; denn Leipzig ist freilich, seit mehr als hundert Jahren, die Stapelstadt der Waren, die diese gelehrten Handwerker zu jeder Messe verfertigen."

51. Jörg Fischer, "Anmerkungen zu Carl Dahlhaus, 'Die Musik des 19. Jahrhunderts,'" *Jahrbuch für Volksliedforschung* 31 (1986): 50: "eine kritische Gesellschaftsgeschichte der Musik, bei der die 'hohe Musik' des 19. Jahrhunderts weniger unter Ideologieverdacht geraten müßte, als daß die Bedingungen ihrer Existenz, ihre Stellung und gesellschaftliche Abhängigkeit stärker akzentuiert würden." Fischer's point is that that history is precisely what Dahlhaus's work had failed to provide.

52. Lydia Goehr, *The Quest for Voice: Music, Politics, and the Limits of Philosophy* (Berkeley and Los Angeles: University of California Press, 1998), 94.

53. Friedrich Kittler, *Discourse Networks 1800/1900*, translated by Michael Metteer, with Chris Cullens (Stanford: Stanford University Press, 1990).

54. Johann Adam Hiller [Vorbericht], *Wöchentliche Nachrichten und Anmerkungen die Musik betreffend* 1 (1766): 3–4: "Mit Anzeigung solenner Musiken an den Höfen oder in den Kirchen wollen wir uns ebenfalls in keiner andern Absicht beschäfftigen, als den Fleiß geschickter Meister auch in diesen

beyden Fächern der musikalischen Schreibart zu rühmen, und ihn von einer Art von Vergessenheit oder beynahe Verachtung zu retten, zu welchem er ohne sein Verschulden verdammt zu seyn scheint, da ihm die öfters weit seichtere Arbeit der Opernbühne überall den Vorzug streitig machen will. Die musikalischen Gesellschaften in Städten verdienen allerdings auch ihrer Gestalt und Einrichtung nach erwähnt zu werden, da sie meistentheils Pflanzschulen der Musik sind, oder wenigstens seyn sollten."

55. August Kahlert, "Das Concertwesen der Gegenwart," *Neue Zeitschrift für Musik* 16 (1842): 97–99. For further discussion of this article, see chapter 5. For an extensive consideration of discussions of domestic musical activity, see Nicolai Petrat, *Hausmusik des Biedermeier im Blickpunkt der zeitgenössischen musikalischen Fachpresse (1815–1848)*, Hamburger Beiträge zur Musikwissenschaft 31 (Hamburg: Karl Dieter Wagner, 1986).

56. See Freia Hoffmann, *Instrument und Körper: Die musizierende Frau in der bürgerlichen Kultur*, Insel Taschenbuch 1274 (Frankfurt am Main: Insel, 1991).

57. Sanna Pederson, "A. B. Marx, Berlin Concert Life, and German National Identity," *Nineteenth Century Music* 18 (1994): 89.

CHAPTER 2. SCHOLARSHIP AND THE DEFINITION OF MUSICAL CULTURES

1. Veit Erlmann, *Music, Modernity, and the Global Imagination: South Africa and the West* (New York: Oxford University Press, 1999), 8.

2. For disciplinarily and intellectually oriented studies of early ethnomusicology, see Frank Harrison, *Time, Place, and Music: An Anthology of Ethnomusicological Observation c. 1550 to c. 1800*, Source Materials and Studies in Ethnomusicology 1 (Amsterdam: Frits Knuf, 1973); Philip V. Bohlman, "R. G. Kiesewetter's *Die Musik der Araber:* A Pioneering Ethnomusicological Study of Arabic Writings on Music," *Asian Music* 18 (1986): 164–96; Bohlman, "The European Discovery of Music in the Islamic World and the 'Non-Western' in 19th-Century Music History," *Journal of Musicology* 5 (1987): 147–63; Bohlman, "Traditional Music and Cultural Identity: Persistent Paradigm in the History of Ethnomusicology," *Yearbook for Traditional Music* 20 (1988): 26–42; and Joep Bor, "The Rise of Ethnomusicology: Sources on Indian Music c. 1780–c. 1890," *Yearbook for Traditional Music* 20 (1988): 51–73.

3. Bohlman, "The European Discovery," 162–63.

4. Erlmann, *Music, Modernity, and the Global Imagination*, 8.

5. The review appeared in the *Allgemeine musikalische Zeitung* 5 (1803): 283–94 and 287–303. The book appeared under the title *Ueber die Musik der Indier: Eine Abhandlung des Sir William Jones: Aus dem Englischen übersetzt, mit erläuternden Anmerkungen und Zusätzen begleitet, von F. H. von Dalberg* (Erfurt: Beyer und Maring, 1802).

6. The journal had not previously reviewed any books on non-Western music, and the only previous lead article on another culture's music was a con-

siderably shorter one, "Einige Bemerkungen über die Musik der Türken, zur Berechtigung mehrerer Reisebeschreiber," which had appeared in 4:17–23.

7. Review of *Ueber die Musik der Indier*, 282: "den Zustand der Tonkunst bey jenen Nationen kennen zu lernen, von denen die erste Kultur ausging, und die zugleich auf mancherley Weise verhindert wurden, an den spätern Fortschritten der Kunst Theil zu nehmen."

8. On Dalberg (and his brother, a writer on aesthetic issues and correspondent with Schiller) see Gustav Schilling, ed., *Encyclopädie der gesammten musikalischen Wissenschaften, oder Universal-Lexicon der Tonkunst* (Stuttgart: Franz Heinrich Köhler, 1835), 2:350–52.

9. Review of *Ueber die Musik der Indier*, 283:

> Die Kultur der Hindoos nämlich betraf mehr die Erweiterung der Einbildungskraft, als die Aufhellung des Verstandes. Dabey blieben sie stehen, und daher ihr vorzüglicher Hang, alles Geistige zu versinnlichen, zu symbolisiren und zu personificiren. Dies haben sie zwar mit allen Morgenländern gemein, wie mit allen Völkern, die nicht mehr im rohen Zustande leben, aber von eigentlicher Aufklärung noch entfernt sind; doch scheinen die Hindoos es damit noch weiter zu treiben, als andre Asiaten. Denn sie . . . gehören zu den harmlosesten, ruheliebensten (man konnte auch sagen: zu den passivsten und weichlichsten oder weiblichsten) Nationen. Kein Wunder, dass sie für Musik einen zarten Sinn haben! Aber auch kein Wunder, dass sie, durch Klima, Religions- und politische Verfassung u.s.f. an weiterer Ausbildung gehindert, schon die ersten Elemente der Tonkunst so mit Phantasieen übergossen, dass sie damit vollauf zu thun hatten und sich aus diesem selbstgezognen magischen Kreise nicht herauswickeln konnte, wenn sie auch gewollt hätten, sondern sich immer mehr vertieften.

10. Ibid., 292: "der Verf. und Herausg. sich durch (eine verzeihliche) Vorliebe für ihren Gegenstand verleiten liessen, bey Angabe des Werths der indischen Tonkunst, Dürftigkeit mit Simplicität, und Unbehülflichkeit mit Originalität und sinnvoller Kühnheit zu verwechseln."

11. See Philip Brett, "Musicality, Essentialism, and the Closet," in *Queering the Pitch: The New Lesbian and Gay Musicology*, edited by Brett, Elizabeth Wood, and Gary C. Thomas (New York: Routledge, 1994), 9–26, esp. 9–15. Quotations are from pp. 14 and 12, respectively.

12. See, for example, Bor, "The Rise of Ethnomusicology," 55–58; and Bohlman, "Traditional Music and Cultural Identity," 31–33.

13. Review of *Ueber die Musik der Indier*, 284: "Ob aber dadurch der *besondere Werth* der indischen Musik dargethan wird, worauf der Verf. so sehr dringt, dass er sogar unsre Fortschritte in der Tonkunst dagegen in Schatten zu stellen sucht, und worin ihn der Herausg. möglichst unterstüzt,—das ist eine Frage, die Rec. geradehin zu *verneinen* kein Bedenken trägt. . . . Aber eine Kunst verdient diesen Namen nur, wenn sie *selbstständig* ist."

14. Ibid., 285: "welche theils für sich allein gefallen, (z. B. in Quartetten) und keine Empfindungen bezeichnen, die durch *Begriffe* bestimmbar sind, theils aber, mit Begriffen (Worten) *verbunden, bestimmtere* Empfindungen ausdrücken."

15. Ibid, 285–86: "Und dieses weit umfassende Gebiet der Tonkunst—. . . sollten wir, wenn's möglich wäre, mit Fleiss einschränken, um dadurch eine vermeynte grössere Energie der Tonkunst zu erhalten, die doch wahrlich nicht durch einen kleinen Vorrath von Kunstmittlen, sondern nur durch einen grösseren, *unserer* Kultur angemessenen, gewonnen werden kann? wir sollten,— was nothwendig daraus folgen würde . . .—die vorzüglichsten Kompositionen eines Ph. E. Bachs, eines Jos. Haydn u.a. für Künsteleyen erklären, und uns mit musikal. Eichelkost, oder—süsslichem Brey genügen? Nein, das wird Deutschlands Genius verhüten, wenn es sich auch nicht von selbst verböte."

16. On the extraordinarily broad circulation of this question and its significance for German musical aesthetics in the eighteenth century, see Morrow, *German Music Criticism in the Late Eighteenth Century*, 4–13.

17. Dalberg quoted the question in a note on p. 7 of *Ueber die Musik der Indier*. Cited in the review, 287. The following quotation reads, "aber ist dies ein Beweis, dass wir unsre schwer errungenen, mannigfachen Kunstmittel aufgeben und unsre Musik freiwillig in die Abhängigkeit zurückführen sollen, von der sie sich, vorzüglich in Deutschland, losgemacht hat?" (288).

18. Ibid., 299: "grösserer Humanität"; 293–94.

19. Ibid., 293: "Dieselbe Stimme erschallt aus England, Italien und Frankreich, wo man mit geringer Ausnahme, für selbstständige, ästhetisch-reine Tonkunst wenig Sinn und Talent hat. Und wir Deutsche, die wir mit Recht auf den Vorzug, die Musik zu einem höhern Range erhoben zu haben, stolz seyn müssen, sollten [wir] uns ihn wegdeklamiren oder wegspötteln lassen?"

20. The reference occurs in the context of the author's speculation that, if Alexander had succeeded in conquering India, he might have brought them the benefits of Greek culture—Napoleon's Egyptian campaign is cited as a counterpart (ibid., 299). On nationalism in relation to musical culture, see Applegate, "How German Is It?"

21. For a valuable summary of the journal's situation, see Pederson, "Enlightened and Romantic German Music Criticism," 62–67.

22. For further information on Dalberg, see the article about him in Schilling, ed., *Encyclopädie;* Bor, "The Rise of Ethnomusicology," 57; and Karl Michael Komma, "Dalberg, Johann Friedrich Hugo, Freiherr von," *Die Musik in Geschichte und Gegenwart* (hereafter *MGG*), edited by Friedrich Blume (Kassel: Bärenreiter, 1952), 2:1570–71.

23. Some sense of Dalberg's position, which was rather more moderate than that painted by the reviewer, is revealed by his annotations to Jones's text in the pages following the note cited above that complains about instrumental passagework (*Ueber die Musik der Indier*, 7). On the following page, he criticizes the dramatic value of most Italian opera, even though he acknowledges the

beauty of Pergolesi's melodies and, shortly thereafter (12–13), praises Forkel's history of music as being superior to Burney's.

24. Review of *Ueber die Musik der Indier*, 293: "eine *solide ästhetische* Theorie der Tonkunst. . . . Denn bis jetzt haben wir nur solche, welche ihren *mechanischen* Theil betreffen, wohin nicht blos Klavierschulen u. dergl., sondern auch Lehrbücher über reinen Saz, Fuge u.a.D. gehören."

25. Steuber, "Ueber die ästhetische Bildung des componirenden Tonkünstlers," *Allgemeine musikalische Zeitung* 12 (1810): 321–22: "Die ästhetische Cultur, das Sinnliche mit dem Intellectuellen vereinigend, f[ü]hrt zur Humanität. Die Poesie cultivirt am meisten. Darum misslang die Kunst bey den unpoetischen Aegyptern und jetzt bey den unpoetischen Chinesen. Nicht diese Kraft besitzt die Musik, weil es ihr an Objectivität fehlt und sie deswegen leicht einseitig macht."

26. For a typical expression of the stereotype of the uncultivated musician, see the dialogue, "Raphael," published in *Beyträge zur Bildung für Jünglinge* 2 (Vienna: Härter, 1818), a yearbook published by a number of Franz Schubert's acquaintances:

> W[ILLIBALD]. Lieber Freund, ich habe mich so oft geärgert über Tonkünstler, die, während sie andere entzücken, nichts zu empfinden scheinen, oder wenn sie ihr Instrument weglegen, unbedeutende, ja bisweilen rohe und abstoßende Menschen sind.
>
> FR[IEDRICH]. Ist Rohheit oder Einseitigkeit schon widerlich an solchen, die Gedanken ausführen, wie vielmehr an jenem, der sie denkt. Sind doch die Musen Schwestern, die sich lieben, und wer eine beleidigt, setzt sich der Gefahr aus, von allen im entscheidenden Augenblicke verlassen zu seyn. (303)

27. See, for instance, "Nachrichten von dem Zustand der Musik bey den Egyptiern und Chinesern, aus dem philosophischen Untersuchungen des Herrn von Paw," "Von den Instrumenten der Perser," "Von der Mogolischen Musik," "Von der Musik bey den Einwohnern der philippinischen Inseln," and "Von der Musik der Türken," all in Forkel's *Musikalisch-kritische Bibliothek* 1 (1778): 227–30, 230, 230–31, 231, and 231–32, respectively; "Auszug aus Karsten Niebuhr's Reisebeschreibung von Arabien und anderen umliegenden Ländern," *Musikalisch-kritische Bibliothek* 2 (1778): 306–16; and "Von der Musik der Chineser," in *Musikalischer Almanach für Deutschland auf das Jahr 1784* (Leipzig: Schwickertschen Verlag, 1784; reprint, Hildesheim: Georg Olm, 1974): 233–74.

28. "Nachrichten von dem Zustand der Musik bey den Egyptiern und Chinesern," 227: "Nach so ausdrücklichen Erklärungen, sollte man fast glauben, daß die Egyptier gar keine Musik gehabt hätten; allein, sie hatten allerdings eine, wiewohl sehr schlechte, und eben so abscheuliche, wie noch heut zu Tage die Musik bey allen Völkern in Africa und im südlichen Asien ist."

29. On Amiot, see Bohlman, "Traditional Music and Cultural Identity," 31–32.

30. Forkel summarizes Amiot's principal conclusions in "Von der Musik der Chineser," 251.

31. Ibid., 263: "Das eingebildete erhielt den Vorzug vor dem Wahren, und Vorurtheile hinderten die Ueberzeugung."

32. Ibid., 271: "So sprechen die neuern Chinesen, freylich unrichtig, aber doch mit so viel Ueberzeugung, daß es nicht möglich ist, ihnen ihren Irthum begreiflich zu machen. Sie sind Opfer von Vorurtheilen einer Erziehung, die sie lehrt, daß alles was wirklich gut sey, sich bey ihnen finde, und daß die von ihren Vorältern erfundene Musik die vollkommentse in der Welt sey. Sie erkennen ferner nur ihre groben und stumpfen Organe für Richter ihrer Gefühle, und werden uns beständig auslachen, wenn wir sie überreden wollen, daß ihre Musik, um gut zu seyn, nach denen Regeln eingerichtet seyn müsse, die wir in Europa beobachten."

33. Bohlman, "Traditional Music and Cultural Identity," 32. For Forkel's questioning of Amiot's argument for the priority of Chinese theory, see "Von der Musik der Chineser," 244.

34. Forkel, "Von der Musik der Chineser," 233–34:

> Es ist allerdings der Betrachtung werth, wenn ein Volk im ersten Aufkeimen der Künste seines Landes die vortreflichsten Aussichten verspricht, und aller dieser schönen Aussichten ungeachtet immer auf einem Punkte stehen bleibt. Die Chineser, von denen man in Europa noch nicht mit Zuverläßigkeit weiß, ob man sie eigentlich für klug oder für dumm zu halten habe, sind in dem angegebenen Fall. Ihre Landesmusik ist noch jetzt, wie sie vor vielen Jahrhunderten war; noch eben so steif, so unmelodisch, unharmonisch und sonderbar, als man sich dieselbe nur denken kann; und als sie in ihrer ersten Kindheit nur immer gewesen seyn mag. Dennoch ist sie im Stande die Herzen der Eingebohrnen aufs kräftigste zu rühren.
>
> Bey einer solchen Bechaffenheit der chinesisch-praktischen Musik, sollte man nun kaum vermuthen, daß die Chineser eben besonders richtige Begriffe von dieser Kunst überhaupt haben könnten. Dennoch findet man eine Art von Theorie über diese Kunst bey ihnen, die so richtige Begriffe enthält, daß man sich kaum genug darüber verwundern kann. Und was noch mehr ist, man findet, daß diese in ihrer musikalischen Theorie enthaltenen richtigen Begriffe sich aus den allerältesten Zeiten der Nation herschreiben. Wie mag es nun kommen, daß dieses Volk bey so frühen guten Aussichten, in der Vervollkommung [*sic*] dieser Kunst bis jetzt noch nicht weiter gekommen ist?

35. Bohlman, "Traditional Music and Cultural Identity," 31–32.

36. Edward Said, *Orientalism* (New York: Vintage, 1979). For a more recent and historically oriented overview of the issue of Europe in relation to the Orient, see Gerard Delanty, *Inventing Europe: Idea, Identity, Reality* (Basingstoke: Macmillan, 1995), esp. 84–99.

37. Austria's border with the Ottoman empire made accounts of Turkish

music something of an exception, but even the observations of "Einige Bemerkungen über die Musik der Türken" are based on a chance encounter with a Turk in Leipzig and reports collected from other visitors.

38. For a more general consideration of colonial discourse in relation to the position of Germany, see Susanne Zantop, "Dialectics and Colonialism: The Underside of the Enlightenment," in *Impure Reason: Dialectic of Enlightenment in Germany*, edited by W. Daniel Wilson and Robert C. Holub (Detroit: Wayne State University Press, 1993), 301–21.

39. Pierre Bourdieu, *Distinction: A Social Critique of the Judgement of Taste*, translated by Richard Nice (Cambridge: Harvard University Press, 1984), 56–57. The class distinctions inseparable from Bourdieu's analysis will be considered in subsequent chapters; for the present, his investigation of the interests of apparently disinterested or arbitrary taste is my primary concern.

40. Heinrich Christoph Koch, *Musikalisches Lexikon* (Frankfurt: A. Hermann der jünger, 1802; reprint, Hildesheim: Georg Olms, 1964), 776: "Die Janitscharenmusik verrath die Hauptkennzeichen der Musik eines noch rohen Volkes, nemlich das Lärmende, und die äußerst fühlbare Darstellung des Rhythmus durch eintönige Schlaginstrumente; und die seit einige Zeit überhand genommene Liebhaberey an dieser Musik, scheint dem guten Geschmacke eben kein allzugroßes Compliment zu machen." On the fashion for Janissary music, see Eric Rice, "Representations of Janissary Music *(Mehter)* as Musical Exoticism in Western Compositions, 1670–1824," *Journal of Musicological Research* 19 (1999): 41–88.

41. Christian Friedrich Michaelis, "Ueber die Musik einiger wilden und halb cultivirten Völker," *Allgemeine musikalische Zeitung* 16 (1814): 509:

> Wie tief in der Naturanlage des Menschen die Fähigkeit und Neigung zur Unterhaltung mit Gesang, Tanz und Musik liege, ergiebt sich nicht nur aus der Geschichte des Alterthums, sondern auch aus den Nachrichten, die uns Reisende über wilde und halb rohe Völker gegeben haben. Denn so wie die ältesten Urkunden des Menschengeschlechts und die Geschichtbücher [*sic*] der Griechen und Römer schon des rohen Anfangs, der zunehmenden Fortschritte und des wachsenden Ansehens der musikalischen Künste erwähnen, so vergessen die Reisebeschreiber unserer Zeit auch selten die Schilderungen musikalischer Unterhaltungen, die sie bey wilden und halb barbarischen Völkern getroffen haben. Nach dem Verhältnis der grössern oder geringern Ausbildung dieser Völker finden wir gewöhnlich auch ihren Sinn für Harmonie und Melodie entwickelt, und ihre Musik mehr oder minder einfach, roh und wild. Manche geben uns noch ein Bild von der armseligen und dürftigen Beschaffenheit, welche die Ausübung dieser Kunst in den ersten Zeiten nach ihrer Erfindung gehabt haben mag.

42. The essay initially appeared as the first installment of an anticipated series, under the title, "Fragen eines Layen über mancherley Gegenstände welche Musik und Musiker angehen," *Allgemeine musikalische Zeitung* 3

(1800): 121–27 and 146–47. In revised and expanded form, it appeared as "Verschiedenheit der Wirkungen der Musik auf gebildete oder ungebildete Völker (Schreiben an einen Freund)" in Rochlitz's retrospective collection, *Für Freunde der Tonkunst* (Leipzig: Carl Knoblach, 1824), 1:196–210. Except as noted, all references in this discussion are to the latter version.

43. Rochlitz, "Verschiedenheit der Wirkungen," 198: "Ist denn das wirklich Musik, was auf Ungebildete so wirkt? und, wo sie es ist, wirkt sie da *als Musik*?"

44. Ibid., 199: "wie sie in der Wirklichkeit unter mehr oder weniger gebildeten Völkern, die eine Geschichte besitzen, gefunden werden."

45. Ibid., 199–200: "Rohe Völker, so wie ganz unbildsame (giebt es deren) und ganz ungebildete Menschen unter uns, haben nun gar keine eigentliche Tonkunst und auch keinen Sinn dafür, sondern nur Rhythmik, und nur Sinn für diese. Das, was vor ihren Ohren tönt, tönt eigentlich nicht, sondern hallt und schallt nur; es ist für sie nur da, als Bedingung, das Rhythmische zu bemerken. Die Nebenfragen: Warum wirkt unsere Musik auf sie fast nichts, die ihrige auf uns widerlich? und dergl., sind also keine Fragen mehr. Sie haben keine *Musik*, und auch keinen Sinn dafür. Was auf sie wirkt, ist etwas ganz Anderes . . . ; obschon es unter die Bestandtheile der Musik mit aufgenommen ist."

46. Ibid., 203: "*ganz gemeiner* Märsche."

47. Ibid., 205: "ist es denn nicht vielmehr die Bestimmung, der Preis der kunst, alles Gewaltsame im und am Menschen zu mildern, das Lieden schaftliche zu bändigen, das Rohe zu beseitigen?"

48. Ibid., 206: "Oder, was ist denn am Ende aller Bildung? Sie erstreckt sich ja nicht blos auf gesellschaftliche Verhältnisse und Sitten; auch nicht blos auf Wissen und Meinen. Was ist sie, und was ist sie werth, wenn sie nicht auch in unsre Willens- und sittlichen Kräfte, und eben damit in unser inneres und äußeres Schaffen und Handeln entschieden eingreift?—Wir alle wissen und gestehen: Maaß halten in jedem, sey, wie die erste Frucht, so das erste Zeichen wahrer Bildung. Maaß halten ist nicht möglich, wo nur die Sinnlichkeit aufgereizt wird: es ist aber nicht nur möglich, sondern wird auch am leichtesten, wenn und wo alle Theile unsers Wesens gleichmäßig in Anspruch genommen, gleichmäßig aufgeregt und beschäftigt werden."

49. The discussion that follows is indebted to Georg G. Iggers, *The German Conception of History: The National Tradition of Historical Thought from Herder to the Present* (Middletown, Conn.: Wesleyan University Press, 1968), 29–43; Frederick C. Beiser, *Enlightenment, Revolution, and Romanticism: The Genesis of Modern German Political Thought, 1790–1800* (Cambridge: Harvard University Press, 1992), 189–221; Wulf Koepke, "*Kulturnation* and Its Authorization through Herder," in *Johann Gottfried Herder: Academic Disciplines and the Pursuit of Knowledge*, edited by Koepke (Columbia, S.C.: Camden House, 1996), 177–98; and Matti Bunzl, "Franz Boas and the Humboldtian Tradition: From *Volksgeist* and *Nationalcharakter* to an Anthropological Conception of Culture," in *"Volksgeist" as Method and Ethic: Essays on Boasian Ethnography and the German Anthropological Tradition*, edited by

George W. Stocking Jr., History of Anthropology 8 (Madison: University of Wisconsin Press, 1996), 17–78, esp. 19–28. Although Norbert Elias's famous distinction between "culture" and "civilization" in German usage is related to the tension between universal cultivation and national identity, it proved too absolute to be useful here. See Norbert Elias, The Civilizing Process: The History of Manners, translated by Edmund Jephcott (Oxford: Basil Blackwell, 1978), esp. 3–10; but see also 289, n. 2, for less oppositional uses of the terms.

50. Herder, Auch eine Philosophie der Geschichte zur Bildung der Menschheit: Beytrag zu vielen Beyträgen des Jahrhunderts (1774), in Sämmtliche Werke, volume 5, edited by Bernhard Suphan (Berlin: Weidmann, 1877–1913), 509. Translation from Iggers, The German Conception of History, 35.

51. Cited in Koepke, "Kulturnation," 189: "Am wenigsten kann also unsre Europäische Cultur das Maas allgemeiner Menschengüte und Menschenwerthes seyn; sie ist kein oder ein falscher Maasstab."

52. For a summary of the anticolonial critique in Auch eine Philosophie der Geschichte, see Beiser, Enlightenment, Revolution, and Romanticism, 203. See Bohlman, "Traditional Music and Cultural Identity," 32–33, for a brief discussion of Herder's significance in ethnomusicology.

53. Such difficulties are noted by Beiser, Enlightenment, Revolution, and Romanticism, 209; and by Wolfgang Wieland, "Entwicklung," Geschichtliche Grundbegriffe: Historisches Lexikon zur politisch-sozialen Sprache in Deutschland, edited by Otto Brunner, Werner Conze, and Reinhart Koselleck (Stuttgart: Ernst Klett, 1975), 2:207.

54. From the sixty-fifth letter of Herder's sixth collection of Briefe zu Beförderung der Humanität (Berlin and Weimar: Aufbau, 1971), 1:362: "Und wodurch kamen die Griechen zu diesem allen? Nur durch ein Mittel: durch Menschengefühl, durch Einfalt der Gedanken und durch ein lebhaftes Studium des wahrsten, völligsten Genusses, kurz, durch Kultur der Menschheit. Hierin müssen wir alle Griechen werden oder wir bleiben Barbaren."

55. See Pederson, "A. B. Marx, Berlin Concert Life, and German National Identity," 87–107; but see also Applegate, "How German Is It?" for an alternative view, which, however, does not dispute the significance of ideas of national character.

56. See, for instance, the following, all of which continue the tradition of translating and transmitting travel reports with relatively little comment: Michaelis, "Von der Musik der Aegypter und der Morgenländer überhaupt," Cäcilia 15, no. 59 (1833): 179–83; "Etwas über Musik und Tanz in Brasilien," Allgemeine musikalische Zeitung 35 (1833): 19–21; and Gustav Keferstein [K. Stein, pseud.], "Musik der Malgaschen auf Madagascar," Neue Zeitschrift für Musik 13 (1840): 136.

57. For instance, the emphasis on geography and climate as determinants of human character in "Aufgefundene Blätter aus dem Tagebuch eines früh verstorbenen Musikers: Musikanlage der Orientalen"(Berliner allgemeine musikalische Zeitung 5 [1828]: 179–80) is in keeping with Herder but also reinforces notions of the irremediable unmusicality of the Oriental.

58. All the volumes were published in Stuttgart by Franz Heinrich Köhler.

59. The music bibliographer Carl Ferdinaɪd Becker reviewed the first two volumes of the project in the *Neue Zeitschrift für Musik* 3 (1835): 177–78, 181–82, and 185–86; and the entire work in 11 (1839): 78–79. Heinrich Dorn had already complained about inaccuracies in 3 (1835): 140, and complaints alternated with Schilling's defensive replies for several years, culminating in "Die Plagiate des Dr. Schilling in Stuttgart betreffend" (14 [1841]: 86), signed by "Die Redaction der Neuen Zeitschrift für Musik" (i.e., Robert Schumann).

60. See Alec Hyatt King, "Schilling, Gustav," *New Grove Dictionary* 16: 648; and Hans Heinrich Eggebrecht, "Schilling, Gustav," *MGG* 11 (1963): 1719–20. Both Eggebrecht and Hyatt King draw much of their information— and their evaluation—from the extraordinarily negative account of Schilling by Robert Eitner, *Allgemeine deutsche Biographie* (Leipzig: Duncker & Humblot, 1890), 31:256–59.

61. From Becker's second review, p. 79: "Die ausgezeichnetsten Artikel in der Encyclopädie sind fast sämmtlich jene, welche die Geschichte der Tonkunst der einzelnen Völker betreffen."

62. Although those shorter articles considerably outnumber the national articles, most are extremely brief. Among the more substantial and interesting are "Balalaika" (Schilling, ed., *Encyclopädie*, 1:403—ascribed to br.); "Barde und Bardiet" (1:435–38—LMF); "Cang-Hi" (2:100–101, on the Chinese emperor discussed by Amiot and Forkel); "Derwisch oder Dervis" (2:387–88); "Jones, Sir William" (3:740–41—Schilling); "Leviten" (4:369–74—Schilling); and "Volkslied" (6:796–99—k.). The concentration of these more substantial articles near the beginning of the alphabet is not coincidental; the *Encyclopädie* shows a marked decline in the quality of its national and non-European articles as it proceeds, with Schilling writing more of the articles himself rather than receiving them from other contributors.

63. Schilling, ed., *Encyclopädie*, 6:531:

> Dann unterscheidet man ferner den Styl in subjektiver Beziehung nach der Nation, welcher der Künstler angehört, denn fast eine jede der verschiedenen Nationen besitzt auch ihr Eigenthümliches, nicht allein in der Darstellungsweise ihrer Kunst, sondern auch in dieser selbst und ihren mannigfachen Mitteln. Die *Türkische Musik* z. B. ist ganz anders als die *deutsche*, und die *französische* wieder anders als die *griechische* u.s.w. Dem einen Volke und dem einen Lande gehören diese, dem anderen jene Instrumente als eigenthümlich an, und das eine hat mehr Fähigkeit und Neigung zur Cultur der Vocal-, das andere zur Cultur der Instrumentalmusik. Bekanntlich ist im diesem Buche der Musik eines jeden Volkes und eines jeden Landes, alter und neuer Welt, eine besondere Beschreibung gewidmet.

64. Ibid., 3:532: "Reden wir von der hebräischen Musik zu Mosis Zeiten, so dürfen wir durchaus nicht an eine so vollkommene rhythmisch geordnete Kunst denken, wie wir jetzt die Musik zu erfassen gewohnt sind. Es war war-

scheinlich nur ein roher *recitativischer* Naturgesang, der auf unvollkommenen Instrumenten, und namentlich *Schlag*instrumente, neben denen übrigens auch schon *Saiten-* und *Blas*instrumente existirten, je wie es den Sängern gut schien, begleitet wurde."

65. Ibid., 3:536: "die Verplichtung zu vergessen scheinen, auch Rücksicht auf die wahre Natur der Sache, den Volkscharacter und andere dahin gehörige Umstände zu nehmen. . . . Und erwägen wir dazu noch, daß die Beschaffenheit der Instrumente ein Maaßstab ist, wonach der Grad der musikalischen Cultur eines Volks ziemlich sicher abgemessen werden darf, so geht daraus zugleich das sicherste Urtheil über den tiefen Stand der hebräischen Musik im Vergleich zu der unsrigen hervor."

66. Ibid., 1:70–71: "Jedenfalls kann sie, schon wegen des Nationalcharakters der Aegyptier, die, jeder Neuerung feind, kein Haar breit von den Gebräuchen ihrer Vorfahren abweichen durften, nur eine solche gewesen seyn, die in der tiefsten Kindheit lag."

67. Ibid., 1:71: "Nicht viel besser redet Tacitus von dem Bardengesange, der nach ihm dem Geknatter der Räder an gehemmten Frachtwagen ähnlich gewesen seyn soll, welche einen steilen Berg herabfahren."

68. Despite this analogy, the work's treatment of Roman *music* is far from flattering. The Romans simply adopted from those they conquered, especially the Greeks, and made no real contributions of their own.

69. Ibid., 3:311–12:

> Aus dem Besitze der einen Kunst folgt nicht der der andern (sonst wäre Raphael ein großer Tonkünstler und Mozart ein großer Maler gewesen), sondern viel eher das Gegentheil. Die Griechen sind überall das *nach Außen* lebende, in der *Anschauung* kunstthätige Volk; darum ist ihre Plastik zur Vollendung gekommen und ihre ganze Poesie nach der Seite der Anschauung gewendet; Denken und Empfinden ist ihnen sogleich Vorstellung, Bild; schon ihre Sprache trägt den Stempel dieser Grundneigung. Aber eben daraus darf schon gefolgert werden, daß die andere Seite, daß die vorzugsweise *innerliche Kunst* der Töne bei ihnen *nicht* zu gleicher Vollendung gekommen seyn könne.

70. Ibid., 3:319:

> In einem *tiefern*, das *Wesen* der Sache fassenden *Sinne* müssen wir aber unter Harmonie die Zusammenstellung der *von Natur*, durch ihren Ursprung und Inhalt, *einigen Töne*, die dem Naturgesetze und der künstlerischen Vernunft gemäße Fortführung (Auseinander- und Wieder-Zusammenführung) dieser Töne verstehen. Wenn unsere jetzige Harmonik ihren ersten Accord aus irgend einem Urtone, z. B. C, abzuleiten, diesen Accord in einen andern naturgemäß fortzuführen, diesen wieder nach bestimmten Naturgesetze auf den Ursprung zurückzuleiten [musical example inserted here] und von diesem Anfange aus (dessen Richtigkeit hier nicht weiter erörtert wird) das ganze System der Harmonie, Mehrstimmigkeit und Modulation zu entfalten vermag, so besitzen wir

Harmonie in jenem tieferen Sinne, die aber dann nicht eine Sammlung zufällig ertappter Zusammenklänge ist, sondern die vernunftgemäße u. naturnothwendige Entfaltung des ganzen Tonwesens, so weit es über die dürre Einstimmigkeit hinausgeht. Die Frage, ob ein Individuum oder Volk solche Zusammenklänge in größerer oder geringerer Zahl besessen? ist von geringer Bedeutung; die Frage, ob es in jenem höheren Sinne Harmonie besessen? ist gleichbedeutend mit der, ob es sich aus der bewußtlosen Kindheit des Kunstlebens zur Selbstständigkeit und Herrschaft in der Kunst emporgeschwungen? Denn wer nicht in dem tiefen Begriffe der Harmonie die Zügel aller Tonbewegung in Händen hat, muß jeden Augenblick dem Zwiespalte zwischen seiner Absicht und der natürlichen Neigung der Töne verfallen.

71. Ibid., 3:203: "Treue dem gegebenen Wort, Ehre den Frauen, Heldentrotz dem Feinde, Demuth vor den Göttern. Diese verehrten sie in reichlich sagenhafter Gestaltung, aber in bedeutungsvollem Abglanz des einiggültig ewigen Lichts, so daß vielleicht keine andere Mythologie darin den Wettkampf mit der Germanischen zu bestehen vermag. Wie unter allen tapfern und waffenfreudigen Völkern, lebte und webte auch bei den Germanen Poesie, und ihre unabtrennliche Schwester, Musik, in heiteren Ehre."

Fouqué also takes care to clarify the political order of the tribes in a way that guards against any idealization of dangerous political ideas: although there was no single king among the tribes, "one must nevertheless not, therefore, consider it a democratically constituted community. Much rather, it was a patriarchal federation: every head of a household was an independent king over family and servants." (Man wolle jedoch dabei nicht an demokratische Gemeinde-Verfassung denken. Vielmehr eine patriarchalische Bundes-Verfassung war es: jeglicher Wehrfester ein unabhängiger König über Familie und Knechte [3:203].)

72. Ibid., 3:204: "eine so kräftige Continuität in dem Strom der Germanischen Geschichte und Bildung"; "der natürliche gesunde Sinn."

73. Ibid., 3:216–17 [recte 206–7]:

So, während der Name *Germanen* aus der Weltgeschichte in ihrem Fürderschreiten nach und nach als Volks- und Stammes-Benennung völlig verschwand, erhielt, ja verbreitete sich zu erhöhetem Leben die germanische Bildung auf's mannigfachste in allen europäischen Landen, ja großentheils auch noch darüber hinaus. Die Grundzüge dieser Bildung haben wir schon vorhin angedeutet, und brauchen nur darauf hinzuweisen, um die Erkenntniß des Heilbringenden ihrer Verbreitung hervorzurufen. Die Musik insbesondere gewann bei diese nach und nach erfolgenden Fürder- und Umgestaltung des Lebens an harmonischer Fülle, die Vielseitigkeit der ineinandergreifenden Gebilde auch ihrerseits darstellend. . . .—Wenn zwar wir keineswegs die antike Musik, wie von manchen Seiten her versucht worden ist, auf die Melodie allein beschränken wollen, ihr etwa höchstens die Octavenbegleitung zugestehend, müssen wir doch erkennen, wie in ihr das reiche Element der Harmonie nur noch sehr unentwickelt in der Knospe lag. Zu seiner jetzigen Blüthe hat es sich erst im Gedeihen der germanischen Bildung entfaltet, welche man öfters auch wohl die *romantische* zu nennen gewohnt ist.

74. Ibid., 6:615:

Nur durch Schlüsse gelangen wir zu der höchst wahrscheinlichen Meinung, daß die altteutschen Gesangsweisen mit der im Alterthume überall verbreiteten Norm der keltischen (s. keltische Musik) übereingestimmt haben mögen. Wie sich nun die älteste Kunst der Musik unter allen Völkern mehr durch Gewalt des Rhythmus als durch Tonschönheit, die erst in der Folge dazu kam, hervorthat, so finden wir es auch bei den alten Teutschen. Ja sie mögen auf Ton noch weniger gesehen haben, als z.B. die alten Schotten. Dies beweisen uns die vielfachsten Beschreibungen alter Schriftsteller, die sie uns vom Gesange der Teutschen hinterlassen haben. Es muß mehr Getöse und Geschrei, als eigentlicher Gesang gewesen seyn, vom Rhythmus wirksam gemacht, einer Kraft, die selbst jetzt noch allgemeiner Eindringlichkeit sich erfreut u. unter die ersten Kräfte der Tonkunst gerechnet werden muß.

75. Ibid., 4:71: "Von Asien aus bewegt sich von Osten nach Westen alles Unruhige, Suchende, Wandernde, alle Kraft und alles Bedrängte, wie alle Cultur, Kunst und Religion."

76. Ibid., 4:72–73: "in der That, wo uns nur noch eine Spur alterthümlicher Anfangkunst europäischer Völker noch übrig geblieben ist, da trägt sie auch deutlich die wesentlichen Merkmale asiatischen Ursprunges an sich. . . . Alle Volksüberreste, die noch durch Absonderung oder Vernachlässigung ihrem frühesten Zustande nahe geblieben sind, liefern unumstößliche Zeugnisse, daß die früheste Kunst der Musik keine andere als die von China und Hindostan ausgewanderte seyn kann."

77. Ibid., 4:74: "Alles, was zur Spekulation darüber gehörte, lag ihrem thatmächtigen Leben nicht nahe genug."

78. Ibid., 6:531: " *moderne* Musik . . . unter welcher man auch wohl die Musik der abendländischen oder europäischen Völker versteht."

79. Ibid., 6:627: "Immerhin behauptet Teutschland in der Tonkunst unter allen Völkern seit lange den ersten Rang, der ihm auch von einsichtsvollen Ausländern selbst nicht mehr abgesprochen wird. Was zu bessern ist, und es ist zu bessern, das wird von Teutschland ausgehen."

80. In contemporary France, by contrast, "even in Paris, instrumental performance for the people is so wretched that it would scarcely be believable in Germany" (das Instrumentenspiel für das Volk ist von einer in Deutschland kaum glaublichen Dürftigkeit, sogar in Paris [3:43]). Fink attributes this to the poor state of music education in French schools. For an earlier account of the inherently musical character of the German nation, see "Musikalischer Cha-

rakter der deutschen Nazion," *Wiener allgemeine musikalische Zeitung,* no. 1 (1813): 159–60.

81. Schilling, ed., *Encyclopädie,* 2:593: "Diese folgerecht durchgeführte Strenge in Gleichheit und gesetzlicher Einerleiheit kirchlicher Musik ist noch nirgends ein Segen für die Kunst gewesen, weder bei den Aegyptern, noch in Griechenland, auch nicht in England; *sie bringt Unfreiheit in die Kunst,* die eben so wie Zügellosigkeit untergräbt."

82. In only one case (not by Fink) is the church ascribed a significant positive role. In the unsigned article on Scottish music (discussed below), the poverty of Scottish music is attributed in part to the *absence* of the cultivating influence of church music due to the Calvinist reformation.

83. Ibid., 1:706: "Zwar liebt das Volk noch immer die Musik, und es vergeht selbst auf dem Lande selten ein Ehren- und Freudentag, an dem nicht Trompeten und Pauken erklängen; die Feldmusik der böhmischen Regimenter gehört immer noch zu den vorzüglichen, wie die österreichische; die Bergleute lieben nach [*sic*] wie vor ihren Triangel, manche Gebirgsgegenden ihr Hackebret und das Egergebiet ganz besonders den Dudelsack, und behandelen diese Lieblingsinstrumente vorzüglich, allein es gehört mehr dazu, soll das Land sich seiner alten Ehre wiederum mit Recht erfreuen. Es ist daher immer noch, Prag ausgenommen, im Ganzen das Land der verstimmten Harfen."

84. Ibid., 6:397–98:

> Wie in Dänemark, und noch weniger fast, hat auch in Schweden die Musik nie eine bedeutende Höhe erreicht. . . . Die wenigen Mußestunden füllt bei den niedern Ständen zum Theil ein zu lautes, rauschendes Vergnügen, als daß die stille Muse sich in ihre Mitte wagen sollte. Bei dem Mittelstande ist sie wohl öfter zu finden; aber die Augenblicke, wo sie einzelnen, in sich selbst gekehrten Gemüthern erschien, waren immer vorübergehend, und die seltene Erscheinung konnte keinen dauernden, lebendigen Kreis um sich bilden, da ein Jeder zu voll von seinem alltäglichen Thun und Treiben war, als daß er mit ganzer Liebe sich diesem zarten Wesen hätte zuwenden können. Von den höheren Ständen wird musikalische Bildung zwar in Schweden wie in anderen Ländern gefordert; sie muß da sogar oft ganz unfreiwillig erscheinen, doch auch nur in einer Modetracht, von deren Zwang ihr Leben und Wirken beschränkt wird, und welche keine Spur einer *nationalen* Eigenthümlichkeit entdecken läßt. . . . Nur wenn wir der schwedischen Musik bis dahin folgen, wo sie in inniger Verwachsung mit dem ganzen Nationalcharakter erscheint, gelangen wir . . . zu erfreulicheren Resultaten.

85. The Danish collection is discussed on 6:395, the Swedish on 6:398–99: "dem treueren Gedächtnisse der niederen Stände" and "die flachen Modegesänge des Tags" (6:398).

86. Ibid., 6:253: "dennoch ist die Musik, welche der Schotte als ihm eigenthümlich angehörend besitzt, streifen wir den Werth der Nationalität davon ab,

so gut als gar keine, oder befindet sie sich in dem Zustande einer höchst armseligen Kindheit."

87. Ibid., 5:517: "Nichts ist als ein Gemisch von Kelten (Urbewohnern), Carthagern, Römern, Deutschen, Arabern, Juden."

88. "Rauh und widrig" (ibid., 5:147) and "unerträglich für gebildete Ohren" (5:148). The article is based on the account in Edward Dodwell's *Classical and Topographical Tour through Greece*.

89. Schilling, ed., *Encyclopädie*, 5:147: "Ein Grieche kann selten singen, ohne zugleich zu tanzen, und die übrigen Anwesenden können nie der Versuchung widerstehen, wie von einem natürlichen Drange hingerissen, mit einzustimmen; und wenn sie nun alle zusammen singen, so giebt dies einen wahrhaft abscheulichen Lärm."

90. Ibid., 5:148: "keinen Antheil an europäischer Culturentwickelung nehmen konnten."

91. Ibid., 3:697: "eine der unsrigen gleiche Vollkommenheit" and "Wäre dieselbe aber jemals so vollkommen gewesen, gewiß wäre sie aufbewahrt und von den einwandernden Völkern angenommen, statt von diesen verdrängt worden. In den englischen Besitzungen ist die Musik jetzt fast rein europäisch." The article "Mauren" also raises the question of the impact of colonization, albeit in a different light: "We must calmly wait to see whether the current French colonization in Africa will bring more cultivation among the Moors and thereby also exercise an advantageous influence. In advance we venture to contend that many promise more of it than will come to fruition." (Ob die jetzige französische Colonisation in Afrika mehr Bildung unter die Mauren bringen und somit auch auf ihre Musik einen vorteilhaften Einfluß ausüben wird, müssen wir ruhig abwarten. Im voraus wagen wir zu behaupten, daß sicher Viele sich mehr davon versprechen, als in Erfüllung gehen wird [4:609].)

92. Raphael Georg Kiesewetter's *Die Musik der Araber nach Originalquellen dargestellt* (Leipzig: Breitkopf & Härtel, 1842) had not yet appeared, but it too would approach Arab music as an early example of rationalization. Kiesewetter's conception of musical progress was similar to those I have discussed here; see Bohlman, "R. G. Kiesewetter's *Die Musik der Araber*"; and Bernhard Meier, "Zur Musikhistoriographie des 19. Jahrhunderts," in *Die Ausbreitung des Historismus über die Musik*, edited by Walter Wiora, Studien zur Musikgeschichte des 19. Jahrhunderts 14 (Regensburg: Gustav Bosse, 1969), 169–206, esp. 170–77.

93. Schilling, ed., *Encyclopädie*, 5:303: "Mehr als alle anderen Nationen Asiens scheinen die *Siamesen* Fortschritte in der Musik gemacht zu haben. Ihre Melodien sind gewöhnlich lebhaft und nicht ohne Anmuth, selbst für ein gebildetes europäisches Ohr."

94. Ibid.: "J. Crawford versichert, daß die meisten ihrer Melodien den schottischen u. irländischen gleichen."

95. Ibid., 6:709–10:

Uebrigens blieb die Musik der Meder meist in den Händen der Weiber. Sie hatten Sängerinnen u. Citharistinnen, die zu dem Gefolge und in das

Harem der Könige gehörten, welcher Gebrauch sich denn auch noch heute in Persien findet. Die besten oder so zu sagen einzigen persischen Tonkünstler sind stets im Dienste des Fürsten. Dann hatten die weichlichen und verführerischen Schauspiele der Meder einen so verderblichen Einfluß auf die Sitten der Perser, daß es mit der Verachtung der Musik nicht besser werden konnte. In Persien bilden die Tänzerinnen und Schauspielerinnen wie meist auch die Tonkünstler, welche nichts eigens vom Fürsten gehalten werden, herumwandernde Banden, die in Privathäusern ihre Künste zur Schau stellen. Eine solche Bande besteht aus einer Prima Donna u. ihrem Gefolge, das nur bisweilen erscheint, um den Hauptdialog mit Chören, Gesängen und Tänzen zu unterbrechen.

Like much else in the *Encyclopädie*, this passage is borrowed almost verbatim and without acknowledgment, in this case from Dalberg's "Musik der Perser und Araber. Ein Nachtrag zur Seite 14 u.f. des Abhandlung," in *Ueber die Musik der Indier: Eine Abhandlung des Sir William Jones: Aus dem Englischen übersetzt, mit erläuternden Anmerkungen und Zusätzen begleitet, von F. H. von Dalberg,* by William Jones, translated with annotations and supplements by Friedrich Hugo von Dalberg (Erfurt: Beyer and Maring, 1802), 105.

96. Schilling, ed., *Encyclopädie*, 6:711: "Auch macht die Musik einen wesentlichen Theil der guten Erziehung bei ihnen aus, u. von den außerordentlichen Civilisations-Bestrebungen des jetzigen Sultans dürfen wir auch in Beziehung auf Hebung der musikalischen Cultur Viel erwarten. Schon hat derselbe in Constantinopel eine bedeutende Anzahl der ausgezeichnetsten Musiker an seinem Hofe versammelt, wenn deren Kunst auch noch mehr einerseits zu süßlichen Tändeleien und andererseits zu militärischen Zwecken verwendet wird."

97. Ibid., 2:625: "Die Musik der Eskimo's, dieses wildesten aller wilden Völker . . . ist zwar eben so beschränkt und ärmlich, als Geist, Sitte und Gestalt 2c., wodurch dieselben sich von allen übrigen Nationen unterscheiden; doch ist sie Musik, und liefert den überzeugendsten Beweis zugleich, daß kein Volk, auch das allerroheste nicht, ohne alle Musik ist, und wie diese verschöndernde Sprache von der Mutter Natur selbst gleichsam jedem vernünftigen, fühlenden Wesen bei der Schöpfung als theuerstes Gut—in der Anlage dazu wenigstens—mitgegeben oder eingeimpft wird."

98. Ibid., 4:387: "Der Orient kennt diesen Ausdruck lebendiger Gefühle eben so wie der Occident, und selbst das wildeste unter den wilden Völkern entbehrt sein Lied nicht, mit dem es sich heiter stimmt, und in dessen Tönen es sein ganzes rohes Herz ausgießt. Vergl. nur den Art. *Eskimo*."

99. Jonathan P. J. Stock, "New Musicologies, Old Musicologies: Ethnomusicology and the Study of Western Music," *Current Musicology* 62 (1998): 40–68.

100. "Dissonanzen vielleicht in der ganzen Oper nicht aufgelöst oder ganz anders da sich in diesen Zeiten unsere verfeinerte Musik nicht denken läßt." Cited in Alexander Wheelock Thayer, *Ludwig van Beethovens Leben*, trans-

lated by Hermann Dieters, revised and expanded by Hugo Riemann (Leipzig: Breitkopf & Härtel, 1923; reprint, Hildesheim: Georg Olms, 1971), 3:504. The translation in *Thayer's Life of Beethoven,* edited by Elliot Forbes (Princeton: Princeton University Press, 1964), 2:618, is less literal than mine.

101. Eduard Krüger, "Künstler-Armuth. (Aus dem Briefwechsel zweier Freunde)," *Neue Zeitschrift für Musik* 17 (1842): 139:

> "Sind's die Künstler minder werth als die Beamten, die Staatsmänner, die Universitätslehrer, daß ihnen das äußere Leben erleichtert werde, damit sie alle Kraft auf das Innere ungestört und unverirrt von niederem Kummer hinwenden mögen? Wer sich einer geistigen Arbeit mit vollem Streben hingeben soll, muß zuvor satt sein. Darum können Mongolen und Kamschadalen keine Künstler haben und keine Gelehrte, weil sie immerfort um's tägliche Brod kämpfen müssen, und keinen Ueberfluss besitzen, um unnütze Sinner und Träumer zu nähren. Dagegen der schöne Ueberfluß, der sich im civilizirten Leben großer gebildeter Völker von selbst einfindet, dem sogennanten Zehrstand zu Gute kommen muß, zu dem wir uns zu rechnen gar kein Bedenken tragen, da wir ja auch unser Theil zur allgemeinen Arbeit beisteuern.

Krüger's article is a fictitious exchange of letters between a statesman and an artist; this excerpt is from one of the artist's contributions.

CHAPTER 3. THE DILEMMA OF THE POPULAR

1. Leopold to Wolfgang, 11 December 1780: "Ich empfehle dir Bey deiner Arbeit nicht einzig und allein für das musikalische, sondern auch für das *ohnmusikalische Publikum* zu denken,—du weist es sind *100 ohnwissende* gegen *10 wahre Kenner,*—vergiß also das so genannte *populare* nicht, das auch die *langen Ohren* Kitzelt." Wolfgang to Leopold, 16 December 1780: "wegen dem sogenannten Popolare sorgen sie nichts, denn, in meiner Oper ist Musick für aller Gattung leute;—ausgenommen für lange ohren nicht." Cited in Wolfgang Amadeus Mozart, *Briefe und Aufzeichnungen,* edited by Wilhelm A. Bauer and Otto Erich Deutsch (Kassel: Bärenreiter, 1963), 3:53, 60.

2. On Viennese opera audiences, see Mary Hunter, *The Culture of Opera Buffa in Mozart's Vienna: A Poetics of Entertainment* (Princeton: Princeton University Press, 1999), 13–15. Hunter deals specifically with comic opera, but there is no reason to suppose that the situation for serious opera would have been any less exclusive than the general one, and "even with the most 'progressive' interpretation of the evidence . . . the Burgtheater audience (and that of the Kärntnerthortheater when it showed opera buffa) represented an incredibly small segment of the broader Viennese population " (14).

3. Heinrich W. Schwab, *Sangbarkeit, Popularität, und Kunstlied: Studien zu Lied und Liedästhetik der mittleren Goethezeit, 1770–1814,* Studien zur Musikgeschichte des 19. Jahrhunderts 3 (Regensburg: Gustav Bosse, 1965), esp. 85–135.

4. Stanley Sadie and John Tyrrell, eds., *New Grove Dictionary of Music and Musicians,* 2nd edition (London: Macmillian, 2000), however, does include a brief article on the "Volkstümliches Lied"; I am grateful to its author, James Parsons, for sharing material from it with me in advance of its publication.

5. I am grateful to James Parsons for providing, in response to an earlier version of this chapter, stimulating comments that have helped me clarify this point. On the aesthetic of simplicity and its relation to the lied, see Parsons, "Ode to the Ninth: The Poetic and Musical Tradition behind the Finale of Beethoven's Choral Symphony" (Ph.D. dissertation, University of North Texas, 1992); and Ann Le Bar, "The Domestication of Vocal Music in Enlightenment Hamburg," *Journal of Musicological Research* 19 (2000): 97–134.

6. Margaret Mahony Stoljar, *Poetry and Song in Late Eighteenth Century Germany: A Study in the Musical "Sturm und Drang"* (London: Croom Helm, 1985), 155.

7. On citation of preexisting authorities as the process through which both the received text and the citer are confirmed in their legitimacy, see Judith Butler, *Bodies That Matter: On the Discursive Limits of "Sex"* (New York: Routledge, 1993), 107–8.

8. Stoljar, *Poetry and Song,* 149, 155, and 170. For an attempt of the type Stoljar rejects, seeking to explain Schulz's accessibility through his similarity to the melodic style of German folksongs, see J. W. Smead, *German Song and Its Poetry, 1740–1900* (London: Croom Helm, 1987), 20–37.

9. J. A. P. Schulz, preface to the second edition of *Lieder im Volkston* (Berlin: Georg Jacob Decker, 1785). Cited in Max Friedlaender, *Das deutsche Lied im 18. Jahrhundert* (Stuttgart: J. G. Cotta, 1902; reprint, Hildesheim: Georg Olms, 1962), volume 1, part 1:256–57:

> In allen diesen Liedern ist und bleibt mein Bestreben, mehr *volksmäßig* als *kunstmäßig* zu singen, nehmlich so, daß auch ungeübte Liebhaber des Gesanges, sobald es ihnen nicht ganz und gar an Stimme fehlt, solche leicht nachsingen und auswendig behalten können. Zu dem Ende habe ich nur solche Texte aus unsern besten Liederdichtern gewählt, die mir zu diesem Volksgesänge gemacht zu seyn scheinen, und mich in den Melodien selbst der höchsten Simplicität und Faßlichkeit beflissen, ja auf alle Weise den *Schein des Bekannten* darinzubringen gesucht, weil ich aus Erfahrung weiß, wie sehr dieser Schein dem Volksliede zu seiner schnellen Empfehlung dienlich, ja nothwendig ist. In diesen Schein des Bekannten liegt das ganze Geheimnis des Volkstons; nur muß man ihn mit dem *Bekannten* selbst nicht verwechseln; dieses erweckt in allen Kunstlern Ueberdruß; Jener hingegen hat in der Theorie des Volksliedes, als ein Mittel, es dem Ohre lebendig und schnell faßlich zu machen, Ort und Stelle, und wird von dem Komponisten oft mit Mühe, oft vergebens gesucht.
>
> Denn nur durch eine frappante Aehnlichkeit des musikalischen mit dem poetischen Tone des Liedes; durch eine Melodie, deren Fortschrei-

tung sich nie über den Gang des Textes erhebt, noch unter ihm sinkt, die, wie ein Kleid dem Körper, sich der Declamation und dem Metro der Worte anschmiegt, die außerdem in sehr sangbaren Intervallen, in einem allen Stimmen angemeßnen Umfang, und in den allerleichtesten Modulationen fortfließt; und endlich durch die höchste Vollkommenheit der Verhältnisse aller ihrer Teile, wodurch eigentlich der Melodie diejenige Rundung gegeben wird, die jedem Kunstwerk aus dem Gebiete des Kleinen so unentbehrlich ist, erhält das Lied den Schein, von welchem hier die Rede ist, den Schein des Ungesuchten, des Kunstlosen, des Bekannten, mit einem Wort, den *Volkston,* wodurch es sich dem Ohre so schnell und unaufhörlich zurückkehrend, einprägt.

10. The first paragraph of Schulz's preface, only summarized by Friedlaender, does, however, make explicit that it is the public *(Publikum)* —and thus a cultivated literary audience—that he is addressing. Schulz, "Vorrede," in *Lieder im Volkston,* 2nd edition (Berlin: Georg Jacob Decker, 1785), n.p.

11. Carl Friedrich Cramer, review of *Lieder im Volkston,* by Johann Abraham Peter Schulz, *Magazin der Musik* 1 (1783): 61–63:

> Es ist nun ohngefähr ein zehn Jahre her, daß Herder, der zu seinem Fouragiren in allerley Gebieten der Literatur umherstreifte, der Witterung von den *Relicks* [*sic*] of *Ancient Poetry* nachgehend, auf das brachgelegene Feld der Volkspoesie kam, das bisher eben von niemand war betreten worden. Sogleich machte er das Abentheuer in den fliegenden Blättern über deutsche Art und Kunst bekannt. Bürger, der gerade um die Zeit derselben Lectüre oblag, that etwas noch wichtigers als der Theoretiker; er realisirte, wiewohl von selbst und ohne Jenes Anstoß zu bedürfen, diese Ideen in seiner vortreflichen *Lenore,* und verschiedenen andern Balladen. Unmittelbar in seine Fußstapfen traten Hölty und Stolberg mit einigen gleichfals sehr schönen Stücken. Nun stellte vollends Bürger in dem Aufsatze des Daniel Wunderlich im Musäo, das misverstandene Theorem *von der alleinigen Herrlichkeit der Volkspoesie* auf: und siehe da! alle Sümpfe am Fusse des Parnasses wurden wach, und ihre kleinen Bewohnerchen quackten allenthalben so viel Volksgesang, daß Bürger endlich selbst die Ohren davon gellten, und er es nöthig fand . . . dem Froschgesindel Stillschweigen aufzuerlegen. . . . die Epidemie theilte sich auch den Musikern mit; sie setzten die Gassenhauern in Noten, erfanden selbst welche; priesens auch wohl, als das Nonplusultra der musikalischen Kunst und als die Ersten *Consolations des Miseres de la vie humaine* an. Dieß ist in Nuce die litterarische Geschichte der Manie des Volksgesangs, welche einige Zeit gewütet hat, und gottlob meist vorbey ist; und an deren dagewesene Existenz man in wenig Jahren nur durch die etwanigen guten Sedimente sich erinnern wird, so die vorübergehende Gährung nachgelassen hat.

Thomas Percy's *Reliques of Ancient English Poetry* had appeared in 1765. The essay by Herder to which Cramer refers is his "Auszug aus einem Briefwechsel über Oßian und die Lieder alter Völker," which appeared in *Von deutscher Art und Kunst: Einige fliegende Blätter* (Hamburg: Bode, 1773); that by Bürger is his "Herzensausguß über Volks-Poesie," the second brief essay in "Aus Daniel Wunderlichs Buch," *Deutsches Museum* 1 (1776).

12. Cramer, review of *Lieder im Volkston*, 63–64:

> Der Inhalt dieser Vorrede, wird man denken, solle nun auch Herrn *Schultz* treffen, der hier Lieder *im Volkstone* herausgiebt:–aber mit nichtem! Der Zusatz: *im Volkstone* ist bey ihm nicht viel mehr als ein Vehiculum, durch das er seinen, jedes Lob verdienenden, herzlichen, gedachten, und innigst empfundenen Gesängen, einen leichtern Zugang zu den Ohren guter, aber von der Menge herauskommender Liedercompositionen fast abgeschreckter Zuhörer hat bahnen wollen. Zwar sieht man ihnen allen die auch nicht mislungne Bestrebung nach wahrer Faßlichkeit, Popularität, und Leichtigkeit an, die er manchmal sogar durch Aufnahme bekannter Gänge und Wendungen der simpeln Manier guter Volksweisen zu erreichen gesucht hat: allein dieß alles sind auch Eigenschaften des guten Liedes überhaupt, das von gar mancherley Schattirungen des Affects seyn kann; und demnach wollen wir sie als Lieder überhaupt betrachten.

13. Schulz, *Gedanken über den Einfluß der Musik auf die Bildung eines Volks, und über deren Einführung in den Schulen der königl. Dänischen Staaten* (Copenhagen: Christian Gottlob Prost, 1790), 3–6:

> Daß die Musik, wenn solche zweckmäßig ausgeübt und angewandt wird, die Sitten mildern, die Empfindung veredeln, Freude und Geselligkeit unter das Volk verbreiten, und überhaupt auf die Bildung des moralischen Charakters großen Einfluß haben könne, kann nur von denen bezweifelt werden, die keine Gelegenheit gehabt haben, über das Wesen und die Wirkungen dieser Kunst Betrachtungen anzustellen, oder von solchen, bey welchen es überhaupt noch nicht ausgemacht ist, daß die Cultur einer Nation ihre Glückseligkeit befördert.
>
> Die Musik würkt auf den reizbarsten Theil des Menschen, auf seine Sinnlichkeit, deren Leitung doch eine der ersten Zwecke der zur Bildung eines Volks anzuwendenden Mittel ist. Aufklärung des Verstandes allein würkt darauf oft nur langsam, oft nur schwach, oft gar nicht; die Musik hingegen allezeit, und oft so gewaltsam, daß sie zu unbegreiflichen Thaten entflammt. Nur ein Beyspiel: Der Soldat, der von der Ehre, fürs Vaterland zu sterben, unterrichtet ist, geht darum vielleicht nicht weniger verzagt in die Schlacht; bey dem Schalle einer lauten Kriegsmusik hingegen geht er, auch ohne diesen Unterricht, dem Tode beherzt entgegen. Das Zeugniß eines jungen aber versuchten Heerführers, dessen Namen hier zu nennen Prallerey seyn würde, nemlich, daß die Ermunterung

zum Singen das würksamste Hülfsmittel ist, dem Soldaten die Be-
schwerlichkeit eines forcirten Marsches nicht empfinden zu laßen, giebt
dem Vorhergesagten völlig Gewicht. Man kann leicht denken, wie sehr
die Würkung des Gesanges bey einer Armee noch erhöht werden müßte,
wenn bey jeder solchen und anderen Veranlaßungen zweckmäßige
Kriegs- und Soldatenlieder gesungen würden.

In den Provinzen Dännemarks, und hauptsächlich unter dem Land-
volke, weiß man noch wenig oder nichts von Musik. So gar der allgemeine Choralgesang in den Kirchen ist noch ein rohes Geschrey ohne
reine Intonation und Zusammenstimmung. Wenn ein Volk gegen die
Vergnügungen des edelsten Sinnes des Menschen, das Gehör, noch in
dem Grade gleichgültig ist, daß schreyen und singen, falsch und rein,
ihm einerley sind,—doch, das ist unter Europäern nicht möglich; sondern, wenn ein Volk die Musik nur dem Namen nach, oder höchstens nur
die unterste Stuffe ihrer Zauberkraft kennt, und von dem Eindrucke, den
sie auf seine Gefühle machen müßte, keine weitre Erfahrung hat, als den
sein rohes Geschrey oder falsch gespielte lärmende Instrumente darauf
hervorbringen, so kann man annehmen, daß die sittliche Bildung bey
diesem Volke noch keine bedeutende Fortschritte gemacht habe; wenigstens sind ihm viele der angenehmsten Gefühle, die den Genuß des Lebens erhöhn, noch unbekannt, und es fehlt ihm daher ein großer Theil
seiner Glückseligkeit. Man mache ihn aber stufenweise mit den höheren
Kräften der Musik bekannt, und zwar nur mit solchen, die seiner
Faßungskraft und seinen Gefühlen immer angemeßen bleiben, und die
vornemlich die Beförderung seines sittlichen Vergnügens zum Augen-
merk haben: man verschaffe ihn den öftern Genuß derselben in so manchen Fällen seines Lebens; und es ist nicht zu zweifeln, daß in eben dem
Grade, worin sein Gehör sich bildet und für die höheren Kräfte dieser
wohlthätigen Kunst empfänglich gemacht wird, auch Gefühle für Schönheit in ihm erweckt werden, deren Einfluß auf die Sitten, auf alle häus-
liche und gesellige Freuden, auf seinen Muth und seine Denkungsart, auf
Versüßung der Arbeit und Erleichterung jeder Last und Leiden, auf den
Genuß und die Glückseligkeit seines Lebens, unwidersprechlich ist.

Wie aber kann die Musik unter ein Volk bekannt und allgemein gemacht werden? Durch die Schulen. Mit dem Schul-Unterrichte muß zugleich der Unterricht in der Musik verbunden werden.

14. Such distaste of the educated for rural singing was by no means an isolated phenomenon. For an extended discussion of primarily English and American examples, see Nicholas Temperley, "The Old Way of Singing: Its Origins
and Development," *Journal of the American Musicological Society* 34 (1981):
511–44.

15. See Gerhard Sauder, "'Verhältnismäßige Aufklärung': Zur bürgerlichen Ideologie am Ende des 18. Jahrhunderts," *Jahrbuch der Jean-Paul-
Gesellschaft* 9 (1974): 102–26.

16. Schulz, *Gedanken*, 20: "Liedercompositionen . . . , und andre Musik-
und Singstücke über zweckmäßige geistliche und weltliche Texte, als Bauer-
lieder, Bürgerlieder, Soldatenlieder, Familienlieder, Rundgesänge über alle Gegenstände die ein Volk intereßiren." Schulz's formulation is reminiscent of the
full title of one of the most successful later collections of such edifying lieder,
the *Mildheimisches Lieder-Buch von 518 lustigen und ernsthaften Gesängen
über alle Dinge in der Welt und alle Umstände des menschlichen Lebens,
die man besingen kann,* edited by Rudolph Zacharias Becker (Gotha: Becker,
1799, and numerous later editions), which was directed to "Freunde erlaubter
Fröhlichkeit und edler Tugend" (friends of permissible merriment and noble
virtue).

17. G. E. Lessing, from a letter to Johann Wilhelm Ludewig Gleim of
22 May 1772. Translated from Johann Wilhelm Ludewig Gleim, *Sämmtliche
Werke,* edited by Wilhelm Körte (Halberstadt: Büreau für Literatur und Kunst,
1811; reprint, Hildesheim: G. Olm, 1971), 1:339–40:

> Sie nur haben das Volk eigentlich verstanden, und den mit seinem Kör-
> per thätigern Theil im Auge gehabt, dem es nicht sowohl am Verstande,
> als an der Gelegenheit, ihn zu zeigen, fehlt. Unter dieses Volk haben Sie
> sich gemischt, nicht, um es durch gewinnstlose Betrachtungen von
> seiner Arbeit abzuziehen, sondern es zu seiner Arbeit aufzumuntern,
> und seine Arbeit zur Quelle ihm angemessener Begriffe, und zugleich
> zur Quelle seines Vergnügens zu machen. Besonders athmen, in Anse-
> hung des letzteren, die meisten von diesen Ihren Liedern das, was den
> alten Weisen ein so wünschenswerthes, ehrenvolles Ding war, und was
> täglich mehr und mehr sich aus der Welt zu verlieren scheint, ich meine
> jene fröhliche Armuth, *laeta paupertas,* die dem Epikur und dem Seneka
> so sehr gefiel, und bei der es wenig darauf ankommt, ob sie erzwungen
> oder freiwillig ist, wenn sie nur fröhlich ist.

18. Stoljar, *Poetry and Song,* 170. Reichardt's (fragmentary) biography
appeared as "I. A. P. Schulz," *Allgemeine musikalische Zeitung* 3 (1800–01):
153–57, 169–76, 597–606, 613–20, and 629–35. For Schulz's correspondence,
see *Briefwechsel zwischen Johann Abraham Peter Schulz und Johann Heinrich
Voß,* edited by Heinz Gottwaldt und Gerhard Hahne, Schriften des Landesinstituts für Musikforschung Kiel 9 (Kassel: Bärenreiter, 1960).

19. Reichardt, "I. A. P. Schulz," 155–57.

20. Rudolf Vierhaus, introduction to *Das Volk als Objekt obrigkeitlichen
Handelns,* edited by Vierhaus, Wolfenbütteler Studien zur Aufklärung 13:
Kultur und Gesellschaft in Nordwestdeutschland zur Zeit der Aufklärung I
(Tübingen: Max Niemeyer, 1992), 4: "Beiden Seiten, den Regierenden wie den
Schreibenden, gemeinsam war die Neigung, das 'Volk' als Objekt der vernünf-
tigen Einsicht und der Beglückung zu verstehen und zu glauben, daß sie seine
wahren Interessen besser verstünden als es selber."

21. For a more general consideration of power in relation to Enlightenment
literature in Germany, see Wilson, "Enlightenment's Alliance with Power."

22. Ernst Klusen, "über den Volkston in der Musik des 19. Jahrhunderts," *Jahrbuch für Volksliedforschung* 17 (1972): 38: "Sie klammern alles Problematische, alles Kritische aus, gewinnen allen Umständen des Lebens eine positive Seite ab und tragen zur Volkserziehung bei, indem sie ordentliche Untertanen heranbilden."

23. Ibid., 37: "Der Künstler sucht neue Ausdrucksmittel und neue Ausdrucksformen zum Zwecke der persönlichen Entfaltung; der Komponist läßt sich, wie der Seefahrer vom Polarstern—zu neuen Ufern führen. Das ist ein individuelles, subjektives Gestaltungsproblem des autonomen Künstlers, das zu sehr komplizierten Gebilden führen kann." This combination of social critique with a faith in the nearly redemptive value of autonomous high art reveals the influence of Adorno, but Klusen's perspective also draws on the work of Dahlhaus. The variety of ways in which the volkslied has been defined and valued was recognized well before Klusen; see especially Julian von Pulikowski, *Geschichte des Begriffes Volkslied im musikalischen Schrifttum: Ein Stück deutscher Geistesgeschichte* (Heidelberg: Carl Winter, 1933; reprint, Wiesbaden: Dr. Martin Sändig, 1970).

24. Reichardt, "An junge Künstler," *Musikalisches Kunstmagazin* 1 (1782): 3:

> Liedermelodien in die jeder, der nur Ohren und Kehle hat gleich einstimmen soll, müssen für sich ohn' alle Begleitung bestehen können, müssen in der einfachsten Folge der Töne, in der bestimtesten Bewegung, in der genauesten Uebereinstimmung der Einschnitte und Abschnitte u.s.w. gerade die Weise—wie's *Herder* treffender nennt, als man sonst nur die Melodie des Liedes benannte—die Weise des Liedes so treffen, daß man die Melodie, weiß man sie einmal, nicht ohne die Worte, die Worte nicht ohne die Melodie mehr denken kann; daß die Melodie für die Worte alles nichts für sich allein seyn will.
>
> Eine solche Melodie wird allemal—um es dem Künstler mit einem Worte zu sagen—den wahren Charakter des Einklangs (*Unisono*) haben, also keiner zusammenklingenden Harmonie bedürfen oder auch nur Zulaß gestatten.
>
> So sind alle die Lieder der Zeiten beschaffen, da unser deutsches Volk noch reich an Gesang war.

25. Herder's own collections, like many that followed, included texts of all three varieties. On the contradictions this introduces into attempts to uphold the volkslied as an ideal creative expression uncontaminated by the taint of commerce, see Rolf Wilhelm Brednich, "Das Lied als Ware," *Jahrbuch für Volksliedforschung* 19 (1974): 11–20.

26. Herder, "Auszug aus einem Briefwechsel über Oßian und die Lieder alter Völker," in *Von deutscher Art und Kunst: Einige fliegende Blätter* (Hamburg: Bode, 1773; reprint, Stuttgart: Reclam, 1968), 12: "Wißen Sie also, daß je wilder, d.i. je lebendiger, je freiwürkender ein Volk ist, (denn mehr heißt dies

Wort doch nicht!) desto wilder, d.i. desto lebendiger, freier, sinnlicher, lyrisch handelnder müßen auch, wenn es Lieder hat, seine Lieder seyn!"

27. Herder, introduction to *Volkslieder. Nebst untermischten andern Stücken*, part 2 (Leipzig: in der Weygandschen Buchhandlung, 1779; reprint, Hildesheim: Georg Olms, 1981), 19: "Zum Volkssänger gehört nicht, daß er aus dem Pöbel seyn muß, oder für den Pöbel singt; so wenig es die edelste Dichtkunst beschimpft, daß sie im Munde des Volks tönet. Volk heißt nicht, der Pöbel auf den Gassen, der singt und dichtet niemals, sondern schreyt und verstümmelt." Such expression of contempt for the actual song of the rural and urban lower classes—often expressed through a contrast between volkslieder and *Gassenhauer*—continued well into the nineteenth century. For further examples, see Pulikowski, *Geschichte des Begriffes Volkslied*, 87–88, 112–14, and 398–99.

28. Reichardt, "An junge Künstler," 5:

> Warum aber findet auch der aufmerksamste Beobachter bey allen europäischen Völker keine neue wahre Volkslieder? Staatsverfassung thut freilich viel: die drückte aber auch sonst. Ich denke das wichtigste ist, daß das schöne Naturbedürfniß Kunst, die Kunst gar Handwerk geworden! Vom Oberkapellmeister des Fürsten bis zum Bierfiedler, der die Operette in die Bauernschenke trägt, ist ja fast alles izt nachahmender Handarbeiter für gangbaren Marktpreiß. Zum vollen Unglück sind ihrer gar so viele, daß die Konkurrenz nie unter die Käufer kommen kann, immer bey den Verkäufern ist. Daher denn auch der höchste Gipfel des izigen sogenannten Künstlers dieser ist, die größte Summe der Narrheiten seines Bezahlers mit einmal zu befriedigen. Und dieß hat einen so allgemein fatalen Einfluß aufs ganze Volk, daß wenn auch Obrigkeit und Pächter einmal ein frohes Gefühl im Menschen zum Aufwallen kommen läßt, dieser nicht mehr geraden, ungetrübten Sinn genug hat es aus sich selbst und nach seiner eignen Natur zu äußern, immer singt der überall fertige Spielmann aus ihm. Anstatt daß alte Jägerlieder ganz den Charakter des nachtfrohen Lauschers u Erhaschers an sich tragen, aus Fischerliedern das heimliche Wasserleben athmet, aus Hirtenliedern ruhige Heiterkeit ausgeht, und alle lebendigen Ausdruck wahrer Freud' und wahres Leid tönen.

29. Reichardt himself had no such illusions, at least not about contemporary rulers, as the *Kunstmagazin*'s dedicatory epistle, "An großgute Regenten," makes clear. For more on Reichardt's political views, see Günter Hartung, "Johann Friedrich Reichardt, der Musiker und der Publizist," in *Johann Friedrich Reichardt (1752–1814): Komponist und Schriftsteller der Revolutionszeit*, edited by Konstanze Musketa, Gert Richter, and Götz Traxdorf, Schriften des Händel-Hauses in Halle 8 (Halle: Händel-Haus, 1992), 11–21. Carl Dahlhaus notes that the idea of a Golden Age of volkslieder frequently came to absorb projections of "whatever one hoped but did not expect to receive from the pres-

ent," although he does not connect that projection with the social status of musicians (*Nineteenth-Century Music*, translated by J. Bradford Robinson [Berkeley and Los Angeles: University of California Press, 1989], 111).

30. Julia Moore, "Mozart Mythologized or Modernized?" *Journal of Musicological Research* 12 (1992): 83–109, esp. 89–91. In equating the economic lot of the musician with that of the *Handwerker*, however, Moore overlooks the consistent denigration of the latter social category in musical literature of that period.

31. Reichardt, "I. A. P. Schulz," 155–56: "Vater, es soll mir eine Kleinigkeit seyn mit der Musik künftig tausend Thäler jährlich zu gewinnen." For another example of a father who could not conceive of his son's ambition to become a musician as other than a choice of low status and poverty, see the account of J. W. Hässler in Klaus Hortschansky, "The Musician as Music Dealer in the Second Half of the 18th Century," in *The Social Status of the Professional Musician from the Middle Ages to the 19th Century*, edited by Walter Salmen, annotated and translated by Herbert Kaufman and Barbara Reisner, Sociology of Music 1 (New York: Pendragon, 1983), 217.

32. Schubert to several friends in Vienna, Zseliz, 3 August 1818, cited in *Schubert: Die Dokumente seines Lebens*, edited by Otto Erich Deutsch, Neue Ausgabe sämtlicher Werke, series 8, volume 5 (Kassel: Bärenreiter, 1964), 64: "sonst wär' noch ein verdorbener Musikant aus mir geworden."

33. DeNora, *Beethoven and the Construction of Genius*, 48–59.

34. On the values of the *Handwerker* and their transformation, see Hans-Ulrich Thamer, "Arbeit und Solidarität: Formen und Entwicklungen der Handwerkermentalität im 18. und 19. Jahrhundert in Frankreich und Deutschland," in *Handwerker in der Industrialisierung: Lage, Kultur, und Politik vom späten 18. bis ins frühe 20. Jahrhundert*, edited by Ulrich Engelhardt (Stuttgart: Klett-Cotta, 1984), 469–96.

35. Sabine Schutte, "Zur Kritik der Volkslied-Ideologie in der zweiten Hälfte des 19. Jahrhunderts," *Jahrbuch für Volksliedforschung* 20 (1975): 44–45.

36. The quotation is from Jürgen Schlumbohm, *Freiheit: Die Anfänge der bürgerlichen Emanzipationsbewegung in Deutschland im Spiegel ihres Leitwortes*, Geschichte und Gesellschaft: Bochumer Historische Studien 12 (Düsseldorf: Schwann, 1975), 83: "die rechtlichen Grundlagen einer vollen und unbehinderten Durchsetzung kapitalistischer Produktionsverhältnisse."

37. For a brief introduction to the topic of the *Bildungsbürgertum* and its extensive literature, see Hans-Ulrich Wehler, *Deutsche Gesellschaftsgeschichte*, volume 1: *Vom Feudalismus des Alten Reiches bis zur Defensiven Modernisierung der Reformära, 1700–1815* (Munich: C. H. Beck, 1987), 210–17.

38. Ludwig Achim von Arnim, "Von Volksliedern: An Herrn Kapellmeister Reichardt," in *Des Knaben Wunderhorn: Alte deutsche Lieder*, collected by Arnim and Clemens Brentano [1806–08] (Munich: Winkler-Verlag, n.d.), 859: "Haben Sie doch selbst mehr getan für alten deutschen Volksgesang als einer

der lebenden Musiker, haben Sie ihn doch nach seiner Würdigkeit den lesenden Ständen mitgeteilt."

39. Ibid., 859–61; quotations from 859. For a similar account of a socially stratifying function being ascribed to traditional South African music, see Louise Meintjes, "Paul Simon's *Graceland,* South Africa, and the Mediation of Musical Meaning," *Ethnomusicology* 34 (1990): 52.

40. Arnim, "Von Volksliedern," 861:

> In diesem Wirbelwind des Neuen, in diesem vermeinten urschnellen Paradiesgebären auf Erden waren auch in Frankreich (schon vor der Revolution, die dadurch vielleicht erst möglich wurde) fast alle Volkslieder erloschen; noch jetzt sind sie arm daran—was soll sie an das binden, was ihnen als Volk festdauernd? Auch in England werden Volkslieder seltener gesungen; auch Italien sinkt in seinem nationalen Volksliede, in der Oper durch Neuerungssucht der leeren Leute; selbst in Spanien soll sich manches Lied verlieren und nichts Bedeutendes sich verbreiten.—O mein Gott, wo sind die alten Bäume, unter denen wir noch gestern ruhten, die uralten Zeichen fester Grenzen, was ist damit geschehen, was geschieht? Fast vergessen sind sie schon unter dem Volke, schmerzlich stoßen wir uns an ihren Wurzeln. Ist der Scheitel hoher Berge nur einmal ganz abgeholzt, so treibt der Regen die Erde hinunter, es wächst da kein Holz wieder; daß Deutschland nicht so weit verwirtschaftet werde, sei unser Bemühen.

41. Reichardt discusses Schulz's 1770 visit to Haydn in "I. A. P. Schulz," 176. On Gottfried van Swieten and the German lied, see Schwab, *Sangbarkeit, Popularität, und Kunstlied,* 120–21. For a discussion of Mozart's working circumstances, see Neal Zaslaw, "Mozart as a Working Stiff," in *On Mozart,* edited by James M. Morris (Washington, D.C.: Woodrow Wilson Center Press; Cambridge: Cambridge University Press, 1994), 102–12.

42. "Korrespondenz: Wien, den 2ten May, 1801," *Allgemeine musikalische Zeitung* 3 (1801): 577: "athmet die unbefangenste Munterkeit."

43. H. C. Robbins Landon and David Wyn Jones, *Haydn: His Life and Music* (Bloomington: Indiana University Press, 1988), 333.

44. The classic study of this phenomenon and its impact on rural life is Rudolf Braun, *Industrialisation and Everyday Life,* translated by Sarah Hanbury Tenison (Cambridge: Cambridge University Press, 1990). On spinning songs, see 139–40.

45. A long tradition of criticism of the libretto points to such inconsistencies in the tone of the text without, however, exploring their social implications. See, for example, the sources cited in Robbins Landon and Wyn Jones, *Haydn,* 309; "Oratorium," *Wiener allgemeine musikalische Zeitung,* no. 1 (1813): 67, which notes that *Die Jahreszeiten* was a difficult compositional challenge "because of the heterogeneous tone of the text" ("der ungleichartigen

Haltung des Textes wegen"); and Karl Geiringer, *Haydn: A Creative Life in Music*, 2nd edition (Berkeley and Los Angeles: University of California Press, 1968), 389: "It cannot be denied that the heterogeneous elements of van Swieten's 'Winter' do not blend well."

46. Review of *Ueber die Musik der Indier*, 292: "und so besteht auch das *Schöne*, welches aus der Wahl eines wirklichen Volksliedes ... oder eines volksmässigen simpeln Thema's in Händels, Haydns u. a. Werken [sic], nicht darin, dass diese Männer, etwa in Ermangelung eines Bessern, hierzu ihre Zuflucht hätten nehmen müssen, sondern dass sie im Verfolg ihrer Komposition zeigen, wie viel sich aus einem einfachen oder einfach scheinenden Satze durch ihren *eignen* Ideen-Reichthum und nach Beschaffenheit *unsrer* Musik machen lässt."

47. See David P. Schroeder, *Haydn and the Enlightenment: The Late Symphonies and Their Audience* (Oxford: Clarendon Press, 1990), esp. 21–32.

48. "Korrespondenz: Wien, den 2ten May, 1801," 579: "In diesem Zirkel fand Haydn's Genius Liebe zur Kunst, ein gebildetes und empfängliches Publikum, und Aufmunterung, wie sie in Deutschland nicht gewöhnlich ist. Möchte sich der Geschmack dieser Schule lange erhalten, weit verbreiten, und überall solche Früchte hervorbringen!"

49. Ibid., 576: "Vom Anfange bis an's Ende wird das Gemüth vom Rührendsten zum Furchtbarsten, vom Naivesten zum Künstlichsten, vom Schönsten zum Erhabensten unwillkührlich fortgerissen."

50. Walther Vetter's assertion that such songs present "pictures of real life" and represent "healthy classical realism" is itself a remarkable idealization (*Der Klassiker Schubert* [Leipzig: Breitkopf & Härtel, 1953], 1:48).

51. See David Gramit, "The Intellectual and Aesthetic Tenets of Franz Schubert's Circle" (Ph.D. dissertation, Duke University, 1987), 96–103, and, more specifically in relation to the ideals of the *Volksaufklärung*, "Lieder, Listeners, and Ideology: Schubert's 'Alinde' and Opus 81," *Current Musicology* 58 (1995): 38.

52. The link between abstraction and administration was recognized by Humboldt himself: "Nichts ist so wichtig bei einem höheren Staatsbeamten, als welchen Begriff er eigentlich nach allen Richtungen hin von der Menschheit hat, worin er ihre Würde und ihr Ideal im Ganzen setzt, mit welchem Grade intellectueller Klarheit er es sich denkt, mit welcher Wärme er empfindet; welche Ausdehnung er dem Begriff der Bildung giebt, was er darin für nothwendig, was nur gewissermassen für Luxus hält." Wilhelm von Humboldt, "Gutachten über die Organisation der Ober-Examinations-Kommission," 8 July 1809, in *Werke*, edited by Andreas Flitner and Klaus Giel (Darmstadt: Wissenschaftliche Buchgesellschaft, 1964), 4:83–84.

53. Friedrich von Schiller, "Ueber Matthisson's Gedichte" (1794), in *Schillers Werke: Nationalausgabe*, edited by Herbert Meyer (Weimar: Hermann Böhlaus Nachfolger, 1958), 22:268–69: "Um aber versichert zu sein, daß er sich auch wirklich an die reine Gattung in den Individuen wende, muß er selbst zuvor das Individuum in sich ausgelöscht und zur Gattung gesteigert haben. Nur alsdann, wenn er nicht als der oder der bestimmte Mensch (in welchem

der Begriff der Gattung immer beschränkt sein würde), sondern wenn er als *Mensch überhaupt* empfindet, ist er gewiß, daß die ganze Gattung ihm nach-empfinden werde—wenigstens kann er auf diesen Effekt mit dem nämlichen Rechte dringen, als er von jedem menschlichen Individuum Menschheit ver-langen kann."

Schiller's review also includes another example of the opposition of art and *Manufaktur* (266).

54. On later examples of the *volkstümliches Lied,* see Edward F. Kravitt, *The Lied: Mirror of Late Romanticism* (New Haven: Yale University Press, 1996), esp. 113–23 and 132–41.

55. This brief list includes only the pieces with clear peasant associations; the collection includes a variety of other examples associated with traditional trades or activities as well, including sailors' songs, riding songs, etc.

56. Robert Schumann, "Musikalische Haus- und Lebensregeln," in *Gesammelte Schriften über Musik und Musiker,* new edition (Leipzig: Breitkopf & Härtel, 1883), 2:371: "Höre fleißig auf alle Volkslieder; sie sind eine Fund-grube der schönsten Melodieen und öffnen dir den Blick in den Charakter der verschiedenen Nationen."

57. On the instability of musical careers between Reichardt's time and Schumann's, see Georg Sowa, *Anfänge institutioneller Musikerziehung in Deutschland (1800–1843): Pläne, Realisierung und zeitgenössische Kritik mit Darstellung der Bedingungen und Beurteilung der Auswirkungen,* Studien zur Musikgeschichte des 19. Jahrhunderts 33 (Regensburg: Gustav Bosse, 1973), 20–22.

58. Carl Alexander, "Ueber das Volkslied, insonders das Italiänische," *Neue Zeitschrift für Musik* 1 (1834): 233: "Sprache ist der durch gewisse Laute beur-kundete Affect der Seele. Die erste Bezeichnung desselben möchte wohl wenig von den Lauten der Thiere unterschieden gewesen sein, und kaum mehr als Schmerz und Freude bezeichnet haben. Daher hören wir noch jetzt die Spra-chen junger oder in tiefe Kindheit zurückgesunkener Völker der heißen Zonen Afrika's und Amerika's, einem langgedehnten, aus Consonanten [*sic*] bestehen-den Geheul ähnlich, nach der Gewaltigkeit ihren Leidenschaften zur unan-genehmen Monotonie gedehnt, indeß die der nordischen Völker nach der Ab-gemessenheit und Kürze ihres Wesens vielmehr einem vocalgehäuften [*sic*] Gezische, Geklapper oder Gepolter gleichen." In my translation I have emended the printed text, which garbles the sense of the passage by reversing *Consonant* and *Vocal.*

59. Ibid., 234:

> So wie die Sprache, nicht nur in Hinsicht auf Wohlklang, sondern auch auf Charakteristik, Reichtum und Modulationsfähigkeit unbedingt die Bildung der Nationen bezeichnet, so ist das Lied der treueste Spiegel ihrer Seele, ihres Charakters, ihrer Gefühlsfähigkeit; mithin die wichtig-ste Quelle aller poetischen und musikalischen, ja, weiter ausgedehnt, aller historischen und philosophischen Forschungen, und es muß das Volks-

lied allen Tonkünstlern ein ehrwürdiges Denkmal einer klassischen Jugend, ein Muster einfachen, natürlichen Gefühls, ohne daß wir zu glauben nöthig haben, daß etwas anders, als Mangel an Erfahrung, an Elas-
ticität des Geistes die Grenzen der edlen Einfachheit gehalten habe. Was
das wohlbegabte einfältige Gemüth instinctmäßig findet, dazu kehrt
endlich durch Irrthum und Schwanken die höchste Bildung zurück, fest
freilich und überzeugt.

60. The opposition of folksong to the fashionable, and its use to secure and
revitalize "the current situation of art, which not infrequently seems to be that
of a craft" (der gegenwärtige Kunstzustand, der nicht selten ein Handwerks-
stand zu sein scheint), is also developed in Carl Ferdinand Becker, "Das Volkslied," *Neue Zeitschrift für Musik* 12 (1840): 69–70; quotation from 69.

61. On the crucial role played by that literary tradition despite the dominance of Viennese rather than North German music in the canon, see Hartung,
"Johann Friedrich Reichardt," 14.

62. Ernst Ludwig Gerber, *Historisch-Biographisches Lexikon der Tonkünstler* (1790–92; reprint, edited by Othmar Wessely, Graz: Akademische
Druck- und Verlagsanstalt, 1977), 1:610: "Er besitzt die große Kunst in seinen
Sätzen öfters bekannt zu scheinen. Dadurch wird er trotz allen contrapunkti-
schen Künsteleyen, die sich darinne befinden, populair und jedem Liebhaber an-
genehm."

63. Gerber, *Lexikon der Tonkünstler*, 2:472: "Unter den jetztlebenden Mei-
stern erster Größe, sind meine Götzen *Schulz* und *Haydn*. Jeder junge Komponist von Talent, suche sich diese beyden zum Muster aufzustellen. Beyde
sind eben so klassisch richtig, als unerreichbar in ihren Schönheiten."

64. E. T. A. Hoffmann, review of Symphony No. 5, 152. Hoffmann's evocation of an idealized rural setting and the round dance connect what could otherwise be simply a description of childlike simplicity to the idealized *Volk* and
their music.

65. Adolph Bernhard Marx, "Haydn, (Joseph)," *Encyclopädie der gesammten musikalischen Wissenschaften, oder Universal-Lexicon der Tonkunst*, edited by Gustav Schilling (Stuttgart: Franz Heinrich Köhler, 1836), 3:518: "Er
war *ganz* den Ausdruck seines Volks, ganz voll und rein. Bürgerlich ehrbar und
rechtlich, in natürlichem Behagen, das das schöne Oestreich jeder Brust ein-
gießt, in unschuldiger Herzensheiterkeit eines von außen und innen ungetrüb-
ten unaufgestörten, fernen Verlangens und fernhinreißender Ideen freien Le-
bensgenusses, kindlich liebevoll und fromm, innigerer Naturempfindung und
froher, *spaßiger* Laune gern offen: so das Völkchen im nächsten Kreise um den
väterlichen Herrscherthron Oesterreichs, und so sein eigenster Sänger."

66. Ibid., 523: "Das Reich des Gedankens gab ihm nur so viel Einblick, als
sich mit der ungestörten Regsamkeit seines Naturells, seines volksmäßigen
Denkens, Empfindens, und Glaubens vertrug; es ließ ihn unbefangenes Kind
seines Landes bleiben und hob ihn über die Fläche bewußtlosen Instinkts, ohne
ihn dem sicheren natürlichen Boden zu entfremden."

67. Ibid., 525: "Kraft seiner tiefern Idee ist Beethoven—und er zuerst—zu neuen, höhern Offenbarungen geführt worden. Aber in dem, was Haydn gab, steht er einzig und unentbehrlich da."

68. James Webster, *Haydn's "Farewell" Symphony and the Idea of Classical Style: Through Composition and Cyclic Integration in His Instrumental Music*, Cambridge Studies in Music Theory and Analysis 1 (Cambridge: Cambridge University Press, 1991), 347–56; quotation from 352. Haydn's strong association with the simple, popular, and folklike may have contributed to Haydn scholarship's reluctance—documented by Webster—to recognize the sophistication of Haydn's music before ca. 1780. Without postulating a long and arduous apprenticeship, a discipline rooted in the values of the nineteenth-century bourgeoisie could not easily acknowledge the value of the music of such a composer, who came neither from a hereditary family of musicians nor from the bourgeoisie itself. Schubert, whose origins presented a similar problem, was also long constructed as a purely natural (and therefore simple) phenomenon, and he too was ultimately subordinated to Beethoven. See Gramit, "Constructing a Victorian Schubert."

69. Guido Adler, "Die Wiener Klassiker Schule," in *Handbuch der Musikgeschichte*, edited by Adler, 2nd edition (1929; reprint, Tützing: Hans Schneider, 1961), 2:783: "Ihre Kunst steht auf dem Boden der Volksmusik."

70. Wilhelm Fischer, "Zur Entwicklungsgeschichte des Wiener klassischen Stils," *Studien zur Musikwissenschaft* 3 (1915): 29: "Der 'Liedtypus' entstammt den Tanz- und Liedweisen des Volkes."

71. Webster, *Haydn's "Farewell" Symphony*, 351.

72. W. Fischer, "Entwicklungsgeschichte," 79: "Der Anteil der Tanzstücke an der Bildung der Sonatenform ist also ein zweifacher: modulatorisches Grundgerüst und Aufbau der Hauptmelodieen ist tanzartig. Alle anderen Formelemente verdanken ihren Ursprung Formen, die der Tanzmusik ferne stehen. Mit vollem Rechte verweist also Guido Adler auf die große Wichtigkeit des Einflusses, den die Abkömmlinge der polyphonen Vokalformen auf die Ausgestaltung der Sonatenform genommen haben." (Fischer gives as the source of Adler's claim his introduction to the *Denkmäler der Tonkunst in österreich*, volume 9, part 2: viii–ix.)

73. On the development of populist politics in Vienna in the late nineteenth and early twentieth centuries, see Carl E. Schorske, "Politics in a New Key: An Austrian Trio," in *Fin-de-Siècle Vienna: Politics and Culture* (New York: Vintage Books, 1981), 116–80. On popularization in musical life, see Margaret Notley, "*Volksconcerte* in Vienna and Late Nineteenth-Century Ideology of the Symphony," *Journal of the American Musicological Society* 50 (1997): 421–53.

74. Walter Wiora, *Europäische Volksmusik und abendländische Tonkunst* (Kassel: Johann Philipp Hinnenthal, 1957), 29: "Inwieweit es einem Komponisten gelingt, die Idee echter, gehaltvoller Volkstümlichkeit zu verwirklichen, hängt nicht nur an seinem guten Willen und an den politischen Richtlinien, die er befolgt. Er muß, wie ein Redner, Instinkt dafür haben, was 'ankommt'; er

muß auf eine Hörerschaft eingespielt sein und 'Volk' von 'Masse' und 'Pöbel' zu scheiden wissen. Neben zahlreichen Abformen, wie gehaltlos-simplen, volkstümelnder und primitivistischen Musikstücken, stehen denkwürdige Arten echt volkstümlicher Kunst. So haben die Wiener Klassiker die Sache des Geistes mit den Ansprüchen der Mitwelt vereint." Wiora discusses the classical style at length in his chapter "Volksmusik und Wiener Klassik," 104–33.

75. Schwab, *Sangbarkeit, Popularität, und Kunstlied,* 132: "Mit solcher Verfahrensweise haben es die Meister verstanden, eine breite Mitwelt einzubeziehen. Neben dem eingängigen Volkston, dem 'Schein des Bekannten', steht die harte Arbeit am musikalischen Material selbst zum Ziele intensiver Werkorganisation. So erfüllen ihre Werke beide Komponenten des Stilbegriffs 'Klassik': die gesellschaftliche und die qualitative." On the contrasting origins and implications of *Werk, Werker,* and *werken* (terms associated with handicraft production) and *Arbeit, Arbeiter,* and *arbeiten* (originating in feudal labor obligations and later associated with wage labor), see Richard Biernacki, *The Fabrication of Labor: Germany and Britain, 1640–1914,* Studies on the History of Society and Culture 22 (Berkeley and Los Angeles: University of California Press, 1995), 290–91.

76. It is important to note, however, that the music-critical discussions cited in this section are by no means the only ones available for the music of this period. I have explored one alternative in "Lieder, Listeners, and Ideology." A number of other musicologists have provided more extensive studies that grapple stimulatingly with issues of socially grounded musical meaning in this period, including Wye Jamison Allanbrook, *Rhythmic Gesture in Mozart: Le Nozze di Figaro and Don Giovanni* (Chicago: University of Chicago Press, 1983); Jeffrey Kallberg, *Chopin at the Boundaries: Sex, History, and Musical Genre* (Cambridge: Harvard University Press, 1996); and Hunter, *The Culture of Opera Buffa.*

77. Walter Frisch, "Schubert's *Nähe des Geliebten* (D. 162): Transformation of the *Volkston,*" in *Schubert: Critical and Analytical Studies,* edited by Frisch (Lincoln: University of Nebraska Press, 1986), 176.

78. Joseph Kerman, *"An die ferne Geliebte," Beethoven Studies* 1 (1974): 123–57.

79. Charles Rosen, *The Classical Style: Haydn, Mozart, Beethoven* (New York: Norton, 1972). Although the following discussion is based on *The Classical Style,* Rosen's discussions of the transcendence of simplicity in *An die ferne Geliebte* and the role of elements drawn from folk music in Chopin in his more recent *The Romantic Generation* ([Cambridge: Harvard University Press, 1995], 166–74 [esp. 174] and 410–13, respectively) suggest that his views remain largely unchanged.

80. Webster, *Haydn's "Farewell" Symphony,* 353–55.

81. Rosen, *The Classical Style,* 335, 337, 341.

CHAPTER 4. EDUCATION AND THE SOCIAL ROLES OF MUSIC

1. Adolph Bernhard Marx, "Beethoven, Ludwig van," in *Encyclopädie der gesammten musikalischen Wissenschaften, oder Universal-Lexikon der Tonkunst*, edited by Gustav Schilling (Stuttgart: Franz Heinrich Köhler, 1835), 1:519–20:

> Wie im äußern Leben er sich fruchtlos nach dem süßbefriedenden Familienbande sehnt und sein Herz mit väterlichem Antheil an übelgerathenen Verwandten täuscht und gern immer wieder zur Täuschung zurückkehrt, so wendet er in seiner Kunst mit Sehnsucht Erinnerung und Wünsche der Liebe hin zu den Menschen, so wächst ihm das Verlangen nach *Menschen-Musik*, nach *Gesang*, und führt ihn auf den Gipfel seines Schaffens. Die neunte Sinfonie, mit Chor, wird geschrieben. . . . Riesengewaltig beschwört er die riesigen Mächte des vollsten, bewegtesten Orchesters. . . . Das alles kann nicht ferner genügen. Es zertrümmert; und die Instrumente selbst ergreifen (in Recitativform) die Weise menschlichen Gesanges. Noch einmal wehen traumhaft alle jene Gestalten vorüber, menschliche Stimmen ergreifen jenes Recitativ, und sie führen zu Schillers Freudengesang, Ihm ein Bundeslied aller Menschen. Nichts kann rührender seyn, nichts läßt uns so tief schauen in seine Brust, als wie erst Bässe, dann Sänger das 'Freude schöner Götterfunken' so einfältig, so volksmäßig anstimmen, so hingegeben in das sanfte Verlangen und Lieben, das nur Menschen, Menschen! Sucht, nur der Gemeinschaft mit Menschen bedarf, und nichts Höheres mehr kennt und will.

2. See Butt, *Music Education*. A noteworthy exception to the separation of studies of education and musical culture is Wolfgang Scherer, *Klavier-Spiele: Die Psycho-Technik der Klaviere im 18. und 19. Jahrhundert*, Materialität der Zeichen, A2 (Munich: Wilhelm Fink, 1989). Eckhard Nolte, *Die Musik im Verständnis der Musikpädagogik des 19. Jahrhunderts: Ein Beitrag zur Geschichte der Theorie musikalischen Lernens und Lehrens in der Schule*, Beiträge zur Musikpädagogik (Paderborn: Ferdinand Schöningh, 1982), also attempts such a link, but does so in order to show the influence of contemporary intellectual and music-aesthetic developments on pedagogical approaches of that period. Michael Spitzer, "Marx's 'Lehre' and the Science of Education: Towards the Recuperation of Music Pedagogy," *Music and Letters* 79 (1998): 489–526, provides another example of English-language work on German pedagogy; although it does examine some of the links between Pestalozzi and music pedagogy that I will discuss below, it focuses on compositional instruction and does not consider pedagogy as a socially and historically conditioned practice.

3. Butt, *Music Education*, 166–92; Rosen, *The Romantic Generation*, 363.

4. For an overview of Marx's views on music education in relation to music, see his *Die Musik des neunzehnten Jahrhunderts und ihre Pflege: Methode der Musik*, 2nd edition (Leipzig: Breitkopf & Härtel, 1873; 1st edition 1854).

For more detailed consideration of Marx's method, see Spitzer, "Marx's 'Lehre' and the Science of Education."

5. On the issues facing professional musicians and the institutionalization of their training, see Sowa, *Anfänge institutioneller Musikerziehung in Deutschland*. On the mechanization of keyboard instruction, see Scherer, *Klavier-Spiele*, esp. 107–223. No study on gender and music education in the period is available, but see, for example, Nina d'Aubigny von Engelbrunner, *Briefe an Natalie über den Gesang, als Beförderung der häuslichen Glückseligkeit und geselligen Vergnügens* (Leipzig: Voß, 1803 and numerous later editions), and the articles by Friedrich Guthmann discussed below.

6. On the reception of the symphony, see Ruth Solie, "Beethoven as Secular Humanist: Ideology and the Ninth Symphony in Nineteenth-Century Criticism," in *Explorations in Music, the Arts, and Ideas: Essays in Honor of Leonard B. Meyer*, edited by Eugene Narmour and Ruth A. Solie, Festschrift Series 7 (Stuyvesant, N.J.: Pendragon, 1988), 1–42.

7. Hans Georg Nägeli, "Anrede an die schweizerische Musikgesellschaft, bey Eröffnung ihre Sitzung zu Zürich, den 19ten August 1812," *Allgemeine musikalische Zeitung* 14 (1812): 715–16: "Je mehr nämlich die Instrumentalmusik sublimirt wird, je weiter entfernt sie sich von der Popularität; die Vokalmusik hingegen nähert sich ihr, je vollkommener sie erscheint."

8. See, for example, Christman, "Tableau über das Musikwesen im Wirtembergischen," *Allgemeine musikalische Zeitung* 2 (1799): 74: at country dances, "the characteristic and naive fall away so completely that one would sooner believe he is hearing a chorus of wild bacchantes than an orderly folksong" (das Charakteristische und Naive so ganz hinwegfällt, daß man eher einen Chor wilder Bacchanten zu hören glaubt, als einen regelmäßigen Volksgesang); "Ueber die Benutzung der Musik zur Veredelung der Landleute, als Sache des Staates, *Allgemeine musikalische Zeitung* 7 (1805): 667: in village churches, "singing does not occur, but rather screaming at the top of the lungs" (da wird nicht gesungen, sondern aus voller Kehle geschrieen); and Christian Friedrich Michaelis, "Einige Gedanken über die Vortheile der frühen musikalischen Bildung, *Allgemeine musikalische Zeitung* 7 (1804): 120, which bemoans "the heartrending scream or howl of the Sunday church meetings" (das herzzerschneidende Geschrey oder Geheul der sonntaglichen Kirchenversammlungen).

9. Hans Georg Nägeli and Michael Traugott Pfeiffer, *Gesangbildungslehre nach Pestalozzischen Grundsätzen, pädagogisch begründet von Michael Traugott Pfeiffer, methodisch bearbeitet von Hans Georg Nägeli* (Zurich: H. G. Nägeli, 1810), 9–10:

> 1. Der Lehrer, an der Wandtafel den Kindern gegenüberstehend, spricht: "Kinder! Ihr sollt singen lernen. Nehmt dazu die gehörige Stellung an, wie ich es verlange: Steht aufrecht! Die Brust heraus; den Kopf nicht zurückgeworfen!"

2. "Steht fest! die Füße nicht zu nah einander!" Weil sie nöthig haben, die Stellung des Körpers von Zeit zu Zeit ein wenig zu verändern, so heißt er sie abwechselnd, bald den rechten, bald den linken Fuß ein wenig vorwärts stellen.

3. "Ihr sollt nie schrag stehen. Die, gegen beyden Seiten zu, müssen nur die Augen und allenfalls den Kopf ein wenig gegen mich wenden, den Körper nicht."

4. "Zum Singen braucht ihr die gleichen Organe (Theile des Körpers) wie zum sprechen. Ich hebe nun die Hand auf; wie ich sie niederschlage, sprecht den Selbstlauter a aus.["]—"a"—(Das Aufheben der Hand, zur Bezeichnung des Anfangs einer Uebung, muß etwas langsam geschehen, zum Unterschied des später einzuführenden taktmässigen Aufschlags. Die Hand muß immer ein Weilchen, zur Bedenkzeit der Kinder, gehoben stehen bleiben, immer aber schnell, gleichsam zuckend, niedergeschlagen werden.)

5. "Ich hebe wieder die Hand auf; wie ich sie niederschlage, sagt zweymal a."—"a.a."

6. "Noch einmal! Wie ich sie niederschlage, sage etliche Male, fünf-sechsmal a."—"a.a.a.a.a.a."—

7. "Und noch einmal! Verbindet mir viele solche a, ohne daß es einen Absatz giebt; vermeidet dabey das Stottern!" Die Kinder versuchen es, ohne es zu können. Endlich sagt er: "Merkt auf! Ich will euch so ein fortgesetztes a hervorbringen." Nun singt er in der ungefähren Tonhöhe, in welcher das a von der Maße (der Gesammtheit der Stimmen) ausgesprochen ward, wirklich einen reingehaltenen Ton. Er spricht: "Macht mir's nach" und singt den Ton auf gleiche Weise. Die Kinder singen "a."

8. "Nun, Kinder! habt ihr einen Ton hervorgebracht. Wenn man einen Selbstlauter ein ziemliches Weilchen so fortsetzt, ebenmässig, und ohne die mindeste Unterbrechung, so entsteht das, was man einen Ton nennt; und eben so fängt man an zu singen."

10. See Nauenburg, "Gesangmethode," in *Encyclopädie der gesammten musikalischen Wissenschaften, oder Universal-Lexikon der Tonkunst*, edited by Gustav Schilling (Stuttgart: Franz Heinrich Köhler, 1836), 3:217.

11. For an overview of a variety of methods of the period, see Rainer Lorenz, *Musikpädagogik in den ersten 30 Jahren des 19. Jahrhunderts am Beispiel Carl Gottlieb Herings*, Musikpädagogik: Forschung und Lehre 26 (Mainz: Schott, 1988), 132–79.

12. On the reform period in relation to Napoleon, see James J. Sheehan, *German History, 1770–1866*, Oxford History of Modern Europe (Oxford: Clarendon Press, 1989), 250–323; on education in particular, see also 364–65 and 435.

13. See Nolte, *Die Musik im Verständnis der Musikpädagogik*, 23–25, 114–16, and 204.

14. Johann Gottfried Hientzsch, "Gesang," *Eutonia* 1 (1829): 158 (the article is an overview of current and past singing methods): "es hat auch eine außerordentliche Anzahl Lehrer sich nach und nach aus diesem Werke abgezogen, was Methode im Gesangunterricht heißen will, und es werden dies hoffentlich noch recht Viele thun. Es ist und bleibt ein Hauptwerk über den Gesang-Unterricht in Schulen jeglicher Art."

15. Johann Heinrich Pestalozzi, *How Gertrude Teaches Her Children*, translated by Lucy E. Holland and Frances C. Turner (Syracuse, N.Y.: C. W. Bardeen, 1898; reprint, Washington, D.C.: University Publications of America, 1977), 132–33; for the German text, see Pestalozzi, *Wie Gertrud ihre Kinder lehrt*, in his *Ausgewählte Werke*, edited by Otto Boldemann (Berlin: Volk und Wissen, 1963), 2:314.

16. See Pestalozzi, *Wie Gertrud ihre Kinder lehrt*, 322.

17. Nägeli, "Die Pestalozzische Gesangbildungslehre nach Pfeiffers Erfindung kunstwissenschaftlich dargestellt im Namen Pestalozzis, Pfeiffers und ihrer Freunde," *Allgemeine musikalische Zeitung* 11 (1809): 770–71: "Dem eigentlichen Musiker muthen mir daher nichts Geringers zu, als dass er für einmal sein ererbtes Tonsystem gleichwie seine erlernte Tonsetzkunst, besonders auch das, was ihm die Systmatiker—sonderbar genug—als seine Grammatik und Rhetorik geben wollten, zu vergessen suche; dass er bey unserm Gebrauch der Kunstwörter sich nie jenes System, überhaupt nichts weiter denke, als die einfache Definition. Ja sogar seine theoretische Eintheilung des Gebiets der Musik in Harmonie und Melodie können wir ihm nicht lassen. Er muss seinen alten Standpunkt zum Behuf gegenwärtiger Untersuchung ganz und gar verlassen, um von einer neuen Seite in das Gebiet der Kunst und Kunstwissenschaft Eingang zu finden. Er vertraue uns."

18. The quotation is from Nägeli and Pfeiffer, *Gesangbildungslehre*, 1: "Der Lehrer selbst äußere bey Eröffnung der ersten Lehrstunde Freude an der Musik."

19. Ibid., 4: "Der Lehrer hüte sich, den Kindern von Empfindungsausdruck, von geschmackvollem Vortrage, von Kunstschönheit in höherm Sinne u. dgl. zu sprechen. . . . Alle unbestimmten musikalisch-asthetischen Ideen dieser Art sollen den Kindern bei dieser unsrer Tonkunstlehre ganz fremd bleiben."

20. Ibid., 65: "die Fortschreitungen der dissonirender Intervalle. . . . bekanntlich bey Weitem der wichtigste und schwierigste Theil der Intonationskunst."

21. Ibid., 68: "Purifikation, Rektifikation und Amplifikation seines Tonvermögens."

22. Ibid., 120:

> Der musikalische Sinn, vorerst durch den rhytmischen, den melodischen, den dynamischen Kurs allseitig aufgeregt, dann durch die Verbindung der Tonelemente mannigfaltig erweitert, soll nun hier zum ächten Kunstsinne gesteigert und geläutert werden; das Vermögen, den Kunstgegenstand (die jedesmalige Tonreihe oder Uebungsphrase) sich *inner-*

lich auf das Genaueste als Begriffs- und Gefühlssache zu vergegenwärtigen, soll hier—in specieller Anwendung betrachtet—seine Vollendung erhalten. Die Tonreihe, die das Kind hört, soll ihm so deutlich vorschweben, daß es einen Moment später, allenfalls eine halbe Minute nachher, die Töne nach ihren Verhältnissen noch geistig um sein Ohr klingen hört, und die ihnen entsprechenden Noten vor seinem Auge dastehen sieht, gleich als wenn es sie äusserlich an die Tafel geheftet sähe. In geringem Grade besitzt dieses Vermögen jeder, der im Stande ist, eine musikalische Phrase auswendig zu singen: denn um sie auswendig singen zu können, muß man sie inwendig sich vergegenwärtigen, *hören*, und wenn man sie nach den Noten erlernt hat, in der That auch *sehen*. Ja jederman hat, als Mensch, diesen geistigen Sinn, ein Seelenohr und Seelenauge— mit einem Wort: das Vermögen der *Kunstanschauung*. So soll hier die Kunstanschauung eben durch die Notirungskunst cultivirt werden.

23. See Butt, *Music Education*, 170–80.

24. From an anonymous review, *Allgemeine musikalische Zeitung* 13 (1811): 470: "Der Form nach ist das Werk eine durch Erweiterung und Weitschweifigkeit geförderte Prachtausgabe des schon Vorhandenen und besser Gekannten." This review was followed by a second, favorable one ("Zweytes Wort über die Gesangbildungslehre nach Pestalozzi's Grundsätze von M. J. [*sic*] Pfeiffer und H. G. Nägeli," *Allgemeine musikalische Zeitung* 13 [1811]: 833– 42, 858–70, and 876–78) by K. A. Dreist, one of the Prussian teacher-officials sent by that government to study at Pestalozzi's school in Yverdon, which was concluded by a brief testimonial in support of Nägeli from Pestalozzi and his chief assistant, Johannes Niederer. For a more balanced view of the book's merits and shortcomings in comparison to other current texts, see Friedrich Wilhelm Lindner, "Was ist bis jetzt für die Gesangs-Bildung geschehen?" *Allgemeine musikalische Zeitung* 13 (1811): 3–8, 17–23, 33–43, and 49–59. For further discussion of critiques of Nägeli's method that nonetheless retained significant elements from it, see Nolte, *Die Musik im Verständnis der Musikpädagogik*, 114–16; and Hans Knab, "Bernhard Christoph Ludwig Natorp: Ein Beitrag zur Geschichte der Schulmusik in der ersten Hälfte des neunzehnten Jahrhunderts" (Ph.D. dissertation, Münster, 1933), 31–34.

25. Butt, *Music Education*, 172.

26. From a document prepared by Natorp for the royal Konsistorium at Münster, 1 October 1822. Translated from Eckhard Nolte, ed., *Lehrpläne und Richtlinien für den schulischen Musikunterricht in Deutschland vom Beginn des 19. Jahrhunderts bis in die Gegenwart: Eine Dokumentation*, Musikpädagogik: Forschung und Lehre 3 (Mainz: Schott, 1975), 36: "In manchen Schulen hat man sich bisher damit begnügt, die Jugend zum Singen einiger der üblichsten Kirchenmelodien und einiger beliebter Schullieder durch wiederholentliches Vorsingen und Nachsingenlassen *mechanisch abzurichten*. Man legte es nur darauf an, daß die Jugend einige Gesänge mit dem bloßen Gehör auffassen und ihrem Gedächtnis einprägen sollte. Man bediente sich keiner musika-

lischen Vorzeichnung und man befolgte bei den Übungen keinen methodischen Stufengang."

27. For examples of the latter, see Michael R. Heafford, *Pestalozzi: His Thought and Its Relevance Today* (London: Methuen, 1967), 39–40; and Kittler, *Discourse Networks*, 19–20.

28. Nägeli and Pfeiffer, *Gesangbildungslehre*, 230:

> Auch wir ehren den Choralgesang als etwas seit Jahrhunderten kirchlich bestehendes. Als Volksgesang, darf er dem Volk nicht entzogen werden, bis man etwas besseres an seine Stelle zu setzen hat, bis er zum Theil von selbst entbehrlich wird. Ganz soll und wird er nie untergehen. Auch aus der höhern Kunst wollen wir ihn durchaus nicht verbannt wissen. Erst dann thut er seine besondre Wirkung, wenn er mit andern Kunstgattungen oder musikalischen Sätzen theilweise vermengt wird, (wie in Grauns allbekanntem Passions-Oratorium) oder stellenweise, als cantus firmus, vermischt wird (wie z. B. in C. P. E. Bachs 'Heilig'). Allerdings aber müssen wir zu verhüten trachten, daß er hinfort nicht mehr auf eine so nachtheilige Weise pädagogisch betrieben und auch in der Kunstphilosophie nicht so übertrieben erhoben werde.

Another rejection of the chorale in elementary pedagogy is found in Friedrich Wilhelm Lindner, "Ueber den Gesang in der Bürgerschule zu Leipzig," *Allgemeine musikalische Zeitung* 8 (1805): 167–68. For an example of a proposal to reform instruction that still gives a central role to the chorale, see Horstig, "Vorschläge zu besserer Einrichtung der Singschulen in Deutschland," 214–20.

29. See Charles Burney, *An Eighteenth-Century Musical Tour in Central Europe and the Netherlands*, edited by Percy Scholes (London: Oxford University Press, 1959), 134 and 138.

30. For an overview of the enthusiasm for popular cultivation (and its limits), see Rudolf Schenda, *Volk ohne Buch: Studien zur Sozialgeschichte der populären Lesestoffe, 1770–1910*, Studien zur Philosophie und Literatur des neunzehnten Jahrhunderts 5 (Frankfurt am Main: Vitorio Klostermann, 1970), 42–50. On mandatory schooling, see *Geschichte der Erziehung* (Berlin: Volk und Wissen, 1957), 143–45 and 223. For more detailed studies of specific territories, see James Van Horn Melton, *Absolutism and the Eighteenth-Century Development of Compulsory Schooling in Prussia and Austria* (Cambridge: Cambridge University Press, 1988); and Karl A. Schleunes, *Schooling and Society: The Politics of Education in Prussia and Bavaria, 1750–1900* (Oxford: Berg, 1989).

31. See Van Horn Melton, *Absolutism*, 8–14.

32. "Ueber den Zustand der Musik in Böhmen," *Allgemeine musikalische Zeitung* 2 (1800): 517–20.

33. From a report of the Studienhofkomission, 12 October 1783, cited in Wangermann, *Aufklärung und staatsbürgerliche Erziehung*, 39: "Ferner die Bildung des Geschmacks, welche eben das Geschäft der Aesthetik ist, ist eine

national-Angelegenheit, denn der Geschmack vervollkommet die Vernunft und Sittlichkeit, und verbreitet Anmut und Geselligkeit über das ganze Leben."

34. Zelter's proposals (and excerpts from his correspondence, including advice from Goethe and Schiller) are excerpted extensively in Cornelia Schröder, *Carl Friedrich Zelter und die Akademie: Dokumente und Briefe zur Entstehung der Musik-Sektion in der Preußischen Akademie der Künste* (Berlin: Deutsche Akademie der Künste, 1959), 69–134. For an excellent recent overview of Zelter's organizational activity in Prussia, see Applegate, "How German Is It?" esp. 289–96.

35. See Schleunes, *Schooling and Society*, 72–77.

36. Nägeli, "Die Pestalozzische Gesangbildungslehre," 833–34:

In dieses Alles ist erst der Freuden Anfang.

Erst da beginnt das Zeitalter der Musik, wo nicht blos Repräsentanten die höhere Kunst ausüben—wo die höhere Kunst zum Gemeingut des Volkes, der Nation, ja der ganzen europäischen Zeitgenossenschaft geworden, wo die Menschheit selbst in das Element der Musik aufgenommen wird. Das wird nur möglich durch die Beförderung des Chorgesanges. . . .

Nehmt Schaaren von Menschen, nehmt sie zu Hunderten, zu Tausenden, versucht es, sie in humane Wechselwirkung zu bringen, eine Wechselwirkung, wo jeder Einzelne seine Persönlichkeit so wol durch Empfindungs- als Wortausdruck freythätig ausübt, wo er zugleich von allen übrigen homogene Eindrücke empfangt, wo er sich seiner menschlichen Selbstständigkeit und Mitständigkeit auf das intuitivste und vielfachste bewusst wird, wo er Aufklärung empfängt und verbreitet, wo er Liebe ausströmt und einhaucht, augenblicklich, mit jedem Athemzug—habt ihr etwas anders als den Chorgesang? findet ihr unter den tausend Quellen, die der Geber alles Guten euch aufschloss, irgend eine, die dieser auch nur von ferne ähnlich wäre?

37. Nägeli and Pfeiffer, *Gesangbildungslehre*, 5: "Der Lehrer hat, so weit seine Befugniß oder Autorität reicht, zu verhüten, daß die Kinder nicht, ehe sie tonfest sind, außer der Schule durch Singen ihre Stimme verderben. Rhytmische Privatübungen wären zwar unschädlich. Hingegen macht das frühzeitige Melodieensingen (das musikalische Lallen jeder Art) die Stimme des Kindes schwankend und unrein. Der Lehrer hat daher bestimmt auch dies zu verhüten, daß die Kinder vor der Hand, ehe sie hinlänglich tonfest sind, um ein Lied von mehrern Zeilen oder Strophen ohne Instrument durchaus rein und ohne merkliches Sinken zu singen, nicht zu Hause singend zeigen sollen, was sie in der Schule gelernt haben."

38. See, for example, Walter Heise, "Musikunterricht im 19. Jahrhundert—Ideen und Realitäten," in *Geschichte der Musikpädagogik*, edited by Hans-Christian Schmidt, Handbuch der Musikpädagogik 1 (Kassel: Bärenreiter, 1986), 47.

39. Natorp, *Anleitung zur Unterweisung im Singen für Lehrer in Volks-schulen: I. Leitfaden für den ersten Cursus,* 5th edition (Essen: G. D. Bädeker, 1837; 1st edition, 1813), 22: "Sie beschränkt sich auf das Singen *blos nach dem Gehöre.* Die Unterweisung besteht im *Vorsingen,* und die Uebung im *Nachsingen.* Man leite die Schüler durch Vorsingen an, zuerst einzelne Töne, dann kürzere und längere Reihen von Tönen, und zwar zuerst mit allen einfachen und doppelten Grundlauten, dann mit Sylben und Wörtern, deutlich, bestimmt, kräftig und milde, in verschiedenen Graden des stärkern und schwächern Ausdrucke und in verschiedenen Graden der langsamern und schnellern Bewegung nachzusingen. Demnächst lehre man sie, solche Gesänge nach dem Gehöre singen, welche ihrer Fassungskraft und ihrem jugendlichen Gemüthe angemessen sind."

40. Michel Foucault, *Discipline and Punish: The Birth of the Prison,* translated by Alan Sheridan (New York: Vintage, 1995), 136–38. See pp. 156–62 for an extended discussion in which the links to Nägeli's method are still more direct.

41. Natorp likewise demands complete silence as the backdrop for singing instruction (*Anleitung zur Unterweisung im Singen,* 19).

42. Foucault, *Discipline and Punish,* 184–92.

43. From an evaluation of another famous pedagogical method of the early nineteenth century, the piano and theory system of Johann Bernhard Logier, in *Encyclopädie der gesammten musikalischen Wissenschaften, oder Universal-Lexikon der Tonkunst,* edited by Gustav Schilling (Stuttgart: Franz Heinrich Köhler, 1837), 4:437: "denn in jeder Kunst giebt es einen Mechanismus, den der Geist beherrschen muß, wenn er leicht und klar aussprechen soll." Pestalozzi himself also frequently resorted to the concept of mechanism; see, for example, *Wie Gertrud ihre Kinder lehrt,* 313–20.

44. F. A. W. Diesterweg, *Der Unterricht in der Klein-Kinder-Schule, oder die Anfänge der Unterweisung und Bildung in der Volksschule,* 2nd edition (Crefeld: Johann Heinrich Funcke, 1832), 195: "*Der Gesang ist ein ganz vorzügliches Disciplinarmittel.* Er zwingt rohe und unbändige Kinder zur stillen Einkehr in sich selbst und zur Selbstbetrachtung."

45. Foucault, *Discipline and Punish,* 135.

46. For identification of these flaws in popular singing, see Horstig, "Vorschläge zu besserer Einrichtung der Singschulen," 171.

47. Nägeli and Pfeiffer, *Gesangbildungslehre,* 243: "Ausgemacht ist, daß der Gesang erst durch genaue, haarscharfe, elementarisch-schöne Lautkunst Umgrenzung, Umriß und Gestaltung bekommt; und erst wenn der Sänger die Schwierigkeiten der Sprache bezwingen, und ihre Vortheile benutzen gelernt hat, wenn er mit den Consonanten—eigentlich zu sagen, mit seinen Lautirorganen—umzuspringen weiß, wie der Klavierspieler mit den Tasten; erst dann wird die Singkunst in ihm und durch ihn recht lebendig."

48. From Zelter's sixth petition on the state of music in Prussia, 11 March 1809, in Schröder, *Carl Friedrich Zelter und die Akademie,* 119:

In den Schulen müßen, wie ehemals ordentliche Singklassen Statt finden. Die Cantores . . . müßen die Knaben von Jugend auf im Singen unterrichten; dadurch wird sich jeder Cantor für seine Kirche einen kleinen Chor bilden; die Cantoren werden mit einander eifern und die jungen Leute werden schon etwas singen können, wenn sie die höhern Schulen antreten.

Geschieht dieser Unterricht nach einer allgemeinen guten Anweisung, so wird dadurch die deutsche Pronunciation (welche im Ganzen fehlerhaft ist) verbeßert werden; denn, wer beßer pronuncirt und artikulirt, endet leicht beßer und bildet sich leichter.

In den höhern Schulen könnte dann die Sache bald weiter gelangen: zur Abwechslung könnten anstatt geistlicher Lieder Chöre alter Sprachen z.E. der lateinischen und griechischen Dichter mit Nutzen gesungen werden.

49. Michaelis, "Einige Gedanken über die Vortheile der frühen musikalischen Bildung," 119: "Bald belohnt dich für diese Sorge die Gewandtheit und Sicherheit der Stimme deines Kindes, der Wohllaut seines Sprechens, und seine Gelehrigkeit im Singen. Du erfreust dich in Kurzem seiner reinen melodischen Sprache, und wunderst dich nun nicht mehr über die eintönige, rohe Mundart der verwilderten oder verbildeten Kinder der sorglosen Nachbarn."

50. From Herder's *Von der Ausbildung der Schüler in Rede und Sprache: Schulrede Weimar*, cited and translated in Kittler, *Discourse Networks*, 37–38.

51. Nägeli, "Die Pestalozzische Gesangbildungslehre," 801: "Der Gesang des Menschen unterscheidet sich vom Gesange der Nachtigall durch bestimmte Abstufung. Letzterer ist ein blosses Wallen, Undulation, ersterer ein Wandeln, Artikulation. Die Nachtigall lässt nach ihrem Kunstinstinkt, wie sie die Kehle geöffnet hat, der Undulation ihren Lauf, so lange ihr Athem, Ein Luftaushauch, nach dem physischen Gesetze dauert. . . . Der Mensch erzeugt nach seinem Kunstinstinkt eine Tonleiter, er leitet sein physisches Tonvermögen, er bricht den Ton ab, erhebt ihn, steigt, fällt, alles in einem Athemzug."

52. See, for example, Pestalozzi, "Swansong," in *Pestalozzi's Educational Writings*, edited by J. A. Green, with Frances A. Collie (New York: Longmans, Green, & Co., 1912; reprint, Washington, D.C.: University Publications of America, 1977), 320–21.

53. See Schenda, *Volk ohne Buch*, 85–90; and Klaus Müller-Salget, *Erzählungen für das Volk: Evangelische Pfarrer als Volksschriftsteller in Deutschland des 19. Jahrhunderts* (Berlin: Erich Schmidt, 1984), 100–101. On the lack of interest in reading among the working classes, see Schenda, *Volk ohne Buch*, 445–52. On the socially conservative function of education among rulers, see 42–50; and Van Horn Melton, *Absolutism*, esp. 145–68.

54. See Schleunes, *Schooling and Society*, 82–83; Robert Lee, "Family and 'Modernisation': The Peasant Family and Social Change in Nineteenth-Century Bavaria," in *The German Family: Essays on the Social History of the*

Family in Nineteenth- and Twentieth-Century Germany, edited by Richard J. Evans and W. R. Lee (London: Croom Helm, 1981), 84–120, esp. 86 and 96–99; Jürgen Schlumbohm, "'Traditional' Collectivity and 'Modern' Individuality: Some Questions and Suggestions for the Historical Study of Socialization: The Example of the German Upper and Lower Bourgeoisies around 1800," *Social History* 5 (1980): 71–103, esp. 79–83; and Carl-Hans Hauptmeyer, "Aufklärung und bäuerliche Oppositionen im zentralen Niedersachsen des ausgehenden 18. Jahrhunderts," in *Das Volk als Objekt obrigkeitlichen Handelns,* edited by Rudolf Vierhaus, Wolfenbütteler Studien zur Aufklärung 13: Kultur und Gesellschaft in Nordwestdeutschland zur Zeit der Aufklärung I (Tübingen: Max Niemeyer, 1992), 197–217.

55. Dahlhaus, *Nineteenth-Century Music,* 47.

56. Fink, "Frankreich—französische Musik," in *Encyclopädie der gesammten musikalischen Wissenschaften, oder Universal-Lexikon der Tonkunst,* edited by Gustav Schilling (Stuttgart: Franz Heinrich Köhler, 1836), 3:43: "An Musikunterricht, wie ihn in Deutschland jede Dorfschule hat, ist noch bis jetzt in Frankreich gar nicht zu denken."

57. F., "Schwäbische Musikzustände," *Neue Zeitschrift für Musik* 17 (1842): 186: "Es ist gewiß erfreulich, wenn so nicht blos Gebildetere, sondern auch Leute aus den niederen Ständen auf die Ausbildung ihres musikalischen Talents Zeit und Fleiß verwenden, wenn auch das gemeine Volk sich über seinen Naturgesang erhebt und denselben zu einem schönen mehrstimmigen Gesange zu veredeln sucht"; "nicht sowohl von allgemein musikalischer Bedeutung, als vielmehr blos musikalische Volksfeste"; and 187: "Gehen wir von den Liederkränzen über auf die höheren Kunstinstitute und Vereine unseres Landes." (The report's introduction [185] explicitly equates *Männergesangvereine* and *Liederkränze.*)

58. Robert Schumann, "Musikalische Haus- und Lebensregeln," in *Gesammelte Schriften über Musik und Musiker,* new edition (Leipzig: Breitkopf & Härtel, 1883), 2:371: "Höre fleißig auf alle Volkslieder; sie sind eine Fundgrube der schönsten Melodieen und öffnen dir den Blick in den Charakter der verschiedenen Nationen."

59. Nägeli and Pfeiffer, *Gesangbildungslehre,* 6–7:

> Eben so wenig verlangen wir, daß die Mutter, welche ihr Kind von früher Jugend an für die musikalische Bildung empfänglich machen soll, indem sie dasselbe singend ihre Stimme hören läßt, eine Kunstsängerin sey im höhern Sinne des Worts. Reine Stimmen, reinen Gesang, reines Spiel auf reingestimmten Instrumenten lasse man die Kinder von Jugend auf hören; das ist die Hauptsache. Jede Mutter, die sich vornimmt, ihr Kind in dieser Kunst selbst zu erziehen, hat daher vor allen Dingen einen Musiker zu fragen, und gewissenhafte Antwort zu fordern, ob sie das, was sie singen gelernt hat, rein singe.... Nur wenn die Antwort befriedigend ausfällt, darf sie das Kind zur Erweckung seines musikalischen Sinnes ihre Stimme hören lassen; im entgegengesetzten Falle muß sie es ver-

meiden, und auf den Selbstunterricht des Kindes im Gesange gänzlich Verzicht thun.

60. See Hausen, "Family and Role-Division," 51–83; Kittler, *Discourse Networks*, 25–69; and Kittler, *Dichter-Mutter-Kind* (Munich: Wilhelm Fink, 1991), esp. 9–17. For a discussion of this gender role system in relation to aspects of German musical culture, see David Gramit, "Schubert's Wanderers and the Autonomous Lied," *Journal of Musicological Research* 14 (1995): 147–68. For a general exploration (with extensive references to further literature) of this topic in relation to another developing area of learning, see Ludmilla Jordanova, "Naturalising the Family: Literature and the Bio-Medical Sciences of the Late Eighteenth Century," in *Nature Displayed: Gender, Science, and Medicine, 1760–1820* (London: Longman, 1999), 163–82.

61. Van Swieten made his argument in a document of 18 August 1784, cited in Wangermann, *Aufklärung und staatsbürgerliche Erziehung*, 45–47. For a list of texts for mothers, see Kittler, *Discourse Networks*, 27–28.

62. Horstig, "Vorschläge zu besserer Einrichtung der Singschulen," 188: "und wird sich der Lehrer des Gesanges nicht ein besondres Verdienst um seine Mitbürger erwerben, wenn er bey ihren hoffnungsvollen Töchtern ein Talent ausbildet, welches ihnen das Glück, künftig einmal liebenswürdige Gattinnen und gute Mütter zu seyn, unendlich versüssen wird?"

63. Friedrich Guthmann, "Winke über den musikalischen Unterricht der Frauenzimmer," *Allgemeine musikalische Zeitung* 8 (1806): 515: "die beschränkte, aber liebliche Weiblichkeit"; and "Noch muss ich auf die Erfahrung Berufen, welche uns gar zu oft gezeigt hat, dass jenes Heraustreten aus dem beschränkten weiblichen Kreise, auch in der Kunst, in hundert Fällen gegen einen, mehr oder weniger missglückt." Guthmann repeated and elaborated on his ideas in "Grad der musikalischen Bildung bey Frauenzimmern," *Allgemeine musikalische Zeitung* 9 (1807): 380–82.

64. Guthmann, "Grad der musikalischen Bildung," 380: "welche durch überwiegendes Talent oder vermöge anderer Verhältnisse praktische Musik zu ihrer Hauptbeschäftigung machen"; and 381: "nur von den guten Mädchen der Mittelstände."

65. Freia Hoffmann, *Instrument und Körper: Die musizierende Frau in der bürgerlichen Kultur*, Insel Taschenbuch 1274 (Frankfurt am Main: Insel, 1991). On tensions within bourgeois ideology, see esp. 79–87; on the social origins of women musicians, see 255–58.

66. Guthmann, "Grad der musikalischen Bildung," 380: "Das Weib soll nicht glänzen, wol aber rühren und erheitern."

67. See Hausen, "Family and Role-Division," esp. 66–68.

68. For Marx's arguments in favor of occupational freedom in music, and thus of the liberal ideal of free, nonhereditary choice of career, see Marx's "Bemerkung" to Gardichert, in Gardichert, "Musikfest zu Demmin in Hinterpommern," *Berliner allgemeine musikalische Zeitung* 3 (1826): 48. There, Marx took the unusual step of expressing editorial disagreement with the author's

qualms about the introduction of *Gewerbefreiheit*. Marx himself, the son of a medical doctor, exemplified the new, free, and securely middle-class status he sought for musicians.

69. Reichardt, "An junge Künstler," 6–7:

> Allumfassende Liebe erfülle deine ganze Seele. Ueberall, wo reine Liebe dich führt, gehst du sicher dem Gipfel deiner Kunst, wie deines Glückes entgegen.
>
> Scheu' auch gesellschaftliche Bande nicht, wenn reine Liebe dich hineinfügt. Es ist keine wahre Freiheit, wo nicht Ruhe des Gemüths ist. Und diese Ruhe findest du nur im festen unauflöslich verwebten Bande mit dem Weibe, das deine Seele liebt. Und tausendfache neue niegeahndete Liebesgefühle leben in deiner Seele auf und befesten dein Wesen und dein Glück, wenn du dich, dein Weib in schönen lieben kleinen Menschen wiederfindest. O es ist unaussprechliche Seeligkeit unnennbarer Seelenfriede in seinem [*sic*; recte meinem?] kleinen Hause eine bessere, selbstgeschafne bessere Welt zu haben, nur über meine wirthliche Hausschwelle treten zu dürfen, um jeden Mißmuth, erzeugt durch Weltverderbtheit sogleich schwinden zu sehen, jede Kraft hier frey zur Vervollkommnung meiner Lieben anwenden zu können, die ich in der größern Gesellschaft oft nicht anwenden durfte nicht konnte!
>
> So nur erzeugt und erhält Liebe edlen Wirkungstrieb.

70. Nägeli "Die Pestalozzische Gesangbildungslehre," 837.

71. Ibid., 828.

72. Cited in Nolte, *Lehrpläne und Richtlinien*, 43: "ist daher eins der wesentlischsten Mittel des erziehenden Unterrichts, durch dessen richtige und ununterbrochen fortgesetzte Anwendung auch das roheste Gemüt für sanftere Gefühle zugänglich gemacht, ihrem Einflusse hingegeben und an eine Unterordnung unter allgemeine Gesetze bei gemeinsamer Tätigkeit mit andern gewöhnt werden kann."

73. From an excerpt of the *Erziehungslehre* published as "Elementarunterricht in der Musik," *Allgemeine musikalische Zeitung* 11 (1809): 405.

74. Friedrich Braun, *Kurze Anweisung für Schullehrer und Kantoren zur zweckmäßigen Betreibung des Gesangunterrichts* (Koblenz: B. Heriot, 1828), cited in Nolte, *Lehrpläne und Richtlinien*, 43: "Es trete hier aber der Gesangunterricht in ernster und würdiger Form auf, verlange Anstrengung, gebe Schwierigkeiten zu überwinden. Denn frühe schon lerne der Mensch, daß kein Vergnügen ohne Arbeit, sie selbst werde ihm Vergnügen."

75. On the expansion of manufacturing and its relation to schooling, see Van Horn Melton, *Absolutism*, esp. 109–44.

76. See Wangermann, *Aufklärung und staatsbürgerliche Erziehung*, 67.

77. These virtues are described in Michaelis, "Einige Gedanken über die Vortheile der frühen musikalischen Bildung," 122–23: "der Sinn für Regelmässigkeit, Richtigkeit, Ordnung und Harmonie"; and 125: "ein Band der Ge-

selligkeit" (the latter passage is from Michaelis's excerpt of O. C. R. Zöllner, *Ideen über Nationalerziehung* [Berlin: n.p., 1804]).

78. Theodor Hagen, "Die Civilisation in Beziehung zur Kunst mit specieller Berücksichtigung der Musik," *Neue Zeitschrift für Musik* 23 (1845): 194: "Alles ist gebrochen in ihnen; von einem giftigen Pfeile getroffen, ertragen sie ihr Loos einerseits mit thierischer Gleichgültigkeit, andrerseits mit rührender Ergebung. Eine große Zahl unter ihnen ist innerlich und äußerlich so abgespannt, so moralisch und physisch erstorben, daß eine plötzliche, materielle Verbesserung ihre Lage, ein plötzliches Erleben unheilvoll auf sie wirken würde.—Die Musik läutert und stärkt den Menschen, sie bereitet ihn auf das Bessere vor, *sie ist es auch, welche die Reorganisation des Fabrikwesens vorbereiten muß*"; and 206: "Freilich ist ein singendes Volk ein sehr schwaches, der Verdummung Preis gegebenes, aber nur dann, wenn es gleich den Italienern sich den Romanzen und Cantilenen überläßt, wenn es *vereinzelt* seinen Schmerz in die Nacht hinaussingt. . . . Aber ein Volk, das nach vollbrachtem Tagewerk sich in größeren Abtheilungen versammelt, und nach den kräftigen, gesunden Melodien, welche aus seinem Munde tönen, die Schritte fröhlich und frei in der Natur erschallen läßt, ein solches Volk ist stark; denn es ist einig."

Hagen's article and its critical context are discussed in Pederson, "Enlightened and Romantic German Music Criticism," 245–27. Pederson's discussion of the liberal music criticism of the period (225–47) also includes valuable material on the *Gesangvereine* and the *Tonkünstlerversammlung,* the convention of (progressive) musicians organized largely by Franz Brendel.

79. See, for example, Theodor Thräner, "Thesen und Vorschläge in Beziehung auf einen humanen Musikunterricht," *Neue Zeitschrift für Musik* 29 (1848): 21–25 and 33–38; Franz Brendel et al., "Eingabe an das königl. Preußische Ministerium der geistlichen-, Unterrichts- und Medicinal-Angelegenheiten," *Neue Zeitschrift für Musik* 29 (1848): 85–88 and 97–100; A. B. Marx, "Denkschrift über Organisation des Musikwesens im preussischen Staate," *Neue Berliner Musikzeitung* 2 (1848): 241–47 and 249–56; and Berlin Tonkünstler-Verein, "Denkschrift des Tonkünstler-Vereines in Berlin über die Reorganisation des Musikwesens," *Neue Berliner Musikzeitung* 2 (1848): 257–65.

80. This characterization of the musical field is indebted to Bourdieu, in particular to *The Rules of Art: Genesis and Structure of the Literary Field,* translated by Susan Emanuel (Stanford: Stanford University Press, 1995). Applegate, "How German Is It?" takes a similar approach to defining the motivations of musicians of the period.

81. For a brief autobiographical sketch by Zelter, see Schröder, *Carl Friedrich Zelter und die Akademie,* 104–8.

82. See Reichardt, "An großgute Regenten," v–vii, esp. vii; "Ueber die Benutzung der Musik zur Veredelung der Landleute, als Sache des Staates," *Allgemeine musikalische Zeitung* 7 (1805): 665–73, esp. 672–73; and Amadeus Wendt, "Betrachtungen über Musik, und insbesondere über den Gesang, als

Bildungsmittel in der Erziehung," *Allgemeine musikalische Zeitung* 13 (1811): 339–40.

83. On relations between educated and folk musicians, see Dieter Krickberg, "On the Social Status of the *Spielmann* ('Folk Musician') in 17th and 18th Century Germany, Particularly in the Northwest," in *The Social Status of the Professional Musician from the Middle Ages to the 19th Century*, edited by Walter Salmen, annotated and translated by Herbert Kaufman and Barbara Reisner, Sociology of Music 1 (New York: Pendragon, 1983), 97–122, esp. 119–20.

84. For an example that does prescribe more limited training for less privileged locations, see Joseph Klein, "Ueber den Gesang in Dorfschulen," *Berliner allgemeine musikalische Zeitung* 4 (1828): 245–47 and 253–55.

85. That the priority of choral song over opera was indeed a concern of the advocates of the *Gesangvereine* is revealed by comparisons of the frivolity of opera to the strictness and seriousness of the new choral literature. See, for example, Louis Spohr, "Einige Bemerkungen über die deutschen Gesang-Vereine, nebst Ankündigung eines neuen für sie geschriebenen Werkes," *Allgemeine musikalische Zeitung* 23 (1821): 817–20, esp. 819; and C. E. H., "Ueber Singvereine," *Allgemeine musikalische Zeitung* 31 (1829): 37–41, esp. 37 and 39.

86. Dahlhaus, *Nineteenth-Century Music*, 47. On the belated development of opera and the artistic prestige of instrumental music, see W. Weber, "Wagner, Wagnerism, and Musical Idealism," 28–51.

87. See Elias, *The Civilizing Process*.

88. Gustav Keferstein [K. Stein, pseud.], "Aphorismen über akademisches Musikwesen und dessen zweckmäßige Gestaltung," *Neue Zeitschrift für Musik* 12 (1840): 113:

> Wie hat nicht z.B. Leipzig auf die Förderung der musikalischen Bildung und auf die Gestaltung des musikalischen Geschmacks, nicht allein in Sachsen, sondern in ganz Deutschland eingewirkt! Wer möchte es aber in Abrede stellen, daß es wenigstens den größeren Theil seines in die Nähe und Ferne hinwirkenden, musikalischen Gewichts, seiner Universität und seinen sonstigen gelehrten Anstalten zu verdanken habe? Tausende von Jünglingen und jungen Männern gewannen in dieser, in musikalischer Hinsicht so ausgezeichneten Stadt, neben ihrer wissenschaftlichen, zugleich auch eine höhere musikalische Bildung, welche sie dann späterhin, als Beamtete des Staates oder der Kirche, in ihren Wirkungskreisen weiter zu verbreiten wußten—und eine namhafte Zahl begabterer Musiktalente fand hier die erste kräftige Anregung zu dem Entschlusse, sich eifriger einer Kunst zu widmen, welche sie sonst entweder ganz versäumt oder nur oberflächlich dilettirend betrieben haben würden.

89. [Gustav] Keferstein, "Ueber das Verhältniss der Musik zum Pädagogik," *Allgemeine musikalische Zeitung* 43 (1841): 993–1002.

90. Brendel reported repeatedly on his efforts in the *Neue Zeitschrift für Musik,* especially during 1847 and 1848. See, in particular, the extensive coverage of the first such meeting, "Die erste Versammlung deutscher Tonkünstler und Musikfreunde in Leipzig," *Neue Zeitschrift für Musik* 27 (1847): 93–96, 105–8, 117–19, 121–26, 141–44, 153–56, 165–67, and 177–80. The organization's name is itself revealing: unlike the earlier Gesellschaft der Musikfreunde, it not only includes professional musicians explicitly but identifies itself first with them and only secondarily with friends of music. Further, it uses *Tonkünstler,* a term with strong associations with cultivated composition, rather than the more neutral and inclusive *Musiker.*

91. On the oversupply of educated men, especially in Germany, see Lenore O'Boyle, "The Problem of an Excess of Educated Men in Western Europe, 1800–1850," *Journal of Modern History* 42 (1970): 471–95.

CHAPTER 5. PERFORMING MUSICAL CULTURE

1. Important studies of the concert include Preußner, *Die bürgerliche Musikkultur,* esp. 5–88; Heinrich W. Schwab, *Konzert: öffentliche Musikdarbietung vom 17. bis 19. Jahrhundert,* Musikgeschichte in Bildern, volume 4, part 2 (Leipzig: Deutscher Verlag für Musik, 1971); Hanns-Werner Heister, *Das Konzert: Theorie einer Kulturform,* Taschenbücher zur Musikwissenschaft 87–88, 2 volumes (Wilhelmshaven: Heinrichshofen, 1983); several of the studies in Joan Peyser, ed., *The Orchestra: Origins and Transformations* (New York: Charles Scribner's Sons, 1986); and Walter Salmen, *Das Konzert: Eine Kulturgeschichte* (Munich: C. H. Beck, 1988).

2. Nägeli, "Anrede an die schweizerische Musikgesellschaft, bey Eröffnung ihrer Sitzung zu Zürich, den 19ten August 1812," 700: "Die Concerte, wie wir sie jetzt haben, wie sie das ganze cultivirte Europa hat, sind ein Erzeugnis des abgewichenen Jahrhunderts, entsprungen theils aus den Entwickelungen der Kunst selbst, theils aus den Erweiterungen des geselligen Lebens." For another acknowledgment of the development of the concert in the eighteenth century, see Johann Karl Friedriche Triest, "Bemerkungen über die Ausbildung der Tonkunst in Deutschland im achzehnten Jahrhundert," *Allgemeine musikalische Zeitung* 3 (1801): 324.

3. Johann Nicholas Forkel, "Genauere Bestimmung einiger musikalischen Begriffe. Zur Ankundigung des academischen Winterconcerts von Michaelis 1780 bis Ostern 1781," *Magazin der Musik* 1 (1783): 1066: "Bey dem unläugbaren Verfall der Kirchen- und Theater-Music aber, sind nun Concerte das noch einzig übriggebliebene Mittel, wodurch sowol Geschmack verbreitet, als auch überhaupt der höhere Endzweck der Music noch bisweilen erreicht werden kann. Desto wichtiger müssen sie uns demnach seyn, und desto genauer muß man sie bestimmen, was sie eigentlich seyn sollen, und was sie durch Vernachläßigung des wahren Begriffs, den man sich von ihnen zu machen hat, geworden sind." Eduard Krüger, *Beiträge für Leben und Wissenschaft in der*

Tonkunst (Leipzig: Breitkopf & Härtel, 1847), 57: "Wozu dieser Misere so viel Aufmerksamkeit? möchte Einer fragen. Wir antworten: Misere ist's, was der Pöbel dem Pöbel aufspielt . . . ; ein Heiligthum aber ist die Kunsthalle, wo der Geist zum Geiste spricht, wo der ächte fromme Künstler voll Liebe zur Menschheit, voll Achtung zu den bedürftigen Jüngern der Kunst mit Begeisterung dichtet und nachdichtet, was unsterbliche Geister vorgesungen. Und um so ernster Dinge willen darf man wohl zürnen, wo Unreine sie besudeln. Der wahren Verbreitung der Kunst ist nichts förderlich als Ernst, nichts verderblich als Leichtsinn; das kann jeder Clavierlehrer, ja jeder Tanz- und ABC-Meister an sich erfahren."

4. See, to name only a few prominent examples, Richard Taruskin, *Text and Act: Essays on Music and Performance* (New York: Oxford University Press, 1995); John Rink, ed., *The Practice of Performance: Studies in Musical Interpretation* (Cambridge: Cambridge University Press, 1995); Jonathan Dunsby, *Performing Music: Shared Concerns* (Oxford: Clarendon Press; New York: Oxford University Press, 1995); Suzanne G. Cusick, "Gender and the Cultural Work of a Classical Music Performance," *repercussions* 3 (1994): 77–110; Christopher Small, *Musicking: The Meanings of Performing and Listening*, Music/Culture Series (Hanover: Wesleyan University Press, 1998); Stan Godlovitch, *Musical Performance: A Philosophical Study* (London: Routledge, 1998); and Goehr, *The Quest for Voice.*

5. Small, *Musicking*, 13.

6. This is particularly clear in his "Performance as Ritual: Sketch for an Enquiry into the True Nature of a Symphony Concert," in *Lost in Music: Culture, Style, and the Musical Event*, edited by Avron L. White (London: Routledge and Kegan Paul, 1987), 6–32, an essay that presents many of the ideas developed at greater length in *Musicking.*

7. See Martha Feldman, "Magic Mirrors and the *Seria* Stage: Thoughts toward a Ritual View," *Journal of the American Musicological Society* 47 (1995): 423–84.

8. See Nägeli, "Anrede an die schweizerische Musikgesellschaft, bey Eröffnung ihrer Sitzung zu Zürich, den 19ten August 1812," 715–18. For discussion of this passage, see chapter 4.

9. Gottfried Weber, "Ueber Kirchenmusik in Concerten," *Musikalische Zeitung für die österreichischen Staaten* 1 (1812): 45–46: "Im Herzen der Herren (sie lassen's nur nicht gern lesen) steht die Antwort geschrieben: Uns langweilt nun einmal Kirchenmusik, nicht blos im Concerte, sondern auch in der Kirche selbst; und das darum, weil sie uns zu tief, zu ernst, und erhaben ist, nicht luxüriös oder tändelnd, nicht oberflächlich, und was wir amüsant nennen!" Weber's article seems to have enjoyed wide circulation; a slightly modified version of it is quoted in H. [Johann August Heinroth?], "Concert," in *Encyclopädie der gesammten musikalischen Wissenschaften, oder Universal-Lexikon der Tonkunst,* edited by Gustav Schilling (Stuttgart: Franz Heinrich Köhler, 1835), 1:284–86, where the source is cited as the *"Allgem. Encyclopädie der Wissenschaften und Künste* von Ersch und Gruber, Art. Concert."

10. Marx, "Einige Worte über das Konzertwesen, besonders in grossen Städten," *Berliner allgemeine musikalische Zeitung* 2 (1825): 360: "Das bisher Gesagte führt uns zu den Gattungen der Komposition, die im Konzerte den höchsten Rang einnehmen und deren Aufführung allein berechtigt, ein Konzert ein *grosses* zu nennen. Das ist die *Symphonie* und die *Kantate.*"

11. See "Oratorium," *Wiener allgemeine musikalische Zeitung* 1 (1813): 67–68: "*Oratorium*, geistliche Cantate, begreift in sich die größte Erhabenheit und Würde, vollkommene Einheit in der Gattung, mit möglichsten Vermeidung aller heterogenen Theile; also männlichen, kräftigen, strengen, würdevollen Satz mit wohlberechneter Anwendung des Kammer- und völliger Ausschließung des eigentlichen Theater-Styls." Spohr's reply appeared in the following issue of the journal, pp. 87–88.

12. C. E. H., "Ueber Singvereine," 39: "Ein Jahr später versuchte der neue Organist der Hauptkirche, der früher an der berühmten Singakademie in B. Theil genommen, nach jenem schönen Vorbilde eine Verbindung zu stiften, und brachte sie, nicht ohne viele Mühe, zu Stande. Aber die meisten Mitglieder hatten zu dem aufgelösten Vereine gehört, und, verwöhnt von der leicht auszuführenden, gefälligen und glänzenden Opernmusik, konnten sie sich in den ernsten, strengen Ton des Dirigenten und seiner Messen und Oratorien nicht finden: Einer nach dem Andern blieb weg, und mit Ablauf des Jahres hatte der Singverein wieder sein Ende erreicht."

13. Ibid., 37: "einige strenge und dem Opernstyl allzu abholde Kunstfreunde."

14. August Kahlert, "Das Concertwesen der Gegenwart," *Neue Zeitschrift für Musik* 16 (1842): 101: "nichts Besseres thun zu können, als zum Theater zu gehen. . . . Unsre ausgezeichneten Gesang-Werke deutscher Tonkunst gehören doch vielleicht zum größten Theile dem Concertsaale oder der Kirche an."

15. Nägeli, "Die Pestalozzische Gesangbildungslehre," 834: "Bisher war das Theater der Brennpunkt, worin das menschliche Daseyn und Wirken am kräftigsten koncentrirt erchien. Hier aber wird die höhere Kunst nur durch Repräsentanten ausgeübt. . . . Das Kunstwesen des Schauspiels in weitester Bedeutung ist seiner Natur nach aristokratisch."

16. Triest, "Bemerkungen über die Ausbildung der Tonkunst in Deutschland," 370: "Die Instrumentalmusik zeigte sich entweder nur als seine Begleiterinn, oder, wenn sie für sich allein herrschen wollte, borgte sie von ihm ihre Annehmlichkeit und ihren Glanz. Allmählig aber trachtete auch sie nach höherem Range. Sie stützte sich (wie das Volk auf seine physische Uebermacht und auf die erlangte Kultur der sonst untern Stände) ebenfalls auf die Vermehrung und Ausbildung ihrer Werkzeuge. So wurden erst aus den regierten Regierer."

17. William Weber, "Wagner, Wagnerism, and Musical Idealism," esp. 40–51.

18. Friedrich Guthmann, "Expectorationen über die heutige Musik. Dritte Expectoration: Ueber Tanzmusik," *Allgemeine musikalische Zeitung* 7 (1805): 777: "Wer da glaubt, dass sie eines grossen Genies unwürdig sind, der irrt sich

gar sehr"; and 778: "Man sollte bey der Tanzmusik den Volkstanz von dem, der gebildetern Klassen wol unterscheiden."

19. Guthmann, "Etwas zur Vertheidigung der Tänze," *Allgemeine musikalische Zeitung* 6 (1804): 405: "Produkten aus einer höhern Sphäre"; and 406: "recht viele hübsche und gefällige Sachen, die so recht für die Aufheiterung des von drückenden Arbeiten und Nahrungssorgen geplagten Volks gemacht sind."

20. *Primarily* is worth stressing here. Guthmann acknowledges that even "Musikkenner" will occasionally enjoy a dance more than a great oratorio ("Vertheidigung der Tänze"; 406), and the potential for that defection likely underlies some of the more pointed later statements discussed below.

21. 26., "Strauß im Norden," *Neue Zeitschrift für Musik* 1 (1834): 309: "Man fand, daß die von Strauß componirten Tänze von den gut eingetheilten Orchester sehr gut vorgetragen wurden, aber man fand auch, daß dergleichen Musik nicht in den Concertsaal gehöre. . . .—der beste Tanz, sagen wir, erscheint bei mehrmaligen Wiederholungen langweilig, wenn nicht darnach getanzt werden soll, wenn die Hörer in feierlicher Passivität ihn anhören müssen, wie ein Kunstwerk, dessen Auffassen den Verstand beschäftigt"; "Strauß ist ein genialer Walzer-Componist und Virtuos, den wir um so mehr lieb haben, weil er nichts anders sein will" (310).

22. Johann Gottfried Hientzsch, "über die Musik als das herrlichste Mittel einer vorzüglichen Bildung, einer geistreichen Unterhaltung und religiösen Erhebung in Familie," *Eutonia* 5 (1831): 152–61, cited in Nicolai Petrat, *Hausmusik des Biedermeier im Blickpunkt der zeitgenössischen musikalischen Fachpresse (1815–1848)*, Hamburger Beiträge zur Musikwissenschaft 31 (Hamburg: Karl Dieter Wagner, 1986), 156: "Nun, wie stehts, meine Herrn Musiklehrer in den größern und größten Städten? . . . Wollen Sie ewig das sein und bleiben für die Finger, was die Tanzmeister für die Füße sind, oder wollen Sie sich erheben und erheben lassen in eine höhere Region, ja vielleicht in einer der höchsten, wo Sie an dem erhabenen Ideale der ästhetisch-christlichen Menschenbildung mitarbeiten?" I am grateful to Ruth Solie for bringing this source to my attention; the translation is hers.

23. Joseph Klein, "Ansichten über Musik-Unterricht, in Bezug auf sogennante Mode-Kompositionen," *Berliner allgemeine musikalische Zeitung* 4 (1827): 50: "Wie unrecht auch die Eltern thun, gegen freilich geringes Honorar, ihre Kinder musikalisch verderben zu lassen, bedarf wohl keiner Erwähnung, eben so, wie wenig es auch hier sagen will, den lieben Kleinen ein Wälzerlein eingetrichtert zu finden, denn eben Tänze sind die Basis aller spätern Verirrungen. Das jugendliche Gemüth ergiebt sich dem Leichteren nur allzu leicht, besonders wenn damit früher in gewisser Hinsicht Beifall zu ärndten ist, es verliert den nöthigen Ernst, selbst bei gutem Willen und gediegnerem Wissen des Lehrers, die klassischen Erzeugnisse der Kunst sich zu eigen zu machen, und vereitelt somit jede wohlgemeinte Bemühung."

24. "Wider Gewerbsfreiheit im Fache der Musik," *Allgemeine musikalische Zeitung* 39 (1837): 642: "Seitdem die bezahlte öffentliche Ausübung der

Musik in die Klasse der Handwerkspraxis gestellt und jedem Fiedler, der einen Gewerbschein löst, gestattet ist, mit einer beliebigen Bande bei Tanzgelagen etc. Geld zu verdienen, ist es selbst in Provinzstädten von 20,000–30,000 Einwohnern unmöglich geworden, ein nur einigermaassen anhörenswerthes Orchester aufzustellen"; and 643: "aus einem Symphoniesatze eines neueren guten Meisters die Ripienstimme der ersten Violine mit Sicherheit, Kraft und Deutlichkeit vom Blatte ausführen könnte."

25. Eduard Hanslick, *On the Musically Beautiful: A Contribution towards the Revision of the Aesthetics of Music*, translated by Geoffrey Payzant (Indianapolis: Hackett, 1986), 61.

26. Forkel, "Genauere Bestimmung," 1067–69.

27. [Bernhard Christoph Ludwig] Natorp, "Unsre Concerte," *Berlinische musikalische Zeitung* 1 (1805): 207–13. Natorp's four types of music are outlined on pp. 208–9.

28. Nägeli, "Anrede an die schweizerische Musikgesellschaft, bey Eröffnung ihrer Sitzung zu Zürich, den 19ten August 1812," 699: "Nicht nur hatte *Lessing* recht, wenn er sagte: 'ein denkender Künstler ist mir noch eins so viel werth;' man kann noch viel weiter gehen und behaupten, ein Kunstwerk, das nicht blos ästhetisch (mit dem Gefühl) aufgefasst, sondern intellectuell angeschaut, ja recht eigentlich durchdacht wird, ist dem Beschauer letzterer Art tausendmal mehr werth."

29. Keferstein, "Ueber das Verhältniss der Musik zur Pädagogik," 1000: "bewusstvolles Zusammenfassen der empfangenen und wahrgenommenen Einzeleindrücke, Gefühlsanregungen, Gemüthsbewegungen u.s.w."

30. Ibid.: "in ihrer höheren Formen und ganz vorzüglich in der vollkommensten und ausgebildetsten unter allen, nämlich in der Sonatenform"; "Beethovens unsterbliche Meisterschöpfungen im Bereiche der Sonatenform, unter welche bekanntlich auch die Sinfonie, die Ouvertüre, das Trio, Quartett u.s.w. fallt."

31. Eduard Krüger, "Das Virtuosenconcert," *Neue Zeitschrift für Musik* 14 (1842): 173: "Mit einem Wort: spielt Sonaten, Symphonieen, Quartette, statt eures Flageoletgedudels, statt eurer halsbrechenden Variationen, statt eurer stupenden Harpeggien-Etuden, statt eurer diamantenen Terzen- und Sextenläufe, statt eures quikenden, ächzenden, ersterbenden, erdröhnenden Ausdrücks, Nachdrucks und Vortrags!"

32. "Ueber den Zustand der Musik in Böhmen," 518: "Gründliche Lehrer werden seltener, und da das Musiklernen blos zum Zeitvertreib geschieht, so achtet man nicht auf sie, und setzt sich immer ein nahes Ziel." O. F. K. W. Schulz, "Zu grosse Vorliebe fürs Pianoforte," *Berliner musikalische Zeitung* 2, no. 21 (24 May 1845): 1–2: "Lanneriaden und Straussiaden u.s.w."; "Mozarts oder Beethovens Tonschöpfungen." For a more general discussion of the role of the piano in the development of the musical public, see Leon Botstein, "Listening through Reading: Musical Literacy and the Concert Audience," *Nineteenth Century Music* 16 (1992): 129–45, esp. 136–37. Although Botstein

places the impact of the piano's spread in the period following 1848, sources such as these suggest that, at least in the minds of the advocates of serious music, its role was significant considerably earlier.

33. See Thomas Christensen, "Four-Hand Piano Transcription and Geographies of Nineteenth-Century Musical Reception," *Journal of the American Musicological Society* 52 (1999): 255–98, esp. 260–75, on favorable and critical views of piano transcriptions. For examples of somewhat grudging admission of the value of arrangements, see Franz Stöpel, "Ueber das Arrangiren," *Cäcilia* 1, no. 1 (1824): 37–39; and [Ignaz Ritter] von Seyfried, review of Hummel's arrangements of Symphony No. 3, by Beethoven, and Piano Concerto in D Minor for piano, flute, violin, and cello, by Mozart, *Cäcilia* 10, no. 39 (1829): 176–77.

34. Gottschalk Wedel, "Gesellschafts- oder Ziermusik," *Neue Zeitschrift für Musik* 6 (1837): 123: "Das einzige wahre Gesellschaftszeug . . . ist und bleibt der Flügel; mag da eine Sache für die Bühne geschrieben, oder der Kirche geheiliget sein, mag sie für ein halbhundert Beethoven'scher Symphoniespieler, oder für eine Strauß'sche Tanzlenkerbande geschaffen sein, nichts kann verhüten, daß sie nicht bald im Clavierauszug erscheine, und das ihr ganzer Reichthum sich solchergestalt in einen Wechselbrief gedrängt, gefallen lassen muß."

35. Seyfried, review of Hummel's arrangements, 175: "nichts wird verschont: die grössten Symphonien, und Ouverturen—Missen, und Kirchen-Cantaten—Oratorien u. Opern etc. etc. etc. müssen herhalten, und werden uns dargeboten in den verschiedenartigsten Formen und Gestalten: als Clavier-Auszüge mit und ohne Singstimmen; eingerichtet für Militär-Banden,—als Quintette, und Quartette, Trio's, Duo's und Solo's für einzelne Instrumente, *scilicet:* Violine, Guitarre, Flöte, Csakan, etc. (*per parenthesin:* die Mundharmonica, vulgo: Maultrommel bietet ein noch nicht urbar gemachtes Feld; merkts Euch, ihr Herrn!) zuletzt wohl noch gar metamorphosirt in Walzer, Galopps, Polonaisen und Eccosaisen."

36. Wedel, "Gesellschafts- oder Ziermusik," 128: "Das Wort Concerto, Prunkstück, verliert sich eben deshalb nach und nach vom Anschlagzettel, wie die altväterlichen Silberbecken von der Tafel, und dafür erscheinen buntgedruckte Dufttöpfchen *(pot-pourris)*, Ergötzungen *(Divertissements)*, Veränderungen oder Verbrämungen *(Variations)* und solcherlei Kleinwaaren, die mit Auber'schen Tänzelouverturen oder Straußischen Walzern würdig eingefaßt werden können."

37. See "Andeutungen zu einer derzeit sehr nöthigen Abhandlung über das gegenwärtige Concert-Unwesen," *Allgemeine musikalische Zeitung mit besonderer Rücksicht auf den österreichischen Kaiserstaat* 2 (1818): 109–11; . . . r., "Über den Verfall der Musik," *Allgemeine musikalische Zeitung mit besonderer Rücksicht auf den österreichischen Kaiserstaat* 2 (1818): 136–37; ——z., "Über den Verfall der Musik" (a response to the previous article), *Allgemeine musikalische Zeitung mit besonderer Rücksicht auf den österreichischen Kaiserstaat* 2 (1818): 153–56; and [Amand Wilhelm Schmith], "Sechzehnter Auf-

satz. Prognosis: Von dem nahen Verfall der Musik," in *Philosophische Fragmente über die praktische Musik* (Vienna: in commission at the k.k. Taubstummeninstitutsbuchdruck, 1787), 94–98.

38. Forkel, "Vorrede," vii: "niemals ist wohl mehr von Größe, vom Erhabenen, vom Schönen, vom Ausdruck eines männlichen und starken Gefühls deklamirt worden als jetzt, und wenn hatten wir wohl weniger Ausdruck des Großen, des Erhabenen, des wahren Schönen, und des männlich-starken Gefühls?"

39. Friedrich A. Kanne, "Was ist von dem jetzigen Geschmacke in der Musik zu fürchten?" *Allgemeine musikalische Zeitung mit besonderer Rücksicht auf den österreichischen Kaiserstaat* 4 (1820): 764: "Was ist aber die grösste Vormauer gegen das Verderben der Musik? Der Contrapunct!"

40. H. Hirschbach, "Moderne deutsche Musikzustände," *Neue Zeitschrift für Musik* 17 (1842): 123–24: "Man kann die Marx'sche Lehre zum Theil als einen Versuch das Genie zu erklären betrachten. Doch, wie dem auch sei, bildet die neue Lehre nur musikalisch gutgesinnte Dilettanten, sie hat genug gethan; sie hat der Kunst den höchsten, ersprießlichsten Nutzen verschafft, der in jetziger Zeit, wo der Dilettantismus ein so wichtiger Hebel des Musikwesens geworden, möglich ist. Die Theorie würde so die Wunden heilen, welche die Praxis eine Menge lüderlicher Componisten dem musikalischen Geschmack beigebracht. In der That arbeiten Tanz- und Virtuositäts-Componisten, französische und italienische Opernschreiber und ihre deutschen Nachahmer unaufhörlich auf dessen Verderben hin."

41. See, for example, Nägeli, "Anrede an die schweizerische Musikgesellschaft, bey Eröffnung ihrer Sitzung zu Zürich, den 19ten August 1812," where, as discussed earlier, vocal and instrumental concerts are distinguished, with the latter representing the most sophisticated form in the context of an ambitious program of general cultivation; and Kahlert, "Das Concertwesen der Gegenwart," in which concerts are divided into the categories of spiritual, virtuoso, and subscription concerts; only the latter are described as the proper place for the best music (sacred music being more properly suited to the church).

42. Marx, "Einige Worte über das Konzertwesen," 350: "Aber welch eine Masse Musik ist dies zusammengenommen, die den Zuhörern nichts gewährt, als Bewunderung einer mechanischen Geschicklichkeit und jenen Sinnengenuss, der vom Kunstgenusse so weit entfernt ist, wie—das Thier vom Menschen." For a more detailed consideration of the opposition of sensual and intellectual listening implied in such sources, see Bernd Sponheuer, "Der 'Gott der Harmonien' und die 'Pfeife des Pan': über richtiges und falsches Hören in der Musikästhetik des 18. und 19. Jahrhunderts," in *Rezeptionsästhetik und Rezeptionsgeschichte in der Musikwissenschaft*, edited by Hermann Danuser and Friedhelm Krummacher, Publikationen der Hochschule für Musik und Theater Hannover 3 (Laaber: Laaber Verlag, 1991), 179–91.

43. Natorp, "Unsre Concerte," 213:

Einer der wichtigsten Vortheile einer solchen Einrichtung der Concerte wäre ohne Zweifel wohl der, daß dadurch alle unächte Musik allmählig ganz verdrängt, und die wahre Musik, die Musik fürs Herz, allmählig eine solche Würde behaupten würde, daß man sich über sich selbst würde wundern müssen, wie es möglich gewesen sey, eine so lange Zeit hindurch einen musikalischen oder vielmehr antimusikalischen Wirrwarr zu ertragen. . . . Ohne Zweifel würde dann der wahre musikalische Geist sich allmählig allgemeiner verbreiten, die Musik würde wieder in Schulen und Kirchen, in die Werkstätten der Arbeiter, in die Hütten und auf die Acker des Landmanns übergehen, und die schönen Hoffnungen, würden erfüllt werden, womit Herr *C. R. Horstig* seine Schrift über die "Uebung der Seminaristen" schloß, und worin ihm alle Freunde des Schönen und Guten von Herzen beistimmen: "Würde die Natur sich nicht in ein Tempe[l] und manches Land in ein Arcadien verwandeln, wenn die sanfte Flöte den Morgen mit lieblichen Gesängen begrüßte, und das weiche Horn aus den Abenddämmerungen des Waldes zu uns herüberhallte? Würde die Arbeit nicht fröhlicher vollbracht und die Stunde der Erholung besser verwendet werden, wenn der Zauber der Tonkunst die Menschen menschlicher machte, und sie dem thierischen Zustande der Betäubung entrisse, worin sie ihre feinere Sinne durch den Genuß der gröbern Ergötzlichkeiten einschläfern? Doch wer weiß, ob das neue Jahrhundert nicht auch hierin einen neuen bedeutenden Schritt zur Veredlung der Menschheit thun wird."

44. [Justus Thibaut], *Ueber Reinheit der Tonkunst* (Heidelberg: J. C. W. Mohr, 1825), 112: "Allein sehr heilsam wäre es gewiß, wenn man es sich zur Pflicht machte, in jedem Concerte einige auserwählte Stücke im ernsten Styl (freylich nicht im reinen Kirchenstyl) zu geben. Die Leute müssen erst auf leichte Art kennen lernen, was ihnen näher gebracht werden soll, und befreunden sie sich gleichsam spielend damit, so kann man die gute Stimmung schon zu weiteren Fortschritten benutzen."

45. [Johann August Günther] H[einroth?], "Concert," in *Encyclopädie der gesammten musikalischen Wissenschaften, oder Universal-Lexikon der Tonkunst,* edited by Gustav Schilling (Stuttgart: Franz Heinrich Köhler, 1835), 2:284: "besonders *Sinfonien,* welche den Kunstsinn und Kunstgeschmack ungemein fördern und heben"; "namentlich lehnt sich der große Theil der sogennant schönen Welt gegen dieselbe, als gegen die langweiligste Musikgattung auf"; and "Nicht das große, nur das ganz kleine Publicum der Auserwählten hat hier allenfalls eine Stimme."

46. Heinrich Paris, "Offener Brief an die Redaction, bei Gelegenheit einer bekannten Pianistin und einer unbekannten Componistin," *Cäcilia* 23, no. 91 (1844): 171: "Auch bin ich für mein Theil wirklich schon so weit gekommen, dass ich der Litanei, die um Abwendung aller Calamitäten bittet, gerne hinter 'Krieg und Pestilenz' die Worte anfügen möchte: 'und vor Clavirvirtuosen bewahre uns, unser Herre Gott!'"

47. Krüger, "Das Virtuosenconcert," 159: "Sagt' ich's nicht, daß der Brotneid durchschimmere? Daß wir Teufelskinder, wie er uns oft heimlich und öffentlich bezeichnet, den Sinn des Publicums verderben, indem wir sie von der Theilnahme an den sublimen Oratorien herauslocken in die sündige Welt?" For a more direct rehearsal of many of the same problems in concert life, see Krüger, "Laien, Dilettanten, Künstler," *Neue Zeitschrift für Musik* 11 (1839): 33–34, 37–38, 41–43, and 45–46.

48. Triest, "Ueber reisende Virtuosen," *Allgemeine musikalische Zeitung* 4 (1802): 737–49, 753–60, and 769–75.

49. Friedrich Guthmann, "Andeutungen und zufällige Gedanken," *Allgemeine musikalische Zeitung* 8 (1806): 561–65, esp. 562–64: "Die grosse Anzahl der Virtuosen und die vielen Stümper, welche unter diese Firma das Publikum oft täuschten, verdarben den Markt" (563).

50. See Nägeli, "Anrede an die schweizerische Musikgesellschaft bey Eröffnung ihrer Sitzung in Schafhausen den 21. August 1811," *Allgemeine musikalische Zeitung* 13 (1811): 656–64, 665–73, 685–92, esp. 669–73.

51. "Concerte in Monath Dezember 1812," *Wiener allgemeine musikalische Zeitung* 1 (1813): 10–11: "Die Reinheit und Schnelligkeit seiner Doppelzunge ließ nichts zu wünschen übrig ist [*sic*]. Ueberhaupt besitzt Herr B. eine seltene Fertigkeit im Vortrage der Passagen; wobey ihn die physische Construction seiner Athmens-Werkzeuge sehr Vortheilhaft unterstützt, da sie ihm in Stande setzt, die längsten Theile einer Variation ohne Respirazion auszuführen."

52. A concert report in *Zeitung für Theater und Musik*, a Berlin publication that survived for only a single year (1821), provides a good example of this less serious style. Although the concert it describes included among its participants Carl Maria von Weber (who was strongly associated with the cause of serious music), it nonetheless directed as much attention to the fashionability of the audience and the splendor of the hall as to the music performed ("Concert in Berlin," *Zeitung für Theater und Musik zur Unterhaltung gebildeter, unbefangener Leser*, no. 20 [19 May 1821]: 77). Some publications drifted to different positions along the spectrum of the popular and the serious during their lives; between 1817 and 1824, for instance, the *Allgemeine musikalische Zeitung mit besondere Rücksicht auf den österreichischen Kaiserstaat* changed from a highly varied publication to one in which lengthy articles on aesthetic issues established the journal's association with serious music beyond any doubt.

53. "Andeutungen zu einer derzeit sehr nöthigen Abhandlung über das gegenwärtige Concert-Unwesen," 110: "muss wieder anfangen sich nicht als tägliche Seiltänzerinn, sondern in ihrer ganzen Würde und Kraft zu zeigen." The exceptional feminine gendering of *Seiltänzerinn* is related to its reference to *die Kunst* rather than a particular (and usually male) virtuoso, but it also adds a further component of dismissal, particularly in opposition to *Würde und Kraft* (value and power).

54. Thibaut, *Ueber Reinheit der Tonkunst*, 73–74: "Daß unsre reisenden

Virtuosen . . . fast unbedingt nur ihr Aeusserstes, und sonst nichts sehen lassen, kann man allenfalls verzeihen, weil das Publicum in der Regel lieber mag, wenn ein Seiltänzer auf dem Kopfe steht, als wenn er in schönen, leichten Bewegungen das Ideal der Lieblichsten Formen darzustellen sucht."

55. Kahlert, "Das Concertwesen der Gegenwart," 105: "Die Fertigkeit, die körperliche Geschicklichkeit, die Sonderbarkeit reizen nunmehr und bringen etwas gänglich Unkünstlerisches in die Sphäre der Kunst. Der Seiltänzer steht durchaus nicht niedriger als ein Virtuos, der nur das sogennante 'Unglaubliche' sich zum Ziele gestellt hat."

56. Susan Bernstein, "Instruments of Virtuosity," in *Virtuosity of the Nineteenth Century: Performing Music and Language in Heine, Liszt, and Baudelaire* (Stanford: Stanford University Press, 1998), 81.

57. Nägeli, "Anrede an die schweizerische Musikgesellschaft bey Eröffnung ihrer Sitzung in Schafhausen den 21. August 1811," 669–70: "So gross, so höchst wirksam und bildend aber dieser für die Kunst durch Individuen errungene Vortheil ist, eben so gross, so höchst missbildend ist dasjenige, was eben auch durch Individuen, und zwar durch eine grosse Zahl von Individuen, in der Welt geleistet wird: ich meine die *herumreisende Virtuosen.*"

58. For a discussion of virtuosos in these terms, see "Der engere Kreis. Ein Beytrag zur Aesthetik, auch der musikalischen," *Allgemeine musikalische Zeitung* 27 (1825): 285–95, 863–66, esp. 864.

59. Kahlert, "Das Concertwesen der Gegenwart," 106: "wenn man früher Compositionen der Meister durch den Vortrag eines Virtuosen erläutert und ins Bewußtsein gerufen haben wollte, jetzt das Interesse sich umkehrt, und man vielmehr die Geschicklichkeit des Einzelnen bewundern will. Auf den frühern Standpuncte war die *Sache,* jetzt wird die *Person* die Hauptsache."

60. Paris, "Offener Brief," 169–70: "durch ihren wahrhaft classischen Vortrag classischer Musik" (170).

61. Marx, "Einige Worte über das Konzertwesen," 357: "das Publikum wird fühlen, den wahren Künstler vor sich zu haben, sobald ein Konzertist das Werk in jedem Tone leicht, frei und wahr, wie es in der Seele des Komponisten gelebt hat, hervortreten lässt."

62. J. Peterson, "Ueber Vortrag musikalischer Kunstwerke, besonders in Beziehung auf den Chorgesang," *Neue Berliner Musikzeitung* 1 (1847): 137–38: "Die oft vorkommende Aeusserung: 'Im Chore kann ich schon mitsingen!' entbehrt in vielen Fällen eines haltbaren Grundes, beruht auf dem, freilich sehr gewöhnlichen Missverstande des Begriffes Virtuosität. Auch der Chorsänger muss Virtuose sein. Aber diese Art der Virtuosität möchte ich mehr eine innerliche nennen."

63. "Nachrichten. Wien im November," *Musikalische Zeitung für die österreichischen Staaten* 1 (1812): 130–31:

> Am 29. November d. J. feyerte *Wien* ein grosses, in seiner Art einziges musikalisches Fest. Es war die Aufführung der Cantate: *Timotheus, oder die Gewalt der Musik;* componirt von *Händl* und durch *Mozart* mit der

Begleitung mehrerer Blasinstrumente versehen. Die Abhaltung dieses grossen Concerts geschah auf besondere höchste Genehmigung Se. Majestät des Kaisers in der k. k. Reitschule von 621 Kunstfreunden aus allen Ständen. Die Hauptsingstimmen hatten Frau *v. Geymüller*, die Fräulein *Bahrensfeld* und *Riedl*, Hr. Hofrath *v. Kiesewetter*, der k. k. Rath und Doktor der Rechten Hr. *Sonnleithner*, der Seiden-Fabrikant Hr. *Soini*, und Hr. *Hoffmann* übernommen. Hr. *Streicher* als Lehrer auf dem Pianoforte und Verfertiger dieses Instrumentes rühmlich bekannt, welcher in der Betreibung aller Vorbereitungs-Anstalten, so auch vorzüglich in der Bildung des Chors unermüdet war, und dem dieses Concert ihre Entstehung vorzüglich zu danken ist, führte den von ihm gebildeten Chor am Clavier. Der durch sein theoretisch und praktisch musikalischen Kenntnisse rühmlichst bekannte Hr. Hofconcipist des k. k. Obersthofmeisteramts, *Mosel*, führte das Ganze auf das trefflichste an. Der Grosshändler Hr. *J. Tost*, hatte die Direktion der Violinen übernommen. Die übrigen Solo- und Haupt-Instrumente welche zunächst am Clavier standen, waren theils von Dilettanten theils von den vorzüglichsten Künstlern besetzt; das Violoncell vom Hrn. *Hauschka*, der Contrabass vom Hrn. *Langhamer*, die 2 Violen von Hrn. *Tœuber*, und Hrn. *Kratki*, die Flöten spielten Hr. *Bogner* und Hr. *Baron v. Knorr*, die Oboen Hr. *Czerwenka* und Hr. *Kiess*, die Clarinetten Hr. *Graf v. Troier* und Hr. *Friedlovky*, die Fagotte Hr. *Romberg* und *Fürst Corolat*, die Waldhörner Hr. *Radezky*, und Hr. *Gowerlovsky*, ausser diesen zeigte sich bei der zweiten Aufführung unter den Solo Sängern auch Sr. Durchlaucht der regierende *Fürst Joseph von Lobkowitz*; überhaupt bemerkte man bei dem Singchor wie bei dem Instrumentenchor mehrere Dilettanten hohen Ranges, was den Werth des Ganzen noch mehr erhöhte. Ueber die Vollkommenheit der Ausführung war nur eine Stimme von beinahe 5000 Zuhörern. Das Ganze gewährte einen entzückenden Anblick und einen mächtigen Eindruck, der sich nicht beschreiben lässt, sondern selbst nur fühlen liess. Die Einladungen an die Kunstfreunde erliessen *Joseph Fürst von Lob[k]owitz, Moritz Graf v. Fries, Maria Anna Gräfin von Dietrichstein*, und *Fanny Freyin v. Arnstein*. Nach dem allgemeinen Wunsche wurde diese Cantate am 3. Dezember wiederholt; beide Mal geruhete der gesammte allerhöchste Hof der Aufführung, welche jedesmal um die Mittagsstunde statt hatte, beizuwohnen. Die Einnahme beider Anfführungen [sic] betrug bei 30000 fl. W. W., deren Bestimmung und Vertheilung der *Gesellschaft adelicher Frauen zur Beförderung des Guten und Nützlichen* überlassen ist.

For further discussion of this event, out of which Vienna's Gesellschaft der Musikfreunde grew, see Schwab, *Konzert*, 90; the account also reproduces a plan for the arrangement of the performers. Schwab, however, relying on the report of the event in "Korrespondenz: Wien, den 8ten Dec., Ubersicht des Monats November," *Allgemeine musikalische Zeitung* 14 (1812): 849–54, gives the number of participants as 590 and states that only among the contrabasses were professionals found; the Viennese report gives the impression of considerably more participation by professionals.

64. In this way, the performance represents a variant of the tradition of politically significant performances of Handel's oratorios in England that William Weber has described in *The Rise of Musical Classics in Eighteenth-Century England: A Study in Canon, Ritual, and Ideology* (Oxford: Clarendon Press, 1992), 103–42 and 223–42. Nor was the performance without German precedents; see the account of a 1786 performance of *Messiah* in Berlin, also involving professionals and dilettantes and organized by the nobility to charitable ends, in "Berlin, den 27sten May, 1786," *Magazin der Musik* 2 (1786): 974–76. See also Johann Adam Hiller, *Nachricht von der Aufführung des Händelschen Messias, in der Domkirche zu Berlin, den 19. May 1786* (Berlin: Christian Sigismund Spener, 1786). For a counterexample—a despairing report on a city in which amateurs refused on principle to play with those they discovered to be of lower degree, and in which empty seats were left in the audience next to women of the middle classes—see the account of Schwerin in "Darstellung des Musikzustandes im Meklenburgischen überhaupt, und in Schwerin in's besondere," *Allgemeine musikalische Zeitung* 2 (1800): 845–46.

65. Forkel, "Genauere Bestimmung," 1072: "unmöglich so wenig eine Privatsache seyn, als auch der Willkühr eines jeden überlassen bleiben, sondern nur durch obrigkeitlichen Veranstaltungen erhalten werden."

66. Schmith, *Philosophische Fragmente über die praktische Musik*, 97: "man kaum Hændel, Gluc, Gasmann, Paisello, Sarti, Naumann, Salieri, Hayden, Dittersdorff, Mozart's u.s.f. in der Zukunft zu erwarten hat."

67. . . . r., "über den Verfall der Musik," 137: "Wenn aber die erste Classe im Staate, auf welche sonst immer die schönen Künste, um der Ausbildung des Geistes und des Geschmackes willen, ihre Fortschritte stützten, ihren wesentlichen Werth nicht zu schätzen weiss, dann fällt die ganze Last der Pflege ihrer Jünger auf den Mittelstand, und werden diesem die Schultern endlich zu schwach, dann sinken Musik, Dichtkunst, Mahlerey und Bildhauerkunst herab, und machen der Rustik Platz."

68. See Volker, "Ueber die Hofkapellen in Deutschland und über ihre Bedeutsamkeit als selbstständige Kunst-Institute," *Neue Zeitschrift für Musik* 32 (1850): 113–15.

69. Reichardt, "An junge Künstler," 6: "Ein geschrieben Blatt was mir mancher wahre Künstler auf meinen Reisen aus seinem verborgnen Schatze gab, war oft unendlich mehr werth als zwanzig gestochene und gedruckte Werke desselben Mannes, zubereitet für das enge Herz seiner gnädigen Käufer und den Eisenkrämereien seines Notenverlegers." For a later consideration of the crowding out of good music by too voluminous publication of inferior works, see Guthmann, "Andeutungen und zufällige Gedanken."

70. Nägeli, "Anrede an die schweizerische Musikgesellschaft, bey Eröffnung ihrer Sitzung zu Zürich, den 19ten August 1812," 699: "ich *kenne* und *schätze* in den nämlichen Personen, welche in unserm Kreise die Kunst höher

zu heben trachten, diejenigen, die in andern Kreisen, in allgemeinen und besondern vaterländischen, in *pädagogischen, ökonomischen* und andern Gestalten—sämmtlich Zierden unsers Vaterlandes—ihre Gemeinnützigkeit längst und vielfach bewährt haben." For Nägeli's discussion of industry and art, see his "Anrede an die Versammlung des musik. Vereins der Schweiz, gehalten zu Freyburg, d. 7ten August dieses Jahres," *Allgemeine musikalische Zeitung* 18 (1816): 677–87.

71. Thibaut, *Ueber Reinheit der Tonkunst,* 111: "Denn wo alle Welt Sitz und Stimme hat, und wo Jeder für sein Geld auch etwas Erquickliches haben muß, da kann das Classische nicht ganz gedeihen."

72. Heinrich Paris, "Die Materialität der heutigen Musik und der heutigen Tänze," *Cäcilia* 20, no. 80 (1839): 201–2: "Weil wir überall den Cultus aller *Ideen* zerstört; überall nur noch *materiellen* Interessen zum einzigen Mobil aller socialen Verhältnisse gemacht haben; weil überall das *Geld* unser alleiniger Gott geworden."

73. Theodor Adorno, *Minima Moralia: Reflections from Damaged Life,* translated by E. F. N. Jephcott (London: NLB, 1974), 36. Among Adorno's examples of tact is "Beethoven's attitude towards traditional patterns of composition."

74. Burney, *An Eighteenth-Century Musical Tour in Central Europe and the Netherlands,* 42–43.

75. For discussions of the virtues and problems of musical life in the absence of major courts, see, respectively, "Musikalischer Verein in Passau," *Allgemeine musikalische Zeitung* 18 (1816): 666–75; and August Kahlert, "Aus Breslau," *Cäcilia* 16, no. 63 (1834): 207–12. It is worth stressing here that I am dealing with perceptions of concert life as represented in musical discourse. On the considerably less tidy reality of musical performance, see Christoph-Hellmut Mahling, "Music and Places for the Performance of Music as a Reflection of Urban Social Stratification in the 19th and Early 20th Centuries," translated by William Templer, in International Musicological Society, *Report of the 12th Congress, Berkeley, 1977,* edited by Daniel Heartz and Bonnie Wade (Kassel: Bärenreiter, 1981), 307–11, and the ensuing discussion, 315–18.

76. Gardichert, "Musikfest zu Demmin in Hinterpommern," 46–47.

77. "Musikalisches Leben Berlin's," *Neue Zeitschrift für Musik* 13 (1840): 66: "Selbst wo das Concert an die Kneipe erinnert und mit derselben zusammenfließt, sind die Aufführungen oft noch besser, als Concerte ersten Ranges in manchen kleinen Städten." On large cities in association with the best touring virtuosos and smaller towns with the poorer ones, see, for instance, Nägeli, "Anrede an die schweizerische Musikgesellschaft bey Eröffnung ihrer Sitzung in Schafhausen den 21. August 1811," 671–72; and Triest, "Ueber reisende Virtuosen."

78. Kahlert, "Das Concertwesen der Gegenwart," 98. For another evocation of the survival of past practices in remote locations, see O. F. K. W. Schulz, "Volksmusik der mittleren und kleinen Städte," *Berliner musikalische Zeitung* 2, no. 28 (1845): 5–6.

79. Marx, "Einige Worte über das Konzertwesen," 349: "an vielen bedeutenden Orten, namentlich auch in Berlin."

80. Krüger, "Laien, Dilettanten, Künstler," 42: "das Publicum ist überall dasselbe, von dem kleinsten Städtchen bis Wien: nur daß in den großen Städten die Infection des Dilettantenkrebses pflegt weiter um sich gegriffen zu haben."

81. Nägeli, "Anrede an die Schweizerische Musikgesellschaft, bey Eröffnung ihrer Sitzungen in Basel, den 14ten Brachmonat 1820," *Allgemeine musikalische Zeitung* 22 (1820): 769–79.

82. See Richard Leppert, *Music and Image: Domesticity, Ideology, and Socio-Cultural Formation in Eighteenth-Century England* (Cambridge: Cambridge University Press, 1988), 11–16. On the standards of the Gesellschaft der Musikfreunde and contemporary criticism, see Leon Botstein, "Music and Its Public: Habits of Listening and the Crisis of Musical Modernism in Vienna, 1870–1914" (Ph.D. dissertation, Harvard University, 1985), 265–76.

83. S., "Aus Stuttgart," *Neue Zeitschrift für Musik* 16 (1842): 154–56: "Die Kunst ist zu edel für ein Handwerk der Langeweile" (155).

84. Kahlert, "Das Concertwesen der Gegenwart," 98: "Diese werthen Herren spielten weit schlechter als heute unsre bezahlten Orchester, aber sie erfreuten sich innig an der Sache. Höchstens in kleinen Städten findet sich jetzt noch etwas Aehnliches, denn der Dilettant ist jetzt aus dem ausübenden Kreise in den der Kunstrichter übergegangen."

85. For enthusiastic reports on dilettantes' activity, see, for instance, "Kurze Uebersicht des jetzigen Musikwesens in Riga," and a correspondence report from Königsberg, both found in the *Allgemeine musikalische Zeitung* 2 (1800): 393–96 and 477–79, respectively. Rochlitz's warning occurs in his "Bruchstücke aus Briefen an einen jungen Tonkünstler: Sechster Brief: Liebhaberey an Musik," *Allgemeine musikalische Zeitung* 2 (1799): 177–83. That Rochlitz's warning is in the form of a citation of a letter to his late sister introduces issues of gender and musical competence as well.

86. J. C. H., "Einige Worte über die musikalische Bildung jetziger Zeit," *Allgemeine musikalische Zeitung* 21 (1819): 569: "Die Allerwenigsten haben auch nur eine leise Ahndung davon, dass wahre musikalische Bildung zur Veredlung des innern Menschen wesentlich beytrage, und im Stande sey, das Gemüth reinigend abzuziehen von allem Gemeinen; die Meisten zerren die Königin, die geboren ist, auf einem der erhabensten Throne im Reiche des Geistigen zu herrschen und zu walten, mit ihren ungeweihten Händen herab in den Schmutz ihres eignen sündhaften Lebens, und zwingen sie, ihrer himmlischen Schönheit entkleidet, als gemeine Dirne aufgeputzt, um sie her zu tanzen und so die Augen des schaulustigen Pöbels auf sie zu ziehen."

87. The first quotation is from a report on performances by students "from the most cultivated families of Berlin" (der gebildetsten Familien Berlins), in "Aus Berlin," *Zeitung für Theater und Musik zur Unterhaltung gebildeter, unbefangener Leser*, no. 4 (27 January 1821): 13: "nicht zu scharf richtender Kritiker." The second is from "Musikalisches Leben Berlin's," 65: "Concerten des zweiten Ranges."

88. See S., "Aus Stuttgart," 155: "Diese Spur läßt uns auf den leidigen Dilettantismus kommen, der in Stuttgart eine schauderhafte Höhe gewonnen hat." Krüger, "Laien, Dilettanten, Künstler," 41: "nie sei er *Diener* des Publicums, denn das ist pöbelhaft dilettantisch und entwürdigt die Hoheit der Idee, dem Reiche des Fleisches und der Finsterniß zu dienen." For attempts to uphold the value of dilettantism in the face of criticism, see "Ueber Dilettanten in der Tonkunst (eingesandt). Mit einem Anhange von G. W. Fink," *Allgemeine musikalische Zeitung* 32 (1830): 65–67; CB, "Das Strassburger Musikfest, beleuchtet unter dem Gesichtspunct: Welchen Einfluss hat auf die Kunst der Dilettantismus," *Cäcilia* 13, no. 51 (1831): 194–201; and G. W. Fink, "Ueber den Dilettantismus in der Teutschen Musik," *Allgemeine musikalische Zeitung* 35 (1833): 7–13.

89. "Musikzustand und musikalisches Leben in Wien," *Cäcilia* 1, no. 2 (1824): 193: "Man kann jetzt in Wien so viel Musik, und zum Theil sehr gute Musik, unentgeldlich hören, dass Wenige dafür Geld ausgeben mögen."

90. Fink, "Ueber den Dilettantismus," 8; "Ueber Dilettanten in der Tonkunst," 65.

91. Reichardt, "An großgute Regenten," vii: "ächte Kunstschulen . . . wo der junge Zögling nicht bloß in seiner Kunst theoretisch und praktisch mit Einsicht und Gefühl und Geschmack unterrichtet wird, wo auch sein Herz durch ächte Religion, Naturgenuß, Geschichte und Beispiel edler Lehrer edel und groß gebildet, sein Kopf durch Kenntniß der Natur, der Alten und der Welt aufgeklärt und so hoher edler Kunstsinn in ihm erzeigt [*sic*—recte erzeugt?] wird—O daß ich solche Kunstschulen noch sähe!"

92. Christman, "Tableau über das Musikwesen im Wirtembergischen," 120: "dass sich unter ihnen ein gewisser Ton der Humanität, des sittlichen Anstandes, und eine Harmonie unter sich selbst bis jetzt erhielt, das einem in ihrem gesellschaftlichen Zirkel eben so wohl und behagli[c]h ist, als in ihrem Odeum."

93. Kahlert, "Das Concertwesen der Gegenwart," 98: "Der alte Musiker, in Erinnerung an ein gewisses Zunftwesen, woraus alle Kunst in Deutschland besonders sich herausgebildet hat, schloß sich mit seinem Wirken und Streben mehr ab, als der heutige, der an der sogenannten *allgemeinen* Bildung sein Recht zu nehmen fordert. Wie alle Stände, alle Beschäftigungen sich mehr und mehr vermischen, ist auch ser Musiker bei Weitem mehr Weltmann geworden, als er es sonst war."

94. August Müller, "Ueber das Wirken des Musikers im Orchester," *Neue Zeitschrift für Musik* 31 (1849): 217: "Beethoven namentlich fordert den Orchester-Musiker auf, Künstler im wahren Sinn des Wortes zu sein, und reicht Jedem, der die erhabenen Ideen dieses schöpferischen Geistes gut wiederzugeben vermag, ein Patent für diese Eigenschaft, welches, von göttlicher Hand besiegelt, in der ganzen, weiten Kunstwelt honorirt werden wird." Müller precedes this passage with a reference to "die Emancipation des reproducirenden Musikers" and goes on to insist that the time is past in which the orchestral musician could be considered a *Handwerker*.

95. See Johann Nicolaus Forkel [Phil. harmonico, pseud.], "Ein launigter Brief, wodurch jemand zu einem Concerte eingeladen wird," *Musikalisch-kritische Bibliothek* 2 (1778): 326–28.

96. The quotation is from Triest, "Bemerkungen über die Ausbildung der Tonkunst in Deutschland," 321–22: "nicht mehr als eine Treibhauspflanze gezogen, sondern auch unter die übrigen Früchte zum Lebensgenuss versezt und vertheilt werden sollte."

97. J. Sartorius, "Ein unvorgreifliches Bedenken über die itzige musikalische Kultur à la mode," *Cäcilia* 3, no. 12 (1825): 286: "Bei den *Konzerten* vollends wird eigentlich nur ein Zeitvertreib und eine Erlustigung gesucht. Das hiesse die Leute um ihr gutes Geld prellen, und wäre ganz gegen die Abrede, wenn das Orchester weiter gehen wollte." For a similar viewpoint, see Kahlert, "Das Concertwesen der Gegenwart," 98.

98. "Musikalisches Leben in Braunschweig," *Neue Zeitschrift für Musik* 6 (1837): 61: "Wahrlich, das Publicum thut Recht daran, solche unreine Aufführung gänzlich zu übersehen, es verlangt mehr Achtung vor seinem Urtheil. Außerdem zahlt es sein Geld nicht für Proben, sondern verlangt, daß diese vorher beseitigt werden."

99. For a discussion of the significance of even superficial dilettantes to music due to their economic influence, see Fink, "Ueber den Dilettantismus," 9–10. Krüger also recognized the role of money in empowering the public ("Laien, Dilettanten, Künstler," 37).

100. Paris, "Die Materialität der heutigen Musik," 231–32:

> Denn alles den Massen Dargebotene, was *Geist* und *Gemüth leer* lässt, indem es die *Sinne erregt*, ist, nach meiner Ueberzeugung, stets ein Stoss, welcher der öffentlichen Moral beigebracht wird; und jemehr durch die heutige Aufklärung, durch das Nivellement der Stände, und den immer wachsenden allgemeinen Geschmack für die künstliche und kunstmäßig vorgetragene Musik, das gute alte gemüthliche, aus eigner Kehle heraus gesungene *Volkslied*, so wie die fröhlichen, natürlichen, durch die eigne Lust begleiteten *Tanzweisen* unter den geringeren Ständen verschwinden, dagegen aber deren halbcivilisirter Andrang zu Theater, Conzerten und rauschenden Musikfesten zunimmt, desto mehr halte ich die lärmende, schwindelnde, betäubende, aus allen Fugen rückende Tendenz, mit einem Wort die *Materialität* der heutigen Musik für ein Zeichen der Zeit, das ich, in Bezug auf Volks- und Jugendbildung, geradezu als eine Art Calamität der Zeit anzusehen, keinen Augenblick Anstand nehme.

101. The proposal—and the analogy to museums—occurs in Kahlert, "Das Concertwesen der Gegenwart," 109–10.

102. Krüger, "Laien, Dilettanten, Künstler," 46: "Wir erkennen—das Volk als den Leib, die unbewußte und unwissende Sinnlichkeit der kunstliebenden Menschheit, als unschuldige Gemeinde dem wissenden Priester gegenüber, der

ihm die Seele geben soll. . . . Laien und Künstler bilden die integrirenden Momente des gesammten Kunstlebens; eins kann ohne das andere nicht sein und darf es auch nicht wollen: eins soll das andere nähren, erfrischen, wechselseitig stützen: so wird das ächte Kunstleben erzeugt und vollendet."

103. See Dahlhaus's discussion of the religion of music in *Nineteenth-Century Music,* 94–96.

104. John Spitzer, "Metaphors of the Orchestra—the Orchestra as a Metaphor," *Musical Quarterly* (1996): 234–64.

105. "Einiges über die Pflichten des Violoncellisten als Orchesterspielers und Accompagnateurs," *Allgemeine musikalische Zeitung* 43 (1841): 132: "Es wirkt hier das Ganze im Vereine; es ist nur ein Ziel, nach welchem alle streben, so dass man die Sinfonie eine rein gesellschaftliche Unterhaltung der verschiedenen Instrumente unter sich nennen könnte."

106. Nägeli, "Anrede an die schweizerische Musikgesellschaft, bey Eröffnung ihrer Sitzung zu Zürich, den 19ten August 1812," 711:

> Um einen Kunststaat zu organisiren, müssen wir, gleichwie im politischen—ich spreche aber nicht politisch—einen Adel und ein Volk haben, einen Adel, als Blüthe der individuellen, ein Volk, als Grundlage der nationellen Bildung. Der Adel muss sich immer höher heben, das Volk seine Gesammtkraft immer mächtiger geltend machen. Hingegen wäre ein Adel ohne Volk, so wie ein Volk ohne Adel, eine fürs öffentliche Leben unedle und wirkungslose Erscheinung.
>
> Der Kern unsers Volks sind unsere Choristen und Orchesterleute, die Repräsentanten unsers Adels unsere Solo-Sänger und Spieler.

107. Müller, "Ueber das Wirken des Musikers im Orchester," 218n.

108. Fink, "Symphonie," in *Encyclopädie der gesammten musikalischen Wissenschaften, oder Universal-Lexicon der Tonkunst,* edited by Gustav Schilling (Stuttgart: Franz Heinrich Köhler, 1838), 6:547: "Beschauen wir diese ganz nothwendigen Anforderungen an ein solches Werk, so wird für die Tondichtung daraus folgen, daß jedes Orchesterinstrument als besonderes Individuum seiner eigenthümlichen Art nach erfaßt werden, jedem sein selbsteigenes Klingen und Singen gelassen werden müsse, als herrsche die vollkommenste Freiheit eines republikanischen Hohenpriesterstaates, worin jeder gern der Idee als einer göttlichen sich unterthan erweist. Im Letzten liegt der Grund höchster Oberherrschaft, höchster Gesetzlichkeit im möglichst engsten Bunde mit individueller Freiheit."

109. "Ueber Bildung eines guten Orchesters," *Allgemeine musikalische Zeitung* 8 (1818): 799: "muss . . . die grösste, ich möchte sagen, eine militärische Pünktlichkeit herrschen—so sehr sonst militärische Einrichtungen dem Kunstcharakter widerstreben." This point is a brief one subordinate to the article's more extensive metaphor of the body, discussed below.

110. "Züge von dem Bilde eines Musikdirectors, wie er nicht seyn soll," *Allgemeine musikalische Zeitung* 16 (1814): 391–92: "im Bewusstseyn seiner

eigenen und der Kraft seiner Untergebenen, dastand, so wie ungefähr ein Feld-
herr an der Spitze seines Heeres vor der Schlacht stehen muss." Ignaz von Seyfried used the corresponding image, through which the director led a well-re-
hearsed performance by holding "the well-organized and -disciplined corps of
troops in fine order" ("das wohlorganisirte und disciplinirte Truppencorps in
schöner Ordnung") in a discussion of the advantages of conducting with a ba-
ton. See his "Selbsterfahrungen auf Berufswegen," *Cäcilia* 13, no. 52 (1831):
233–39; quotation from 236.

111. On the household, see "Vergeich einer Familie mit einem Concerte.
Neue Bearbeitung," *Allgemeiner musikalischer Anzeiger,* no. 14 (13 September 1826): 111–12; and Techo di Teczoni, "Das Konzert des häuslichen Lebens," *Berliner allgemeine musikalische Zeitung* 6 (1830): 13–16. The latter
article is identical to the former in many of its parallels, suggesting familiarity with it (or the predecessor suggested by the earlier article's title). Images
of the body appear in "Ueber die Bildung eines guten Orchesters," 799; 26.,
"Strauß im Norden," 310; and Müller, "Ueber das Wirken des Musikers im
Orchester," 218.

112. 26., "Strauß im Norden," 310: "Sein Orchester ist auf das trefflichste
eingespielt, was allerdings leichter beim engen Umfang ihres Zwecks: die Seele
davon ist Strauß, dessen Geist die Körper aller Mitwirkenden beherrscht; daß
dieser Einfluß sich etwas körperlich kund thut, mag an den physischen Genre
seiner Leute liegen; wenn seine Streichinstrumente etwas zu schwach waren,
so erklären wir dies daraus, daß er einige Geigen als zu arge Brodf[r]esser zu
Hause gelassen haben wird."

113. Rochlitz, "Bruchstücke aus Briefen an einen jungen Tonkünstler:
Vierter Brief: Der Musikdirektor," *Allgemeine musikalische Zeitung* 2 (1799):
57–63, esp. 57–59.

114. "Vom Dirigiren und insbesondere von der Manie des Dirigirens,"
Neue Zeitschrift für Musik 4 (1836): 130: "Wer möchte leugnen, daß die hohe
Achtung, welche die Orchestermitglieder für die wissenschaftliche Kenntniß
ihres Directors haben, nicht mächtig bei Musikaufführungen elektrisirt. Ist es
dann nicht, als ob der Geist der Composition seine Strahlen vom Direction-
spulte aus über das Orchester würfe?"

115. "Musikalisches Leben in Braunschweig," 69: "Diese unvergleich-
lichen Vier haben, sobald es ihr Quartett gilt, gleich Verschworenen nur *eine
Seele.* Daß eine solche Uebereinstimmung leichter erlangt werden kann, als
eine ähnliche bei Symphonien, wo gleichsam ein ganzes Volk zur Realisirung
einer großen Idee (Thema) aufsteht, schwächt die Vortrefflichkeit des Müller-
schen Quartetts nicht; der reproducirende Künstler hat alle Bedingungen erfüllt, sobald er sich mit dem *vorliegenden* Kunstwerke in Einklang zu setzen
wußte."

116. Cusick, "Gender and the Cultural Work of a Classical Music Performance," 82. Cusick's hypothetical example gives not a generalized composer
but Schumann.

117. Nägeli, "Anrede an die schweizerische Musikgesellschaft bey Eröffnung ihrer Sitzung in Schafhausen den 21. August 1811," 670–71:

> Süßlinge, noch zerschmelzender als ihre Töne; Schwächlinge, die nicht einmal aufrecht stehen können, und in ihrem Körper so wenig Takt und Haltung haben, als in ihrem Spiel. Und was für Musik produciren sie gewöhnlich, in den Sälen, die sonst von *Haydns* und *Mozarts* Prachtwerken wiederhallen? Concerte, von sich; Variationen, auch von sich; Divertissements, kurzweilige, auch von sich; Concertantstücke sogar, dass der Himmel erbarmen möchte, auch von sich; alles, wie natürlich, mit Ansprüchen auf grossen Applaus, der ihnen auch nicht entgeht, wenn sie eine noch so elende Composition schön oder brillant vortragen. . . . Man bemerke auch wohl dass gerade die bessern Künstler seltener etwas von sich spielen, desto öfter Werke grosser Meister.

A considerably later discussion of virtuosos, Krüger, "Das Virtuosenconcert," includes a similar (if more circumspect) critique of neglecting the work of "unsere ewigen Classiker" (160) in favor of compositions by the performer.

118. Peterson, "Ueber Vortrag musikalischer Kunstwerke," 137: "die Componisten sagten: 'Verstehe und empfinde mein Werk, und der anmuthige Vortrag wird von sich selbst finden.'" The author of "Ueber die Bildung eines guten Orchesters" prefaces his social, military, and corporeal metaphors for performance with a discussion of the needs of the composer as requiring such activity (798). For more discussion of the role of performance indications in relation to the composer's authority, see Lydia Goehr, *The Imaginary Museum of Musical Works: An Essay in the Philosophy of Music* (Oxford: Clarendon Press, 1992), 224–27.

119. Cusick, "Gender and the Cultural Work of a Classical Music Performance," 85.

120. "Musikzustand und musikalisches Leben in Wien," 200:

> Würdiger und glänzender hätte der diesmalige musikalische Winter-Kurs nicht beschlossen werden können, als durch eine grosse musikalische Akademie, in welcher das grösste Genie unserer Zeiten bewies, dass der wahre Künstler keinen Stillstand kennt. Vorwärts, aufwärts, ist seine Losung, sein Sieges-Ruf. *Beethoven* gab eine grosse Ouverture, drei Hymnen seiner neuen Messe, und seine neue Symphonie, deren letztes Stück sich mit einem Chor über Schillers Lied an die Freude endigt. Man kann nicht Mehr sagen, als, die Kenner erkannten und sprachen es einstimmig aus: *Beethoven* hat alles übertroffen, was von ihm vorhanden ist, *Beethoven* ist noch weiter vorwärts geschritten!!
>
> Diese neuen Kunstwerke erscheinen als die ungeheuern Producte eines Göttersohnes, welcher die heilige, belebende Flamme eben unmittelbar vom Himmel holte.

The article concludes with a promise to treat these works at length in a later report.

121. "Musikalisches Leben in Braunschweig," 57:

Die erste Aufgabe eines Orchesters ist offenbar, sich als ein festge-
gliedertes, einiges Ganzes anzusehen. Hier hat kein Mitglied für sich
allein Bedeutung. Es ist die Pflicht eines Jeden, seine Eigenthümlichkeit
in so weit aufzuopfern, als sie nicht in Beziehung zum Großen und Ganzen steht. Dies erfordert eine Verständigung über den Vortrag bedeu-
tender Instrumentalstücke, sei es durch die dominirende Vermittelung
eines ausgezeichneten Dirigenten, sei es durch ein gemeinschaftliches
Uebereinkommen der Einzelnen. Jedenfalls darf von dem eigentlich
Technischen nichts dem Zufall überlassen bleiben. Wird dies, bei großem
Fleiße übrigens, gehörig berücksichtigt, so ist es möglich, daß die Masse
wie von *einem* Geist belebt erscheine. Es ergeben sich dann jene un-
glaublichen Erfolge, welche in neuster Zeit durch den Vortrag von Symphonieen, und der *Beethovenschen* vorzugsweise, erreicht worden sind.
So haben sich vor anderen die Städte *Paris, Wien, Berlin* und *Leipzig*
durch gute Aufführungen großer Instrumentalstücke ausgezeichnet. Referent hatte Gelegenheit, in einer dieser Städte jene herrlichen Erfolge
zu erleben. Welch' ein begeisternder Schwung war in diesem Orchester,
diesem Publicum! Beiderseitige Begegnung in der Theilnahme für einen
gewaltigen Genius förderte das Herrlichste zu Tage. Wie jener Stein
Funken sprüht, wenn ihn Stahl berührt, so schlug das Feuer der Begeisterung überall aus diesen dichtgedrängten horchenden Massen. Man
denke sich ein Publicum, welches wie zum Gottesdienste sich vorberei-
tet, den Riesenbau einer Beethovenschen Symphonie zu erfassen. Nun
vollends während der Aufführung. Hier ein kaum verhaltener Ausruf
der höchsten Bewunderung und Freude, oder des Schrecks, wenn Beethoven auf seine dämonische Weise in schnellsten Uebergängen Nacht
aus Tag macht, oder Tag aus Nacht. Dort Männer von Fach mit der Par-
titur zur Had, diesem oder jenem zublinzelnd, wenn's packt wie mit Gei-
sterarmen. Und keine Störung, von keiner Art, überall Gleichgesinnte,
Brüder in schönster Bedeutung des Wortes. Das bewirkt ein Orchester,
vom ältesten bis zum jüngsten Mitgliede so mit ganzer Seele bei der
Sache. Referent sah, wie im vierten Satze der C-Moll-Symphonie
von Beethoven, wo ein Geigensatz von Oberst zu Unterst wie ein Riß
herunterfährt', die Herren von der Capelle mit dem Publicum in eine
Gemeinschaft traten, daß man Blicke wechselte, alle hergebrachte Form
vergessend.

122. It is true that three of the cities mentioned were in fact court cities, and
the report's use of the term *Capelle* implies a court ensemble, but the description avoids any mention of nobility or court; they are irrelevant to the event.
The conception is rather of a city where a mass audience and skilled professionals can encounter one another.

AFTERWORD

1. Adorno, "Analytical Study of the *NBC Music Appreciation Hour*," *Musical Quarterly* 78 (1994): 328. This study was written between 1938 and 1940 but first published in 1994.

2. Theodor W. Adorno, *Beethoven: The Philosophy of Music*, edited by Rolf Tiedemann, translated by Edmund Jephcott (Stanford: Stanford University Press, 1998).

3. Ibid., 3 (fragment 1).

4. See Bourdieu, *Distinction*, 74–76; quotation from 76.

5. Stock, "New Musicologies, Old Musicologies, 53.

6. Adorno, *Beethoven*, 14 (from fragment 29).

7. Adorno, "On the Fetish Character in Music and the Regression of Listening," in *The Essential Frankfurt School Reader*, edited by Andrew Arato and Eike Gebhardt (New York: Urizen Books, 1978), 270–99; quotations from 288.

8. For a recent attempt to view Adorno's diatribes on jazz and popular song in the context of his other writings on music, see Robert W. Witkin, *Adorno on Music* (London: Routledge, 1998), esp. 160–80 and 191–95.

9. For a similar observation concerning Adorno's links to earlier German music aesthetics, see Sponheuer, "Der 'Gott der Harmonien' und die 'Pfeife des Pan,'" 183.

10. Rose Rosengard Subotnick, "Adorno's Diagnosis of Beethoven's Late Style: Early Symptom of a Fatal Condition," in *Developing Variations: Style and Ideology in Western Music* (Minneapolis: University of Minnesota Press, 1991), 41.

11. I have noted this trait in recent scholarship in David Gramit, "The Roaring Lion: Critical Musicology, the Aesthetic Experience, and the Music Department," *Canadian University Music Review* 19 (1998): 19–33; and "Musical Scholarship, Musical Practice, and the Act of Listening," in *Music and Marx: Ideas, Practice, Politics*, edited by Regula Burckhardt Qureshi (New York: Garland, forthcoming).

12. Goehr, *The Imaginary Museum of Musical Works*, 152.

13. In a more recent study, Goehr also overlooks the implications of Wagner's use of the same dichotomy in *Die Meistersinger;* although she notes the "anti-bourgeois" quality of Walther's character, she does not comment on the class-based boundary established between the mere craftsperson and the artist by Walther's mockery of the equation of art and craft. See Goehr, *The Quest for Voice*, 57–58.

Bibliography

EIGHTEENTH- AND NINETEENTH-CENTURY LITERATURE

Note: To facilitate location, those articles whose authors are indicated only by ciphers or by initials that I have been unable to expand are alphabetized by title.

Alexander, Carl. "Ueber das Volkslied, insonders das Italiänische," *Neue Zeitschrift für Musik* 1 (1834): 233–35.

"Andeutungen zu einer derzeit sehr nöthigen Abhandlung über das gegenwärtige Concert-Unwesen," *Allgemeine musikalische Zeitung mit besonderer Rücksicht auf den österreichischen Kaiserstaat* 2 (1818): 109–11.

Arnim, Ludwig Achim von, and Clemens Brentano. *Des Knaben Wunderhorn: Alte deutsche Lieder.* [1806–08.] Munich: Winkler-Verlag, n.d.

"Aufgefundene Blätter aus dem Tagebuch eines früh verstorbenen Musikers: Musikanlage der Orientalen," *Berliner allgemeine musikalische Zeitung* 5 (1828): 179–80.

"Aus Berlin," *Zeitung für Theater und Musik zur Unterhaltung gebildeter, unbefangener Leser,* no. 4 (27 January 1821): 13.

"Aus Stuttgart," *Neue Zeitschrift für Musik* 16 (1842): 154–56. Ascribed to "S."

"Auszug aus Karsten Niebuhr's Reisebeschreibung von Arabien und anderen umliegenden Ländern," *Musikalisch-kritische Bibliothek* 2 (1778): 306–16.

Becker, Carl Ferdinand. Review of *Encyclopädie der gesammten musikalischen Wissenschaften, oder Universal-Lexicon der Tonkunst,* edited by Gustav Schilling. *Neue Zeitschrift für Musik* 3 (1835): 177–78, 181–82, 185–86; 11 (1839): 78–79.

———. "Das Volkslied," *Neue Zeitschrift für Musik* 12 (1840): 69–70.

"Bemerkungen aus dem Tagebuche eines praktischen Tonkünstlers," *Allgemeine musikalische Zeitung* 8 (1806): 705–12 and 721–28.

"Berlin, den 27sten May, 1786," *Magazin der Musik* 2 (1786): 974–76.

Beyträge zur Bildung für Jünglinge. Volume 2. Vienna: Härter, 1818.

Brendel, Franz. "Die erste Versammlung deutscher Tonkünstler und Musikfreunde in Leipzig," *Neue Zeitschrift für Musik* 27 (1847): 93–96, 105–8, 117–19, 121–26, 141–44, 153–56, 165–67, and 177–80.

Brendel, Franz, et al. "Eingabe an das königl. Preußische Ministerium der geistlichen-, Unterrichts- und Medicinal-Angelegenheiten," *Neue Zeitschrift für Musik* 29 (1848): 85–88 and 97–100.

Burney, Charles. *An Eighteenth-Century Musical Tour in Central Europe and the Netherlands.* Edited by Percy Scholes. London: Oxford University Press, 1959. Originally published as *The Present State of Music in Germany, the Netherlands, and United Provinces. Or, the Journal of a Tour through Those Countries, Undertaken to Collect Materials for a General History of Music.* London: T. Becket, 1773.

Christman. "Tableau über das Musikwesen im Wirtembergischen," *Allgemeine musikalische Zeitung* 2 (1799): 71–80, 118–28, and 139–44.

"Concert in Berlin," *Zeitung für Theater und Musik zur Unterhaltung gebildeter, unbefangener Leser,* no. 20 (19 May 1821): 77.

"Concerte in Monath Dezember 1812," *Wiener allgemeine musikalische Zeitung* 1 (1813): 10–11.

Cramer, Carl Friedrich. Review of *Lieder im Volkston,* by Johann Abraham Peter Schulz. *Magazin der Musik* 1 (1783): 61–63.

"Darstellung des Musikzustandes im Meklenburgischen überhaupt, und in Schwerin in's besondere," *Allgemeine musikalische Zeitung* 2 (1800): 843–48 and 858–61.

Diesterweg, F. A. W. *Der Unterricht in der Klein-Kinder-Schule, oder die Anfänge der Unterweisung und Bildung in der Volksschule.* 2nd edition. Crefeld: Johann Heinrich Funcke, 1832.

Dreist, K. A. "Zweytes Wort über die Gesangbildungslehre nach Pestalozzi's Grundsätze von M. J. [sic] Pfeiffer und H. G. Nägeli," *Allgemeine musikalische Zeitung* 13 (1811): 833–42, 858–70, and 876–78.

"Einige Bemerkungen über die Musik der Türken, zur Berechtigung mehrerer Reisebeschreiber," *Allgemeine musikalische Zeitung* 4 (1801): 17–23.

"Einige Worte über die musikalische Bildung jetziger Zeit," *Allgemeine musikalische Zeitung* 21 (1819): 565–76 and 581–86. Ascribed to "J. C. H."

"Einiges über die Pflichten des Violoncellisten als Orchesterspielers und Accompagnateurs," *Allgemeine musikalische Zeitung* 43 (1841): 129–33.

Eitner, Robert. "Schilling, Gustav." In *Allgemeine deutsche Biographie.* Volume 31. Leipzig: Duncker & Humblot, 1890.

Engelbrunner, Nina d'Aubigny von. *Briefe an Natalie über den Gesang, als Beförderung der häuslichen Glückseligkeit und geselligen Vergnügens.* Leipzig: Voß, 1803.

Engelmann. "Musik als Erziehungsmittel," *Allgemeine musikalische Zeitung* 7 (1805): 633–37.

"Der engere Kreis. Ein Beytrag zur Aesthetik, auch der musikalischen," *Allgemeine musikalische Zeitung* 27 (1825): 285–95 and 863–66.

"Etwas über Musik und Tanz in Brasilien," *Allgemeine musikalische Zeitung* 35 (1833): 19–21.

Fink, G[ottfried] W[ilhelm]. "Ueber den Dilettantismus in der Teutschen Musik," *Allgemeine musikalische Zeitung* 35 (1833): 7–13.

Forkel, Johann Nicolaus [Phil. harmonico, pseud.]. "Ein launigter Brief, wodurch jemand zu einem Concerte eingeladen wird," *Musikalisch-kritische Bibliothek* 2 (1778): 326–28. Hildesheim: Georg Olm, 1964.

Forkel, Johann Nicolaus. "Vorrede," *Musikalisch-kritische Bibliothek* 1 (1778): iii–xxvi.

———. "Genauere Bestimmung einiger musikalischen Begriffe. Zur Ankundigung des academischen Winterconcerts von Michaelis 1780 bis Ostern 1781," *Magazin der Musik* 1 (1783): 1039–72.

———. "Von der Musik der Chineser." In *Musikalischer Almanach für Deutschland auf das Jahr 1784*, 233–74. Leipzig: Schwickertschen Verlag, 1784; reprint, Hildesheim: Georg Olm, 1974.

Frantz, K. W. "Singechöre, eine nützliche Anstalt," *Allgemeine musikalische Zeitung* 4 (1802): 673–79.

Gardichert. "Musikfest zu Demmin in Hinterpommern," *Berliner allgemeine musikalische Zeitung* 3 (1826): 46–48. Followed by an editorial, "Bemerkung zu Obigen," by A. B. Marx, 48.

Gerber, Ernst Ludwig. *Historisch-Biographisches Lexikon der Tonkünstler.* Edited by Othmar Wessely. 1790–92. Reprint, Graz: Akademische Druck- und Verlagsanstalt, 1977.

Gleim, Johann Wilhelm Ludewig. *Sämmtliche Werke.* Edited by Wilhelm Körte. Halberstadt: Büreau für Literatur und Kunst, 1811; reprint, Hildesheim: G. Olm, 1971.

Grillparzer, Franz. *Selbstbiographie.* Edited by Arno Dusini. 1853. Reprint, Salzburg: Residenz Verlag, 1994.

Guthmann, Friedrich. "Etwas zur Vertheidigung der Tänze," *Allgemeine musikalische Zeitung* 6 (1804): 405–7.

———. "Expectorationen über die heutige Musik. Dritte Expectoration: Ueber Tanzmusik," *Allgemeine musikalische Zeitung* 7 (1805): 777–79.

———. "Andeutungen und zufällige Gedanken," *Allgemeine musikalische Zeitung* 8 (1806): 561–65.

———. "Winke über den musikalischen Unterricht der Frauenzimmer," *Allgemeine musikalische Zeitung* 8 (1806): 513–16.

———. "Grad der musikalischen Bildung bey Frauenzimmern," *Allgemeine musikalische Zeitung* 9 (1807): 380–82.

GutsMuths, J. C. F. "Wollen alle Deutschen Musikanten werden?" *Bibliothek der pädagogischen Literatur* (November 1804): 295–99.

Hagen, Theodor. "Die Civilisation in Beziehung zur Kunst mit specieller Berücksichtigung der Musik," *Neue Zeitschrift für Musik* 23 (1845): 153–56, 158–59, 165–67, 173–75, 185–86, 189–90, 193–95, and 205–6.

Hanslick, Eduard. *On the Musically Beautiful: A Contribution towards the Re-*

vision of the Aesthetics of Music. Translated by Geoffrey Payzant. Indianapolis: Hackett, 1986.

Herder, Johann Gottfried. "Auszug aus einem Briefwechsel über Oßian und die Lieder alter Völker." In *Von deutscher Art und Kunst: Einige fliegende Blätter*, 7–62. Hamburg: Bode, 1773; reprint, Stuttgart: Reclam, 1968.

———. *Volkslieder. Nebst untermischten andern Stücken.* Part 2. Leipzig: in der Weygandschen Buchhandlung, 1779; reprint, Hildesheim: Georg Olms, 1981.

———. *Sämmtliche Werke.* Edited by Bernhard Suphan. Berlin: Weidmann, 1877–1913.

———. *Briefe zu Beförderung der Humanität.* Berlin: Aufbau, 1971.

Hientzsch, Johann Gottfried. "Gesang," *Eutonia* 1 (1829): 149–67 and 239–71.

———. "Über die Musik als das herrlichste Mittel einer vorzüglichen Bildung, einer geistreichen Unterhaltung und religiösen Erhebung in Familie," *Eutonia* 5 (1831): 152–61.

Hiller, Johann Adam. [Vorbericht]. *Wöchentliche Nachrichten und Anmerkungen die Musik betreffend* 1 (1766): 1–8.

———. *Nachricht von der Aufführung des Händelschen Messias, in der Domkirche zu Berlin, den 19. May 1786.* Berlin: Christian Sigismund Spener, 1786.

Hirschbach, H. "Moderne deutsche Musikzustände," *Neue Zeitschrift für Musik* 17 (1842): 123–24.

Hoffmann, Ernst Theodor Amadeus. Review of Symphony No. 5, by Ludwig van Beethoven. Translated by F. John Adams Jr. In *Symphony No. 5 in C Minor*, by Ludwig van Beethoven. Norton Critical Scores, edited by Elliot Forbes. New York: Norton, 1971. The review first appeared in *Allgemeine musikalische Zeitung* 12 (1810): 630–42 and 652–59.

Horstig, [Carl Gottlob]. "Vorschläge zu besserer Einrichtung der Singschulen in Deutschland," *Allgemeine musikalische Zeitung* 1 (1798): 166–74, 183–89, 197–201, and 214–20.

Humboldt, Wilhelm von. *Werke.* Edited by Andreas Flitner and Klaus Giel. Darmstadt: Wissenschaftliche Buchgesellschaft, 1960–81.

"In wie fern kann die Erlernung der Musik etwas zur sittlichen und gelehrten Erziehung beitragen?" *Wiener allgemeine musikalische Zeitung* (1813): 343–51 and 359–70.

Jones, William. *Ueber die Musik der Indier: Eine Abhandlung des Sir William Jones: Aus dem Englischen übersetzt, mit erläuternden Anmerkungen und Zusätzen begleitet, von F. H. von Dalberg.* Erfurt: Beyer and Maring, 1802.

Kahlert, August. "Aus Breslau," *Cäcilia* 16, no. 63 (1834): 207–12.

———. "Das Concertwesen der Gegenwart," *Neue Zeitschrift für Musik* 16 (1842): 97–99, 101–2, 105–6, and 109–110.

Kanne, Friedrich A. "Was ist von dem jetzigen Geschmacke in der Musik zu fürchten?" *Allgemeine musikalische Zeitung mit besonderer Rücksicht auf den österreichischen Kaiserstaat* 4 (1820): 725–28, 729–32, 737–41, 745–49, 753–57, and 761–64.

Keferstein, Gustav [K. Stein, pseud.]. "Aphorismen über akademisches Musikwesen und dessen zweckmäßige Gestaltung," *Neue Zeitschrift für Musik* 12 (1840):113–15, 117–18, and 122–23.

———. "Musik der Malgaschen auf Madagascar," *Neue Zeitschrift für Musik* 13 (1840): 136.

———. "Ueber das Verhältniss der Musik zum Pädagogik," *Allgemeine musikalische Zeitung* 43 (1841): 993–1002.

Kiesewetter, Raphael Georg. *Die Musik der Araber nach Originalquellen dargestellt.* Leipzig: Breitkopf & Härtel, 1842; reprint, Wiesbaden: Dr. Martin Sändig, 1968.

Klein. "Vorschläge zur Verbesserung der gewöhnlichen Singschulen in Deutschland," *Allgemeine musikalische Zeitung* 1 (1798): 465–71.

Klein, Joseph. "Ansichten über Musik-Unterricht, in Bezug auf sogennante Mode-Kompositionen," *Berliner allgemeine musikalische Zeitung* 4 (1827): 49–51.

———. "Ueber den Gesang in Dorfschulen," *Berliner allgemeine musikalische Zeitung* 4 (1828): 245–47 and 253–55.

Koch, Heinrich Christoph. *Musikalisches Lexikon.* Frankfurt: A. Hermann der jünger, 1802; reprint, Hildesheim: Georg Olms, 1964.

"Korrespondenz: Königsberg, Mitte März," *Allgemeine musikalische Zeitung* 2 (1800): 477–79.

"Korrespondenz: Wien, den 2ten May, 1801," *Allgemeine musikalische Zeitung* 3 (1801): 575–79.

"Korrespondenz: Wien, den 8ten Dec., Ubersicht des Monats November," *Allgemeine musikalische Zeitung* 14 (1812): 849–54.

Krüger, Eduard. "Laien, Dilettanten, Künstler," *Neue Zeitschrift für Musik* 11 (1839): 33–34, 37–38, 41–43, and 45–46.

———. "Künstler-Armuth. (Aus dem Briefwechsel zweier Freunde)," *Neue Zeitschrift für Musik* 17 (1842): 135–37, 139–40, 143–45, and 147–48.

———. "Das Virtuosenconcert," *Neue Zeitschrift für Musik* 14 (1842): 159–61, 163–65, 167–69, and 171–73.

———. *Beiträge für Leben und Wissenschaft in der Tonkunst.* Leipzig: Breitkopf & Härtel, 1847.

"Kurze Uebersicht des jetzigen Musikwesens in Riga," *Allgemeine musikalische Zeitung* 2 (1800): 394–96.

Lindner, Friedrich Wilhelm. "Ueber den Gesang in der Bürgerschule zu Leipzig," *Allgemeine musikalische Zeitung* 8 (1805): 145–58 and 161–73.

———. "Was ist bis jetzt für die Gesangs-Bildung geschehen?" *Allgemeine musikalische Zeitung* 13 (1811): 3–8, 17–23, 33–43, and 49–59.

Marx, Adolf Bernhard. "Einige Worte über das Konzertwesen, besonders in grossen Städten," *Berliner allgemeine musikalische Zeitung* 2 (1825): 349–51 and 357–61.

———. "Denkschrift über Organisation des Musikwesens im preussischen Staate," *Neue Berliner Musikzeitung* 2 (1848): 241–47 and 249–56.

———. *Die Musik des neunzehnten Jahrhunderts und ihre Pflege: Methode der Musik*. 2nd edition. Leipzig: Breitkopf & Härtel, 1873; 1st edition 1854.

Michaelis, Christian Friedrich. "Einige Gedanken über die Vortheile der frühen musikalischen Bildung," *Allgemeine musikalische Zeitung* 7 (1804): 117–26.

———. "Ueber einen Aufsatz mit der Ueberschrift: Wollen alle Deutsche Musikanten werden? (in der Bibliothek der pädagog. Literatur, herausgegeben von Guthsmuths [*sic*], November 1804)," *Allgemeine musikalische Zeitung* 7 (1805): 229–37.

———. "Ueber die Musik einiger wilden und halb cultivirten Völker," *Allgemeine musikalische Zeitung* 16 (1814): 509–15 and 525–30.

———. "Von der Musik der Aegypter und der Morgenländer überhaupt," *Cäcilia* 15, no. 59 (1833): 179–83.

Mozart, Wolfgang Amadeus. *Briefe und Aufzeichnungen*. Edited by Wilhelm A. Bauer and Otto Erich Deutsch. Kassel: Bärenreiter, 1963.

Müller, August. "Ueber das Wirken des Musikers im Orchester," *Neue Zeitschrift für Musik* 31 (1849): 217–19 and 229–30.

"Musikalischer Charakter der deutschen Nazion," *Wiener allgemeine musikalische Zeitung* 1 (1813): 159–60.

"Musikalischer Verein in Passau," *Allgemeine musikalische Zeitung* 18 (1816): 666–75.

"Musikalisches Leben Berlin's," *Neue Zeitschrift für Musik* 13 (1840): 65–66.

"Musikalisches Leben in Braunschweig," *Neue Zeitschrift für Musik* 6 (1837): 57–58, 60–61, 65–66, 69–70, and 74.

"Musikzustand und musikalisches Leben in Wien," *Cäcilia* 1, no. 2 (1824): 193–200.

"Nachrichten von dem Zustand der Musik bey den Egyptiern und Chinesern, aus dem philosophischen Untersuchungen des Herrn von Paw," *Musikalisch-kritische Bibliothek* 1 (1778): 227–30.

"Nachrichten. Wien im November," *Musikalische Zeitung für die österreichischen Staaten* 1 (1812): 130–31.

Nägeli, Hans Georg. "Die Pestalozzische Gesangbildungslehre nach Pfeiffers Erfindung kunstwissenschaftlich dargestellt im Namen Pestalozzis, Pfeiffers und ihrer Freunde," *Allgemeine musikalische Zeitung* 11 (1809): 769–76, 785–93, 801–10, and 817–45.

———. "Anrede an die schweizerische Musikgesellschaft bey Eröffnung ihrer Sitzung in Schafhausen den 21. August 1811," *Allgemeine musikalische Zeitung* 13 (1811): 656–64, 665–73, and 685–92.

———. "Anrede an die schweizerische Musikgesellschaft, bey Eröffnung ihrer Sitzung zu Zürich, den 19ten August 1812," *Allgemeine musikalische Zeitung* 14 (1812): 695–703, 711–18, and 727–34.

———. "Anrede an die Versammlung des musik. Vereins der Schweiz, gehalten zu Freyburg, d. 7ten August dieses Jahres," *Allgemeine musikalische Zeitung* 18 (1816): 677–87.

———. "Anrede an die schweizerische Musikgesellschaft, bey Eröffnung ihrer Sitzungen in Basel, den 14ten Brachmonat 1820," *Allgemeine musikalische Zeitung* 22 (1820): 769–79.

Nägeli, Hans Georg, and Michael Traugott Pfeiffer. *Gesangbildungslehre nach Pestalozzischen Grundsätzen, pädagogisch begründet von Michael Traugott Pfeiffer, methodisch bearbeitet von Hans Georg Nägeli.* Zurich: H. G. Nägeli, 1810.

Natorp, [Bernhard Christoph Ludwig]. "Unsre Concerte," *Berlinische musikalische Zeitung* 1 (1805): 207–13.

———. *Anleitung zur Unterweisung im Singen für Lehrer in Volksschulen: I. Leitfaden für den ersten Cursus.* 5th edition. Essen: G. D. Bädeker, 1837; 1st edition 1813.

"Oratorium," *Wiener allgemeine musikalische Zeitung* 1 (1813): 66–75.

Paris, Heinrich. "Die Materialität der heutigen Musik und der heutigen Tänze," *Cäcilia* 20, no. 80 (1839): 199–244.

———. "Offener Brief an die Redaction, bei Gelegenheit einer bekannten Pianistin und einer unbekannten Componistin," *Cäcilia* 23, no. 91 (1844): 168–82.

Pestalozzi, Johann Heinrich. *How Gertrude Teaches Her Children.* Translated by Lucy E. Holland and Frances C. Turner. Syracuse, N.Y.: C. W. Bardeen, 1898; reprint, Washington, D.C.: University Publications of America, 1977.

———. *Pestalozzi's Educational Writings.* Edited by J. A. Green, with Frances A. Collie. New York: Longmans, Green & Co., 1912; reprint, Washington, D.C.: University Publications of America, 1977.

———. *Ausgewählte Werke.* Edited by Otto Boldemann. Berlin: Volk und Wissen, 1963.

Peterson, J. "Ueber Vortrag musikalischer Kunstwerke, besonders in Beziehung auf den Chorgesang," *Neue Berliner Musikzeitung* 1 (1847): 137–39.

Petiscus. "Ueber musikalische Lehrbücher und die neuesten unter denselben," *Allgemeine musikalische Zeitung* 10 (1807): 161–66 and 177–83.

Petri, Johann Samuel. *Anleitung zur praktischen Musik.* Leipzig: Johann Gottlob Immanuel Breitkopf, 1782.

Reichardt, Johann Friedrich. "An großgute Regenten," *Musikalisches Kunstmagazin* 1 (1782): v–vii.

———. "An junge Künstler," *Musikalisches Kunstmagazin* 1 (1782): 1–7.

———. "I. A. P. Schulz," *Allgemeine musikalische Zeitung* 3 (1800–01): 153–57, 169–76, 597–606, 613–20, and 629–35.

Review of *Gesangbildungslehre*, by Hans Georg Nägeli and Michael Traugott Pfeiffer, *Allgemeine musikalische Zeitung* 13 (1811): 465–75 and 481–86.

Review of *Ueber die Musik der Indier: Eine Abhandlung des Sir William Jones: Aus dem Englischen übersetzt, mit erläuternden Anmerkungen und Zusätzen begleitet, von F. H. von Dalberg, Allgemeine musikalische Zeitung* 5 (1803): 281–94 and 297–303.

Rochlitz, Friedrich. "Bruchstücke aus Briefen an einen jungen Tonkünstler: Vierter Brief: Der Musikdirektor," *Allgemeine musikalische Zeitung* 2 (1799): 57–63.

———. "Bruchstücke aus Briefen an einen jungen Tonkünstler: Sechster Brief: Liebhaberey an Musik," *Allgemeine musikalische Zeitung* 2 (1799): 177–83.

———. "Fragen eines Layen über mancherley Gegenstände welche Musik und Musiker angehen," *Allgemeine musikalische Zeitung* 3 (1800): 121–27 and 146–47. Revised and expanded as "Verschiedenheit der Wirkungen der Musik auf gebildete oder ungebildete Völker (Schreiben an einen Freund)." In *Für Freunde der Tonkunst,* by Friedrich Rochlitz, 1:196–210. Leipzig: Carl Knoblach, 1824.

Sartorius, J. "Ein unvorgreifliches Bedenken über die itzige musikalische Kultur à la mode," *Cäcilia* 3, no. 12 (1825): 281–91.

Schiller, Friedrich von. "Ueber Matthisson's Gedichte" (1794). In *Schillers Werke: Nationalausgabe,* edited by Herbert Meyer. Volume 22. Weimar: Hermann Böhlaus Nachfolger, 1958.

Schilling, Gustav, ed. *Encyclopädie der gesammten musikalischen Wissenschaften, oder Universal-Lexicon der Tonkunst.* 6 volumes. Stuttgart: Franz Heinrich Köhler, 1835–38. Supplement-Band (edited by Schilling) and Anhang (edited by F. S. Gaßner), 1842.

[Schmith, Amand Wilhem]. *Philosophische Fragmente über die praktische Musik.* Vienna: in commission at the k.k. Taubstummeninstitutsbuchdruck, 1787.

Schulz, Johann Abraham Peter. *Lieder im Volkston.* 2nd edition. Berlin: Georg Jacob Decker, 1785.

———. *Gedanken über den Einfluß der Musik auf die Bildung eines Volks, und über deren Einführung in den Schulen der königl. Dänischen Staaten.* Copenhagen: Christian Gottlob Prost, 1790.

Schulz, Johann Abraham Peter, and Johann Heinrich Voß. *Briefwechsel zwischen Johann Abraham Peter Schulz und Johann Heinrich Voß.* Edited by Heinz Gottwaldt and Gerhard Hahne. Schriften des Landesinstituts für Musikforschung Kiel 9. Kassel: Bärenreiter, 1960.

Schulz, O. F. K. W. "Zu grosse Vorliebe fürs Pianoforte," *Berliner musikalische Zeitung* 2, no. 21 (1845): 1–2.

———. "Volksmusik der mittleren und kleinen Städte," *Berliner musikalische Zeitung* 2, no. 28 (1845): 5–6.

Schumann, Robert. *Gesammelte Schriften über Musik und Musiker.* New edition. Leipzig: Breitkopf & Härtel, 1883.

"Schwäbische Musikzustände," *Neue Zeitschrift für Musik* 17 (1842): 185–86 and 187–89. Ascribed to "F."

Schwarz, Friedrich H. C. "Elementarunterricht in der Musik," *Allgemeine musikalische Zeitung* 11 (1809): 401–8 and 417–22.

Seyfried, [Ignaz Ritter] von. Review of Hummel's arrangements of Symphony No. 3, by Beethoven, and Piano Concerto in D Minor for piano, flute, violin, and cello, by Mozart, *Cäcilia* 10, no. 39 (1829): 174–78.

———. "Selbsterfahrungen auf Berufswegen," *Cäcilia* 13, no. 52 (1831): 233–39.

Spohr, Louis. "Einige Bemerkungen über die deutschen Gesang-Vereine, nebst Ankündigung eines neuen für sie geschriebenen Werkes," *Allgemeine musikalische Zeitung* 23 (1821): 817–20.

Steuber. "Ueber die ästhetische Bildung des componirenden Tonkünstlers," *Allgemeine musikalische Zeitung* 12 (1810): 321–25 and 793–99.

Stöpel, Franz. "Ueber das Arrangiren," *Cäcilia* 1, no. 1 (1824): 37–39.

"Das Strassburger Musikfest, beleuchtet unter dem Gesichtspunct: Welchen Einfluss hat auf die Kunst der Dilettantismus," *Cäcilia* 13, no. 51 (1831): 194–201. Ascribed to "CB."

"Strauß im Norden," *Neue Zeitschrift für Musik* 1 (1834): 309–10. Ascribed to "26."

Teczoni, Techo di. "Das Konzert des häuslichen Lebens," *Berliner allgemeine musikalische Zeitung* 6 (1830): 13–16.

[Thibaut, Justus]. *Ueber Reinheit der Tonkunst.* Heidelberg: J. C. W. Mohr, 1825.

Thräner, Theodor. "Thesen und Vorschläge in Beziehung auf einen humanen Musikunterricht," *Neue Zeitschrift für Musik* 29 (1848): 21–25 and 33–38.

Tonkünstler-Verein, Berlin. "Denkschrift des Tonkünstler-Vereines in Berlin über die Reorganisation des Musikwesens," *Neue Berliner Musikzeitung* 2 (1848): 257–65.

Triest, Johann Karl Friedrich. "Bemerkungen über die Ausbildung der Tonkunst in Deutschland im achzehnten Jahrhundert," *Allgemeine musikalische Zeitung* 3 (1801): 225–35, 241–49, 257–64, 273–86, 297–308, 321–31, 369–79, 389–401, 406–10, 421–32, and 437–45. Translated by Susan Gillespie as "Remarks on the Development of the Art of Music in Germany in the Eighteenth Century." In *Haydn and His World*, edited by Elaine Sisman, 321–94. Princeton: Princeton University Press, 1997.

———. "Ueber reisende Virtuosen," *Allgemeine musikalische Zeitung* 4 (1802): 737–49, 753–60, and 769–75.

"Ueber Bildung eines guten Orchesters," *Allgemeine musikalische Zeitung* 8 (1818): 797–804 and 813–20.

"Über den Verfall der Musik," *Allgemeine musikalische Zeitung mit besonderer Rücksicht auf den österreichischen Kaiserstaat* 2 (1818): 136–37. Ascribed to ". . . r."

"Über den Verfall der Musik," *Allgemeine musikalische Zeitung mit besonderer Rücksicht auf den österreichischen Kaiserstaat* 2 (1818): 153–56. Ascribed to "———z."

"Ueber den Zustand der Musik in Böhmen," *Allgemeine musikalische Zeitung* 2 (1800): 488–94, 497–507, 513–23, and 537–42.

"Ueber die Benutzung der Musik zur Veredelung der Landleute, als Sache des Staates, *Allgemeine musikalische Zeitung* 7 (1805): 665–73.

"Ueber Dilettanten in der Tonkunst (eingesandt). Mit einem Anhange von G. W. Fink," *Allgemeine musikalische Zeitung* 32 (1830): 65–67.

"Ueber Singvereine," *Allgemeine musikalische Zeitung* 31 (1829): 37–41. Ascribed to "C. E. H."

"Vergeich einer Familie mit einem Concerte. Neue Bearbeitung," *Allgemeiner musikalischer Anzeiger,* no. 14 (13 September 1826): 111–12.

Volker. "Ueber die Hofkapellen in Deutschland und über ihre Bedeutsamkeit als selbstständige Kunst-Institute," *Neue Zeitschrift für Musik* 32 (1850): 113–15.

"Vom Dirigiren und insbesondere von der Manie des Dirigirens," *Neue Zeitschrift für Musik* 4 (1836): 129–30.

"Von den Instrumenten der Perser," *Musikalisch-kritische Bibliothek* 1 (1778): 230.

"Von der Mogolischen Musik," *Musikalisch-kritische Bibliothek* 1 (1778): 230–31.

"Von der Musik bey den Einwohnern der philippinischen Inseln," *Musikalisch-kritische Bibliothek* 1 (1778): 231.

"Von der Musik der Türken," *Musikalisch-kritische Bibliothek* 1 (1778): 231–32.

Weber, Gottfried. "Ueber Kirchenmusik in Concerten," *Musikalische Zeitung für die österreichischen Staaten* 1 (1812): 43–46.

Wedel, Gottschalk. "Gesellschafts- oder Ziermusik," *Neue Zeitschrift für Musik* 6 (1837): 123–24 and 127–28.

Wendt, Amadeus. "Betrachtungen über Musik, und insbesondere über den Gesang, als Bildungsmittel in der Erziehung," *Allgemeine musikalische Zeitung* 13 (1811): 281–87, 297–303, 317–24, and 333–41.

"Wider Gewerbsfreiheit im Fache der Musik," *Allgemeine musikalische Zeitung* 39 (1837): 642–43.

"Züge von dem Bilde eines Musikdirectors, wie er nicht seyn soll," *Allgemeine musikalische Zeitung* 16 (1814): 391–94.

TWENTIETH-CENTURY LITERATURE

Adler, Guido, ed. *Handbuch der Musikgeschichte.* 2nd edition. 1929. Reprint, Tützing: Hans Schneider, 1961.

Adorno, Theodor W. *Minima Moralia: Reflections from Damaged Life.* Translated by E. F. N. Jephcott. London: NLB, 1974.

———. "On the Fetish Character in Music and the Regression of Listening." In *The Essential Frankfurt School Reader,* edited by Andrew Arato and Eike Gebhardt, 270–99. New York: Urizen Books, 1978. First published in *Sozialforschung* 7 (1938).

———. "Analytical Study of the *NBC Music Appreciation Hour,*" *Musical Quarterly* 78 (1994): 325–77.

———. *Beethoven: The Philosophy of Music.* Edited by Rolf Tiedemann, translated by Edmund Jephcott. Stanford: Stanford University Press, 1998.

Allanbrook, Wye Jamison. *Rhythmic Gesture in Mozart:* Le Nozze di Figaro *and* Don Giovanni. Chicago: University of Chicago Press, 1983.

Anderson, Benedict. *Imagined Communities: Reflections on the Origin and Spread of Nationalism.* Revised edition. London: Verso, 1991.

Applegate, Celia. "How German Is It? Nationalism and the Idea of Serious Music in the Early Nineteenth Century," *Nineteenth Century Music* 21 (1998): 274–96.

Beiser, Frederick C. *Enlightenment, Revolution, and Romanticism: The Genesis of Modern German Political Thought, 1790–1800.* Cambridge: Harvard University Press, 1992.

Bernstein, Susan. *Virtuosity of the Nineteenth Century: Performing Music and Language in Heine, Liszt, and Baudelaire.* Stanford: Stanford University Press, 1998.

Biernacki, Richard. *The Fabrication of Labor: Germany and Britain, 1640–1914.* Studies on the History of Society and Culture. Volume 22. Berkeley and Los Angeles: University of California Press, 1995.

Bohlman, Philip V. "R. G. Kiesewetter's *Die Musik der Araber:* A Pioneering Ethnomusicological Study of Arabic Writings on Music," *Asian Music* 18 (1986): 164–96.

———. "The European Discovery of Music in the Islamic World and the 'Non-Western' in 19th-Century Music History," *Journal of Musicology* 5 (1987): 147–63.

———. "Traditional Music and Cultural Identity: Persistent Paradigm in the History of Ethnomusicology," *Yearbook for Traditional Music* 20 (1988): 26–42.

Bonds, Mark Evan. "Idealism and Aesthetics of Instrumental Music at the Turn of the Nineteenth Century," *Journal of the American Musicological Society* 50 (1997): 387–420.

Böning, Holger, and Reinhart Siegert. *Volksaufklärung: Bibliographisches Handbuch zur Popularisierung aufklärerischer Denkens im deutschen Sprachraum von den Anfängen bis 1850.* Volume 1. Stuttgart: Holzboog, 1990.

Bor, Joep. "The Rise of Ethnomusicology: Sources on Indian Music c. 1780–c. 1890," *Yearbook for Traditional Music* 20 (1988): 51–73.

Botstein, Leon. "Music and Its Public: Habits of Listening and the Crisis of Musical Modernism in Vienna, 1870–1914." Ph.D. dissertation, Harvard University, 1985.

———. "Listening through Reading: Musical Literacy and the Concert Audience," *Nineteenth Century Music* 16 (1992): 129–45.

Bourdieu, Pierre. *Distinction: A Social Critique of the Judgement of Taste.* Translated by Richard Nice. Cambridge: Harvard University Press, 1984.

———. *The Logic of Practice.* Translated by Richard Nice. Stanford: Stanford University Press, 1990.

———. *The Rules of Art: Genesis and Structure of the Literary Field.* Translated by Susan Emanuel. Stanford: Stanford University Press, 1995.

Braun, Rudolf. *Industrialisation and Everyday Life.* Translated by Sarah Hanbury Tenison. Cambridge: Cambridge University Press, 1990.

Brednich, Rolf Wilhelm. "Das Lied als Ware," *Jahrbuch für Volksliedforschung* 19 (1974): 11–20.

Brett, Philip. "Musicality, Essentialism, and the Closet." In *Queering the Pitch: The New Lesbian and Gay Musicology,* edited by Brett, Elizabeth Wood, and Gary C. Thomas, 9–26. New York: Routledge, 1994.

Bruford, Walter Horace. *The German Tradition of Self-Cultivation:* Bildung *from Humboldt to Thomas Mann.* London: Cambridge University Press, 1975.

Bunzl, Matti. "Franz Boas and the Humboldtian Tradition: From *Volksgeist* and *Nationalcharakter* to an Anthropological Conception of Culture." In *"Volksgeist" as Method and Ethic: Essays on Boasian Ethnography and the German Anthropological Tradition,* edited by George W. Stocking Jr., 17–78. History of Anthropology 8. Madison: University of Wisconsin Press, 1996.

Butler, Judith. *Bodies That Matter: On the Discursive Limits of "Sex."* New York: Routledge, 1993.

Butt, John. *Music Education and the Art of Performance in the German Baroque.* Cambridge: Cambridge University Press, 1994.

Certeau, Michel de. *The Practice of Everyday Life.* Translated by Steven F. Randall. Berkeley and Los Angeles: University of California Press, 1984.

Christensen, Thomas. "Four-Hand Piano Transcription and Geographies of Nineteenth-Century Musical Reception," *Journal of the American Musicological Society* 52 (1999): 255–98.

Cusick, Suzanne G. "Gender and the Cultural Work of a Classical Music Performance," *repercussions* 3 (1994): 77–110.

Dahlhaus, Carl. *Nineteenth-Century Music.* Translated by J. Bradford Robinson. Berkeley and Los Angeles: University of California Press, 1989.

Delanty, Gerard. *Inventing Europe: Idea, Identity, Reality.* Basingstoke, England: Macmillan, 1995.

DeNora, Tia. *Beethoven and the Construction of Genius: Musical Politics in Vienna, 1792–1803.* Berkeley and Los Angeles: University of California Press, 1995.

Deutsch, Otto Erich, ed. *Schubert: Die Dokumente seines Lebens.* Neue Ausgabe sämtlicher Werke. Series 8, volume 5. Kassel: Bärenreiter, 1964.

Dunsby, Jonathan. *Performing Music: Shared Concerns.* Oxford: Clarendon Press; New York: Oxford University Press, 1995.

Eagleton, Terry. *The Ideology of the Aesthetic.* Oxford: Basil Blackwell, 1990.

Elias, Norbert. *The Civilizing Process: The History of Manners.* Translated by Edmund Jephcott. Oxford: Basil Blackwell, 1978.

Erlmann, Veit. *Music, Modernity, and the Global Imagination: South Africa and the West.* New York: Oxford University Press, 1999.

Evans, Richard J., and W. R. Lee, eds. *The German Family: Essays on the Social History of the Family in Nineteenth- and Twentieth-Century Germany.* London: Croom Helm, 1981.

Feldman, Martha. "Magic Mirrors and the *Seria* Stage: Thoughts toward a

Ritual View," *Journal of the American Musicological Society* 47 (1995): 423–84.

Fischer, Jörg. "Anmerkungen zu Carl Dahlhaus, 'Die Musik des 19. Jahrhunderts,'" *Jahrbuch für Volksliedforschung* 31 (1986): 46–50.

Fischer, Wilhelm. "Zur Entwicklungsgeschichte des Wiener klassischen Stils," *Studien zur Musikwissenschaft* 3 (1915): 24–84.

Foucault, Michel. *Discipline and Punish: The Birth of the Prison*. Translated by Alan Sheridan. New York: Vintage, 1995.

Friedlaender, Max. *Das deutsche Lied im 18. Jahrhundert*. Stuttgart: J. G. Cotta, 1902; reprint, Hildesheim: Georg Olms, 1962.

Frisch, Walter. "Schubert's *Nähe des Geliebten* (D. 162): Transformation of the *Volkston*." In *Schubert: Critical and Analytical Studies*, edited by Frisch, 175–99. Lincoln: University of Nebraska Press, 1986.

Geiringer, Karl, in collaboration with Irene Geiringer. *Haydn: A Creative Life in Music*. 2nd edition. Berkeley and Los Angeles: University of California Press, 1968.

Geschichte der Erziehung. Berlin: Volk und Wissen, 1957.

Godlovitch, Stan. *Musical Performance: A Philosophical Study*. London: Routledge, 1998.

Goehr, Lydia. *The Imaginary Museum of Musical Works: An Essay in the Philosophy of Music*. Oxford: Clarendon Press, 1992.

———. *The Quest for Voice: Music, Politics, and the Limits of Philosophy*. Berkeley and Los Angeles: University of California Press, 1998.

Gramit, David. "The Intellectual and Aesthetic Tenets of Franz Schubert's Circle." Ph.D. dissertation, Duke University, 1987.

———. "Constructing a Victorian Schubert: Music, Biography, and Cultural Values," *Nineteenth-Century Music* 17 (1993): 65–78.

———. "Schubert's Wanderers and the Autonomous Lied," *Journal of Musicological Research* 14 (1995): 147–68.

———. "Lieder, Listeners, and Ideology: Schubert's 'Alinde' and Opus 81," *Current Musicology* 58 (1995): 28–60. Reprinted in *Music/Ideology: Resisting the Aesthetic*, edited by Adam Krims, 179–212. Critical Voices in Art, Theory, and Culture. Amsterdam: G & B Arts International, 1998.

———. "The Roaring Lion: Critical Musicology, the Aesthetic Experience, and the Music Department," *Canadian University Music Review* 19 (1998): 19–33.

———. "Musical Scholarship, Musical Practice, and the Act of Listening." In *Music and Marx: Ideas, Practice, Politics*, edited by Regula Burckhardt Qureshi. New York: Garland, forthcoming.

Guillory, John. *Cultural Capital: The Problem of Literary Canon Formation*. Chicago: University of Chicago Press, 1993.

Harrison, Frank. *Time, Place, and Music: An Anthology of Ethnomusicological Observation c. 1550 to c. 1800*. Source Materials and Studies in Ethnomusicology 1. Amsterdam: Frits Knuf, 1973.

Hartung, Günter. "Johann Friedrich Reichardt, der Musiker und der Publizist." In *Johann Friedrich Reichardt (1752–1814): Komponist und Schriftsteller der Revolutionszeit*, edited by Konstanze Musketa, Gert Richter, and Götz Traxdorf, 11–21. Schriften des Händel-Hauses in Halle 8. Halle: Händel-Haus, 1992.

Hauptmeyer, Carl-Hans. "Aufklärung und bäuerliche Oppositionen im zentralen Niedersachsen des ausgehenden 18. Jahrhunderts." In *Das Volk als Objekt obrigkeitlichen Handelns*, edited by Rudolf Vierhaus, 197–217. Wolfenbütteler Studien zur Aufklärung 13: Kultur und Gesellschaft in Nordwestdeutschland zur Zeit der Aufklärung 1. Tübingen: Max Niemeyer, 1992.

Hausen, Karin. "Family and Role-Division: The Polarization of Sexual Stereotypes in the Nineteenth Century: An Aspect of the Dissociation of Work and Family Life." In *The German Family: Essays on the Social History of the Family in Nineteenth- and Twentieth-Century Germany*, edited by Richard J. Evans and W. R. Lee, 51–83. London: Croom Helm, 1981.

Heafford, Michael R. *Pestalozzi: His Thought and Its Relevance Today*. London: Methuen, 1967.

Heister, Hanns-Werner. *Das Konzert: Theorie einer Kulturform*. Taschenbücher zur Musikwissenschaft 87–88. 2 volumes. Wilhelmshaven: Heinrichshofen, 1983.

Hoffmann, Freia. *Instrument und Körper: Die musizierende Frau in der bürgerlichen Kultur*. Insel Taschenbuch 1274. Frankfurt am Main: Insel, 1991.

Hortschansky, Klaus. "The Musician as Music Dealer in the Second Half of the 18th Century." In *The Social Status of the Professional Musician from the Middle Ages to the 19th Century*, edited by Walter Salmen, 189–218. Annotated and translated by Herbert Kaufman and Barbara Reisner. Sociology of Music 1. New York: Pendragon, 1983.

Hunter, Mary. *The Culture of Opera Buffa in Mozart's Vienna: A Poetics of Entertainment*. Princeton: Princeton University Press, 1999.

Iggers, Georg G. *The German Conception of History: The National Tradition of Historical Thought from Herder to the Present*. Middletown, Conn.: Wesleyan University Press, 1968.

Jordanova, Ludmilla. "Naturalising the Family: Literature and the Bio-Medical Sciences of the Late Eighteenth Century." In *Nature Displayed: Gender, Science, and Medicine, 1760–1820*, 163–82. London: Longman, 1999.

Kaiser, Gerhard. "The Middle Class as the Agency of Culture." In *Enlightenment in Germany*, edited by Paul Raabe and Wilhelm Schmidt-Biggemann, 62–78. Bonn: Hohwacht, 1979.

Kallberg, Jeffrey. *Chopin at the Boundaries: Sex, History, and Musical Genre*. Cambridge: Harvard University Press, 1996.

Kaschuba, Wolfgang. "Deutsche Bürgerlichkeit nach 1800: Kultur als symbolische Praxis." In *Bürgertum im 19. Jahrhundert: Deutschland im europäischen Vergleich*, edited by Jürgen Kocka, 3:9–44. Munich: Deutscher Taschenbuch Verlag, 1988.

Kerman, Joseph. "*An die ferne Geliebte*," *Beethoven Studies* 1 (1974): 123–57.

Kittler, Friedrich. *Discourse Networks 1800/1900.* Translated by Michael Metteer with Chris Cullens. Stanford: Stanford University Press, 1990.

———. *Dichter-Mutter-Kind.* Munich: Wilhelm Fink, 1991.

Klusen, Ernst. "Über den Volkston in der Musik des 19. Jahrhunderts," *Jahrbuch für Volksliedforschung* 17 (1972): 35–48.

Knab, Hans. "Bernhard Christoph Ludwig Natorp: Ein Beitrag zur Geschichte der Schulmusik in der ersten Hälfte des neunzehnten Jahrhunderts." Ph.D. dissertation, Münster, 1933.

Kocka, Jürgen, ed., with Ute Frevert. *Bürgertum im 19. Jahrhundert: Deutschland im europäischen Vergleich.* 3 volumes. Munich: Deutscher Taschenbuch Verlag, 1988.

Koepke, Wulf. "*Kulturnation* and Its Authorization through Herder." In *Johann Gottfried Herder: Academic Disciplines and the Pursuit of Knowledge,* edited by Koepke, 177–98. Columbia, S.C.: Camden House, 1996.

Kravitt, Edward F. *The Lied: Mirror of Late Romanticism.* New Haven: Yale University Press, 1996.

Krickberg, Dieter. "On the Social Status of the *Spielmann* ('Folk Musician') in 17th and 18th Century Germany, Particularly in the Northwest." In *The Social Status of the Professional Musician from the Middle Ages to the 19th Century,* edited by Walter Salmen, 97–122. Annotated and translated by Herbert Kaufman and Barbara Reisner. Sociology of Music 1. New York: Pendragon, 1983.

La Vopa, Anthony J. "Conceiving a Public: Ideas and Society in Eighteenth-Century Europe," *Journal of Modern History* 64 (1992): 79–116.

Le Bar, Ann. "The Domestication of Vocal Music in Enlightenment Hamburg," *Journal of Musicological Research* 19 (2000): 97–134.

Lee, Robert. "Family and 'Modernisation': The Peasant Family and Social Change in Nineteenth-Century Bavaria." In *The German Family: Essays on the Social History of the Family in Nineteenth- and Twentieth-Century Germany,* edited by Richard J. Evans and Lee, 84–120. London: Croom Helm, 1981.

Leppert, Richard. *Music and Image: Domesticity, Ideology, and Socio-Cultural Formation in Eighteenth-Century England.* Cambridge: Cambridge University Press, 1988.

Lorenz, Rainer. *Musikpädagogik in den ersten 30 Jahren des 19. Jahrhunderts am Beispiel Carl Gottlieb Herings.* Musikpädagogik: Forschung und Lehre 26. Mainz: Schott, 1988.

Mahling, Christoph-Hellmut. "Music and Places for the Performance of Music as a Reflection of Urban Social Stratification in the 19th and Early 20th Centuries," translated by William Templer. In International Musicological Society, *Report of the 12th Congress, Berkeley, 1977.* Edited by Daniel Heartz and Bonnie Wade, 307–11, with ensuing discussion, 315–18. Kassel: Bärenreiter, 1981.

———. "The Origin and Social Status of the Court Orchestral Musician in the 18th and Early 19th Century in Germany." In *The Social Status of the Pro-*

fessional Musician from the Middle Ages to the 19th Century, edited by Walter Salmen, 219–64. Annotated and translated by Herbert Kaufman and Barbara Reisner. Sociology of Music 1. New York: Pendragon, 1983.

Maróthy, János. *Music and the Bourgeois, Music and the Proletarian*. Translated by Eva Róna. Budapest: Akadêmiai Kiadó, 1974.

Meier, Bernhard. "Zur Musikhistoriographie des 19. Jahrhunderts." In *Die Ausbreitung des Historismus über die Musik*, edited by Walter Wiora, 169–206. Studien zur Musikgeschichte des 19. Jahrhunderts 14. Regensburg: Gustav Bosse, 1969.

Meintjes, Louise. "Paul Simon's *Graceland*, South Africa, and the Mediation of Musical Meaning," *Ethnomusicology* 34 (1990): 37–73.

Moore, Julia. "Mozart Mythologized or Modernized?" *Journal of Musicological Research* 12 (1992): 83–109.

Morrow, Mary Sue. *Concert Life in Haydn's Vienna: Aspects of a Developing Musical and Social Institution*. New York: Pendragon, 1989.

———. *German Music Criticism in the Late Eighteenth Century: Aesthetic Issues in Instrumental Music*. Cambridge: Cambridge University Press, 1997.

Müller-Salget, Klaus. *Erzählungen für das Volk: Evangelische Pfarrer als Volksschriftsteller in Deutschland des 19. Jahrhunderts*. Berlin: Erich Schmidt, 1984.

Musketa, Konstanze, Gert Richter, and Götz Traxdorf, eds. *Johann Friedrich Reichardt (1752–1814): Komponist und Schriftsteller der Revolutionszeit*. Schriften des Händel-Hauses in Halle 8. Halle: Händel-Haus, 1992.

Neitzert, Lutz. *Die Geburt der Moderne, der Bürger und die Tonkunst: Zur Physiognomie der ver-öffentlichten Musik*. Stuttgart: Franz Steiner, 1990.

Nolte, Eckhard. *Die Musik im Verständnis der Musikpädagogik des 19. Jahrhunderts: Ein Beitrag zur Geschichte der Theorie musikalischen Lernens und Lehrens in der Schule*. Beiträge zur Musikpädagogik. Paderborn: Ferdinand Schöningh, 1982.

———, ed. *Lehrpläne und Richtlinien für den schulischen Musikunterricht in Deutschland vom Beginn des 19. Jahrhunderts bis in die Gegenwart: Eine Dokumentation*. Musikädagogik: Forschung und Lehre 3. Mainz: Schott, 1975.

Notley, Margaret. "*Volksconcerte* in Vienna and Late Nineteenth-Century Ideology of the Symphony," *Journal of the American Musicological Society* 50 (1997): 421–53.

O'Boyle, Lenore. "The Problem of an Excess of Educated Men in Western Europe, 1800–1850," *Journal of Modern History* 42 (1970): 471–95.

Parsons, James. "Ode to the Ninth: The Poetic and Musical Tradition behind the Finale of Beethoven's Choral Symphony." Ph.D. dissertation, University of North Texas, 1992.

Pederson, Sanna. "A. B. Marx, Berlin Concert Life, and German National Identity," *Nineteenth Century Music* 18 (1994): 87–107.

————. "Enlightened and Romantic German Music Criticism, 1800–1850." Ph.D. dissertation, University of Pennsylvania, 1995.

Petrat, Nicolai. *Hausmusik des Biedermeier im Blickpunkt der zeitgenössischen musikalischen Fachpresse (1815–1848)*. Hamburger Beiträge zur Musikwissenschaft 31. Hamburg: Karl Dieter Wagner, 1986.

Petzoldt, Richard. "The Economic Conditions of the 18th-Century Musician." In *The Social Status of the Professional Musician from the Middle Ages to the 19th Century*, edited by Walter Salmen, 158–88. Annotated and translated by Herbert Kaufman and Barbara Reisner. Sociology of Music 1. New York: Pendragon, 1983.

Peyser, Joan, ed. *The Orchestra: Origins and Transformations*. New York: Charles Scribner's Sons, 1986.

Porter, Roy, and Mikuláš Teich, eds. *The Enlightenment in National Context*. Cambridge: Cambridge University Press, 1981.

Preußner, Eberhard. *Die bürgerliche Musikkultur: Ein Beitrag zur deutschen Musikgeschichte des 18. Jahrhunderts*. 2nd edition. Kassel: Bärenreiter, 1950.

Pulikowski, Julian von. *Geschichte des Begriffes Volkslied im musikalischen Schrifttum: Ein Stück deutscher Geistesgeschichte*. Heidelberg: Carl Winter, 1933; reprint, Wiesbaden: Dr. Martin Sändig, 1970.

Raabe, Paul, and Wilhelm Schmidt-Biggemann, eds. *Enlightenment in Germany*. Bonn: Hohwacht, 1979.

Rice, Eric. "Representations of Janissary Music *(Mehter)* as Musical Exoticism in Western Compositions, 1670–1824," *Journal of Musicological Research* 19 (1999): 41–88.

Rietzschel, Evi, ed. *Gelehrsamkeit ein Handwerk? Bücherschreiben ein Gewerbe? Dokumente zum Verhältnis von Schriftsteller und Verleger im 18. Jahrhundert in Deutschland*. Frankfurt am Main: Röderberg, 1983.

Rink, John, ed. *The Practice of Performance: Studies in Musical Interpretation*. Cambridge: Cambridge University Press, 1995.

Robbins Landon, H. C., and David Wyn Jones. *Haydn: His Life and Music*. Bloomington: Indiana University Press, 1988.

Rosen, Charles. *The Classical Style: Haydn, Mozart, Beethoven*. New York: Norton, 1972.

————. *The Romantic Generation*. Cambridge: Harvard University Press, 1995.

Said, Edward. *Orientalism*. New York: Vintage, 1979.

Salmen, Walter. *Das Konzert: Eine Kulturgeschichte*. Munich: C. H. Beck, 1988.

————, ed. *The Social Status of the Professional Musician from the Middle Ages to the 19th Century*. Annotated and translated by Herbert Kaufman and Barbara Reisner. Sociology of Music 1. New York: Pendragon, 1983.

Sauder, Gerhard. "'Verhältnismäßige Aufklärung': Zur bürgerlichen Ideologie am Ende des 18. Jahrhunderts," *Jahrbuch der Jean-Paul-Gesellschaft* 9 (1974): 102–26.

Schenda, Rudolf. *Volk ohne Buch: Studien zur Sozialgeschichte der populären Lesestoffe, 1770–1910*. Studien zur Philosophie und Literatur des neunzehnten Jahrhunderts 5. Frankfurt am Main: Vitorio Klostermann, 1970.

Scherer, Wolfgang. *Klavier-Spiele: Die Psycho-Technik der Klaviere im 18. und 19. Jahrhundert*. Materialität der Zeichen A2. Munich: Wilhelm Fink, 1989.

Schleunes, Karl A. *Schooling and Society: The Politics of Education in Prussia and Bavaria, 1750–1900*. Oxford: Berg, 1989.

Schlumbohm, Jürgen. *Freiheit: Die Anfänge der bürgerlichen Emanzipationsbewegung in Deutschland im Spiegel ihres Leitwortes*. Geschichte und Gesellschaft: Bochumer Historische Studien 12. Düsseldorf: Schwann, 1975.

———. "'Traditional' Collectivity and 'Modern' Individuality: Some Questions and Suggestions for the Historical Study of Socialization: The Example of the German Upper and Lower Bourgeoisies around 1800," *Social History* 5 (1980): 71–103.

Schmidt, Hans-Christian, ed. *Geschichte der Musikpädagogik*. Handbuch der Musikpädagogik 1. Kassel: Bärenreiter, 1986.

Schmitt, Hanno. "Philanthropismus und Volksaufklärung im Herzogtum Braunschweig-Wolfenbüttel in der zweiten Hälfte des 18. Jahrhunderts." In *Das Volk als Objekt obrigkeitlichen Handelns*, edited by Rudolf Vierhaus, 171–95. Wolfenbütteler Studien zur Aufklärung 13: Kultur und Gesellschaft in Nordwestdeutschland zur Zeit der Aufklärung 1. Tübingen: Max Niemeyer, 1992.

Schorske, Carl E. *Fin-de-Siècle Vienna: Politics and Culture*. New York: Vintage Books, 1981.

Schröder, Cornelia. *Carl Friedrich Zelter und die Akademie: Dokumente und Briefe zur Entstehung der Musik-Sektion in der Preußischen Akademie der Künste*. Berlin: Deutsche Akademie der Künste, 1959.

Schroeder, David P. *Haydn and the Enlightenment: The Late Symphonies and Their Audience*. Oxford: Clarendon Press, 1990.

Schutte, Sabine. "Zur Kritik der Volkslied-Ideologie in der zweiten Hälfte des 19. Jahrhunderts," *Jahrbuch für Volksliedforschung* 20 (1975): 37–52.

Schwab, Heinrich W. *Sangbarkeit, Popularität, und Kunstlied: Studien zu Lied und Liedästhetik der mittleren Goethezeit, 1770–1814*. Studien zur Musikgeschichte des 19. Jahrhunderts 3. Regensburg: Gustav Bosse, 1965.

———. *Konzert: Öffentliche Musikdarbietung vom 17. bis 19. Jahrhundert*. Musikgeschichte in Bildern. Volume 4, part 2. Leipzig: Deutscher Verlag für Musik, 1971.

Sheehan, James J. *German History, 1770–1866*. Oxford History of Modern Europe. Oxford: Clarendon Press, 1989.

Small, Christopher. "Performance as Ritual: Sketch for an Enquiry into the True Nature of a Symphony Concert." In *Lost in Music: Culture, Style, and the Musical Event*, edited by Avron L. White, 6–32. London: Routledge and Kegan Paul, 1987.

———. *Musicking: The Meanings of Performing and Listening.* Music/Culture Series. Hanover: Wesleyan University Press, 1998.

Smead, J. W. *German Song and Its Poetry, 1740–1900.* London: Croom Helm, 1987.

Solie, Ruth. "Beethoven as Secular Humanist: Ideology and the Ninth Symphony in Nineteenth-Century Criticism." In *Explorations in Music, the Arts, and Ideas: Essays in Honor of Leonard B. Meyer,* edited by Eugene Narmour and Ruth A. Solie, 1–42. Festschrift Series 7. Stuyvesant, N.J.: Pendragon, 1988.

Sowa, Georg. *Anfänge institutioneller Musikerziehung in Deutschland (1800–1843): Pläne, Realisierung und zeitgenössische Kritik mit Darstellung der Bedingungen und Beurteilung der Auswirkungen.* Studien zur Musikgeschichte des 19. Jahrhunderts 33. Regensburg: Gustav Bosse, 1973.

Spitzer, John. "Metaphors of the Orchestra—the Orchestra as a Metaphor," *Musical Quarterly* (1996): 234–64.

Spitzer, Michael. "Marx's 'Lehre' and the Science of Education: Towards the Recuperation of Music Pedagogy," *Music and Letters* 79 (1998): 489–526.

Sponheuer, Bernd. "Der 'Gott der Harmonien' und die 'Pfeife des Pan': Über richtiges und falsches Hören in der Musikästhetik des 18. und 19. Jahrhunderts." In *Rezeptionsästhetik und Rezeptionsgeschichte in der Musikwissenschaft,* edited by Hermann Danuser and Friedhelm Krummacher, 179–91. Publikationen der Hochschule für Musik und Theater Hannover 3. Laaber: Laaber Verlag, 1991.

Stock, Jonathan P. J. "New Musicologies, Old Musicologies: Ethnomusicology and the Study of Western Music," *Current Musicology* 62 (1998): 40–68.

Stoljar, Margaret Mahony. *Poetry and Song in Late Eighteenth Century Germany: A Study in the Musical "Sturm und Drang."* London: Croom Helm, 1985.

Subotnick, Rose Rosengard. "Adorno's Diagnosis of Beethoven's Late Style: Early Symptom of a Fatal Condition." In *Developing Variations: Style and Ideology in Western Music,* 16–41. Minneapolis: University of Minnesota Press, 1991.

Taruskin, Richard. *Text and Act: Essays on Music and Performance.* New York: Oxford University Press, 1995.

Temperley, Nicholas. "The Old Way of Singing: Its Origins and Development," *Journal of the American Musicological Society* 34 (1981): 511–44.

Thamer, Hans-Ulrich. "Arbeit und Solidarität: Formen und Entwicklungen der Handwerkermentalität im 18. und 19. Jahrhundert in Frankreich und Deutschland." In *Handwerker in der Industrialisierung: Lage, Kultur, und Politik vom späten 18. bis ins frühe 20. Jahrhundert,* edited by Ulrich Engelhardt, 469–96. Stuttgart: Klett-Cotta, 1984.

Thayer, Alexander Wheelock. *Ludwig van Beethovens Leben.* Translated by Hermann Dieters, revised and expanded by Hugo Riemann. Leipzig: Breitkopf & Härtel, 1923; reprint, Hildesheim: Georg Olms, 1971.

————. *Thayer's Life of Beethoven*. Edited by Elliot Forbes. Princeton: Princeton University Press, 1964.

Van Horn Melton, James. *Absolutism and the Eighteenth-Century Development of Compulsory Schooling in Prussia and Austria*. Cambridge: Cambridge University Press, 1988.

Vetter, Walther. *Der Klassiker Schubert*. Leipzig: Breitkopf & Härtel, 1953.

Vierhaus, Rudolf. "The Historical Interpretation of the Enlightenment: Problems and Viewpoints." In *Enlightenment in Germany*, edited by Paul Raabe and Wilhelm Schmidt-Biggemann, 23–36. Bonn: Hohwacht, 1979.

————, ed. *Das Volk als Objekt obrigkeitlichen Handelns*. Wolfenbütteler Studien zur Aufklärung 13: Kultur und Gesellschaft in Nordwestdeutschland zur Zeit der Aufklärung 1. Tübingen: Max Niemeyer, 1992.

Wallace, Robin. *Beethoven's Critics: Aesthetic Dilemmas and Resolutions during the Composer's Lifetime*. Cambridge: Cambridge University Press, 1986.

Wallerstein, Immanuel. "Class Conflict in the Capitalist World-Economy." In *Race, Nation, Class: Ambiguous Identities*, by Etienne Balibar and Wallerstein, 115–24. London: Verso, 1991.

Wangermann, Ernst. *Aufklärung und staatsbürgerliche Erziehung: Gottfried van Swieten als Reformator des österreichischen Unterrichtswesens, 1781–1791*. Munich: Oldenbourg, 1978.

Weber, William. "The Contemporaneity of Eighteenth-Century Musical Taste," *Musical Quarterly* 68 (1984): 175–94.

————. "Wagner, Wagnerism, and Musical Idealism." In *Wagnerism in European Culture and Politics*, edited by David C. Large and Weber, in collaboration with Anne Dzamba Sessa, 28–71. Ithaca: Cornell University Press, 1984.

————. *The Rise of Musical Classics in Eighteenth-Century England: A Study in Canon, Ritual, and Ideology*. Oxford: Clarendon Press, 1992.

————. "L'Institution et son public: L'Opera à Paris et à Londres au XVIIIe siècle," *Annales: Économies, Sociétés, Civilisations* 48 (1993): 1519–39.

Webster, James. *Haydn's "Farewell" Symphony and the Idea of Classical Style: Through Composition and Cyclic Integration in His Instrumental Music*. Cambridge Studies in Music Theory and Analysis 1. Cambridge: Cambridge University Press, 1991.

Wehler, Hans-Ulrich. *Deutsche Gesellschaftsgeschichte*. Volume 1: *Vom Feudalismus des Alten Reiches bis zur Defensiven Modernisierung der Reformära, 1700–1815*. Volume 2: *Von der Reformära bis zur industriellen und politischen "Deutschen Doppelrevolution," 1815–1845/49*. Munich: C. H. Beck, 1987.

Whaley, Joachim. "The Protestant Enlightenment in Germany." In *The Enlightenment in National Context*, edited by Roy Porter and Mikuláš Teich, 106–17. Cambridge: Cambridge University Press, 1981.

Wieland, Wolfgang. "Entwicklung." In *Geschichtliche Grundbegriffe: Historisches Lexikon zur politisch-sozialen Sprache in Deutschland*, edited by

Otto Brunner, Werner Conze, and Reinhart Koselleck, 2:199–228. Stuttgart: Ernst Klett, 1975.

Wilson, W. Daniel. "Enlightenment's Alliance with Power: The Dialectic of Collusion and Opposition in the Literary Elite." In *Impure Reason: Dialectic of Enlightenment in Germany*, edited by Wilson and Robert C. Holub, 364–84. Detroit: Wayne State University Press, 1993.

Wilson, W. Daniel, and Robert C. Holub, eds. *Impure Reason: Dialectic of Enlightenment in Germany*. Detroit: Wayne State University Press, 1993.

Wiora, Walter. *Europäische Volksmusik und abendländische Tonkunst*. Kassel: Johann Philipp Hinnenthal, 1957.

Witkin, Robert W. *Adorno on Music*. London: Routledge, 1998.

Woodmansee, Martha. *The Author, Art, and the Market: Rereading the History of Aesthetics*. Social Foundations of Aesthetic Forms. New York: Columbia University Press, 1994.

Zantop, Susanne. "Dialectics and Colonialism: The Underside of the Enlightenment." In *Impure Reason: Dialectic of Enlightenment in Germany*, edited by W. Daniel Wilson and Robert C. Holub, 301–21. Detroit: Wayne State University Press, 1993.

Zaslaw, Neal. "Mozart as a Working Stiff." In *On Mozart*, edited by James M. Morris, 102–12. Washington, D.C.: Woodrow Wilson Center Press; Cambridge: Cambridge University Press, 1994.

Index

Adler, Guido, 88
Adorno, Theodor W., 147, 161–64,
196n23; *Beethoven: The Philosophy
of Music,* 161–62
"Advice to Young Artists." *See* "An
junge Künstler" (Reichardt)
Alexander, Carl, 85–86
Allgemeine musikalische Zeitung
(journal), 6, 150; on concert per-
formance sites, 148; on *Gesangbil-
dungslehre,* 102, 209n24; Indian
music review in, 28–32, 175n6;
Leipzig location of, 122–23; Nä-
geli's article in, 99–100; on peda-
gogy's goal of cultivation, 123
Amiot, Joseph-Marie, 34–36
An die ferne Geliebte (Beethoven), 90
"An junge Künstler" (Reichardt), 74,
116–17
Anleitung zur praktischen Musik
(Petri), 13
*Anweisung zum musikalisch-
richtigen Gesange* (Hiller), 102
Applegate, Celia, 31, 120
Arab music, 59, 188n92
Aristocracy. *See* Court
Arnim, Ludwig Achim von, 78–79;
Des Knaben Wunderhorn, 78
Arrangements, musical, 136–37,
223n32
Art: dilettantism's threat to, 149–51;

and disinterestedness, 17–18, 37;
folksong's oppositional reinforcement of, 85–86, 91, 202n60; as
guarantor of value, 145–46; moderation goal of, 40–41; product-
oriented focus on, 163–64, 239n13;
Reichardt on commodification of,
75–77, 146, 197n29; simplicity's
link to, 88, 90; social practice linked
to, 2–4, 17–19; *Volkston's* claims
to, by Schulz, 66–68, 69
Asian music. *See* Oriental music
Audiences: collective conceptions of,
152–54; concert's cultivation of,
139; urbanization of, 148–49. *See
also* Popular

Bach, Johann Sebastian, 14, 95
Baden, Archduchess Stephanie von,
142
Bayer, Anton, 140
Becker, Carl Ferdinand, 44, 183n59
Beethoven, Ludwig van, 62; Adorno's
reflections on, 161–62; *An die ferne
Geliebte,* 90; Fifth Symphony, 3;
and Haydn, 88; Marx on Ninth
Symphony of, 93–94, 96, 116, 124;
as paradigmatic composer, 158–59;
simple-complex synthesis in, 90;
sonata form of, 135; symbolizing
autonomy, 152, 233n94

263

Beethoven: The Philosophy of Music (Adorno), 161–62

Berliner Allgemeine musikalische Zeitung (Marx), 95–96

Bernstein, Susan, 142

Bohemian music, 55, 104, 118, 136

Bohlman, Philip V., 28, 35, 36

Bonds, Mark Evan, 5

Botstein, Leon, 223n32

Bourdieu, Pierre, 18, 37, 162

Bourgeoisie: concert's significance to, 125–26; *Freyheit* goals of, 77–78; literary culture's ties to, 18–19; as model for natural family, 116–17, 215n68; social limits of discourse of, 8–9; universalized values of, 8, 78, 117

Braunschweig orchestra, 153, 159–60

Brazilian music, 57

Brendel, Franz, 22, 123

Brett, Philip, 30

Burmese music, 59

Burney, Charles, 104, 147

Butt, John, 95, 102, 103

Celtic music, 52–53, 57

Chinese music, 34–36, 57, 58, 59

Choral singing: in Beethoven's Ninth Symphony, 93–94, 96–97; Nägeli's view of, 103, 105, 117, 121; non-literary instruction in, 104; and opera, 121–22, 129–30, 218n85; subsidiary ranking of, 54–55, 112–13, 187n82

Choral societies, 112–13, 122, 129–30

Classical canon: folksong's opposi-tional reinforcement of, 85–86, 91, 202n60; place of simplicity within, 87–88, 90; *Volkston*'s role within, 79–84, 89, 199n45

The Classical Style (Rosen), 91–92, 204n79

Claudius, Matthias, 82

Colonialism, justification for, 36, 58–59, 188n91

Composers: concert role of, 26, 157–59; cultivated/privileged status of, 33–34, 63–64; socioeconomic cir-cumstances of, 75–76, 77, 198n30. *See also* Musicians

Concerts: audiences of, 139, 152–54; class leveling's threat to, 146–47, 153–54; composer's centrality to, 26, 157–59; cultivation role of, 25–26, 138–39, 154; dance's exclusion from, 131–33; dilettantes' perfor-mance of, 149–51; genres advo-cated for, 134–35; metaphorical descriptions of, 155–57, 235n110, 236n111; musical arrangements' threat to, 136–37; musical essen-tiality of, 125–26; Natorp's pro-posed reform of, 138–39; opera's exclusion from, 128–31; relational nature of, 126–27, 143–45, 149; sites of, 22, 147–49; urbanized standards of, 159–60, 238n122; virtuoso performance in, 139–41, 227n52

Court: altered music relations of, 22, 130–31, 145–47; as concert site, 147–48; idealized concert of, 143–45, 149, 230n64; patronage role of, 11–13

Craft. See *Handwerk* (trade)

Cramer, Carl Friedrich, 68–69

Cultivation: Enlightenment mandate for, 9–10, 20, 24, 104; Leipzig dis-course on, 122–23; literary formu-lation of, 18–20; mothers' role in, 113–15; musical formulation of, 34–39; music education's goal of, 16–17, 25, 70–71, 94–95, 96–97, 104–5, 109–10, 122–23, 146; Ori-ental origins of, 28–29, 52–53; pro-nunciation as marker of, 109–11; religious imagery of, 154; social im-plications of, 63–64, 71–73, 111–12, 115–16, 123–24. *See also* Musical culture

Cultural identity. *See* National character

Cusick, Suzanne, 157, 159

Dahlhaus, Carl, 21, 112, 122, 154, 196n23, 197n29
Dalberg, Friedrich Hugo von, 28, 30, 31, 32–33, 58, 177n23
Dance, 88, 131–33, 222n20
Danish music, 56
DeNora, Tia, 77
Diesterweg, F. A. W., 108–9
Dilettantism, 26, 149–51
Discipline: performance metaphor of, 156, 235n110; of pure/authorized practice, 109–10; singing instruction as, 94, 106–9, 117–18
Dorn, Heinrich, 183n59
Dreist, K. A., 209n24
Dynamics, in Nägeli's system, 101

Egyptian music, 34, 48
Elias, Norbert, 122, 181n49
Encyclopädie der gesammten musikalischen Wissenschaften, oder Universal-Lexikon der Tonkunst (Schilling), 87; on Celtic music, 52–53, 57; on church-imposed music, 54–55; on colonialism, 58–59, 188n91; on Egyptian music, 48; on Eskimo music, 61; on European music, 54–57; on Germanic tribal music, 50–52, 185n71; on Greek music, 48–50, 57–58; on Hebrew music, 45, 47–48; on instrumental music, 139; national articles in, 24, 44–45, 46–47 table, 183n62; on Oriental music, 58–60, 188n92; reviews of, 44, 183n59; on Scandanavian music, 56–57; size/scope of, 43–44; on Turkish music, 60–61
English music, 54–55
Enlightenment: aesthetic theory of, 67–68; and bureaucratic state, 9–10; claim for universal validity of, 8–9; pedagogy as goal of, 9–10, 16–17, 20, 24, 104; rationalist arguments of, 7–8;
Erlmann, Veit, 27, 28

Die erste Wanderung der ältesten Tonkunst (Fink), 53
Erziehungslehre (Schwarz), 118
Eskimo music, 58, 61
Esterházy family, 81
Ethnomusicology: history of, 27–28; and musicology, 61–62
Europäische Volksmusik und abendländisches Tonkunst (Wiora), 88–89
European music: Asian origins of, 52–53; *Encyclopädie's* articles on, 46–47 table, 54–57; national character and rankings of, 54

Feldman, Martha, 127
Fink, Gottfried Wilhelm, 12–13, 22, 44; on Celtic music, 52–53; on church-imposed music, 54–55, 187n82; developmental progress model of, 52, 54; on dilettantism, 151; on music education, 112; performance metaphor of, 156
Fischer, Jörg, 21
Fischer, Wilhelm, 88
Fontenelle, Bernard Le Bovier de, 1, 31
Forkel, Johann Nicolaus, 22, 37, 43; audience satire by, 152; on Chinese music, 34–36; on Egyptian music, 34; on music's decline, 12–13, 137; *Musikalisch-kritische Bibliothek*, 137, 152; on secular support for music, 145; on vocal music, 134
Fortspinnungstypus (term), 88
Foucault, Michel, 25, 94, 106–7, 108, 109
Fouqué, Baron Friedrich de la Motte, 50–51, 185n71
Frederick the Great, 157
French music, 54, 55, 186n80, 188n91
French Revolution, 79
Frisch, Walter, 90

Gade, Niels, 85
Gellert, Christian Fürchtegott, 78
Gerber, Ernst Ludwig, 87

Germanic tribal music, 50–52,
185n71
*Gesangbildungslehre nach
Pestalozzischen Grundsätze* (Nägeli
and Pfeiffer): Foucauldian discipline
of, 106–9; journal reviews of, 102,
209n24; on mother's cultivation
role, 113–14; Pestalozzian prin-
ciples of, 98–99; systematic/pro-
gressive method of, 97, 100–102,
106, 108
Gesangverein. See Choral societies
Gesellschaft der Musikfreunde, 150
Gleim, Johann Wilhelm Ludwig, 72
Goehr, Lydia, 22, 158, 164, 239n13;
*Imaginary Museum of Musical
Works,* 164
Goethe, Johann Wolfgang von, 83–84
Göttinger Hainbund, 82
Greek music, 48–50, 57–58
Grillparzer, Franz, 1, 2, 6, 26
Grosheim, Georg Christoph, 61
Grove, George, 94
Guilds, 77, 151, 152
Guillory, John, 19
Guthmann, Friedrich, 115–16, 131–
32, 222n20
GutsMuths, J. C. F., 13–14

Hagen, Theodor, 118–19, 120
Handel, George Frideric: *Messiah,*
230n64; *Timotheus (Alexander's
Feast),* 143–44
Handwerk (trade): literary production
as, 19; musician separated from,
151–52, 233n94; social implications
of concept, 75–76, 77, 164, 239n13;
virtuoso concert as, 141
Hanslick, Eduard, 22, 133, 134; *Vom
Musikalisch-Schönen,* 133
Harmony: Germanic development of,
51–52; Marx on, 49–50
Haydn, Franz Joseph, 32; folklike sim-
plicity of, 87–88, 203n68; *Die
Jahreszeiten,* 80–82, 199n45; popu-
lar-artistic synthesis in, 91–92;
Schöpfung, 129

Hebrew music, 45, 47–48, 59
Herder, Johann Gottfried, 24, 32, 84;
on cultivation of speech, 110–11;
cultural relativism of, 41–42, 55;
on human development, 42–43,
182n57; Reichardt's alignment with,
74–75, 196n25; Schilling's article
on, 44
Hientzsch, Johann Gottfried, 98, 132
Hiller, Johann Adam, 22, 102
Hindu music. *See* Indian music
*Historisch-Biographisches Lexikon
der Tonkünstler* (Gerber), 87
Hoffmann, E. T. A., 3–4, 6, 87,
202n64
Hoffmann, Freia, 23, 115
"Hoffnung" (Goethe), 83
Hölty, Ludwig, 82
Horstig, Carl Gottlob, 115
Humboldt, Wilhelm von, 84, 98, 110,
200n52
Hunter, Mary, 190n2

*Imaginary Museum of Musical
Works* (Goehr), 164
Indian music, 28–31, 53, 58–59,
175n6
Instruction. *See* Music education
Instrumental music: chorus joined
with, 93–94, 96–97; cultivation
role of, 139; German skills in, 31,
54, 186n80; superior ranking of,
112–13, 121–22, 130–31
Instruments, as standard of musical
development, 45, 47–48
Italian music, 54, 55

Janissary music, 37
Jones, Sir William, 28, 30, 58
Journals. *See* Musical discourse

Kahlert, August, 23, 130, 141, 142,
150, 152
Kanne, Friedrich August, 137
Keferstein, Gustav, 122–23, 135
Kerman, Joseph, 90–91

Kiesewetter, Raphael Georg, 43,
188n92
Kirnberger, Johann Philipp, 67, 120,
122
Kittler, Friedrich, 22
Klusen, Ernst, 73, 79, 86, 196n23
Des Knaben Wunderhorn (Arnim), 78
Koch, Heinrich Christoph, 37
Krüger, Eduard, 148, 151, 154,
190n101
Kunst (term), 19, 77, 164. *See also* Art

La Vopa, Anthony J., 9
*Das Leben und die Meinungen des
Herrn Magister Sebaldus
Nothanker* (Nicolai), 19
Leipzig, 122–23
Leppert, Richard, 149–50
Lessing, Gotthold Ephraim, 72, 134
Liederkranz. See Choral societies
Liedertafel. See Choral societies
Lied im Volkston (term), 65. *See also
Volkston*
Liedtypus (term), 88
Literary culture: binary status within,
112–13; bourgeoisie's ties to, 18–
19; musical culture's tension with,
19–20, 32–34, 50–53, 68–69
Lower classes: choral societies of,
113; dance tied to, 131–32, 222n20;
folksong role of, 56–57; Goethe's
abstraction of, 83–84; Hagen's solution for, 118–19; in Haydn's work,
80–81; *Musikanten*'s services to,
15, 16; in Schubert's work, 82–83,
200n50; as threat to concert, 153–
54

Magazin der Musik (Cramer), 68
Marpurg, Friedrich Wilhelm, 122
Marx, Adolph Bernhard, 44, 87, 124;
on Beethoven's use of chorus, 93–
94, 96–97; on Chinese music, 58,
59; on concert performance, 137–
38, 148; on education, 95–96; on
Greek music, 48–50; "natural"
family ideal of, 113, 116, 215n68;

on opera, 129; on secular support,
17; on virtuosity, 142–43
Medean music, 60
Michaelis, Christian Friedrich, 14–15,
38, 110
Moore, Julia, 77, 198n30
Morrow, Mary Sue, 1
Mothers, cultivation role of, 113–15
Mozart, Leopold, 63
Mozart, Wolfgang Amadeus, 63
Müller, August, 152, 155, 158, 233n94
Müller quartet (Braunschweig), 157
Music: ambivalent status of, 12–16;
expressive role of, 1–2; impact of,
on primitives, 39–41; popular cultivation role of, 16–17, 20, 21–22;
social practice of, 2, 3–5
Musical culture: Adorno's immersion
in, 161–63; advocates of, 5–6, 17–
18; arrangements' threat to, 136–
37; concert's centrality to, 25–26,
125–26, 127, 138–39; developmental perspective on, 36–39, 43, 48,
81, 182n57; Enlightenment values
of, 7–10, 67–68; generic boundaries of, 128–33; limited access to,
21, 23, 162–63; literary culture's
tension with, 19–20, 32–34, 68–
69; Marx's vision of, 93–94, 96; and
music education studies, 95, 205n2;
musicology's representation of, 61–
62; national character tied to, 23–
24, 31–33, 41–43, 54–55, 186n80;
Oriental origins of, 28–29, 52–53;
and product-oriented focus, 163–
64; singing instruction's role in, 94–
95, 96–97, 104–5; social categories
of, 2, 3–5, 63–65; state's role in, 17,
104–5, 120–21; virtuosos' threat
to, 139–42
Musical discourse: as adaptations/
translations, 36, 179n37; Adorno's
relevance to, 162–63; on Chinese
music, 34–36, 58, 59; colonialism
perspective of, 58–59, 188n91; cultivation perspective of, 21–22; developmental perspective of, 36–39,

Musical discourse *(continued)*
43, 48, 81, 182n57; Enlightenment
ideology of, 7–10, 67–68, 192n10;
historical sources for, 38–39; on Indian music, 28–31, 58–59, 175n6;
from journals, 6; Leipzig source of,
122–23; literary culture's tension
with, 19–20, 32–34, 50–53, 68–
69; and non-European music, 27–
28, 175n6; pragmatic orientation of,
10–11; relevance of, to musicians,
62; situation in public sphere of, 6–
7, 23; social categories of, 3–5, 63–
64; women's exclusion from, 23. See
also *Encyclopädie der gesammten
musikalischen Wissenschaften,
oder Universal-Lexikon der
Tonkunst* (Schilling)
Music education: cultivation goal of,
16–17, 25, 94–95, 96–97, 104–5,
109–10, 146; Enlightenment spirit
of, 9–10, 20; GutsMuths on, 13–
14; intelligentsia's role in, 122–23;
as journal topic, 95–96; mother's
role in, 114–15; and musicology,
95, 205n2; political/economic uses
of, 118–19; and popularity, 24;
in Portugal, 57; print's impact on,
10–11; Schulz on, 70–72; social
implications of, 72–73, 111–12,
115–16, 121–24; state's role in, 17,
104–5, 120–21. See also Singing
instruction
Musicians: cultivated/privileged status of, 63–64, 121, 123–24, 154;
dance's threat to status of, 132–33;
Freyheit as goal of, 77–78; instruc-
tional role of, 10–11; music scholarship's relevance to, 62; *Musikant*
versus *Musikus* as types of, 14–16;
Nägeli's methods for, 99–100; nuclear family as model for, 116–17,
215n68; patronage concerns of, 11–
13, 145–46; redefinition of professional, 151–52, 233n94; socioeconomic circumstances of, 75–76, 77,
198n30; state support of, 17, 62,

120–21, 190n101. *See also* Com-
posers; Virtuosos
Musicking (term), 127
Musicology, 61–62, 163–65; Adorno
as viewed by, 162; and colonialism,
28; and ethnomusicology, 61–62;
German, and *Volkston*, 86–89;
music education as treated by, 95;
North American, and *Volkston*, 89–
92; roots in cultivated bourgeoisie
of, 124
Musikalisches Kunstmagazin (Reich-
ardt), 74
Musikalisches Lexikon (Koch), 37
Musikant (term), 13–15, 16
Musikus (term), 14–15

Nägeli, Hans Georg, 9, 123, 128, 148;
on audiences, 153; on bourgeois patronage, 146; on choral singing,
103, 105, 121; on concerts, 126, 134,
135; disciplinary requirements of,
106–9, 117; elementary singing
method of, 25, 97–98, 99–102, 106,
108, 209n24; on mother's role, 113–
14; on performance as political, 155;
Pestalozzian principles of, 98–99;
on pure/cultivated practice, 109–
10, 111; on virtuosos, 140, 142, 158
Napoleon, 32, 177n20
National character: *Encyclopädie*'s
concept of, 44–45, 54; folk music's
relevance to, 55–57; Herder's rela-
tivistic view of, 41–43, 182n57;
musical culture linked to, 23–24,
31–33
Natorp, Bernhard C. L.: on concerts,
134, 135, 138–39; on singing instruction, 103, 104–5, 106, 212n41
Nauenburg, Gustav, 44–45, 61, 97–
98
NBC Music Appreciation Hour, 161,
162
Neue Zeitschrift für Musik (journal),
44, 85, 122, 130
Nicolai, Friedrich, 19
Niederer, Johannes, 209n24

Nineteenth-Century Music (Dahlhaus), 21
Nolte, Eckhard, 205n2
Notation, in Nägeli's system, 101–2
Nuclear family, ideal of, 113, 116–17, 215n68

Opera, 22, 64, 190n2; choral singing and, 121–22, 218n85; concert's exclusion of, 128–31
Oratorio, 129, 135
Orchestral metaphors, 155–56, 235n110, 236n111
Orientalism, 29–30, 36
Oriental music, 59–60; Celtic dissemination of, 52–53, 57; colonialist replacement of, 58–59, 188n91; Hebrew music as, 45–48; Indian music as, 28–30; past/present interchangeability of, 59–60

Paris, Heinrich, 139, 142, 146, 153–54
Peasant virtues: Goethe's abstraction of, 83–84; in Haydn's work, 80–81; in Schubert's work, 82–83, 200n50
Pedagogy. *See* Music education
Pederson, Sanna, 4, 6–7, 24
Performance: composer's centrality to, 157–59; devalued modes of, 135–37; by dilettantes, 149–51; metaphorical descriptions of, 155–57, 235n110, 236n111; relational nature of, 26, 126–27, 143–45, 149; urbanized standards of, 159–60, 238n122. *See also* Concerts
Persian music, 60
Pestalozzi, Johann Heinrich, 9, 98–99, 112, 114, 209n24
Petri, Johann Samuel, 13
Pfeiffer, Michael Traugott, 97–98
Piano arrangements, 136, 223n32
Pitch, in Nägeli's system, 100–101, 106
Popular: alternative views of, 24; Haydn's representation of, 80–81; Mozart family on, 63; in political

terms, 66; Schubert's expression of, 82–83, 200n50; social implications of, 64–65, 121, 190n2; as threat to concert, 146–47, 153–54; vocal music's ties to, 93–94, 96–97, 121–22, 218n85
Portuguese music, 57
Primitive peoples: in developmental hierarchy, 38–39, 52, 86; *Encyclopädie*'s articles on, 46 table; language of, 85; musical instruments of, 45, 47–48; music's impact on, 39–41
Print culture, and music instruction, 10–11
Pronunciation, 109–11
Prussian national assembly (1848), 119

Rationalism, 8–9, 30
Reichardt, Johann Friedrich, 6, 24, 64; aligned with Herder, 74–75, 196n25; on art as commodity, 75–77, 146; *Frohe Lieder für deutsche Männer*, 74; musical culture goals of, 4–5; *Musikalisches Kunstmagazin*, 74; on nuclear family ideal, 116–17; on Schulz's education, 72–73; Schumann's perspective versus, 85; on secular support, 120; Stoljar on, 66
Rellstab, Ludwig, 44
Rhythm: Nägeli instruction in, 100; of primitives, 39–40
Rochlitz, Friedrich, 43, 52, 150, 157; on music's impact, 39–41, 180n42
Roman music, 48, 184n68
Rosen, Charles, 91–92, 95, 108, 204n79; *The Classical Style*, 91–92, 204n79

Said, Edward, 36
Salis-Seewis, Johann von, 82
Scandanavian music, 56
Scheibe, Johann Adolf, 14
Scherer, Wolfgang, 205n2

Schiller, Friedrich von, 84
Schilling, Gustav, 23–24; on Hebrew music, 45, 47–48, 59; on Portuguese music, 57; reputation of, 44. See also *Encyclopädie der gesammten musikalischen Wissenschaften, oder Universal-Lexikon der Tonkunst* (Schilling)
Schlegel, August Wilhelm von, 51
Schlumbohm, Jürgen, 77–78, 198n36
Schmith, Amand Wilhelm, 145
Schroeder, David, 81
Schubert, Franz, 77, 82–83, 90, 200n50, 203n68; and *Volkston*, 82–84. Works: *Abenlied*, D. 276, 82; *Erntelied*, D. 434, 82; *Fischerlied*, D. 351, D. 364, D. 562, 82; *Heidenröslein*, D. 257, 90; *Hoffnung*, D. 295, 83; *Lied*, D. 362, D. 501, 82; *Das Lied vom Reifen*, D. 532, 82; *Morgenlied*, D. 266, 82; *Nähe des Geliebten*, D. 162, 90; *Pflügerlied*, D. 392, 82; *Täglich zu singen*, D. 533, 82; *Tischlerlied*, D. 274, 82
Schulz, Johann Abraham Peter, 24, 64, 118, 122; *Gedanken über den Einfluß der Musik auf die Bildung eines Volks*, 70–72; and Haydn, 87; *Lieder im Volkston*, 65–69, 74; on musical cultivation, 70–72; on popular singing, 96; and Reichardt, 74; socioeconomic circumstances of, 77; *Volkston* concept of, 66–68, 69, 192n10
Schumann, Robert, 84–85, 86, 113. Works: *Album für die Jugend*, op. 68, 84, 85, 95, 201n55; "Ernteliedchen," 84; "Frölicher Landmann von der Arbeit zurückkehrend," 84, 95; *Fünf Stücke im Volkston*, op. 102, 84–85; "Ländliches Lied," 84; "Nordisches Lied," 84; "Schnitterliedchen," 84; "Volksliedchen," 84
Schutte, Sabine, 77
Schwab, Heinrich W., 64, 65, 89
Schwarz, Friedrich H. C., 118

Schwarzenberg Palace (Vienna), 81
Scottish music, 57, 187n82
Secularization: and musical development, 54–55; of music education, 103–5
Seyfried, Ignaz von, 235n110
Siamese music, 59
Simplicity: of Haydn, 87–88; role of, in classical style, 88, 90
Singing instruction: cultivating role of, 94–95, 96–97, 104–5; disciplinary requirements of, 106–9, 117–18; impact of, on musical hierarchy, 121–22, 218n85; mother's role in, 114–15; Nägeli method of, 25, 97–98, 99–102, 106, 108; Natorp method of, 106, 212n41; natural versus rote, 103; pronunciation linked to, 109–10; social implications of, 111–12. See also Music education
Small, Christopher, 126–27, 143
Social categories: aesthetic investment and, 2, 17–19; of art versus *Handwerk*, 75–76, 77, 164, 239n13; commodification's leveling of, 146–47, 153–54; concert's inclusion of, 143–45, 149; of dance, 131–33, 222n20; Goethe's abstraction of, 83–84, 200n52; in Haydn's work, 80–81; Hoffman's implication of, 3–4; music education's reinforcement of, 72–73, 111–12, 115–16, 121, 122–24; music's ambivalent status and, 12–16; the popular and, 63–65, 121, 190n2; Reichardt's strategy of, 4–5; Rosen's acknowledgement of, 91–92; in Schubert's work, 82–83, 200n50; universalized values and, 8–9. See also Bourgeoisie; Court; Lower classes
Sonatas, 88, 135
Spitzer, John, 155
Spitzer, Michael, 205n2
Spohr, Ludwig, 129; *Das jüngste Gericht*, 129
State: hierarchical structure of, 9–10;

music discipline's benefit to, 117–18; role of music education in, 17, 104–5, 120–21

Stock, Jonathan, 61, 162

Stolberg, Friedrich von, 82

Stoljar, Margaret Mahony, 65–66, 89

Strauss, Johann, 131–32, 156–57

Streicher, Andreas, 149

Style, and national character, 44–45

Subotnick, Rose, 163

Sulzer, Johann Georg, 67

Swabia, condition of music in, 113

Swedish music, 56

Thibaut, Justus: *Ueber Reinheit der Tonkunst,* 139, 141, 146

Thomasschule (Leipzig), 104

Tonal art *(Tonkunst):* harmony element of, 49–50, 51–52; primitives without, 39–40

Tonkünstlervereine (musicians' societies), 123

Turkish music, 37, 59, 60–61

Ueber die Musik der Indier (Jones), 37, 52, 81; review of, 28–33, 175n6, 177n23

Ueber Reinheit der Tonkunst (Thibaut), 139, 141, 146

"Ueber das Volkslied, insonders das Italiänische" (Alexander), 85–86

Universalized values: ambivalent claims to, 7, 8; domestic linked to, in Beethoven, 93–94; exclusions from, 8–9, 21, 23, 84, 163; Goethe's abstraction of, 83–84, 200n52; and social fluidity, 146–47, 153–54

Van Swieten, Gottfried, 80, 81, 98, 104, 114–15

Vetter, Walther, 200n50

Vierhaus, Rudolf, 73

Virtuosos, 26, 139–43, 158

Volk (term): ambivalent notion of, 65; idealized view of, 75–76

Volkslieder: Armin's experience of, 78–79; Cramer on revival of, 68–69; in European hierarchy, 55–57; Reichardt's discomfort with, 74–77, 197n29; and reinforcement of canon, 85–86, 91, 202n60; simplicity's source in, 88

Volkston: ambivalent notion of, 65; classical style's link to, 88–89; Cramer on, 68–69; in Haydn's works, 80–81, 87–88, 199n45; Klusen's binary view of, 73, 196n23; marginal study of, 64–65; Marx's vision of, 93–94, 96; North American accounts of, 89–92; in Schubert's songs, 82–83, 200n50; Schulz's concept of, 66–68, 69–72, 192n10; Schumann's usage of, 84–85; Stoljar on, 65–66

Volksweise (folk-style melody), 90–91

Vom Musikalisch-Schönen (Hanslick), 133

Voß, Johann Heinrich, 72

Wagner, Richard, 22, 130–31, 239n13

Wallerstein, Immanuel, 18

Weber, Carl Maria von, 227n52

Weber, Gottfried, 128–29

Weber, William, 2, 5–6, 130–31, 230n64

Webster, James, 88, 91, 203n68

Wendt, Amadeus, 120

Whaley, Joachim, 9

Wiener allgemeine musikalische Zeitung (journal), 140

Wiener Zeitschrift für Kunst, Literatur, Theater und Mode (journal), 141

Wiora, Walter, 88–89

Wirtemberg, Duke of, 152

Wochenblatt für Menschenbildung (Pestalozzi), 99

Wöchentliche Nachrichten und Anmerkungen die Musik betreffend (Hiller), 22

"Wollen alle Deutsche Musikanten werden?" (GutsMuths), 13–14

Women: cultivation role of, 23, 113–

Women *(continued)*
15; Medean/Persian music of, 60;
music education restrictions on,
115–16
Working class. *See* Lower classes

*Zeitung für Theater und Musik zur
Unterhaltung gebildeter, unbefangener Leser* (journal), 141, 227n52
Zelter, Karl Friedrich, 98, 104, 110,
120, 122

Text: 10/13 Aldus
Display: Aldus
Compositor: G&S Typesetters, Inc.
Printer: Haddon Craftsmen, Inc.
Index: Pat Deminna